NATURAL DISASTERS THAT CHANGED THE WORLD

For Alison and Gerard

NATURAL DISASTERS THAT CHANGED THE WORLD

by Rodney Castleden

CHARTWELL
BOOKS, INC.

This edition published in 2007 by
CHARTWELL BOOKS, INC.
A division of BOOK SALES, INC.
114 Northfield Avenue
Edison, New Jersey 08837, USA

Copyright © Omnipress 2007

ISBN-13: 978-0-7858-2228-8
ISBN-10: 0-7858-2228-3

Produced by Omnipress, Eastbourne

Printed in the EU

Futura
An imprint of Little, Brown Book Group
Brettenham House
Lancaster Place
London WC2E 7EN

Photo credits: Getty Images

CONTENTS

II: THE MEDIEVAL AND RENAISSANCE WORLD

III: THE ENLIGHTENED WORLD

IV: THE NINETEENTH-CENTURY WORLD

V: THE MODERN WORLD

INTRODUCTION

WE ARE USED to reading about natural disasters in the newspapers, or watching film footage of them on the television news. There is no question about it – they are tremendously exciting. It is easy to see why. They cut right across the mundane and sometimes too predictable routines of our everyday lives, and they fill us with renewed wonder at the sensational power of the forces of nature. Then we feel a twinge of guilt at being excited, because we know, as we read and watch, that people are losing their homes, their businesses, their belongings, their well-being, their peace of mind and even their lives – in some disasters whole communities are wiped out – and then we feel sorry for the disaster victims. Our responses invariably contain this guilty triple-take of excitement, shame and pity, and we feel we have to suppress our sense of exhilaration.

Because of my background as a physical geographer I have other responses as well; all too frequently I can see that a disaster was foreseeable and that measures could have been taken either to escape from it or to prevent it from happening in the first place. I hope the reader will develop that same sense while reading this book.

It is very important to understand why disasters happen. It was all too easy in past centuries to portray disasters as chaotic, unforeseen and unforeseeable. People were actively encouraged especially by spiritual leaders to think of them as acts of punishment by a vengeful God. This is a particularly cruel mindset; a family bereaved by earthquake, storm or plague has to

11

bear the additional grief that God has deliberately struck their loved ones down and that they must have done something wicked to deserve punishment. As we shall see, the 1755 Lisbon earthquake did something significant to change that. The twentieth century brought a great increase in our understanding of the way the world works. We now have to accept that many disasters are – and increasingly will be – foreseeable. Some historic disasters could certainly have been foreseen and avoiding action could have been taken.

Some natural disasters, like the mass extinctions of species with which this book opens, are purely natural. Many natural disasters are the result of powerful natural forces, but there is also a human element in play that makes the disasters much worse. The mudslides that happened at Sarno in Italy in 1998 were produced by a combination of heavy rain and layers of loose volcanic debris lying on steep mountain sides – entirely natural phenomena – but the disaster was made far worse by people who had misguidedly built settlements on the valley floors and deforested the mountain side, and by administrative authorities who turned a blind eye to these activities. Nature and man. Often, throughout this book, we will find that there is this insidious partnership between destructive natural processes and environmentally insensitive human behaviour.

There is an element of subjectivity, of value judgement, when we use the word disaster.

Was it a disaster when, as some astronomers believe happened early in Earth's history, our planet collided with a planetoid, causing a huge chunk of Earth to break off to form the Moon? It would certainly have looked spectacular and catastrophic if we had been around to watch it from some safe vantage point. But it could be argued that, because this happened before the human race came into existence and injured nobody, it could not be described as a disaster. Some might say that the great mass extinctions were also not disasters, because once again no people were harmed.

This leads us into another line of thought, which is that what may be disastrous for one life form or even one group of people may be a godsend for another. Disasters can have major creative impacts. Sudden large-scale changes in the environment can stimulate jumps in evolution as well as bring about extinctions. As the environment changes, plants and animals undergo pulses of adaptations to fill the new habitats as they are created. The great mass extinction at the close of the Cretaceous period wiped out the dinosaurs. But annihilating disaster for the dinosaurs meant opportunity for the mammals. It was only after the extinction of the dinosaurs that the mammals were able to multiply, diversify and grow in size, that the human race itself was able to emerge. It is hard to imagine a frail and vulnerable species like our earliest ancestors surviving in a world dominated by efficient and well-established predatory reptiles; we needed the dinosaurs to be overtaken by disaster in order that our own species could evolve.

We tend to view the discovery and colonization of new lands in a very positive light, as landmarks in human progress. But frequently native species of plants and animals have suffered as a result of these intrusions; unfortunately, all too frequently any indigenous human communities have suffered too. In the tenth century AD Polynesian settlers reached New Zealand; within a few hundred years thirty-four species of birds, including the spectacular giant flightless moa, had vanished. Madagascar was colonized about 500 years earlier, and by the time of the Battle of Hastings ten families of larger mammals, as well as seven types of lemur and a strange flightless elephant bird, had been eaten to extinction. A major advance for one species is often a natural disaster for many others.

The subjectivity poses other problems too. A violent earthquake or volcanic eruption that happens in an uninhabited region might cause no human casualties; an event of the same magnitude occurring close to a city may kill tens of thousands of people. Is the event that causes the deaths a disaster and the other

13

not? I have to an extent left this question hanging in the air by including some large-scale events that did cause thousands of deaths and others that did not. This is because I think it is important to try to see the world we live in objectively. The huge eruption of Katmai in 1912 may not have resulted in any deaths because it happened in an uninhabited wilderness, but it formed part of a larger pattern of extremely violent events that forms our global environment, and what happened to Mount Katmai helps us to understand what is happening elsewhere in the world.

The disasters featured in this book have been selected for a variety of reasons. Many of them are obvious choices, such as the Black Death of the fourteenth century, the 1906 San Francisco earthquake and the Boxing Day tsunami of 2004. Some are less obvious. Some may seem to the reader to be minor disasters in that few or no people died, but I have included them either because our perception of the world was changed significantly by them or because they illustrate an important aspect of human response to the environment.

The Hubbards Hill landslips near Sevenoaks did not make front page news when they happened in 1962. No one was killed or injured. But they made it plain that landscape studies really do have a valuable contribution to make to civil engineering projects; it was a turning point in perception. Geography became important, and would become more so as other environmental issues surfaced. The Tunguska event of 1908 opened our minds to the alarming possibility of collisions with asteroids or comets. The Boscastle flood of 2004 showed how reluctant people are to learn from history, a point also made by the tragic destruction of the town of Armero in the Nevado del Ruiz eruption of 1985.

Some disasters have been included because of their sheer peculiarity, such as the Waimangu geyser disaster of 1903 and the 1996 eruption of a volcano under an Icelandic ice cap. There is a sense in which every natural disaster is an epiphany, a revelatory experience that changes us by reminding us of the precariousness of our relationship with the world, by reminding us that the universe is an exciting but also an extremely perilous place in which to live.

The statistics of disasters present a particular problem; they are simply not reliable. For one thing, different sources give different figures. I have tried to evaluate the evidence to my best ability. I have made every effort to give accurate statistics in this book, but regrettably the information available is by its very nature unreliable. When the speed of a high wind, avalanche or pyroclastic flow is given, it is in many cases not a measurement but an estimate reported by a survivor and the trauma of the ordeal may well have distorted the survivor's assessment. Sometimes there are variations according to the locations of the observers; that certainly seems to be the case with the reports of the Tunguska event. Sometimes there are instrumental measurements, and these will be more accurate and trustworthy, though even here there can be an element of unreliability. The techniques used to measure river discharge today are more sophisticated than those in use 100 years ago, which makes it difficult to compare, for instance, Mississippi floods of the nineteenth century with those of the late twentieth century.

The reader will become aware that death tolls are often imprecise and uncertain. This is because communities stricken by a major disaster are thrown into chaos by it; they are not in a position to count their dead precisely and routine bureaucracies often have to be set aside in order to ensure that bodies are buried quickly. The events described move incredibly swiftly, often creating confusion, and sometimes the dead are removed entirely from the scene of a disaster. The very biggest disasters are the ones about which there is the least certainty.

This warning about statistics applies especially to the figures given in the Appendix at the end of the book. They represent my best endeavour, but there is considerable uncertainty about them. The list does, even so, give a fair impression of the scale of human loss, suffering, grief and hardship inflicted by the worst natural disasters.

There are three very striking features about this list. One is that natural disasters are not evenly distributed round the world, and that is to an extent a function of population density; where there are more people there are more lives to be lost. Some regions even so get far more than their fair share. The Ganges Delta is one and eastern China is another. Nearly one-third of the seventy worst natural disasters in terms of human lives lost have happened in China. A second striking feature is that many of the worst disasters seem to be happening today, in our lifetime; over one-quarter have happened in the last fifty years, one-tenth of them in the last decade. This shows that the world is still a very dangerous place, and apparently becoming more so. A third striking feature of the list is that the worst disaster of all is the one that we have almost completely blotted from our memory. Most people haven't even heard of it. Putting disasters behind us and forgetting them seems to be a very deep-seated human trait; maybe at some primeval level we need to forget in order to get on with our lives, perhaps just to keep our sanity. The scale of human loss as presented here is truly horrifying.

The same or very similar disasters keep on happening in the same places and one of the themes of this book is recurrence or cyclicity. If a location has been prone to flooding in the past, it will inevitably be prone to flooding again in the future. The flat floodplains of rivers all round the world have been created during many repeated river floods. Geologists and geographers know exactly where they are, and know that they are places where houses should not be built. If an area has volcanoes, they must have been created by the ejection of lava and they will almost certainly erupt again at some time in the future. Places that have suffered earthquakes in the past will have them again in the future. An alarming aspect of this patterning is that as settlements grow, the death tolls too are likely to grow. Some towns and cities have tragically been built in the wrong places. We have only to think of Pompeii, Herculaneum and their modern successor, the city of Naples, doomed to be destroyed one day by Vesuvius, or of Tokyo, similarly doomed to destruction by a future major earthquake, which has already been given a name, the Great Tokai Earthquake.

Because most disasters follow patterns and cycles, it is becoming increasingly possible to forecast the disasters of the future. The terrible disasters that will one day overtake Naples and Tokyo have already been mentioned; San Francisco can expect a repeat of the 1906 earthquake and is waiting for 'the Big One', which could come at any time.

But one long-anticipated and greatly feared future catastrophe may well not happen at all, so – against all expectations – this book will have a happy ending.

I
THE ANCIENT WORLD

THE PERMIAN MASS EXTINCTION
(251 MILLION BC)

FROM TIME TO time, at very long intervals in the story of Earth, there are cataclysmic disasters, disasters on a scale that is very hard to imagine. Some of the biggest disasters are silently recorded in the layers of rock that we sometimes see exposed in quarries or cuttings for new motorways. They show up, to the trained geologist, as abrupt changes in the fossil contents of the rocks. There may be lots of remains of a particular species, in the form of shells or skeletons, but then above a certain layer they are missing. Sometimes lots of species disappear all at the same level, which means that all disappeared at the same time. This is what is called a mass extinction.

One such moment came towards the end of the Permian period, 251 million years ago, when a catastrophic natural disaster killed enormous numbers of plants and animals. Ninety-five percent of all marine life was killed. Seventy percent of all the land families became extinct. One of the most conspicuous species to become extinct was the trilobites, marine creatures that looked rather like giant woodlice. They came in a range of sizes, but they all seem to have lived on the bottom of the sea, where they hovered up food like cordless vacuum cleaners. These engaging creatures were well adapted to their environment, with countless generations of them thriving in the oceans for many millions of years. Then suddenly they became extinct. Why?

There has been a great deal of discussion of the possible cause of the extinction of the trilobites and all the other species that disappeared at the same time. Something spectacular must have happened, but it is not evident from the rocks what it was. Several different ideas have been put forward. Perhaps it was climate change. A cooling of the climate could have brought about the onset of glacial conditions in high latitudes and drought in low latitudes. There is evidence in the rocks themselves that an ice sheet covered the southern part of South America, South Africa and Australia, those three regions then being all joined together. The glaciation would have lowered the sea level and left the continental shelves exposed as lowlands; this would have reduced the shallow sea areas and therefore heightened competition among marine species preferring shallow water environments.

One problem in reconstructing a catastrophe in the Permian world is that it was a differently shaped world. The Earth was round, just as it is now, with continents and oceans, just as now, but the continents and oceans were different shapes. The continents are, and always have been, continuously on the move, so that over tens of millions of years the world map changes out of recognition.

The continents slowly drifted together to form a single super-continent known as Pangaea. This assembling of the land areas into one huge land mass would also have reduced ecological diversity. It would have done this by shortening the world's coastline and again removing many of the shallow sea areas. This is a logical hypothesis and based on very sound geological evidence, but Pangaea was formed in the middle of the Permian period and the mass extinction came hundreds of thousands of years later, so the connection is not clear. There might be a time lag between the creation of adverse environmental conditions and the extinction of a species, but it seems unlikely that the time lag would be hundreds of thousands of years.

Geologists can also tell us that there was explosive volcanic activity in Siberia, which produced huge clouds of ash. The dust veil from these eruptions would have caused a drop in temperature, which could in turn have triggered the glaciations and drought. The date of the lava tallies well with the date of the mass extinction.

Other scientists favour the impact of a meteorite or asteroid as an explanation. There is no direct evidence of this, but the worldwide environmental deterioration is certainly consistent with such an event. The rocks in South Africa show that rivers there were suddenly clogged with sediment 251 million years ago. The only explanation for this is that a major ecological disaster destroyed the vegetation cover that had been holding the soil and sediment in place. The fern shrublands and pine woodlands were destroyed and the rivers of the Karoo turned from being lightly loaded meandering rivers to being braided, multichannel rivers choked with sediment.

The Permian rock layers in Australia and Northern Europe tell a similar story of traumatic environmental change. It took tens of thousands of years for the river systems to deal with the change and re-establish their former meandering courses. The huge scale of climatic and environmental change everywhere suggests that a very large meteorite or asteroid may have collided with the Earth. It may have been an object as big as ten or twelve miles across. The meteorite or asteroid theory is a valid and credible one, but there is as yet no positive evidence that this is what happened. If an extraterrestrial object big enough to cause global environmental change fell into the ocean, it would have created huge tsunami waves. If it fell on the land area, it would have made a huge impact crater. So far, no evidence of a mega-tsunami has been found. So far, no impact crater has been identified that could be connected with the Permian extinctions.

There is a great deal of debris scattered through interplanetary space, most of it too small to be visible to the naked eye, or even through telescopes. As Earth travels round its orbit, it inevitably collides with some of this debris. Small grains the size of sand or grit become visible as the friction with the air heats them up; they are the shooting stars that are a common feature of the night sky. Rocks the size of bricks fall out of the sky somewhere in the world every year. In the last fifty years or so, several houses and even a car have been hit by objects of this size. Larger objects collide with Earth far less frequently.

In about 20,000 BC, an iron mini-asteroid about 300 feet across fell on Arizona; it made the Arizona Meteor Crater, which is now a tourist attraction. A much bigger asteroid, maybe five miles across, could have caused a large scale environmental catastrophe at the end of the Permian period – one that would wipe out many species.

THE CRETACEOUS MASS EXTINCTION

(65 MILLION BC)

THE JURASSIC AND Cretaceous periods were the great age of the dinosaurs. After that, there were no dinosaurs at all. Something happened right at the end of the Cretaceous period that exterminated them. What is more, the dinosaurs had been the biggest life form on the land for 160 million years. Along with the dinosaurs many other species – an estimated seventy per cent of all the species in the world – became extinct too.

This mass extinction was a great mystery for a long time. In the nineteenth century and for most of the twentieth century, geologists resisted the idea that that impacts of meteorites, comets or asteroids could have catastrophic effects on the evolution of life on Earth. Catastrophism was seen as an outmoded eighteenth century model for ecological and geological development – a biblical approach to processes. But in 1980 Walter and Luis Alvarez from California and others found some unexpected evidence that a great catastrophe did in fact happen at the end of the Cretaceous. They were studying rocks at Gubbio in Italy that dated from the boundary between the Cretaceous and the following Tertiary, when they found an unusual clay layer right at the boundary. It contained thirty times the normal level of a rare element called iridium. This is an element that exists deep inside Earth, dating from early in its formation, and in meteorites and asteroids. The source of the high level of iridium could not be from inside Earth, as volcanoes are fed by lava generated not far below the surface. The only possible source of the iridium was extraterrestrial. It was a major discovery that led on to a spectacular new theory about the end of the dinosaurs.

The end of the dinosaurs was, and still is, difficult to explain. At the time of the dinosaur extinction a lot of other species became extinct too. Most of the vegetation was wiped out, though ferns suddenly proliferated. Extinction can be explained by simple natural wastage. Species evolve into existence, and they evolve out of existence. They can just fade away, without any special mechanism being required. Some scientists think the dinosaurs may have just faded out, arguing that the dating methods available cannot tell us whether the dinosaurs died out within a year or over the course of five million years. But it looks significant when there are lots of dinosaurs before the end of the Cretaceous and none afterwards.

There is no shortage of theories about the extinction of the dinosaurs. Many of them cannot be disproved, but that does not give them any validity or status. Here is a sample. Dinosaurs died out because they suffered from hay fever. There was a pandemic that wiped them out. They grew too big. The mammals evolved and out-competed the dinosaurs. The mammals ate all the dinosaurs' eggs. The dinosaurs were all killed by cosmic rays.

There are, strange to say, sound scientifically based arguments against all of these theories, but they are not worth discussing here. They are not worth taking that seriously.

In 1980, Walter and Luis Alvarez and their supporters put forward the far more worthwhile theory that an object, perhaps an asteroid or a meteorite about six miles across, collided with the Earth sixty-five million years ago, at the end of the Cretaceous. They also proposed that this enormous impact produced a string of environmental effects that led to the extinction of large numbers of species.

If the impact was on land, it would have formed a huge impact crater 100 miles across. If the impact was in the ocean, huge tsunamis, waves a mile high, would have been sent careening round the oceans, sweeping hundreds of miles into the continental interiors, destroying everything in their path. Scalding debris from the impact would have rained down over a wide area, setting fire to the forests. Dust thrown up into the upper atmosphere by the impact would have been spread round the world by high-altitude winds and the resulting dust veil would have greatly reduced the amount of sunlight reaching the ground. The whole world would have descended into a kind of twilight. Plants failed to get enough sunlight to allow them to carry out photosynthesis. As the plants died, the herbivores that depended on them for food would have starved to death. Once the herbivores died, the carnivores that depended on them for food also died. The land food chain collapsed. The only land plant that seems to have prospered is the fern, which actually showed an increase of diversity at this time: the so-called 'fern spike'.

Conditions in the oceans were far worse. The acid rain poisoned the oceans, and corroded the shells of many species of shellfish. Far more creatures died in the oceans than on land. Altogether, about seventy per cent of all the species in the world died out.

The asteroid or meteorite impact theory has gradually become more and more popular, but from 1980 the hunt was on to find the impact crater to go with this spectacular event. Without a crater, the theory remained a hypothesis, a speculation; with a crater of an appropriate size and date, it would begin to look more like a fact. Eventually a huge impact crater 120 miles in diameter was discovered, concealed beneath later sediments, half on land and half on the seabed, on the coast of the Yucatan peninsula in Mexico. The crater was called the Chixculub Crater after a village near its centre and is now generally recognized as the likeliest location for the epoch-making impact that wiped out the dinosaurs along with many other species.

The site of the crater is faintly visible on photos taken from the Space Shuttle. The outermost concentric ring shows up as an arc-shaped trough ten feet deep and three miles wide. The crater itself is buried, and this trough has developed because of subsidence in the limestone layers deposited on top of it. The limestone has developed lots of caverns and sinkholes, and as the land surface has become pocked with sinks and collapsed caverns, an arc of collapse features has become visible, punctuating the shallow trough. The sinks were, incidentally used by the Mayas as places of sacrifice. This very shallow feature shows where the edge of the original crater lies, though it would originally have been half a mile deep.

The Chixculub Crater, which has a complex, concentric multi-ring structure, is believed by many geologists to have been created by the collision with an asteroid perhaps ten miles across. But not all geologists believe that the asteroid impact can have been responsible for the mass extinction. One group of scientists has questioned it on the grounds that the date of the impact does not match the mass extinction; the asteroid impact came first, which is as it should be, but the dinosaurs did not become extinct for another 300,000 years. These scientists argue from the dated core sample they obtained that the Chixculub impact combined with perhaps another two later collisions could explain the extinction. It is possible that the dating of the core rock is inaccurate, but the scientists took care to use five separate indicators of its age. If the date is correct, then the time difference really does look too great for the two events to be connected.

Another candidate has recently been found, the Shiva Crater on the Arabian Sea bed off the coast of Mumbai in India. The Indian geologists who discovered it suggest that it might be contemporary with Chixculub, and that the two craters might have been formed by fragments of the same large object, hitting Earth twelve hours apart as Earth rotated on its axis. The geologists who have dated Chixculub 300,000 years earlier disagree, believing that the Shiva Crater was made by a completely separate and later asteroid collision and that it did coincide with the mass extinction; they are happy to blame Shiva for the mass extinction. On the other hand, large scale events like these do not happen any more often than once in 100 million years in the life history of Earth, so it is very unlikely that two completely independent asteroid collisions would affect Earth within 300,000 years. It is more likely that the Indian geologists are right, and that these impacts were caused by pieces of the same disintegrating asteroid.

The '300,000 years too early' date for Chixculub is in any case a problem as far as the majority of geologists are concerned, as there is strong rock-layer evidence that the crater was formed at the boundary between the Cretaceous period and the succeeding Tertiary, the boundary where the mass extinction took place. In Haiti, for instance, there is once-molten rock deposited at this boundary that is similar to the deposits from the Chixculub Crater. The layers of debris thrown out by the collision become thicker as they are traced back to the crater, like a trail pointing to the impact site.

The impact theory is supported by several lines of evidence in addition to the craters. In the rock layers at the very end of the Cretaceous, there are shocked quartz crystals. The passage of a very powerful shock wave has rearranged the crystal structure of the quartz grains. In the same rock layers there are glass beads that look like as if they may been thrown out of a crater impact. There is also a soot layer in many places, probably resulting from the forest fires triggered by the scalding debris thrown out by the impact.

The team of geologists who pointed out that the Chixculub impact crater is 300,000 years too early to be connected with the mass extinction suggests that climate change was the real culprit. They believe that the climate first cooled (which could have been the effect of fall-out after the Chixculub impact) and then warmed up as a result of the greenhouse effect. Today, global warming is being blamed on man-made carbon dioxide. In the later Cretaceous period it can be blamed on carbon dioxide released during the large-scale lava eruptions all over the Indian Deccan; the Deccan Plateau is made of huge sheets of lava erupted at that time.

Today's global warming is trifling compared with the scale of the Cretaceous global warming of perhaps ten degrees Celsius. At the same time as the warming, the volume of the ocean basins was coincidentally reduced when the mid-ocean ridges became more active, heaving up huge areas of the sea bed and displacing the ocean water. The result was that sea level rose an astonishing 1,000 feet, drowning all the lowland areas of the continents. That, with the loss of grazing land and living space implied, was a huge environmental disaster in itself.

THE PLEISTOCENE ICE AGE

(2.6 MILLION BC)

THE SLOW-MOTION drifting of the continents that we saw assembling a gigantic supercontinent in the Permian has continued to the present. During the last few million years this drifting by chance produced a layout of land masses that favoured cooling. Antarctica inched its way into position over the South Pole, preventing tropical water from reaching the far south. The northern continents grouped themselves round the North Pole, trapping a great lake of cold water in the far north and isolating it too from any warming effect from tropical water. The result of these random movements of the continents was that both the Arctic and Antarctic regions became colder, and the contrast between cool poles and hot tropics intensified. Gradually the colder and colder winters of high latitudes led to a build-up of snow and ice and the average temperature of the world decreased. At 2.6 million years ago, the world entered the Pleistocene ('most recent') Ice Age.

There were other ice ages before this, at 750 million, 675 million, 440 million and 280 million years ago, so it looks as if ice ages return at a long time interval, perhaps every 200 million years on average. The previous ice ages were lengthy, lasting several million years, and the Pleistocene is only two and a half million years old. We are probably now in the middle of the Pleistocene Ice Age, which is ironic, given the current panic about global warning. The fact is that we are living in a warm episode in the Ice Age, probably quite a short-lived warm episode at that, and the glacial conditions will return.

Since the start of the Pleistocene Ice Age the world has been dominated by dramatic and wrenching environmental changes, as every 100,000 years huge areas in middle to high latitudes have been completely covered with ice for thousands of years at a time. Each time, the whole of Canada, Scandinavia and Siberia were engulfed in ice sheets as much as a mile deep. Most of Britain was repeatedly buried under ice. Regions next to the ice sheets were reduced to treeless, windswept tundras. Again and again, the vegetation and wildlife were wiped out, and a fresh colonization had to take place when the climate warmed up again in the interglacials or warm stages. The cold stages often began and ended quite suddenly.

Whole books have been written about the possible causes of these regular cycles of cold and warmth, but it is clear that the temperature changes are at least partly a response to complex astronomical changes, which include very small changes in the shape of Earth's orbit and a slight wobble as Earth spins on its axis. These cyclical changes were first discovered by James Croll in 1867, but not fully explored until the 1930s by Milutin Milankovitch. Graphs generated on a computer in the 1970s by Berger showed that their combined effects account for about half of the temperature changes. Some of the remaining temperature changes can be explained by what are called feedback effects. As more of the earth's surface is covered by snow and ice, more of the sun's energy is reflected back into space, causing the Earth to cool down some more. This allows the area under snow and ice to extend, and so on. The feedback mechanism explains why global cooling and global warming episodes tend to be rapid and catastrophic.

Within the most recent cold stage, known in northern Europe as the Weichsel cold stage, in Britain as the Devensian and in North America as the Wisconsin, there were several episodes of extreme cold (stadials), which produced glaciers and ice sheets.

The Milankovitch cycles, which are astronomical and therefore regular and predictable, can be made to generate a graph of summer solar radiation values for latitude 65 degrees North, and the low points in that well-defined wave pattern correspond exactly with the timing of the five stadials or glaciations within the Devensian (Wisconsin). What at first sight looks chaotic turns out to be very structured.

But climatologists have been aware for a long time that more than one 'forcing' process must lie behind the pattern of cold and warm stages. Many are coming round to the idea that volcanic eruptions have a major effect on temperature. As early as 1784 the American polymath Benjamin Franklin guessed that volcanoes could influence the weather. He believed the exceptionally cold winter of 1783–84 was the result of the eruptions of the Asama volcano in Japan and Laki in Iceland.

Modern climatologists agree with Franklin, believing that Asama caused overall cooling in the Northern Hemisphere by nearly 1.5 degrees Celsius and lasting for more than a decade. Today we tend not to see volcanoes as making a very obvious impact, but this is only because within living memory there have been no world-class eruptions. The biggest recent one was the Pinatubo eruption of 1991, which reduced global temperatures by one-third of a degree for several years. This was a significant and measurable effect, but not big enough to reverse the twentieth century global warming process. In fact, it could be the lack of big ash eruptions that has allowed temperature to rise over all between 1900 and 2000.

Right at the start of the Pleistocene period, 2.6 million years ago, there were some enormous volcanic eruptions along the northern coastline of the Pacific Ocean, in a line from Kamchatka to Alaska, following the Aleutian Islands. The volcanic eruptions were not the only cause of Northern Hemisphere glaciation, but they acted as the specific triggers, tipping the climate system into a full glacial mode. Studies of the sediment on the seabed of the

North Pacific, adjacent to this line of active volcanoes, show many layers of volcanic ash, some of them surprisingly thick. There were layers dating to 7 million, 6 million and 4.5 million years ago. Then, after a long quiet period, there were many ash layers beginning 2.6 million years ago. The Pleistocene Ice Age was a phase of much greater volcanic activity – and that is probably not a coincidence.

The onset of the Pleistocene Ice Age was a natural disaster on an epic scale in terms of landscape change. Each time the glaciers and ice sheets covered the northern continents, the landscapes of the highland areas were gouged out by the ice to form distinctive U-shaped valleys, corries and pyramid peaks, while the lowland areas were coated with thick layers of glacial debris. Major troughs such as the Yosemite Valley in California and the Lauterbrunnen Valley in central Switzerland were excavated by glaciers in successive cold stages. The Western Cwm next to Mount Everest was scooped out by the Khumbu Glacier. The Matterhorn was sharpened like a pencil by an ice sheet eroding its flanks. The flat plains of Wisconsin, East Anglia and the North Sea bed (now inundated) were coated with glacial deposits, in some places 300 feet thick and completely burying earlier landscapes. These were landscape changes on a grand scale.

The mountain regions were made more dramatic and diverse, the valleys and the ridges between them were strongly differentiated, while the lowlands were smoothed out into monotonous till plains. These effects were accentuated in each successive cold stage. In the cold stages, much of the world's water was locked up in glaciers and ice sheets. The water was in effect stranded on the land for thousands of years, interrupting the water cycle. This caused the level of the sea to fall, worldwide, to about 400 feet below its present day level. In the warm stages, most of that water was released, allowing the sea to return to its pre-glacial level. This up and down movement of the sea, like huge outgoing and incoming tides, has meant that coastal processes have been brought to bear on a much larger area than had previously been realized. The gently sloping bed of the English Channel is really a composite shore platform, with different areas of it eroded by the waves at different times as the sea level rose and fell. Much of the physical geography of countries such as Great Britain and the United States was produced by the distinct alternating landscape processes of the Pleistocene.

The Pleistocene Ice Age was a disaster in terms of the animal extinctions it caused. As it started, twenty-one major families of large mammals became extinct. The Ice Age was a natural holocaust, with every major episode of cooling or warming weeding out more species of plants and animals. But it also stimulated evolutionary development. It is no accident that it was during the Pleistocene, a period of enormous environmental challenge, that human beings evolved into *Homo sapiens*.

THE ERUPTION OF THE YELLOWSTONE SUPERVOLCANO

(638,000 BC)

THE YELLOWSTONE NATIONAL Park in Wyoming is a favourite tourist destination for Americans and foreign visitors, who travel there to see the wild scenery, which includes the Yellowstone Canyon, which is 1,000 feet deep, the forests and the mountains of this 8,000 feet high volcanic plateau. They also come to see the hot springs and geysers.

The geysers – there are 3,000 of them – are powered by groundwater seeping down through the ground and touching the hot magma (molten rock) that lies not far below the surface; the water shoots back up to the surface under enormous pressure, superheated by contact with the molten rock. The most famous geyser is Old Faithful. It is famous for the regularity of its eruptions (every 65 minutes), which last four and a half minutes each time. It is also greatly admired for the grace and beauty of the water column that it throws up between 95 and 130 feet into the air.

In fact, beneath the geysers lies a huge magma chamber six miles thick, twelve miles wide and thirty miles long. This subterranean lake of molten lava extends across about half of the national park yet, perhaps because it is out of sight, most visitors hardly give it a thought. They really should, because at any time it could erupt with a violence not experienced in human history!

Caldera eruptions are far and away the most violent and

dangerous type of volcanic eruption. Usually they involve a convulsive series of eruptions that completely empties the huge magma chamber. Once the chamber is empty, its unsupported roof collapses, causing a final violent destructive explosion.

On the land surface, the eroded remains of a large ancient collapse crater called a caldera stretches across about the same area as the magma chamber. Because it is on the surface, one might expect it to be visible, and therefore be a major element in the Yellowstone 'tourist trail'. But the caldera is so big that from the ground one could not be aware of more than one small part of it at a time. It only becomes apparent on satellite images; it cannot be seen on the ground at all and visitors to the park are completely unaware of it. The Old Faithful geyser is close to its western edge. This huge crater represents the scene of three huge volcanic eruptions, 1,800,000 years ago, 1,300,000 years ago and the most recent one 640,000 years ago.

Yellowstone is a supervolcano. It can eject over a trillion tons of lava and ash when it erupts, thirty times as much as Krakatoa in 1883. There have been no volcanic eruptions anywhere in the world on that scale in recorded history, so it is hard for us to imagine what it would be like to witness. We have nothing in our experience to compare it with. 'Thirty times as big as Krakatoa' is probably the best we can hope for. It was 638,000 years when ago the Yellowstone supervolcano threw out 240 cubic miles of ash. The ash cloud it produced spread out to cover the entire western half of the United States, just as the previous eruption did, burying the landscape under several feet of ash.

The pattern of earthquake activity in the Yellowstone area is (naturally) being monitored closely, and the pattern of earthquakes shows that the entire area of the ancient caldera is becoming active again, together with an extension westwards across the border into Idaho. If – and it would be closer to reality to say when – the Yellowstone supervolcano erupts again, it will not be safe to be within a 500-mile radius of the eruption. A herd of fossilized rhinos was found, choked to death by the ash of the 638,000 year old eruption, and that was 1,000 miles from Yellowstone. Even the city of San Francisco, with other environmental threats on its mind, would not be safe from a Yellowstone supervolcano eruption.

The eruptions happen approximately every 600,000 years, so the next Yellowstone eruption is due at any time. If the time interval was exactly 600,000 years, as some writers on the subject have implied, then the next eruption is seriously overdue. But the last three eruptions have not been exactly 600,000 years apart, so it may be that the next eruption will not happen for another 20,000 years. There is absolutely no way of predicting from just three eruptions. Some non-scientific Americans have tried to predict when the next one will happen by looking for elaborately coded hints in the Bible. This desperate measure produced the year 2010.

What the Yellowstone eruptions demonstrate is a common feature of natural events. Small-scale events are common. Large-scale events are uncommon. Spectacularly large-scale events are very uncommon indeed. Natural phenomena in other words are what statisticians call positively skewed – and this is something for which we should all be thankful. There is no way of stopping a supervolcano eruption; nor is there is any adequate way of preparing for one.

THE ATITLAN
ERUPTION

(82,000 BC)

IN THE GUATEMALAN Highlands, midway between North America and South America, two volcanoes stand side by side, called Toliman and Atitlan. Atitlan rises to a height of 11,500 feet. Their peaks each have the classic conical shapes we associate with volcanoes, but their lower slopes are coated with grotesque lobes and tongues of solidified lava. On one side, the Atitlan lavas snake down to the shores of Lake Atitlan, which stands at an altitude of 4,000 feet and rests in a large volcanic crater 1,000 feet deep and twenty-four miles across. The town of Solola has grown up close to the lake's northern shore, while the town of Atitlan itself has grown up on its southern shore.

This was the site of a large-scale eruption in 82,000 BC, much bigger than anything known in modern times. In this eruption, the Atitlan volcano ejected a huge cloud of ash, which settled across a large area of Central America. The ash layer was first recognized in 1959, when it showed up in cores taken from seabed sediments in both the Pacific and the Caribbean. This ash layer, which was known as Los Chocoyos ash, was eventually traced back, from the minerals it contained, to Atitlan. Finding evidence of a big prehistoric volcanic eruption was an important scientific achievement in itself, but geologists noticed something else that was of great importance: the faunal remains above and below the ash layer were quite different. The volcanic eruption must have happened at the same time as a major climatic change.

This major discovery was reinforced by the discovery from the Greenland ice sheet that at exactly the same time as the Atitlan eruption there was a marked increase in the accumulation of ice in Greenland, implying that the eruption in Guatemala had the effect of causing more snow to fall in Greenland. Cores taken from the North Atlantic seabed show that after the Atitlan eruption the sea surface temperature dropped three degrees.

Cause and effect relationships that far back in time are extremely hard to prove, but the evidence that is available to us very clearly points to a connection between the volcanic eruption in Guatemala and a global fall in temperature at the same time, in 82,000 BC. Global cooling on a grand scale was triggered by the eruption of Atitlan.

THE TOBA ERUPTION

(73,000 BC)

NEAR THE NORTHERN tip of Sumatra there is a huge caldera crater, 1,000 square miles in area. It was the scene of the biggest and most violent volcanic eruption to have occurred on the planet in the past 2.6 million years. It was in fact ten times greater than any other eruption during that time, and the most recent of the supervolcano eruptions. This was Toba. In its magnitude, the Toba eruption of 73,000 BC dwarfs all the other eruptions of the Ice Age.

As with the Atitlan eruption of 9,000 years earlier, we have difficulties in imagining the Toba eruption simply because nothing on that scale has happened in modern times. The colossal Toba crater, which was formed during the eruption, is still surrounded by the debris that was thrown out 75,000 years ago, layers of lava and ash that are still in some places hundreds of feet thick. That thickness of ash is an indication of the colossal energy levels involved, but there are others. Another is the unusually large size of the particles found at different distances from the volcano, as compared with other, later eruptions. It takes more energy to eject large particles than small ones, so the size of the particles can be used as an indicator of the level of energy involved in an eruption. In the so-called 'Campanian' eruptions of Vesuvius, which happened between 28,000 and 23,000 BC, the average particle size found 1,000 miles from the volcano was 0.001 inches; Toba ejected particles with an average size that was four times larger the same distance from the source. That shows that the energy of the eruption was far greater.

On the Asian mainland, at Tampan on the Malayan peninsula, the Toba ash is three feet thick, and that is 300 miles north-east of the caldera. Toba ash has been found in cores taken from the seabed all across the Bay of Bengal, as well as on the mainland of India. The ash footprint was unusually big and unusually thick compared with those known from other eruptions, another indicator of the enormous power of the 73,000 BC eruption. In the Campanian eruptions, Vesuvius deposited an ash layer 0.4 inches thick 300 miles away; Toba deposited a layer, on average, four times as thick.

The eruption deposits that can still be seen suggest that the equivalent of as much as 240 cubic miles of solid rock were erupted. Volcanologists think that the eruption lasted about ten days, which means that lava must have been thrown out at the amazing rate of 100 million cubic feet per second.

Some geologists argue that the energy of the eruption would have hurled ash and dust up to make a great cloud-like column rising fifty miles into the air. If so, this would have meant that the ash column passed right up through two major boundary layers in the atmosphere, the tropopause and the stratopause. On the whole that seems unlikely to me, as high-altitude winds blowing at considerable strength are likely to have pushed the ash sideways, but the scale of this eruption was so much greater than anything else we have observed or have any knowledge of, so maybe it is what happened – a towering column of ash that billowed right up through the troposphere (the lower atmosphere where we live) and right through the stratosphere as well. Within the first day of the eruption, the rotation of Earth would have spun the eruption cloud into a vortex about 4,000 miles in diameter, which, from space, would have looked rather like the spiral cloud system of a hurricane.

The ash veil from Toba spread around the world, cutting out a significant proportion of the sun's light and heat. Global temperatures plummeted. A phase of widespread and rapid ice sheet growth followed. As it happened, this was a moment when the Milankovitch cycles favoured cooling; it was a time when there was a marked decrease in summer solar radiation for astronomical reasons. But the Toba eruption was decisive, tipping the world into a major cooling episode and the Northern Hemisphere into large-scale glaciation. It was the Toba eruption that decisively launched the Devensian cold stage.

These catastrophic environmental effects brought the human race close to extinction. By the time the eruption was over there were only about 5,000 people left in the world. Over ninety per cent of the human race had been wiped out. This was the single biggest threat to the human species in its entire history. In view of the fact that it was the single biggest challenge to our survival, it is remarkable that we give the Toba eruption so little thought. It was a major landmark, but we have let it slide from our consciousness.

Looking at the large tranquil lake that fills the caldera today, it is almost impossible to imagine the violence of the eruption. In modern times, we tend to think of the Krakatoa eruption of 1883 as 'the biggest'. But Toba was thirty times bigger than that.

THE PHLEGRAEAN
FIELDS CALDERA
ERUPTION

(37,000 BC)

IN ABOUT 37,000 BC, there were large scale eruptions in the vicinity of Vesuvius. The violence of these eruptions can be read from the huge ash footprints that still survive across the floor of the Mediterranean. The scale of these eruptions was much bigger than the famous eruption of AD 79, which destroyed Pompeii.

Vesuvius's history as a volcanic cone goes back 25,000 years, but there are places nearby that have been active for longer. Immediately to the west of Naples is an area of subsidence known as the Phlegraean Fields Caldera. The volcanic field has several separate foci of volcanic activity, and the area is now being seen by geologists as an even bigger threat to the city of Naples than Vesuvius itself.

The eruption of the Phlegraean Fields Caldera in 37,000 BC was very violent. It was the biggest eruption in the Mediterranean region of the last 200,000 years. Large volumes of ash were thrown out, covering a huge area. As the magma chamber exhausted itself, its roof sagged, causing the whole area to subside. This is how the caldera was formed. The subsidence affected not only the Phlegraean Fields, but part of Naples and the adjacent coastline of the Bays of Naples and Pozzuoli.

At Pozzuoli the Romans built a Temple of Serapis. Early twentieth-century tourists were intrigued to see the remains of this temple partly submerged under water. This showed that the subsidence of the area had continued after the Roman period. In the 1960s, the remains were still under several feet of water. Then in 1983-85 an area of thirty square miles in the Phlegraean Fields was lifted as much as six feet as the magma chamber beneath refilled. A great deal of structural damage was done by this movement of the earth's crust; 36,000 people had to be relocated. The Temple of Pozzuoli has been lifted back up to its original position, above sea level. While that may be seen as a good thing, the reactivation of the Phlegraean Fields is very bad news for the people of Naples.

RISING
SEA LEVEL

(13,500 BC)

As THE HUGE ice sheet covering Canada collapsed and its edges melted rapidly back, large quantities of water were returned to the oceans. The global sea level started to rise dramatically, flooding huge areas of lowland. In 16,000 BC, the 'Long Island' coastline lay about seventy-five miles to the south-east of its present position. Starting in 13,500 BC it moved rapidly north-westwards as the lowlands were inundated, and by 9,000 BC it was forty-five miles closer to present-day Long Island. In the Persian Gulf, the coastline was displaced sideways by as much as 300 miles in 5,000 years. After that the submergence halted.

This spectacular submergence of lowlands, with all its ecological implications, was repeated all round the world. Only Africa was relatively unchanged by it, because of its very narrow continental shelves. The impact on wildlife was enormous. These often extensive lowlands were important grazing lands; submerged, they were put out of reach. The seabed on the continental shelf east of New York is scattered with mammoth teeth, which tell their own sad story.

The process of submergence is sometimes described as the Flandrian transgression, because it marked the beginning of the Flandrian interglacial. The transgression was rapid across gently sloping lowlands, though even at a speed of four feet in every 100 years still much slower than an incoming tide. Along the Lancashire coast of England, the sea rose vertically twenty-one feet in 200 years, the equivalent of the daily tidal range in Sussex today.

The rise in sea level was not smooth, because of small-scale variations in climate. As a result the sea rose in jerks, often making low cliffs that now lie hidden under the water. In the Mediterranean, erosional notches have been found showing that the sea hovered for a time at 180 feet, ninety feet and thirty-three feet below its present level.

The flooding of the continental shelves had lots of implications. Some see it as the most important geographical event of recent times. Certainly it changed the shapes of coastlines from the unfamiliar to the familiar. The British Isles, France, the Irish Sea and the North Sea were all joined together by rather featureless lowlands; it was only after the submergence that the distinctive ragged outline of the half-drowned British Isles appeared. Similarly, between south-east Asia and Australia a huge landmass, the Sunda shelf, was turned by the invasion of the sea into the Malay peninsula and a complex cluster of islands that includes the islands of Sumatra, Java and Borneo.

The inundation initiated the building of many modern deltas, such as the Mississippi and Nile deltas. It did this by invading and obstructing the lower courses of the rivers. By checking their flow, the mass of sea water induced the rivers to drop their loads of silt and sand. The Nile channel became choked with sand bars, causing the water to divert round their sides, and this led to the river dividing in two, and then in two again. In this way the delta was produced.

The inundation also stimulated the development of coral reefs; it drowned the lower courses of river valleys and stimulated the development of flood plains such ase that of the River Thames; it drowned the lower parts of glaciated valleys and formed fjords such as the Sogne Fjord in Norway or Glacier Bay in Alaska. The advancing sea bulldozed seabed sediment forward to create all our modern beaches, such as Blackpool beach, and barrier islands like Cape Hatteras.

By reshaping the outlines of the continents, it strongly influenced the migration patterns of a wide range of organisms – including human beings. While the sea level was low, it was possible for people to walk into North America from Asia across what is now the Bering Strait and was then a broad plain called Beringia. This is how North America was peopled, near the end of the last cold stage. It was possible, too, for people to walk from France to Great Britain across the dried-out floor of the southern North Sea and English Channel. Once the rising sea flooded the land bridges those routes were no longer passable.

The flooding and permanent loss of huge areas of useful lowland stuck on the folk memories of many communities round the world. The transgression formed the basis of the flood myths that many communities have at the core of their religious texts. The earliest known myth, written down for the first time in about 3000 BC, was Gilgamesh. It tells of a great flood, in which early people were saved by building an ark. A version of the same flood story has been handed down to us as the biblical story of Noah's flood. So this highly significant event, or process, played its part in myth-building, in helping people to assemble stories that explained or illuminated their place in the world.

THE MISSOULA
SUPERFLOODS

(11,150 BC)

IN THE LAST cold stage of the Ice Age, the Wisconsin, a huge ice sheet covered Canada. Its southern edge more or less followed the frontier between Canada and the United States, though in some places the ice crossed the border. At the ice sheet's maximum extent, the state of Wisconsin was covered by the ice sheet. Meltwater collected at low points along its southern edge, especially towards the end of the cold stage, when the climate began to warm and the melting was more aggressive. As the southern edge of the ice sheet ran approximately along the Canada–US border, the temporary lakes formed in an irregular chain from the state of Washington in the west, eastwards to the Great Lakes.

Some of these temporary ice-dammed lakes were very large indeed. Lake Missoula, which lay across the states of Washington and Idaho, contained up to 300 cubic miles of water. Although we tend to think of ice ages as being continuously cold, there were big variations in the climate, just as there have been in the post-glacial period. As the climate warmed and cooled, the ice sheets fluctuated in area and thickness, so that from time to time huge volumes of water were released from Lake Missoula in as many as forty catastrophic floods. These eroded the scablands of the Columbia River Basin in Washington, and dumped huge amounts of sediment out on lowlands that are now submerged continental shelf. The last of the Missoula floods was in 11,150 BC. The amount of water released in this last flood was, amazingly, twenty times the total volume of water flowing through all the rivers in the world at the present day.

This biblical deluge and the huge amounts of energy it released changed the landscape of the region beyond recognition. In many areas, it left behind huge boulder bars. In others, the raging torrents swept round pre-existing low hills, sculpting them into streamlined forms. In places the basalt bedrock was exposed, eroded and carved with complex patterns of grooves and potholes. The sediment the flood waters carried along was shaped into giant ripples with crests sixteen feet high and 300 feet apart.

THE MISSISSIPPI SUPERFLOOD

(10,500–9500 BC)

MELTWATER FROM THE Canadian ice sheet collected in the centre of the continent to create a huge lake, Lake Agassiz. The lake has appropriately been named after Louis Agassiz, the man who first conceived the idea of the Pleistocene Ice Age.

The temperature rose rapidly at the close of the cold stage, between 10,500 and 9,500 BC, causing Lake Agassiz to overflow southwards into the Mississippi valley. When 3,250 cubic miles of water flooded down the Mississippi, it raised sea level by two or three inches.

The centre of North America was in upheaval. The ice front shifted its position and the meltwater kept finding different escape routes. The situation was made more complicated by the ever-decreasing weight of the melting ice sheet. So much weight was shed that the centre of the continent itself began to rise, and this accentuated the tendency for Lake Agassiz to empty. Only a few centuries after the Mississippi superflood, Lake Agassiz once again overflowed catastrophically, but this time towards the east, down the St Lawrence Valley into the Atlantic.

GLOBAL
WARMING

(8300 BC)

TODAY THE MEDIA are full of talk about global warming, the increase in the temperature of about half a degree Celsius that took place during the twentieth century. Journalists, environmentalists and politicians of every party are working hard to condition us to see this current episode of global warming as a catastrophic episode. But if we look back to the much larger-scale, much more dramatic global warming episode of 10,000 years ago, a time when the temperature rose several degrees, we see something different. We invariably see that global warming episode in an entirely positive light. It was the end of the last cold stage, the start of the Flandrian interglacial. It was a springboard for human progress, a real beginning for *Homo sapiens sapiens* that would shortly make agriculture and settled life in villages and towns possible. It was therefore, as everyone agrees, a very positive benchmark in human prehistory. It seems we are very inconsistent in our responses to global warming and our evaluation of it.

The warming that started in 8,300 BC brought with it some spectacular environmental changes, especially in middle latitudes. The ice sheet covering Scotland and northern England melted away completely, though not continuously. There were zigzags in the temperature graph, times when the climate was cooling, times when the warming resumed. The warming episode also generated profound changes in southern Britain. In Norfolk, as we know

51

from pollen preserved in pond sediments, the treeless tundra gave way to birch woodland for a short time, and that in turn gave way to a woodland of Scots pine; that developed into a mixed woodland dominated by elm, oak and hazel trees; and all this change happened within the space of 1,500 years.

In the context of human history and prehistory, these things happened not so long ago. The first totem poles were raised at Stonehenge (on the site of the visitor car park) in a clearing in the early pine woodland, and they were put up, one after another, not long after the interglacial started. The stones at Stonehenge were erected about halfway between then and now.

THE EMPTYING OF
LAKE AGASSIZ INTO
THE NORTH ATLANTIC

(6200 BC)

THE LAST OF the large ice-dammed lakes, Lake Agassiz, was not emptied until 6200 BC. As the retreating Canadian ice sheet warmed, decayed and shrank back, a huge volume of water collected underneath it. Lake Agassiz once again became swollen, along with a second lake to the east, Lake Ojibway. Then a series of major environmental changes led to the biggest superflood known on the planet. The ice sheet became unstable and suddenly imploded, releasing the trapped meltwater in a great rush. The ice dams ponding up the freshwater melted back, releasing the water from the lakes. The waters of Lake Ojibway burst northwards between two fragments of the Canadian ice sheet into the Hudson Bay lowland, and from there to the North Atlantic. An unimaginably large volume of water, which scientists estimate at 14,000 cubic miles of melted ice sheet, was added to the North Atlantic, raising its level by twelve inches. It was one of the biggest floods of the last two million years.

The freshwater was lighter than the salt ocean water and floated on top of it. This flooding of the North Atlantic with fresh water shut down the Atlantic Conveyor for a second time, stopping the familiar circulation of ocean currents, including the Gulf Stream, for 400 years. Much colder, drier weather conditions descended on Europe. Once again, Northern Europe was plunged suddenly into an ice age. In Great Britain, the mountain corries refilled with ice in what is called the Loch Lomond Readvance.

The effects of the freshwater added to the North Atlantic from the North American ice sheet were reinforced by similar meltwater being added from the Scandinavian ice sheet from 7000 BC onwards. Meltwater collected in glacial lakes in Poland, which overflowed westwards across the North German Plain into the North Sea. As the Scandinavian ice front retreated, this meltwater found new routes to the west, successively further north. This created a series of broad parallel valleys which are known as Urstromtaler (primeval storm valleys).

At the same time as this was happening, sea level was rising rapidly. By 6200 BC, it was rising about 1.8 inches a year, flooding many lowland areas. The northern and central areas of the North Sea went under water, and large areas of Scandinavia were similarly drowned. Great Britain was finally separated from the European mainland by the relentlessly rising water. In Eastern Europe, the Sea of Marmara, the limb of the Mediterranean that extended closest to the great Euxine Lake, was filling higher and higher.

The dry conditions in eastern Europe and Asia Minor created huge problems for the early farmers in these areas. They found it harder and harder to produce food. Many gave up their old settlements, which turned out to be in arid and unproductive areas. The ancient settlement of Catal Huyuk, high in the Anatolian plateau, was abandoned. People moved to lower ground, where it was warmer and moister, and made new settlements there. Many of these settlers gathered by the western and southern shores of the Euxine Lake.

For the 400 years of this 'Mini Ice Age', from 6200 to 5800 BC, the benign coastlands of the Euxine Lake acted like a huge oasis. It was a place where farmers could grow crops, set up new villages, and probably trade networks. If you are wondering why you have not heard of the Euxine Lake, there is a very good reason. It no longer exists, and the story of another great disaster lies ahead for it – and for the people who lived beside it. The lost villages of the Euxine's shores cannot be seen any more, as they lie up to 500 feet below the waters of the Black Sea.

THE STOREGGA
LANDSLIDE

(6100 BC)

LANDSLIDES ON STEEP mountain sides are common enough, and well known enough. What is not widely known is that landslides can happen on the seabed too, and on a very large scale. Often these happen on relatively steep slopes but, because the sediment is saturated and surrounded by water, even landslides on fairly gentle slopes are possible. Around the coastline of north-west Europe there is an area of shallow water called the continental shelf. The English Channel and North Sea are part of this shelf area. The water is less than 600 feet deep and the gradients on the seabed are very gentle. Where the continental shelf comes to an end, along its outer edge, there is a steep drop down into the deep ocean basin of the North Atlantic. This steep drop down is called the continental slope. It is on this steep slope marking the geological edge of Europe that the Storegga landslides happened.

The existence of this landslide complex has only been known about for the last few decades because it was only discovered when geologists were commissioned by the oil companies to carry out detailed surveys of the seabed and the rocks below it. It was then that they found a huge area of landslipped sediment, roughly the area of Great Britain, spread out over the seabed between Norway and Iceland. The landslides are surprisingly large – much more extensive than any that are found on land – and the amount of sideways movement involved is also surprisingly large. Rocks breaking away from the continental slope not far from the coast of central Norway have slid, rolled and flowed halfway to Greenland.

The layout of the sediment shows that there were three separate Storegga landslides, and that they all happened in the last 50,000 years. While the geologists were mapping the Storegga slides, geomorphologists were discovering layers of sediment in the Netherlands and Scotland that appeared to have been deposited by a big tsunami. Then it was realized that the two – the landslides and the tsunami – were connected. It was the displacement of huge volumes of rock down the continental slope off the coast of Norway that had generated the big tsunami.

The second Storegga landslide is thought to have happened in 6,100 BC and was probably triggered by an earthquake. The scale of the landslide deposits on the seabed is such that a very big tsunami with waves up to 100 feet high, a mega-tsunami, is likely to have been created, and it would have affected all the shores of the North Sea as well as travelling further afield, across to North America. At several places near the North Sea coast of Scotland there is a sand deposit resting up to twenty-five feet above sea level, and dating to around 6,000 BC. A Scottish stone age settlement was engulfed by the sand. In 1989, it was proposed that that this sand deposit was washed into place by the mega-tsunami produced by the second Storegga slide.

The fact that Storegga is not just a single landslide but a landslide complex prompts the thought, as with many other disasters, that there could be another one in the future. This could be very significant, as the Storegga landslide area is just where Norway's richest reserves of oil lie. A future landslide in the area could, and almost certainly would, snap seabed oil pipelines, causing massive pollution, and do untold damage to any drilling platforms that happened to be in the way. The economic consequences for Norway are very great. At the same time, there is nothing the Norwegians can realistically do to prevent another landslide from happening. All they can do is watch and wait, and be aware that another landslide would be likely to produce another tsunami that would wreak havoc throughout the North Sea basin. It is, after all, not just the Pacific Ocean and the Indian Ocean that need a tsunami warning system: a global tsunami warning system is what we really need.

THE BLACK SEA FLOOD

(5550 BC)

THE INHABITANTS OF those villages around the shore of the Euxine Lake must have been bewildered and horrified when they found the lake waters creeping across their fields and into their houses. The water was rising slowly, but continuously, at about six inches per day. That might sound a gentle enough rate of rise, but on a very gently sloping plain huge areas were being covered quite fast. Many unfortunate people must have been trapped and drowned by the rising waters.

This was one of the greatest natural disasters ever to strike Europe. It was discovered by a team of scientists that included Walter Pitman and William Ryan. By looking at samples of sediment from the floor of the Black Sea, they were able to map the shores of a huge freshwater lake that had once existed 500 feet below the present surface of the Black Sea. In the sediments, there was a horizon above which tiny marine shells suddenly appeared.

The Euxine Lake had owed its origin to a combination of melting ice in Scandinavia and the isostatic uplift that went with the removal of the weight of the ice. Huge volumes of meltwater were released, flowing southwards along the valleys of the Danube, Dnieper, Volga and Don. When the cold phase right at the end of the Devensian came, that inflow of meltwater virtually stopped. After that, the Euxine Lake level began to drop as a result of evaporation from its surface. The level of water in the

Mediterranean to the south-west meanwhile was rising; it was about fifty feet below its present level, and creeping up.

In 5500 BC, the Sea of Marmara finally started to overflow to the north-east. At first a trickle spilled over. That turned into a stream, and that quickly developed into a river. Before long, it was a raging torrent with rapids surging forwards at sixty miles per hour. The speed and force of the water were such that it was able to rip out a gorge up to 450 feet deep. It was this terrific surge of water that made the level of the Euxine Lake rise by six inches a day. People living close to the new 'river' bringing the water in would possibly have realized that something catastrophic and irreversible was under way and made their escape, but further to the north-east, around the shores of the lake, many must have been completely mystified, watching spellbound as the waters rose to engulf them. Some people have wondered, naturally, whether this catastrophe is the prehistoric disaster that lay behind the story of the biblical flood. To those involved, those who were living on what is now the bed of the Black Sea, it must indeed have seemed as if the entire world had disappeared under water.

THE MOUNT MAZAMA
CALDERA ERUPTION

(4860 BC)

CRATER LAKE IN Klamath County, Oregon, is a spectacularly beautiful circular lake sitting in an enormous circular basin five miles in diameter, rimmed by cliffs 600 to 2,000 feet high. The water level in the lake is 6,160 feet above sea level. In spite of its high altitude, Crater Lake has never been known to freeze over.

In the lake is Wizard Island, a small, picturesquely forested cone built up from the floor of the enormous crater; Wizard Island has its own small crater. The steep cliffs overlooking the lake show alternating and outward-sloping layers of ash and lava, the internal structure of a broad shield volcano or stratovolcano. Small U-shaped valleys are truncated abruptly by the crater walls, showing that before the big eruption that blasted out the crater valley glaciers had flowed down the flanks of the cone. Layers of ash blanket the surrounding country.

All the geological evidence points to a great volcanic mountain that once stood on the site of Crater Lake, rising to an altitude of 14,000 feet above sea level and 8,000 feet above the surrounding tableland. This imposing lost mountain is known as Mount Mazama.

The eruption of Mount Mazama in 4860 BC was violent: forty-two times more powerful than the Mount St Helens eruption of 1980. The destruction of the mountain was a combination of explosion and collapse. It was a classic 'caldera' eruption, in which the magma chamber beneath the volcano completely emptied and then collapsed – the most violent type of volcanic eruption there is.

Mount Mazama in effect decapitated itself. The uppermost 6,000 feet of this ancient peak has been blown off – ten cubic miles of rock. Some of this is spread across the surrounding area, with some blocks twelve feet across hurled as much as twenty miles away, though the volume there only accounts for a fraction of the former mountain. An estimated nine cubic miles of rock must have shot high into the air as dust and scattered all around the world without leaving a recognizable trace. In fact, scientists are now detecting traces of this and other large-scale eruptions trapped as fine layers inside the ice sheets of Greenland and Antarctica.

METEORITE
SWARM

(3100 BC)

ALL AROUND THE world in 3100 BC, something was happening to make people do things differently. In Great Britain, notably, the first modest earth circle was marked out at Stonehenge, an earth bank within a rock-cut ditch; just outside the north-eastern entrance was a collection of stake holes that were markers for the northernmost moonrise. Within the circular bank was a post circle. It was the modest beginning of what would become a major set-piece monument. At nearby Avebury, an even more ambitious monument, a gigantic stone circle within a big earthen henge (a circular ditch inside a circular bank), was laid out at the same time. The great passage grave of Newgrange was built in Ireland. At other sites up and down the British Isles the first generation of stone circles was raised. It was a major cultural shift. Before there had been long barrows, some of them admittedly very elaborate structures, but now there were these new types of monument, the henges and stone circles. To go with them there were, in some places, huge round burial mounds too. What happened in Great Britain to make people suddenly start building new types of monument? A religious conversion? Or an environmental crisis? Or perhaps both?

In other regions there were also major cultural shifts. Civilizations started. It has been suggested by some prehistorians that 3100 BC was a turning point in world prehistory. In Mesopotamia there was a dark age. It began in 3100 BC, lasted a century, and separated two well-documented periods. In 3100 BC, the Uruk period ended. In 3000 BC, the Early Dynasty began. In between there was a dwindling of culture. In the Mayan civilization, something of profound significance must have happened in 3114 BC, the first year in the Mayan calendar.

There are some small craters dating to about this time, suggesting the impact of large meteorites, or fragments of something much bigger such as a comet or an asteroid. If a swarm of meteorites hit the earth, there would have been a range of natural disasters and environmental shifts. A great deal of dust would have been thrown up into the atmosphere, creating a dust veil. If some fell into the sea, there would have been tsunamis. People would have been thrown into a panic, perhaps rejected old religious beliefs for the sake of new ones or become fanatically obsessed with the observation of old rituals.

This became a cultural boom time, when the first great civilizations had their origins. Northern and southern Egypt were unified, although it is not known exactly how this union was organized, as there is no evidence of conquest. The first king of this united Egypt was called Menes, and his reign began some time between 3150 and 3110 BC. It would take several hundred years before this embryonic civilization was transformed, in around 2700 BC, into what is called Old Kingdom Egypt. Events in Mesopotamia seem to have marched to the same rhythm. The great city-states of Uruk and Ur had come into being, then in about 2600 BC they became components of a larger union. In Crete, the Early Minoan culture was evolving.

There is no suggestion that these widely scattered cultures had contact with one another, rather that they were all switched on by what they saw in the heavens above them, and by what was happening in their immediate environment. The lunar post holes at Stonehenge and the midwinter sunrise roof box at the Newgrange passage grave imply that the people of the middle neolithic in the British Isles were now much more interested in things that were happening in the sky than before. This must not be exaggerated too much, because they had for hundreds of years been building long barrows with their entrances or forecourts pointing towards the sunrise. But now it became more obsessional, more time-consuming, more meticulous.

Perhaps the ancient saga, the Edda, contains some folk memory of the event.

> *Everything is shaking and quaking and falls from Heaven. The wolf is so big that it can snap from Earth to Heaven; it can swallow the Sun. The snake is so big that it fills the sea, runs into the beach and throws fire and poison so that the Earth begins to catch fire. The tremblings shake loose the ash of the Aasa Land and burn it, and its burning branches spread all over the world and even the stars in the Heaven move their place. Heimdal blows his horn louder than a thunderstorm. The soldiers of Valhalla crowd onto the lowland of Ida, but giant birds and dragons spitting fire fill the air and fall on the lowland and fall on the soldiers, crushing them. Down in the Middle Land people run out of their homes like ants from a disturbed stack, and the mighty army pushes beneath them to the rainbow bridge, which collapses. The wolf jumps to the Aasa Land, the snake climbs on its tail, binds itself into the Odin's Lidskjalv and draws itself up thus . . .*

The picture language is very strange, but it could be taken as an attempt at a word picture of a large-scale natural disaster. Elements in it sound distinctly cosmic in character. It could be a description of a super-Tunguska event as seen by an archaic and superstitious prehistoric society.

It is possible that the meteorites that appeared in the sky and fell to Earth in 3100 BC belonged to the swarm known as the Taurids. The Taurids represent the debris from the break up of a very large object, perhaps an asteroid sixty miles across, and one that probably disintegrated between 10,000 and 30,000 years ago. If it had happened any earlier, the debris would have become dispersed around the inner solar system and no longer be recognizable as an identifiable stream or tube. The Taurid complex is believed by astronomers to have intercepted Earth in about 3100 BC, when it could have caused a whole sequence of Tunguska events spanning a hundred years. The Taurid complex is accompanied by a couple of comets, Encke and Oljato.

Perhaps meteorite storms caused by an encounter with the Taurids around 3100 BC attracted the attention of the British megalith builders to the sky, to the old and the new things that could be seen there. It is very unlikely that Stonehenge or any other monument was built to observe meteorites, because they do not lend themselves to that kind of observation; only cyclically repeating phenomena could be built into a monument. In fact, the wooden posts littering the north-eastern entrance were part of exactly that sort of exercise. The northernmost moonrise does not take place at the same point on the horizon every year: it moves along. The posts made it possible to detect the pattern. There was an ultimate northernmost point – from the centre of Stonehenge it was a little to the north of north-east – and the Moon reached it only once every eighteen-and-a-half years. With several generations of Stonehenge people observing the moon for more than a hundred years between them, they were able to mark out six complete cycles – more than enough to prove that this was a perpetually repeating pattern. Those repeating patterns, however frightened they may have been by the meteorites, are what the Stonehenge people were ultimately concerned about.

That leaves us with the Mayan calendar. It is possible that the zero date in the calendar was chosen arbitrarily or on the basis of some poetic version of the creation. But the coincidence in date is compelling, and it has been suggested that maybe there was a major cosmic event, perhaps the spectacular disintegration of one of the large fragments in the Taurid complex, on 13 August 3114 BC. If so, that spectacle would have made an obvious starting point for the Mayan calendar.

THE THERA ERUPTION

(1520 BC)

IN THE MIDDLE of the south Aegean Sea, immediately to the north of Crete, is a ring of islands called Santorini. Cradled within this ring of islands, Thera, Therasia and Aspronisi, is a huge oval bay seven miles across. This bay was the scene of an unimaginably violent eruption, which destroyed the bronze age civilization on Santorini. Where once hill slopes rose to a cluster of volcanic peaks, the seabed is now 1,300 feet deep. Along the cliffed walls of the caldera it is possible to see the alternate layers of ash and lava, which tell of a long sequence of eruptions. Phira, the main town of Santorini today, stands high on the rim of the huge crater, with a spectacular view across the bay towards the setting sun.

Until the huge eruption destroyed the ancient civilization in 1520 BC – some archaeologists and geologists prefer 1620 BC – there were villages and at least one city on Santorini. That city was a port on the south coast, facing Crete. It was probably called Therassos and the island itself was called Thera, just as it was in the classical period. The Minoans on Crete worshipped a goddess called Therassia, 'She-from-Therassos'. Today, Therassos has become the archaeological site of Akrotiri (which is currently closed to visitors following an accident). A village existed there as early as 2500 BC, so the city had been evolving over a period of a thousand years. By the time the destruction came, a fully developed, civilized and prosperous Minoan way of life was in full swing. We know this because the ash that overwhelmed and asphyxiated Therassos as a living city entombed and preserved much of it for us to see. Tantalizingly, even more of the city remains buried under the ash.

Long before the big eruption, there were signals that magma was on its way to the surface, that the magma chamber under Thera was filling. The town of Therassos was damaged by earthquakes in 1580 BC, but it was repaired. After a period of stability, the final catastrophe started to unfold in about 1525 BC. The initial earthquakes warned the Therans to leave, gave them time to gather their treasured possessions and escape from the city to neighbouring islands, with perhaps Ios, the nearest, as the first stop. The sequence of tremors culminated in a really big earthquake that shook down many houses. Their ruins are found under layers of rose pumice thrown out during the eruption that followed, showing that they were shaken down before the eruption began.

The big eruption was preceded by a series of earthquakes and small eruptions of pumice, which fell on the doomed city like a snowstorm. Then the earth stopped shaking and some of the refugees came back to the island. Special work teams went in to make the city safe. Unsafe buildings were demolished to stop them from collapsing into the narrow streets, exactly as was done after the 1580 BC earthquake. The work teams cleared as much as they could of the pumice, which had the consistency and lightness of popcorn; it was everywhere and they were working knee-deep in it. The work teams cleared paths through the debris. Some of it was retained behind some drystone walling to stop it from falling back across the streets. Generally the work teams smoothed the pumice out and left the streets at a slightly higher level. Ground-floor rooms suddenly became semi-basements.

We cannot tell how many Therans returned, but they must have been deeply frustrated when, in 1520, after a lull of five years, the island started to shake again and emissions of gas, steam and smoke spurted from the mountain in the centre of the island. The Therans knew that either a major earthquake or a volcanic eruption was coming. At that stage most of the people left, not only the city but the island as a whole. Only a few stayed behind – in these situations it usually the foolhardy and the old – to perish in the holocaust that followed. The eruption sequence was under way.

First the island was sprayed with a fountain of fine white pumice, which settled on the city like a six-feet thick layer of snow. It was in effect lava with millions of tiny gas bubbles in it, thrown up from seven miles below the island. Then there was a pause, time for large quantities of basalt rock from the crater's sides to roll down into the floor of the crater; fragments of this were later hurled out sideways. Then another fountain of pumice was sprayed all over the island. A huge eruption cloud towered twenty miles above the island.

By this stage, most of the houses of Therassos were buried under pumice. The roofs of many of them had given way, the houses had filled up. The walls of many of the houses are broken off at about six feet above the ground, suggesting that the lowest six feet were protected by being buried in pumice.

By then the eruption crater had grown big enough to allow sea water to seep into it and this caused some huge explosions which sent massive blocks of rock hurtling outwards like shells at 100 feet a second. The upper storeys of many houses were shot away by these bombs, some of them five feet across. Perhaps ten cubic miles of magma from the chamber underneath the island had been thrown up. Eventually the lava chamber under the volcano was emptied. The island sagged into this yawning vault and networks of radial and ring fissures opened up. What was left of the ancient volcano that had once risen about 1,600 feet into the air collapsed into the abyss. Sea water poured after it into the searingly hot chamber, causing more violent eruptions and a series of tsunamis 200 feet high that raced outwards through the widened entrance to the South Bay across the Aegean Sea to Crete. The progressive collapse of the centre of the island into the magma chamber created a similar open channel, which now separates the (main) island of Thera from the northern tip of the (smaller) island of Therasia.

The collapse of the volcano must have been accompanied by colossal shallow-seated earthquakes measuring as high as nine or ten on the Richter scale. Ear-splitting explosions were heard as deafening roars all around the Aegean – and identified in terror as the roars of Poseidon, who was a sea-god but identified also with bulls and earthquakes. No wonder Poseidon was the principal god in the Minoan pantheon. The roaring would have been audible as far away as Pakistan, the Congo and Egypt. People living in England, in the shadow of Stonehenge, then recently completed with its bluestones reinstated, heard the rumble of Thera's spectacular implosion and will have thought no more of it than distant thunder.

The Minoan civilization on Santorini itself was completely expunged by this catastrophic eruption. The places near the centre of the island where people had lived were blasted out or had sunk into the caldera; the places round the edge where they had lived, like the town of Therassos, were buried beneath the ash. The island of Santorini had been cauterized.

The civilization on the 'mainland' of Crete was seriously damaged but not destroyed. The tsunamis took twenty-five minutes to reach the coastal towns along the north coast of Crete. Those towns were wrecked by the giant waves. I have seen the remains of waterfront houses at the harbour town of Amnisos on the north coast of Crete, with their huge wall stones sucked out of place by the tsunamis of 1520 BC. Many of the merchant ships that made the Minoans rich must have been sunk or smashed by the tsunamis. Then there was the ash falling from the huge ash plume that reached out from Santorini to cover eastern Crete. Only a thin layer of acidic ash was needed to put the fields out of production for a couple of years – enough to cripple the Minoan economy. It was not long before the Mycenaeans, the people of mainland Greece, exploited the Minoans' weakened state and reached out to take their trading empire from them.

The Minoan civilization was not to be destroyed all at once, though. It limped on for another hundred years. But it was critically weakened, and the Mycenaean civilization, which was completely unaffected by the eruption, simply because Greece was upwind at the time, was able to develop and overtake it. At a stroke, the Santorini eruption of 1520 (or 1620) BC brought about the extinction of a civilization and the birth of another. By burying substantial parts of Therassos at Akrotiri, it also supplied us with an incredibly detailed picture of the way of life in Minoan Santorini.

The frescoes have in many cases survived complete and in full colour. They provide us with far more information about Minoan religious beliefs than we have been able to reassemble at Knossos. In particular there is a remarkably poetic portrait of a beautiful goddess, who is probably Therassia, the goddess of Therassos. She sits on an elaborate stepped altar, where she is courted by her heraldic beasts, a monkey and a griffin, and offered a gift of crocuses by a girl. There is also an elaborate and complex series of images connected with rites of passage for adolescent boys and girls, which gives us an idea of some of the ceremonies that would have taken place within the Knossos Labyrinth on Crete.

The area of the bronze age city that has so far been excavated is frustratingly small – about twenty buildings and a handful of streets – and the rate of excavation is frustratingly slow, but it has given us a wonderful opportunity to see what town life was like in the Minoan period.

There has been nothing on the scale of the Minoan caldera eruption of Santorini anywhere in the world since 1520 BC. The awe-inspiring sequence of events and its consequences to human history should make us stop and consider the real nature of our relationship with Earth. We and all our possessions and our entire culture can be wiped out at a stroke in a single geological disaster. The Earth and its natural processes are far more powerful than we are. This is a painful lesson that we have to relearn periodically.

THE DESTRUCTION OF THE KNOSSOS LABYRINTH

(1380 BC)

THE BRONZE AGE Minoan civilization on the island of Crete was a very distinctive one, in many significant ways different from the Mycenaean civilization that replaced it. The Minoans were great nature-lovers, responding to all the various aspects of the natural world – the land and especially the sea. This interest is plain to see in the decorative images they put on their walls and pottery. They had a distinctive ideal of human beauty, too. They liked to see long, slender, graceful but muscular limbs, narrow waists and dark hair falling in long flowing ringlets to the waist, on both men and women. They liked to see broad shoulders and deep chests on men, and firm full breasts and full hips on women. Their art has nature as its focus, not contemporary events. There are no statues or portraits of kings, no great personal monuments. Their rulers evidently had no ego – the diametric opposite of their contemporaries in Egypt, Turkey and Mesopotamia. There were no pharaohs or great kings on Crete.

The Minoan civilization was severely damaged and shaken by the Thera eruption, though not completely extinguished by it. The trading empire that had its hub at the Minoan capital of Knossos, just south of modern Heraklion, was weakened and the mainland Greeks, the Mycenaeans, were greedily taking the trading network over. The takeover was probably piecemeal, a gradual process spread across several decades.

The Minoan civilization had at its centre a remarkable building with a strange design, one that retained a reputation in later centuries as a puzzle building. This remarkable rambling multi-storey building of stone and mud brick, with hundreds of tapering wooden pillars and scores of staircases, was the Labyrinth. It stood at the centre of the bronze age city of Knossos. Both the words 'Knossos' and 'Labyrinth' are bronze age Minoan words, which can be read on the clay archive tablets actually found in the ruins of the building 2,300 years after they were baked in the fire that destroyed the building. The syllables can still be read in the baked clay: 'Konosos' and 'Labyrinthos' are two of the names the Minoans called the place – and there may have been more.

This very large building, the largest building in ancient Crete, has for the past century been called the Palace of Minos, after the legendary king of Crete, but all of the archaeological evidence that has come from the site shows that it was a temple complex. The building was a collection of shrines, sanctuaries, temple work-shops, sacristies and vestries, rather like a medieval abbey. The central feature, around which all the shrines were arranged, was a huge rectangular courtyard. The wall paintings show all sorts of elaborate and exotic religious ceremonies presided over by priestesses. These women were very elaborately and expensively dressed and it is clear from the frescoes that they were incredibly important people. The priestesses were at the centre of every religious ritual. When the great bull-leaping festivals were organized, they attracted huge crowds, and the priestesses sat together as a group in a kind of royal box, watching the spectacle of teams of scantily dressed acrobats vaulting over a bull.

It was a remarkable and exotic civilization, this civilization where women were in charge. It came to an end in 1380 BC, when the Knossos Labyrinth, the great temple complex, went up in flames. It is no known for certain what caused the fire, but an earthquake is the likeliest cause. Crete is prone to earthquakes and earlier destructions of the Labyrinth, such as the major one in

1470 BC, were caused by earthquakes.

It would not have taken a very big earthquake to start the fire, because heating in the Labyrinth was provided by portable hearths, which could be tipped over quite easily. Lighting was provided by oil lamps of various kinds, and these too could easily be knocked over. It is easy to imagine an earthquake shaking over scores of oil lamps around the building, and some of them setting fire to curtains, hangings, mats and vestments. With a stiff breeze blowing – and archaeologists have established from the soot patterns that there was one – the fire swept through the building.

The Knossos Labyrinth had been damaged before and been rebuilt and refurbished afterwards. But not this time. This time the fire seems to have been the last straw. It was never again in full-scale use as a temple, but stood in ruins for hundreds of years. It was the final disaster for the great building.

Later, a classical city grew up beside it, also called Knossos, and then the Labyrinth became a kind of heritage site. It was rather like Stonehenge today, a mystery, an enigma about which people liked to speculate and tell stories. With some parts fallen down and other parts buried, the old building no longer made any sense. Classical ideas of temples were very different; the classical facades faced outwards, towards the city. The Minoan concept was the opposite; the facades faced inwards, towards the central courtyard. The Labyrinth was an inside-out building. The puzzle building became an emblem for the city, and a simplified plan of it – the Labyrinth – was proudly shown on the city's coins. This was where the European idea of the labyrinth came from, and therefore where, ultimately, all later labyrinths came from.

People living in the classical city naturally speculated about the eerie, empty, abandoned site at the southern edge of their busy, thriving city. They composed and passed on folk tales about the purpose of the building, about who had built it and why. This is where the strange story of King Minos came from, and his master engineer, the architect Daedalus who designed the Labyrinth for him. It is startling to find on one of the baked tablets from Knossos the place name 'Daidalaion', which means the house of Daedalus, or the shrine or temple of Daedalus. Maybe even the Minoans thought Daedalus was the name of the architect, and he once really existed.

Daedalus designed the Labyrinth not as a palace but as a maze to conceal the Minotaur, the terrible mythical bull-man who required regular human sacrifices. How did the people of classical Knossos know about the bulls? It is tempting to speculate that some kind of oral tradition, like the one about the Trojan War, was passed down through the years, and that just may have happened. But there is another, more prosaic explanation. There were some walls sticking up out of the general debris of the ruins of the Labyrinth, and one of them carried an impressive fresco, a relief fresco made of painted and moulded plaster – and it was a huge image of a rampaging bull. But the idea of human sacrifices could not have been deduced from that or any other surviving image. Interestingly, we know from a recent archaeological dig at the Temple of Anemospilia not far to the south of Knossos that young Minoans were sacrificed. But it is difficult to guess how Greeks of the classical period could have known that the Minoans carried out human sacrifice – unless of course they had literary sources that have since been lost.

However those particular details of the story were assembled, and the disaster of 1380 BC generated one of the most extraordinary strands in Greek mythology, the interconnected stories of Minos, Daedalus, Ariadne and Theseus. Theseus was the Mycenaean hero who on Ariadne's advice unwound a ball of string when he entered the Labyrinth in order to be sure to find his way out again. It is startling to find that stories like these, though powerful works of human imagination, were actually inspired by particular places and events. The disaster also brought the Minoan civilization to a close, and this in itself changed the direction of European history. The elegant, feminine and ultra-refined Minoan civilization was supplanted by a more aggressive and war-like civilization, the Mycenaean civilization, and that in turn left Europe with a very different heritage based on aggression, warrior heroes, military exploits and foreign invasions. It is a heritage that lives on into the twenty-first century.

THE ERUPTION
OF VESUVIUS

(AD 79)

THE IMPRESSIVE CONE of Mount Vesuvius towers menacingly above Naples, about seven miles to the east-south-east of the modern city. In the Roman period, the cities of Pompeii and Herculaneum were built on those same perilous foot slopes. Because it is an active volcano, sometimes building and sometimes destroying its cone, the height of the mountain is variable. For instance, in June 1900 Vesuvius was measured as 4,275 feet high, but in 1907 (after the 1906 eruption) it was only 3,668 feet. The mountain consists of two components. There is an active cone, and half encircling it on the north side there is a high semicircular vertical cliff. This cliff represents the remains of a much larger pre-historic crater. The shapes of volcanoes often betray their past in this way.

The Romans thought Vesuvius was extinct, because it had been inactive for as long as anyone could remember. The slopes of the mountain were covered in vineyards, exploiting the rich and fertile volcanic soil. Pompeian wine jars were frequently marked proudly with the name Vesu-vinum. The local wine is now called Lacrima Christi. At that time the summit of Vesuvius was a wide gently sloping basin walled by rugged cliffs covered with wild vines. The arc of Monte Somma represents a surviving fragment of this amphitheatre. It was in this lofty basin that the gladiator Spartacus was trapped and besieged by Claudius Pulcher in 73 BC. Spartacus managed to escape personal disaster on the top of

Vesuvius by twisting together vines to make a rope and using it to climb down through unguarded ravines in the rim of the crater. There is a wall painting among the ruins of Pompeii showing what Vesuvius looked like in the decades just before the eruption.

Then, in AD 63, earthquakes started to shake the countryside around the mountain, signalling the slow ascent of magma deep underneath the cone. The earthquakes did a lot of damage to the Roman towns in the area. People who know little about volcanoes assume that the lava thrown out onto the surface comes from the centre of Earth, but in fact it originates not far down. Vesuvius's magma chamber lies just three miles below the base of the mountain.

On 20 August in the year AD 79, the eruption phase began in earnest with a low roar. Four days later explosion after explosion sent a huge column of ash and lava high into the air. The climax of the eruption came with the release of clouds of scalding gas, smoke and ash that raced down the mountain sides, killing every living thing instantly. The bodies of many of the victims at Pompeii were buried in the ash and pumice that rained down on the cities. Pompeii on the southern flank of the volcano and Herculaneum on the western flank were entombed under the volcanic debris.

One distinguished witness was the scholar Pliny the younger, who watched from a ship out in the Bay of Naples and wrote two remarkable letters to the historian Tacitus, describing the eruption. It is very rare to have an eye witness account like this of an ancient disaster. Pliny was staying at Misenum with his uncle, the elder Pliny, who was the commander of the fleet. The elder Pliny went off in the afternoon of 24 August with the idea of saving the people of Herculaneum, but he arrived there too late. Instead he went to spend the night with a friend at the town of Stabiae, where he died the following morning of suffocation from the poisonous fumes given off by the volcano. Vulcanologists have given his name to the distinctive eruption column that he watched rising from Vesuvius – Plinian.

Three Roman towns are known to have been destroyed in the eruption of Vesuvius: Pompeii, Herculaneum and Stabiae.

The AD 79 eruption of Vesuvius was a landmark because it buried the town of Pompeii, conserving it under layers of ash. When antiquarians started to uncover the ancient city in 1748, they saw in astonishing detail how Romans of every class had lived. Buildings, frescoes, furniture, everyday objects and whole streets of shops were preserved. The discovery of Pompeii represented the dawn of a new science – archaeology. Suddenly it was obvious to everybody that it was possible to gain access to the past by careful excavation.

During the excavation, cavities in the ash were found. From their size and shape it looked as if they might be the moulds of human corpses. By pouring plaster into the cavities and removing the ash after the plaster had solidified, the actual shapes of dead Romans came into view, caught at the very moment of their death. Part of the popular appeal of Pompeii over the last 200 years has been this poignant collection of human remains. A beautiful statue of a youth was discovered in 1925. It was standing in the porch of a house, which shows that the owners had taken it in from the garden to save it from being damaged by falling ash. The beautiful statue survived, though its owners almost certainly did not.

At one time it was thought that the 'unearthing' of the wonderful Laocoon statue in early sixteenth century Rome was the beginning of modern archaeology, but recent scholarship suggests that the sculpture was a fake – made by Michelangelo. It was nevertheless a very up-market forgery and it had the effect of generating a huge surge of interest in ancient sculpture. The finding of Pompeii and its excavation, initially by Winckelman, was the real beginning of archaeology.

It was one day in 1711 that a peasant digging a well at Resina, on the bay five miles south-east of Naples, made the first archaeological find. He dug into a layer of architectural marble of various colours. This chance find led directly to the discovery of the buried Roman town of Herculaneum. In 1748, workmen digging beside the Sarno canal nine miles further round the bay, similarly found marble and bronzes on a site that turned out to be where Pompeii lay buried. It was only fifteen years later that an inscription was unearthed there confirming that this was indeed Pompeii. Unfortunately the first phase of digging at Pompeii was more of a treasure hunt than what we recognize as archaeology today. Both Pompeii and Herculaneum were treated as quarries for works of art, and as a must-see stop on the Grand Tour – which was a European travel itinerary that flourished from about 1660 – but at least antiquities, and antiquity itself, had become important elements in western civilization. The uncovering of Roman art revolutionized artistic tastes in Europe. King Ludwig II of Bavaria built a replica of a Pompeian house at Ashaffenburg. The great romantic art historian Winckelmann developed many of his ideas about classical art on the basis of Pompeian finds. Casanova's brother made money by forging some of the paintings.

It was almost as if the systematic gridiron street plan of Pompeii pressed the excavators into a more structured approach. By 1860, Fiorelli was bringing that more scientific approach to both Pompeii and Herculaneum. From then on, the excavations have added more and more to our knowledge of the ancient Roman way of life: town planning, public life, domestic life, trade, religion, art, attitudes and values. None of this would have been possible without the disaster of the AD 79 eruption and the entombment of the two towns.

The more comprehensive approach that modern archaeology brings has revealed things that the art collectors missed – such things as the graffiti and the slogans painted on the walls. Some are aggressive, some poignant: 'Here Vibius lay alone and longed for his beloved.' Some are advertisements left by prostitutes: ' I am yours for two asses.' An as was a copper coin of low value, and the price was the equivalent of two pennies.

The slogans show us a lot about Roman small town politics.

There is for instance a series of red and black election posters painted onto house and shop walls. Particular groups of people, such as laundrymen, dyers, fishermen, goldsmiths, urged their fellow citizens to vote for specific candidates for public office. Some of the pressure-groups were occupational, some not. There was one poster that was from a fast set, the seribibi, literally 'the late drinkers'. There was another that the candidate himself must have been rather embarrassed about: 'The sneak-thieves support Vatia for the aedileship.' But for the eruption, we would not have known about this amusing side of Roman town life.

The Roman eruption of Vesuvius has also been of long-term interest to modern geologists, who now see the AD 79 eruption as one in a long sequence of eruptions. After the AD 79 eruption, which blew off the summit of the Monte Somma, there was a long period of quiet when the volcano did not erupt. Then, in 1139, there was an eruption of lava. This was followed by 500 years more of quiet, and then another violent eruption in 1631. From then until the twentieth century, Vesuvius has erupted more frequently, every ten to forty years, gradually rebuilding the top of the cone inside the Monte Somma crater. The last major eruption of Vesuvius was in the 1940s.

The next eruption in the sequence is long overdue. What vulcanologists fear is that because of the long delay the next eruption will be a very violent one, of the same type as the one that destroyed Pompeii, and that it will in a similar way destroy the city of Naples. Many people died at Herculaneum and Pompeii, but Naples is a much bigger city with a much bigger population, and the fear is that a great natural disaster entailing huge loss of life is waiting to happen in Naples. Really, the lesson of history (and archaeology and geology) is that Naples should be rebuilt elsewhere, but it has always proved extremely difficult to move cities. Geographical inertia prevails. A similar plan to move Tokyo to a safer location further to the west has, for similar reasons, led nowhere.

ANTHRAX EPIDEMIC SWEEPS THROUGH THE ROMAN EMPIRE

(AD 80)

IN THE YEAR AD 80, anthrax struck the cattle and horses of the tribes living on the borders of China. The plight of these people was made even worse by the severe drought that struck at the same time. As a result, the doubly afflicted people started to migrate westwards in search of new and better pasturage.

As many as 30,000 Asians were involved in this mass migration; they took with them as many of their livestock as they could. It has been estimated that this amounted to as many as 40,000 horses and 100,000 cattle. They joined Iranian tribespeople and Mongols from the forests of Siberia to form an important new community. They would in Europe in time to come become known – and greatly feared – as the Huns.

The same anthrax pandemic that hit the Asians' livestock also affected European livestock. The disease swept through the Roman Empire, killing thousands of animals, and people, too.

The mass migration of the Huns began as a flight from a natural disaster near the Chinese border, a flight from the devastating combined effects of anthrax and drought. Within 300 years, the Huns arrived in Europe, where they found the rich lands they were looking for. Once in Europe, they became an increasing threat to the Romans and eventually, together with other immigrant groups, brought about the destabilization and collapse of the Roman Empire.

II

THE MEDIEVAL AND RENAISSANCE WORLD

THE SILTING OF
EUROPEAN HARBOURS

(BEGINNING IN 400)

ALL AROUND THE coastline of Europe, bays and river estuaries were in use as harbours, some for local fishing fleets, others as ports for regional trading, and a few as commercial ports of international importance. Their utility depended on shelter, often by adjacent headlands, and by the maintenance of deep water so that ships could come close inshore to anchor. For some reason, the silting of river mouths and harbours started to increase around the year 400, and accelerated over the next thousand years.

An early victim of the process was the Roman port of Ostia. The emperor Trajan's artificial harbour was completed in AD 104, and that marked the peak of Ostia's prosperity. Ostia proper, the city, was built on the south bank of the River Tiber and right at its mouth. It was a logical place to found an outport for Rome, which itself straddled the Tiber a few miles inland. But silting at the mouth of the Tiber early on made the city docks inaccessible to big sea-going ships, and so increasingly only the smallest boats could use Ostia. The rate of silting can be appreciated very easily; the beach of modern Ostia, Ostia Lido, is three miles beyond the seawall of the ancient port.

Trajan built his artificial harbour to one side of the mouth of the Tiber, to escape the effects of the silting. Trajan's Ostia was created over two miles to the north-west, over the site of Claudius's earlier harbour, built in AD 42. Trajan created his harbour with two long moles, or breakwaters, and between these two arms there was an artificial island with a lighthouse on it, the Pharos. Trajan's port, Portus, was on the open Mediterranean coastline, and his engineers linked it across to the Tiber with a short canal, the Fossa Traiana, just one mile long. The harbour had a large docking basin of revolutionary design: it was hexagonal. Restored in the 1860s, it still exists. But the same silting process that choked old Ostia to death as a commercial port eventually overwhelmed Portus, Trajan's Ostia. His harbour too is now land-locked. The deposition of silt in the Mediterranean close to the mouth of the Tiber has left the Roman coastline a mile inland. Even the site of the Pharos is half a mile inland.

The silting process may have seemed like an entirely natural process at the time, but today we can see that it was connected with the continuing clearance of forests. That clearance was happening partly to create extra farmland to feed the gradually growing population, partly to supply firewood and timber for house-building and shipbuilding.

Removing the forest left the soil less protected from rainwash, and so some soil got washed into the streams and rivers. Areas that were cleared for agriculture were ploughed up, and this released even more sediment into the rivers every time it rained. The rivers carried the eroded soil down to their lower reaches, and deposited it in bays and tidal reaches where the flow was checked by the sea. The salt in sea water has the effect of making fine clay particles cling together in bigger lumps that are more likely to settle; this too helped in the process of deposition. Gradually, the harbours and estuaries became shallower and shallower.

Eventually, by the middle ages, some European ports went into decline or out of use altogether because of the process of accelerated deposition: Pisano in Italy, Bruges in Belgium, Yarmouth, King's Lynn, Chester and Sandwich, all in Great Britain, all went into decline, bringing economic disaster to the communities depending on them. In the English county of Sussex alone, Steyning, Seaford, Winchelsea and Rye were all badly affected.

THE JUSTINIAN
PLAGUE
(541)

THREATENED WITH INVASION by barbarians to the north, the Romans took the last of their troops out of Britain in 436. The Roman occupation, a highly significant episode in Britain's history, came to an end. From then on, the native aristocratic elites were able to re-establish regimes that had been in place before the Romans arrived. Many British kings and princes went on using Latin, especially for important statements such as tomb inscriptions; Latin, the language of the Romans, was still considered very upmarket. The new regimes were therefore partly Romanized.

This was the Arthurian period in Great Britain. Arthur himself was probably king of Dumnonia, the English West Country, with an additional role as commander-in-chief of the British armies battling against the Anglo-Saxon invaders. Unfortunately, native chieftains like Arthur were not to have very long in power, as Germanic settlers from the Netherlands, Germany and Denmark started colonizing south-east England. This Anglo-Saxon colonization was already under way, though small in scale at first, by about 500. Then, with Arthur either killed or retired after the Battle of Camlann in 537, King Maelgwn of Gwynedd (North Wales) became the British commander-in-chief.

Whether Arthur or his successor Maelgwn knew it or not will probably never be known, but their contemporary in Rome, the Emperor Justinian, had plans to re-invade Britain to make it once more part of the Roman Empire. How they would have reacted to that is impossible to guess. It is possible that they would have been relieved to have Roman legions back in Britain to help them stem the tide of incoming Angles, Saxons and Jutes. But at this critical point, a turning point in British history, the Romans were distracted; they did not invade.

A great epidemic, believed to be bubonic plague, swept through Europe. It came from Egypt, through Palestine and Syria, and from there to Constantinople. The disease was carried by infected rats travelling in the holds of merchant ships. The progress of the epidemic closely followed the busiest trade routes: hence the focus on the great port of Constantinople (now Istanbul).

From Constantinople, the plague spread throughout the Roman Empire, making hundreds of thousands of people ill. Agriculture drew to a standstill because there were too few healthy people to keep the land in production. Serious famines followed. At the peak of the plague, as many as 10,000 people were dying of the disease every day in Constantinople.

The plague spread relentlessly from town to town, from village to village right across Europe. It went on for sixty years, spreading right across Europe and Asia. In 547, the Justinian plague reached Great Britain. King Maelgwn of Gwynedd caught it and died.

The Emperor Justinian himself contracted plague in 541. After a few months he recovered, but he had to abandon his plans to invade Gaul and Great Britain. So even this natural disaster, which killed hundreds of thousands of people, had its positive side; Britain was spared a reconquest by the Romans. The Germanic colonization continued and southern and eastern Britain went on to become England.

The Justinian plague eventually petered out, but Europe and Asia were repeatedly swept by epidemics, though not all of them were true bubonic plague. There were 'plagues' in Constantinople in 732 and 746, and Spain in 750.

THE MILLENNIUM
CALAMITY

(1000)

THE YEAR 1000, the Millennium, was at the time widely believed to be the 1,000th anniversary of the birth of Jesus. It was also believed that it marked the end or the culmination of the Christian era and there would be some kind of transformation of the world. The kingdom of God would be established on Earth and there would be a Last Judgement. Some of these expectations were based on the teachings of Jesus, though on no occasion did he actually say that the kingdom of God would be established in 1,000 years' time. In fact, people's expectations as the year 1000 approached do seem to have varied quite a lot. Theologians knew what the teachings in the New Testament contained, and they were not expecting a transformation to take place. Ordinary people, who were superstitious about numbers, expected something very dramatic to happen. On the other hand, the wording of wills that were made at that time implies that some people at least were expecting the ordinary everyday things to continue; they at least left their goods and property in that spirit.

There was a general expectation of disaster. No one knew what sort of disaster it was going to be, except that it was going to be a natural disaster, a God-given disaster, on a grand scale. Wealthy aristocrats had churches and chapels built or rebuilt, in the hope of persuading God that they had repented of their sins, so they could after all gain entry into Heaven rather than being sent to Hell. Some went on arduous pilgrimages, with the same end in view. A general hysteria set in as the year 999 drew towards a close, because many people thought the beginning of the year 1000 would mark the Millennium. In fact, they were miscounting, as there was no Year 0. The first year of the Christian era was AD 1, so the completion of the first millennium came at the end of 1000. Some people evidently realized this, because there was a further flurry of pilgrimage during that year. They must have been disconcerted when, after all, no major disaster overtook the world then either.

One commentator on this period was a monk called Ralph Glaber. He entered his first monastery as a teenager in 997. He was a born troublemaker and was thrown out of one monastery after another; the good side of this, from our point of view, is that he acquired a very broad perspective on what was going on in Europe in the run-up to the Millennium. He reported on one of the signs that the world was about to end: the appearance of a frightening comet in 989.

> *It appeared in September, not long after nightfall, and remained visible for nearly three months. It shone so brightly that its light seemed to fill the greater part of the sky; then it vanished at cock-crow. But whether it is a new star which God launches into the heavens, or whether He merely increases the normal brightness of another star, only He can decide.*
>
> *What appears established with the greatest degree of certainty is that this phenomenon in the sky never appears to men without being the sure sign of some mysterious and terrible event. And indeed a fire soon consumed the church of St Michael the Archangel built on a promontory in the ocean, which had always been the object of special veneration throughout the whole world.*

The church he described was at Mont-Saint-Michel off the Brittany coast of France. What Glaber was doing was linking together two events that we today would see as separate and unconnected. He interpreted the appearance of the comet as a warning, an omen, and the consumption of the church by fire as a confirmation of that warning. It was an easy process to develop a scenario within which anything and everything that happened could become part of the build-up to the end of the world. The great natural disaster of the Millennium was really a state of mind.

Ralph Glaber reported other disasters that were similar omens of even worse things to come.

In the seventh year from the millennium, almost all the cities of Italy and Gaul were devastated by violent conflagrations, and Rome itself largely razed by fire. As one, the people let out a terrible scream and turned to rush to the Prince of the Apostles.

Many eminent people died at about this time, he said, though that could be said about any period. Heresy erupted in Sardinia. Glaber commented, 'All this accords with the prophecy of St John, who said that the Devil would be freed after a thousand years.'

The Devil was a very real presence in people's minds, a powerful psychological force. Ralph Glaber thought he had seen the Devil, who appeared at the foot of his bed on several occasions. The Devil was a black, hunched figure covered in hair, with a goat's beard. He whispered to Ralph, 'Why do you monks bother with fasts and vigils and mortifications? One day, one hour of repentance, is all you need to earn yourselves eternal bliss, so why bother to get out of bed at the sound of the bell when you could go on sleeping?'

This shows Ralph's inner doubts about the life he had chosen. Many monks must have wondered, just like him, why they were putting themselves through such an exacting and rigorous monastic regime, when they could be leading a much more comfortable and easy life. They could just repent on their deathbeds, like a lot of other people, and get into Heaven that way. It would be far easier.

As the Millennium came and went, the hysteria did not dissipate straight away. As often happens with prophecies that fail to came true, people recalculated: the great disaster would come later. Maybe the fulfillment of the Christian era did not come 1,000 years after the birth of Jesus because it was due 1,000 years after his death. If Jesus was born in AD 1, as people then believed, he was probably crucified in AD 33 and the Millennium might happen 1,000 years after that date instead. Given that the crucifixion and the resurrection were even more momentous events than the birth of Jesus, it now seemed more likely that the Millennium would come in 1033. Signs and omens could easily be pointed to that supported this idea.

After the many prodigies which had broken upon the world around the Millennium of the Lord Jesus Christ's birth, there were plenty of able men of penetrating intellect who foretold other, just as great, at the approach of the millennium of the Lord's Passion, and such wonders were soon manifest.

Just before the third year after the Millennium [AD 1003], throughout the whole world, but especially in Italy and Gaul, men began to reconstruct churches, although for the most part the existing ones were properly built and not in the least unworthy. But it seemed as though each Christian community was aiming to surpass all the others in the splendour of construction. It was as if the whole world was shaking itself free, shrugging off the burden of the past, and cladding itself everywhere in a white mantle of churches.

The mantle was white because churches were traditionally whitewashed outside. Inside, the walls were often garishly painted with biblical scenes, and among them was often a terrifying and prominent image of the Last Judgement, to remind people what to expect. Today we are used to seeing churches in their natural stone colour both outside and in. The Christians of the Millennium literally inhabited a different world.

There were teams of stone masons travelling from one community to another, offering package deals in much the same way that modern firms solicit custom for replacement windows or new kitchens. The new parish churches were virtually built from kits. But they were above all new, and a testimony to the faith of the people who paid for them.

The urge to reconstruct unnecessarily, as Ralph Glaber saw it, was to carry on through the middle ages. The urge to compete was also to continue. The hysteria generated by the Millennium jolted Christian Europe into a different mode of behaviour altogether, driving towards an explosion of extravagant architectural styles in an age of great cathedrals and abbeys.

The year 1033 came and went without the world ending. There was no apocalypse. Ralph Glaber reported that all was well.

At the millennial anniversary of the Passion of the Lord, the clouds cleared in obedience to the Divine mercy and goodness and the smiling sky began to shine and flow gentle breezes. At that point, in Aquitaine [south-western France], bishops, abbots and other men devoted to holy religion first began to gather councils of the whole people. When news of these assemblies was heard, the entire populace joyfully came, unanimously ready to follow whatever should be commanded them by the pastors of the church. A voice descending from Heaven could not have done more, for everyone was still under the effect of the previous calamity and feared the future loss of abundance.

So, even though the prophecies of doom and the prophecies that the kingdom of God would be established on Earth had been proved wrong, faith in Christianity was strengthened, not weakened. People ought to have been disillusioned and angry that they had been so seriously misled. Instead, they were tremendously relieved that their lives were going to be allowed to continue in the old familiar way; they were not after all really ready for the kingdom of God. There had been no apocalypse. There had been no real calamity at all – only a calamity in the mind.

SUPERNOVA
IN TAURUS

(1054)

WHILE TRACKING A comet in 1758, the French astronomer Charles Messier discovered a strange, distinctive, misty patch of light in the constellation Taurus. It was bright but seemingly had no stars in it. This strange phenomenon was eventually to become known as the Crab Nebula. Messier recorded and published his discovery, generously noting later that it was the same phenomenon that had been discovered independently in 1731 by the English astronomer John Bevis. Bevis wrote to Messier about it in 1771, exactly forty years after his discovery.

The nebula was given its name, the Crab Nebula, much later, after people saw the drawing Lord Rosse made of it in 1844. Nineteenth-century astronomers peered at the haze, trying to find the stars they were sure must exist within the haze, but to no avail. Twentieth-century astronomers eventually found a pulsar, a tiny throbbing remnant, that is the collapsed core of the exploded star.

Spectrum analysis in 1915 showed that some parts of the nebula were blue-shifted and therefore moving away from us, while other parts of it were red-shifted and therefore moving towards us. It seemed odd, but the Crab Nebula was evidently expanding. Astronomers realized that what they were looking at was a huge explosion in slow motion, and the slow motion was an illusion created by extreme distance. That idea was confirmed by comparing photographs taken several years apart. If the rate of expansion, calculated in 1921, was reversed until the nebula was reduced to a point, it implied an origin in the eleventh century.

Then everything fell into place. There had indeed been a major event in the heavens in the eleventh century. What Bevis and Messier had seen was the expanding cloud of debris from a colossal explosion, called a nova, that had happened in the year 1054. The debris from the explosion spread out from its point of origin, so that the luminous gas cloud now covers a large and irregular patch of space.

Remarkably, the explosion in the sky was seen and reported in both China and Japan. What those eleventh century astronomers saw, on 5 July 1054, was a small star in the constellation Taurus explode and give off so much light that it was visible in the sky continuously, night and day, for twenty-three days and after that, as it dimmed, still plainly visible at night for two years. The Chinese called it a 'guest star'. The event was considered so remarkable that it was recorded in China and Japan and in pictographs of he New World.

Whether the exploded star had its own solar system, its own collection of planets and moons orbiting round it, cannot be known. If it did, all of those worlds were destroyed in the explosion – along with whatever life forms inhabited them.

That this spectacular cosmic disaster could be seen at all from Earth is remarkable, because it happened 6,300 light years away. The scale of the explosion was enormous – quite beyond anything that has ever happened inside the solar system. Because of the length of time it takes for light to travel across the vastness of space, what the Chinese saw in 1054 actually happened long before Stonehenge was built. It is strange to think that when we look at the night sky we are looking into the distant past – and into different parts of the past at that.

THE APPEARANCE OF HALLEY'S COMET

(1066)

WHEN HALLEY'S COMET appeared in the sky in 1066, it was seen by the English as a portent of disaster. Something terrible was going to happen. The monk Eilmer of Malmesbury wrote ominously, 'You have come then, have you, you source of tears to many mothers? It is a long time since I saw you last; but as I see you now you are far more terrible than before. I see you brandishing the downfall of my country.' As a boy Eilmer had seen this grim visitor with its message of doom once before, seventy-five years earlier, in 989. Quite why everyone in England sensed that the comet was the angel of death is unclear. Sixty-six years earlier, in the year 1000, people had been worked up into a frenzy of fear and despair as they waited for the end of the world; perhaps, decades later, they were still trapped in that millennial mindset, still expecting the Last Judgement.

The most remarkable feature of the comet was the fact that most of the time it was not there, but reappeared briefly every seventy-five or seventy-six years. It was Edmond Halley who discovered that periodicity, hundreds of years later. Halley recognized from the descriptions they wrote of the comets they saw in 1531 and 1607 that the astronomers Apianus and Kepler had seen the selfsame comet that had appeared in 1682; there were not three separate comets but just one comet reappearing at regular intervals. The exactly recurring time interval suggested to him that this was an object orbiting the Sun with a very long orbital path. Halley's Comet has not only a very long orbit, it is a very long and narrow elliptical orbit, so that for much of the time it is a long way from the Sun and therefore invisible; only occasionally does it pass close to the Sun, and at those times it becomes visible to us. Based on the visitations of 1531, 1607 and 1682, Halley was able to predict that the comet would reappear in 1757. In fact it reappeared towards the end of 1758 – it had been slowed down by 600 days by passing too close to Saturn and Jupiter. It was reported in 1758 by a German farmer and amateur astronomer called Palitzsch.

We know from ancient records that the comet visited our skies in 240, 164, 87 and 12 BC, and then went on appearing at the same regular interval until the most recent appearance in 1986.

In that year a probe was sent to visit the head of the comet, which turned out to be not spherical, as might have been expected, but a very irregular block of ice and dust, looking like one of the Avebury megaliths, but the size of the Isle of Wight. The tail consists of bits of the head being blow-torched away by the solar wind.

When the comet appeared unexpectedly in 1066, it was reported to be four times the size of Venus and shining with a light one-quarter that of the Moon: a very bright object. In 1456, when it passed very close to Earth, its tail took on the menacing shape of a huge sabre. Once again, Christians in Europe thought it was the angel of death arriving. Pope Callixtus III thought it looked evil and excommunicated it. The 1910 approach was the first to be photographed. The most recent appearance was in 1986. It will not be seen again until the summer of 2061, and after that not until the spring of 2134.

Most people see Halley's Comet just once in their lives. The lucky few see it twice. The composer Michael Tippett saw it as boy and hoped to live long enough to see it as an old man. He did. Eilmer of Malmesbury saw it twice, but did not consider himself blessed. He was right, too; in the wake of the 1066 visitation came the Norman conquest. Whether the reappearance of Halley's Comet is a natural disaster or not depends on your mindset. Most people today see Halley's Comet as just another body orbiting the Sun, like the classic planets and the newly recognized class of dwarf planets; for them, the comet does no harm. But in the past, in the worlds of Eilmer and Pope Callixtus, the comet was seen as an agent of destruction, a visitor bringing death and disaster. So much depends on how you think the universe works.

THE SINKING OF THE
WHITE SHIP

(1120)

IN 1120, THE usurping Norman dynasty had not long ago established itself on the throne of England. The king, Henry I, was conscious of the need to found a dynasty that would consolidate the Norman claim in future generations. Henry had many offspring, but most were illegitimate and therefore useless as potential heirs. He had just two surviving children who were legitimate and his dynastic hopes seemed secure when his son was born. He named him William, after the first two Norman kings of England, which was a clear statement of intent: the boy would become William III. He also called him William the Aetheling. This princely Saxon title was the equivalent of Heir Apparent or Prince of Wales, and emphasized that he would one day be king. The conscious choice of a Saxon title was a gesture towards the native population, which was by no means Norman-French and never would be. The people of England might have been conquered, harried and cowed by William the Conqueror, but Henry seems to have recognized a need to do some nation-building by showing that he was uniting the Saxon and Norman royal houses.

His heir was everything Henry I could have wished for. At the age of seventeen he was already a warrior prince, fighting at his father's side to re-affirm their dynastic rights on the southern side of the English Channel.

They fought a successful campaign in 1119 in France. It reached a climax in the utter defeat and humiliation of Louis VI of France at the Battle of Bremule. In November 1120, Henry I prepared to return to England. The *White Ship* was a new ship, belonging to Thomas FitzStephen. Thomas's father Stephen had been the Conqueror's sea captain, the man who had sailed him to the Sussex coast to conquer England. Thomas offered his fine new ship to the king for the return voyage, but the king had already settled his travelling arrangements.

Instead, Henry proposed that his son should sail in the *White Ship*. The young prince had already became the focus of court life. He was the glamorous rising star, attracting attention, gathering his own courtiers around him. They were all to travel with him in the *White Ship*, 300 of them, including his half-brother Richard, his half-sister Matilda and his cousins Stephen and Matilda of Blois. There would also be the nephew of Henry V, the German emperor, the youthful Earl of Chester, and the heirs to half the great estates in England and Normandy.

There was a pageant-like atmosphere to the revels that preceded their embarkation from Barfleur. The prince had casks of wine taken on board to lubricate the revels. This turned out to be a mistake, because by the time the ship set sail many of the crew as well as the passengers were drunk, and the crew at least should have remained sober. The revelers started to get out of hand. Some shouted abuse at one another. When priests arrived to give a much-needed blessing to the voyage, they were seen off with abuse too.

Some of the intended passengers decided not to sail in the *White Ship* after all. They sensed that there was worse trouble ahead, as indeed there was. Stephen of Blois was suffering from diarrhoea and decided to sail for England when he had recovered.

The drinking and partying meant that the *White Ship*'s departure had been delayed. The King's ships had already set sail, leaving Prince William far behind. The *White Ship* did not finally set sail until after nightfall on 25 November 1120. It would have been better to wait until daybreak. But the spirited (and intoxicated) young prince had the idea that he might still be first home. He ordered the ship's master to use his oarsmen to row at full speed so that they could catch up and overtake the rest of the squadron.

The ship's master was by this stage as drunk as his aristocratic passengers. He accepted the order, and the *White Ship* set off towards the open sea. It was not long before the ship struck a rock, which pierced the ship's hull on the port side. The prince's bodyguard quickly brought him up on deck and put him in a small boat, which they launched well before the drunken crew had started to attempt to pole the ship off the rocks. The prince was still within earshot when his half-sister called out to him, pleading with him not to leave her to drown. The prince ordered his boat turned back to the ship, but as he approached the *White Ship* began to sink in front of him.

By this time most of the passengers were struggling in the water and they instinctively made for the prince's dinghy. They fought to climb into it. Inevitably the boat capsized and sank. Then everyone was in the water, including the highly valued prince, the heir apparent, but no longer future king.

In the account of the *White Ship* disaster by the chronicler Orderic Vitalis, Thomas FitzStephen was one of those struggling in the water after the sinking, and when he heard that William the Aetheling had drowned, he gave up and let himself drown rather than have to face the king. But the account Orderic Vitalis also includes a full moon lighting up the scene, when calculated tables show that the moon was new, so his account is not reliable. In any case, by this stage the situation would have been so chaotic that it is hard to believe that the one surviving eye-witness to the disaster could possibly have noticed who was doing what or where.

Legend has it that there was only one survivor from the wreck of the *White Ship* and that he was a butcher from Rouen, a man called Berold. But the story continues that he was only on board to collect the aristocrats' debts, and that seems too neat; it turns the wreck of the *White Ship* into a medieval miracle play. But that is the story as we have it. Berold was wearing thick ramskin garments that protected him from hypothermia and he was pulled out of the water by fishermen the next morning.

For weeks afterwards, the bodies of the courtiers, princes and countesses were washed up on the Normandy beaches. It is said that after hearing of the disaster Henry I never smiled again. The death of William the Aetheling meant that he had no legitimate male successor, no reliable heir. In desperation, Henry made his English barons swear loyalty to his one surviving legitimate child, Matilda. They were to acknowledge her as their monarch after Henry's death. But the times were harsh and war-like, and most of the barons thought it was inappropriate to have a woman on the throne. The result was that when Henry died, some acknowledged Matilda while Henry's nephew Stephen usurped the English throne. The situation descended into a chaotic civil war, an unsatisfactory power struggle between Stephen and Matilda, the so-called Anarchy, when no one ruled. It was a particular twist of irony that all of that trouble was caused by the self same Stephen who might have travelled on the *White Ship* with William, and died with him, yet survived because of a bout of diarrhoea.

Would things have turned out any differently if Henry I had accepted the offer of the *White Ship* and travelled with his son? I believe that they would. There would have been no delaying drunken revelry and no mad dash through the black waves after nightfall. Both father and son would have arrived safely in England, and there would, in due time, have been a twelfth century King William III. In other words, without the *White Ship* disaster, there would have been no Plantagenet dynasty, no power struggle between Henry II and Thomas Becket, no King John, no Magna Carta. The course of English history would have taken a very different direction.

FLOODS IN THE
NETHERLANDS

(1163)

THERE WERE SEVERAL floods in the Netherlands in 1163. Much of the country lay at or even below sea level, so it was extremely vulnerable to flooding. Storm surges in the North Sea continually sent sea water into the coastal areas. High flows coming down the River Rhine cause a continual problem with freshwater floods in the south and west of the country.

In a continuing struggle to save their country from the sea, the Dutch kept building more and more stretches of embankment along the coast and along the banks of major rivers. When water levels were very high in the River Maas or the Rhine, the pressure on the embankments was such that water often found its way through. The embankments became saturated, which in itself meant that leakages occurred, but they also lost their strength and collapsed, and that released huge quantities of water out onto farmland, pasture and villages.

The 1163 floods resulted mainly from dyke breaches of this kind along the River Maas. As a result, the mouth of the Oude Rijn at Katwijk, which had already become severely silted, was completely closed by sediment carried along in the flood water.

Seven years later, in 1170, there were even more serious floods in the north of the Netherlands. A large area was flooded by the sea during storms. It was at this time that the Almere lake, behind the coastal sand barrier, was enlarged. Bit by bit, in successive storms, the lake became connected to the North Sea through breaches in the coastal barrier.

In the St Nicholas flood of 1196, large areas of the north and the Zuyder Zee region were flooded by the sea again. There were areas of peat deposits in West Friesland, and once the sea gained access to these they were easily washed away. This process of creeping encroachment in successive sea floods gradually enlarged the Almere lake and the Wadden Zee. It was a prelude to the later catastrophic flooding of the Zuyder Zee area, a much larger area to the south, and then the Dutch were to lose a huge area to the sea.

THE ZUYDER ZEE
FLOOD

(1228)

THE HUGE AREA of the Zuyder Zee was, until 1228, an expanse of very low-lying land, much of it below sea level. The region was defended from invasion by the sea by a natural barrier, the beaches built up by wave action along the Dutch coast. In earlier sea floods, the Almere lake in the north and the Wadden Zee were gradually enlarged as peat deposits were winnowed away by the waves. What happened in 1228 is that there was a great culminating storm, which piled water over and through the barrier beach and into the low-lying area beyond, semi-permanently claiming a very large area for the sea.

It is likely that the storm was of the same type as the one that caused the 1953 floods. An intense low-pressure system passing over Great Britain drove very strong north winds towards the Dutch coast, piling the water up and raising the high tide levels. As the low-pressure system passed over the North Sea, it actually pulled the sea surface up by as much as another three feet. The effect of this was to send huge quantities of water into the low-lying areas behind the coastal sand barriers. There was huge loss of life and property: 100,000 people were drowned. Unlike most other floods, the water did not drain back. The entire area remained under water. Huge areas of productive farmland were lost, apparently for ever.

In the course of a single day, the huge bay know as the Zuyder Zee was formed. Parts of the barrier beach in the north became stranded offshore to make a string of islands, the Frisian Islands. It was only in the twentieth century that people made a concerted effort to reclaim this land, investing great ingenuity as well as huge amounts of time and money in trying to win back what the sea had taken from them in the thirteenth century.

The southernmost third of the Zuyder Zee has been reclaimed (the famous Dutch polders), and the central third has been turned into a large freshwater lake, Lake Yssel (or Ijseelmeer); the northernmost third, immediately behind the West Frisian Islands, has been left as open sea (the Wadden Zee).

TYPHOONS DESTROY KUBLA KHAN'S FLEET

(1274 AND 1281)

IN 1281, THE great Khan assembled on the coast of China an army of as many as 100,000 men and a fleet of 4,400 ships. The invasion of Japan was launched with the largest armada the world had ever seen. Yet both the army and the fleet were to disappear without a trace. Kenzo Hayashida, a prominent marine archaeologist believes he has found evidence on the seabed that will solve the enduring mystery of the lost invasion force, 700 years after its disappearance.

The great Khan, Kubla Khan, was a Mongol. His ancestors were nomadic horsemen. Decades earlier, Kubla Khan's grandfather, Genghis Khan, united the tribes and took them on an extraordinary campaign of conquest. In Kubla Khan's lifetime, a huge tract of Eurasia was under his control, from Ukraine in the west to Mongolia in the east. Then he conquered China, too. Once he had declared himself the new Emperor of China he felt the need to demonstrate his power, and he made overtures to the Emperor of Japan, inviting him to submit to Chinese–Mongol rule. The Japanese emperor understandably refused to receive these dispatches. Kubla Khan responded to this snub by setting his commanding general the overwhelming challenge of conquering Japan.

Since this involved crossing 500 miles of open water and probably fighting at sea, Kubla Khan was entering entirely unknown areas of military operation. Here were sown the seeds of disaster. The initial invasion fleet comprised 300 large vessels together with about 500 smaller ships. Around 8,000 Korean and 20,000 Mongol warriors embarked on the long voyage to Japan, making landfall in Hakata Bay on the island of Kyushu on 19 October 1274.

The great Khan's army was equipped with the most advanced technology. His warriors also resorted to using poisoned arrows, which the Japanese regarded as a violation of the protocols of war.

But the great Khan's apparent military superiority was set at nought on 20 November 1274, when a typhoon struck, sinking over 200 of the Mongol ships. Around 13,000 Mongol warriors were sleeping on board at the time and many of them were drowned. After the disaster, the survivors withdrew to the mainland of China. The invasion that was intended to humble the Japanese emperor ended in humiliation for the Chinese emperor.

Seven years passed before Kubla Khan made his second attempt to invade Japan. This time he ordered a much larger fleet to be built and assembled a much larger army. On the coast of China, thousands of Chinese were set to work building ships for the invasion fleet. The Khan's tyrannical dictatorial powers ensured that the work was done with incredible speed; he allowed them just one year to create the enormous armada. It was ready by August 1281. The huge armada was larger even than the 4,000-strong fleet assembled by the Allies for the 1944 D-Day landings.

Over 40,000 Mongol troops were sent from Korea as an advance party to Japan in May. A second army consisting of 70,000–100,000 men assembled with the fleet. As soon as the new ships were ready, the main Mongol invasion force embarked for Japan. Kubla Khan must have been supremely confident that he would conquer Japan; his forces were overwhelming. Yet they failed utterly.

The earliest record that is known to exist is a scroll in the Hakozaki Shrine. This was painted in 1293, only twelve years after the second attempted invasion. It is the only pictorial record we have of the Mongol fleet. Frustratingly, the scroll offers no explanation of the fleet's disappearance. It does show fighting between Mongols and Japanese warriors, and this suggests that the fleet successfully reached the shores of Japan. The Japanese are also believed to have taken around 2,000 Mongol warriors prisoner.

Presumably the fleet was lost in some sort of disaster, whether as a result of a concerted attack by the Japanese or by storms, so Kenzo Hayashido began to search the Japanese coastline for evidence. But Japan consists of a long chain of over 3,000 islands, stretching over 2000 miles. Finding the long-lost fleet was a virtual impossibility. By chance a fisherman on the small island of Takashima found a metal object with an inscription in a non-Japanese script. When Hayashido saw it he realized at once that it was a well-preserved brass seal and that the inscription was Mongolian. This single find made him narrow his search to this one island. He assembled a team of divers and archaeologists.

They used side-scan sonar, which located a number of large objects on the seabed, which unfortunately were buried under a thick layer of silt. Vacuum pumps were used to clear the silt, which in places was forty feet thick. After months of clearing the silt, they found a huge wooden anchor made of timber that had come from China. Nine more anchors were found. Then came the decisive discovery – human remains, sword blades, quivers of arrow heads and the helmets of the Mongol warriors.

The evidence convinced Hayashido that the Mongol invasion fleet had sunk off the coast of Takashima. But half of the mystery remained. What went wrong? Why had the fleet been lost? It is possible to propose a working hypothesis. The invasion force had been well equipped by the standards of the time, with long range bows and an exploding shrapnel bomb called a tetsuhau. They seem to have had the advantage while they stayed on their ships, but when they landed they were up against the greater skill of the Samurai warriors. The Mongols were probably unable to take control of a beach head. The Japanese were similarly probably unable to mount an attack on the ships. So a kind of stalemate was reached, with neither side able to gain the upper hand.

If this stand-off was maintained for several weeks, the invaders, who were a very long way from home, would have begun to run short of supplies, including food. Morale would have dropped and anxiety would have set in.

The ten anchors had all been found in the same position, pointing towards the shore. This implies that some force was driving the ships towards the coast. There is a Japanese folk tale about the fleet's disappearance; it speaks of a 'divine wind' that saved Japan from invasion. The Hakazoki scroll does not mention a wind, but it is likely that it was a typhoon that drove the ships towards the beach, sank them and drowned many of the warriors. The invasion is known to have taken place in late summer, which is the typhoon season. Even so, it seemed very unlikely that a typhoon would have sunk all 4,000 ships, especially since the Chinese were very skilled at building sea-going junks.

Then a surprising discovery was made. Examination of the finds from the seabed showed that many of the craft were only riverboats, which were not designed to ride out typhoons. The workmanship was also poor, as a great deal of conscripted labour was used – and the fleet was built in a hurry. It turns out that Kubla Khan's invasion was ineptly equipped; it was more like Dunkirk than D-Day.

So the disastrous loss of the second invasion fleet and the huge invasion army was in part an organizational and strategic disaster, in part a natural disaster. But it is easy to see how the Japanese, breathing a collective sigh of relief at the destruction of so many enemies in a single storm, would have seen the typhoon as heaven-sent. Japan kept its independence; it did not become part of the Mongol–Chinese Empire. The natural disaster that saved Japan was remembered in the Second World War, when the phrase 'divine wind' (*kamikaze* in Japanese) was to carry a new and very different meaning.

THE BLACK DEATH

(1333 ONWARDS)

THE BLACK DEATH was a particularly virulent and destructive outbreak of the plague that from time to time swept from east to west right across Eurasia, recurring again and again over the centuries and wiping out tens of thousands of people.

The Black Death had its beginnings in China in 1333. It reached Europe when marauding Tatars pursued and attacked Genoese merchants at the port of Calla in the Crimea. The Tatars, who were intent on retrieving furs and silks the merchants had acquired in China, laid siege to the merchants at Calla. The Tatars were infected with the plague and before they lifted their siege they catapulted their own corpses into the trading post, presumably deliberately to infect the merchants. In this they succeeded, and the merchants carried the disease on to Cyprus. Some of the merchants died before reaching home; others took the disease to various ports, such as Constantinople, Genoa and Venice.

The Black Death reached Cyprus in 1347 and the city of Florence in April 1348, and spread north-westwards from there, reaching Paris in June and England in August. London itself was spared until November.

The plague was called bubonic because of the bubo, or enlarged lymph gland, which was a definitive symptom of the disease. It is thought that the disease was spread mainly by rat-borne fleas. Rats travelled in carts, crates, waggons and the holds of ships; and their fleas could be carried in the bags and clothing of merchants. The disease naturally progressed along the major trade routes by land and sea, distributing itself almost like an economic commodity.

The Black Death was responsible for the deaths of hundreds of thousands of people all over Europe. Many of the victims succumbed quickly becauses they were already weakened by famine. The Black Death was also responsible for increased mobility. A lot of people tried to run away from it. In the Auvergne in France, for instance, most of the physicians fled. The surgeon Guy de Chauliac was one of the few who stayed and tried to alleviate the sufferings of the plague victims. He wrote a description of the disease's progress. 'The visitation came in two forms. The first lasted two months, manifesting itself as an intermittent fever accompanied by spitting of blood from which people died usually in three days. The second type lasted the remainder of the time, manifesting itself in high fever, abscesses and carbuncles, chiefly in the axillae and groin. People died from this in five days. So contagious was the disease, especially that with blood-spitting, that no one could approach or even see a patient without taking the disease. The father did not visit the son nor the son the father. Charity was dead and hope abandoned.'

It is clear from de Chauliac's description that this was a particularly horrible way to die. Victims had to suffer not only the physical anguish of their symptoms, which were terrible enough in themselves: they had to die alone, untended, unvisited – the ultimate misery.

Inevitably, as in any time of crisis, there were those who looked around for people to blame. Most societies in Europe at that time were anti-Semitic, so it was inevitable that the Jews would be blamed. It was said that they deliberately contaminated wells and 'anointed' people and houses with poison. The persecution of Jews began on the shores of Lake Geneva, at Chillon. It spread to Basel and Freiburg, where as many Jews as could be found were herded into barns and burned alive. At Strasbourg over 2,000 Jews were hanged on scaffolds built at the Jewish burial ground. It was a foretaste of the twentieth century Holocaust. Pope Clement VI issued two formal statements declaring that the Jews were innocent of responsibility for the Black Death, but it made no difference. The persecution of the Jews continued. As a result, thousands of Jews fled from western Europe to Poland and Russia, and other countries in eastern Europe where, for the time being, they found greater tolerance.

The persecution of the Jews was one manifestation of the mass hysteria that the pandemic produced. Thousands of people died, year after year. By the time the pandemic was over, half the population of Europe had been wiped out. In some areas, two-thirds of the population died. On a local scale, it could be even worse still. The population of Locarno on Lake Maggiore in Italy fell from 4,800 to only 700. In England, many villages were reduced to a level where it was impossible, economically and socially, for them to continue. These 'plague villages' were permanently abandoned. Their grassed-over street plans can still be traced on air photographs, more than 600 years later, and on the ground it is often possible to pick out the rectangular bumps in fields marking the sites of individual houses and the hollows where the village streets once ran.

The pandemic was to have effects lasting several decades. The high death rate led to a long-term shortage of workers. It is estimated that before the Black Death there were five million people living in England and that after it, in 1377, there were only two million. A Statute of Labourers was introduced, which attempted to force workers to accept work if it was offered; it also unwisely tried to fix wages at their 1346 levels. In 1360, English labourers who tried to negotiate higher wages were imprisoned. The situation slid towards a commoners' revolt. The fall in population reduced demand for food supplies and prices fell. Farming was far less profitable and many landlords turned their arable land over to animal pasture instead. This led to an increase in sheep numbers and wool production, changing the direction of the English economy.

The large scale loss in population on both sides of the English Channel caused the governments of England and France to call a truce in the Hundred Years' War between the two countries in 1349. The Scots seized on this moment of weakness to invade England, but the soldiers caught the plague and took it back to Scotland with them. By this stage the Black Death had spread right across Europe, affecting Poland and Russia. There, people already weakened by famine and poverty quickly succumbed to the disease.

The Black Death came, went and returned, bringing renewed outbreaks. In 1371, there was a new outbreak in England, though not as destructive as before. The Black Death was a personal disaster for the individuals and families who caught the disease. It was also a disaster for many villages, which became non-viable and had to be abandoned when large numbers of villagers died. Halving Europe's population, the Black Death was a major demographic and economic disaster.

THE LITTLE ICE AGE

(BEGINNING IN 1450)

THE LITTLE ICE Age was a cool phase that began in 1450 and came to a gradual end between 1800 and 1900. The coldest part lasted from 1645 to 1723, and the cold was especially intense between 1680 and 1712. In many areas, the Little Ice Age came to an end in around 1800, though in some areas colder conditions persisted until the end of the nineteenth century, to be followed by the episode that is now referred to as global warming.

The Little Ice Age is most fully documented in Europe, but it does seem to have affected the world as a whole. In central England, the average annual temperature in 1600, the warmest point in the Little Ice Age, was eight-and-a-half degrees Celsius compared with ten degrees in 1200. In other words it was at least one-and-a-half degrees cooler in the Little Ice Age than at the peak of the previous period, which is sometimes called the medieval warm phase. What lay behind this global cooling?

The invention of the telescope at the beginning of the seventeenth century made detailed observation of the Sun possible for the first time. One feature that presented itself for study immediately was the sunspots that had been known about from naked-eye observations as early as 527 BC; now they could be observed and counted accurately. Sunspots are dark dots on the Sun's apparent surface, and they involve a dimming of its radiant energy by over fifty per cent; the temperature of the Sun's surface over a sunspot is up to 2,000 degrees Celsius cooler. So, given the delicate balance of Earth's climate system, it would not be surprising if times when there were more sunspots were also times when Earth itself underwent cooling.

Thanks to Galileo's telescope, we have a continuous record of the Sun's variable activity since 1610. A very striking feature of the sunspot record is the conspicuous lack of sunspots in the period 1640–1710, a phase known as the Maunder Minimum. This corresponds to the coldest part, the core episode, of the Little Ice Age. It is almost certain that the colder conditions on Earth in the Little Ice Age were mainly the result of reduced solar activity. Other evidence shows that there was an earlier phase of reduced solar activity 1450–1550, a phase known as the Spörer Minimum, so really the Little Ice Age was composed of two consecutive phases of solar inactivity.

Volcanic activity is another factor. Before the Little Ice Age, in what is sometimes called the medieval warm phase, there were very few volcanic eruptions. Between 1450 and 1900 there were a lot of eruptions. In Iceland, in that period there were between one and five large-scale eruptions per twenty years. The volcanic dust reduced the number of hours of sunshine, promoted condensation and cloud formation. This reinforces the longer-term pattern; in the Pleistocene Ice Age as a whole volcanoes produced four times as much ash as in the preceding period.

The effects on the environment and on people were many and varied. The Norse settlement in Greenland was brought to an end by adverse weather conditions in about 1500. Frobisher reported bitter cold and heavy snowfall on the deck of his ship as he negotiated the Hudson Strait in August 1578. Some of Champlain's men were able to walk across the frozen surface of Lake Superior to an island in June 1608. Major European rivers were frozen over many times; this was the time of the famous frost fairs on the River Thames. Many glaciers thickened and advanced. There were thirty-six reports of glaciers advancing in the period 1587–1798, compared with only three for the period 1011–1211 and five for 1880–1964.

But the environmental effects of the Little Ice Age were not the same everywhere. For some reason in northern Greenland it became slightly warmer. In Africa, the level of Lake Chad rose eighteen feet above its 1950 level, while the level of Lake Malawi fell about 400 feet.

In Europe, the cooling effects were most noticeable in the marginal lands, the hill country. Hill farmers found that they were no longer able to grow cereals. A lot of marginal land went out of cultivation altogether, and many highland settlements were abandoned. But there were some interesting exceptions. In southern Turkey, there was a major shift in population in the Little Ice Age – but it was from the plains into the mountains. Large numbers of people moved up from the lowlands to settle in mountain valleys. This was because of the political instability associated with the declining Ottoman Empire; the need for safety overrode any problems that might lie ahead for food production. We live in a multifactorial world.

THE SINKING OF THE
MARY ROSE

(1545)

THE ENGLISH KING, Henry VIII, was faced with a double threat. Across the English Channel were the French. There was also a strong and potentially hostile Scottish fleet. For the sake of security, Henry VIII launched a programme of fort-building, which included the distinctive rose-shaped Walmer Castle, Camber Castle and Hurst Castle. He also launched a programme of warship-building. The *Mary Rose* and the *Peter Pomegranate* were among the first purpose-built warships to serve in the English Royal Navy. Earlier ships used in warfare by the king's father, Henry VII, were not much more than armed merchant vessels, but the new generation of fighting ships built on Henry VIII's orders was to be tailor-made. This was what made the loss of the *Mary Rose* such a traumatic experience.

It is thought that the ship was named after Mary, the king's sister, and the Tudor rose.

The ship was an English carrack built at Portsmouth in 1509-10, and one of the first ships built sturdily enough to be able to fire a full broadside of cannons. A single cannon firing resulted in a kick back. A broadside, all the guns along one side of the ship firing at once, produced a massive kick back. Unless the ship was designed to take this, it might keel over or even capsize. The *Mary Rose* was fully armed, fitted with seventy-eight guns, and this was increased after an upgrade in 1536. She never served as a merchant ship, was never anything other than a fighting ship. A new method of hull construction made it possible to make the gun ports watertight. The *Mary Rose*'s guns were mounted close to the waterline, so watertight gun ports were crucial to her safety.

The *Mary Rose* was Admiral Sir Edward Howard's flagship in the Italian Wars and was often involved in sea battles. On 19 August 1512 the *Mary Rose* was the flagship of the English fleet (about fifty ships) attacking Brest in Brittany. The *Mary Rose* attacked the French flagship, *Marie la Cordeliere*, and succeeded in crippling her French counterpart. The *Mary Rose* was herself badly damaged in the encounter and ran aground. Three other English ships, the *Sovereign*, the *Regent* and the *Mary James*, took over from the *Mary Rose*, firing on the French flagship until she exploded, killing over 1,000 men. It was a ferocious battle in which more than thirty French ships were either destroyed or captured. When we see paintings or models of these supremely elegant and beautiful galleons, we can all too easily forget that they were designed as entirely functional killing machines; their beauty and picturesqueness were incidental.

When Admiral Edward Howard died in 1513, the *Mary Rose* became the flagship of the Lord High Admiral, Sir Thomas Howard. She went for a major refit, virtually a rebuild, in 1528 and again in 1536. These refits were designed to give he more fire power, which they certainly did, but they also made her top-heavy and liable to roll in rough weather. The refits involved adding guns and an extra deck, and these alterations must have raised her centre of gravity dangerously.

She was a substantial ship of fifty tons displacement, and seventy tons after her refit in 1536. She was a small ship by modern standards, 120 feet long and with a beam of thirty-six feet, but she was the cutting edge of marine technology in the early sixteenth century – a very fine ship and the pride of the English naval fleet.

The last phase of the *Mary Rose*'s distinguished career came in the summer of 1545, when Francis I of France launched an invasion fleet against England. The French king sent 200 ships and 30,000 soldiers across the English Channel. This was a serious invasion fleet, bigger than the Spanish Armada launched against England forty-three years later. The English were able to throw only eighty ships and 12,000 soldiers against this attack. The *Mary Rose* was the flagship of Vice Admiral Sir George Carew.

At the beginning of July, the French fleet entered the Solent, the broad channel of open water between the Isle of Wight and the English mainland, with the evident intention of taking either Portsmouth or Southampton. Carew took his fleet out of Portsmouth to engage with the French on 18 July 1545. The first engagement was at long range. It was little more than a shaking of fists, with no real damage done on either side. The following day, 19 July, was a still, windless day. The English fleet was becalmed, so the French sent their galleys with oarsmen against the English ships.

In the early evening a light wind started up. Carew saw his chance, set sail and started to sail the *Mary Rose* towards the French fleet. She suddenly capsized and sank immediately. There was huge loss of life. Only thirty-five men escaped with their lives, and they were presumably men who were lucky enough to be up on deck.

Why the ship sank was a complete mystery at the time. The French tried to gain a propaganda victory from this terrible accident by claiming to have sunk her by firing at her, but other explanations are more likely. The truth is that the great ship was sunk by a light wind. She began to heel over as soon as she raised her sails. What seems to have happened is that the poorly trained and poorly disciplined crew had neglected to close the lower gun ports after firing at the French galleys. The low-slung gun ports were watertight, but only when they were shut. When the ship heeled in the light wind, the open lower gun ports on the lee side dipped below the water line, letting huge quantities of water onto the gun deck. The ship was top-heavy anyway and did not recover her upright position. She stayed heeled over, and as more water poured in by the second she went right over. There may have been an additional factor – poor ballasting. It was usual for top-heavy ships to have rocks or gravel loaded into their bilges to keep them stable in the water. If a negligent crew had failed to bring sufficient ballast on board, it would make the ship more likely to heel over.

An attempt was made the following month to raise her from the seabed. Even if the ship could not be refloated the high-quality timber and guns were well worth salvaging. The salvage attempt failed and the *Mary Rose* was abandoned. Resting on its starboard side, the wreck became covered in seabed mud, which protected the starboard side from erosion and decay. The port side of the ship was left exposed, and it has decayed away. During the seventeenth and eighteenth centuries, the wreck was completely covered in a layer of clay.

The *Mary Rose* was rediscovered by chance on 16 June 1836, when a fishing net snagged on its timbers. The diver John Deane went down and recovered timbers, guns and longbows. But without modern technology the exact location could not be recorded exactly, so when Deane stopped working on it in 1840 the ship was lost again for another 120 years.

A new search for the *Mary Rose* was begun in 1965 and two years later Harold Edgerton pinpointed the site using side-scan sonar. A spring tide in 1971 coincided with a gale, and this moved aside the layer of mud covering the wreck. Suddenly several of the heavier structural timbers of the ship's hull were visible. Exploration of the wreck by divers and archaeologists over the next few years revealed that the wreck was resting on its starboard side at an angle of sixty degrees. In 1974, the *Mary Rose* was given legal protection from unofficial divers by a new Protection of Wrecks Act. The site is still protected, because a substantial part of the ship is still on the seabed.

The *Mary Rose* Trust was founded in 1979 and a large section of the wreck was raised in 1982 under the direction of Margaret Rule. The surviving section, still in the middle of twenty-year conservation process in which the timber is first saturated in polyethylene glycol and then dried, is on display in the Portsmouth Historic Dockyard. More pieces of the *Mary Rose* remain on the seabed, and they will doubtless eventually be raised when funding allows. The ship's anchor and parts of the bow were brought up in 2005.

The *Mary Rose* disaster is proving to be a landmark in many different ways. New techniques had to be devised for raising and conserving the remains of the ship. The rescue also revolutionized marine archaeology. The ship and the objects found with it are yielding an unprecedented amount of information about everyday life in the mid-sixteenth century. The remains of half of the crew were found and a large number of artefacts: medical equipment such as a syringe and bleeding bowl, navigational instruments, tools for carpentry, longbows, arrows with traces of binding glue still on their tips, guns, cooking utensils, plates, bowls, lanterns, backgammon boards, dice, leather shoes, shaving bowl and razors. The divers even found a shawm in a good state of preservation. This was a predecessor of the modern oboe, and it has been possible to build an exact, working replica of the original shawm. There was also a beautifully turned wooden pepper mill, presumably from the admiral's table. The wreck has turned out to be a valuable time capsule of the mid-sixteenth century, giving us an unrivalled glimpse of life as it was lived by ordinary seamen then.

Like other natural disasters, there was a major human element in the loss of the *Mary Rose*. She was carrying too much weaponry for her own good. She was built one deck too high. She was top-heavy after her refits. Her crew were undisciplined and casual. If, after firing at the French galleys, the gunners on the lower deck had closed their gun ports, the water would not have been able to get in. The forces of nature meanwhile were at their subtlest. Who would ever have thought that a light breeze could be so lethal?

122

THE SHENSI
EARTHQUAKE

(1556)

CHINA IS PRONE to earthquakes. Most big earthquakes happen along well defined lines separating the plates that make up the Earth's crust, such as the boundary between the North American Plate and Pacific Plate that runs through California along the San Andreas Fault. China is different. India is driving northwards, crumpling the southern edge of Asia into the Himalayas. China is being stretched apart in compensation, cracking open along a whole series of faults, and major earthquakes can occur almost anywhere along the many lines of weakness.

On the night of 23-24 January 1556, the Shensi (Shanxi) province of China was shaken by one of these earthquakes. This was no ordinary earthquake. It was in human terms the worst known earthquake in human history. It killed over 830,000 people. It is said that it was felt across eight provinces of China – half the country – and affected ninety-seven other countries, too. The destruction spread through an area 500 miles across.

Most of the deaths were caused by geomorphological events triggered by the earthquake. Steep and unstable hill and mountain sides were shaken down, causing rockfalls and landslides. In narrow, steep-sided mountain valleys, the landslides buried villages on the valley floor and created temporary dams, causing rivers to pond back and flood. Most people lived in poorly built houses. They collapsed on their occupants, often crushing them to death.

Earthquakes and earth tremors are commonplace. There are around 8,000 earth tremors happening all around the world every day, most of them too slight to detect. Once a year, somewhere in the world, there is a very big earthquake measuring 8.0 or more on the Richter scale; often these happen in uninhabited areas, and therefore cause few or no deaths. The Shensi earthquake is estimated to have been about 8.3 on the Richter scale, and unluckily it struck a densely populated region.

The Chinese annals record that the ground rose up, forming new hills, and that new valleys, gullies and springs were created. Huts, houses, temples and city walls all collapsed. An important ancient monument, the monoliths of the Forest of Stone, was badly damaged. A tall pagoda, the Small Wild Goose Pagoda in Xi'an, was shaken so severely that it settled slightly and was six feet shorter (140 feet instead of 146) after the earthquake. The greatest loss of life was in the cave dwellings cut out of the loess in Shanxi, Shaanxi and Gansu provinces; the earthquake caused many landslides, which destroyed the caves and buried alive many of the occupants. In all, perhaps sixty per cent of the population of the interior of China died.

THE DOVER STRAITS EARTHQUAKE

(1580)

SEVERE EARTHQUAKES IN southern England and northern France are uncommon. The Dover Straits earthquake of 1580 was the biggest in the recorded history of England, Belgium and France. It happened at 6 o'clock in the evening on 6 April, in Easter week and caused damage in towns and villages on both sides of the English Channel. Those at sea had the most frightening experience. Freak swells and tsunamis sank twenty or more ships. A passenger sailing from Dover said his vessel had grounded on the seabed five times and the waves had risen higher the ship's mast.

Calais, in France, was very badly hit by the tsunami, a 'deluge' that swamped the town and surrounding countryside. Several people were drowned. Parts of the town wall fell down, killing and injuring several more. Boulogne was similarly flooded. Several buildings at Lille fell down and stones were dislodged from buildings in several other towns: Arras, Douai, Béthune and Rouen. At Beauvais the cathedral bells started ringing on their own.

In England, several buildings collapsed and there was a major fall of chalk from the White Cliffs of Dover. Saltwood Castle was so badly damaged that it was uninhabitable until the structure was repaired in the nineteenth century. In London, many chimney stacks and one of the pinnacles of Westminster Abbey were shaken down. Stones fell from Ely cathedral. At the English port of Sandwich a strange noise was heard as the arches of the church cracked and the gable end of one of the transepts collapsed. The strange noise may have been the same rumbling sound that was heard by peasants working in the fields near Ghent; they also saw the ground rolling like waves.

At dawn the next morning came the first of a series of aftershocks, which brought down several more houses in Dover and generated another tsunami, drowning 120 people. More aftershocks were felt in east Kent on 1–2 May.

Geological work preceding the building of the Channel Tunnel showed that the 1580 earthquake's focus was fifteen miles under the seabed of the English Channel, and it is estimated to have been about 5.5 on the Richter Scale. Records suggest that there are earthquakes in the Dover Straits roughly every 200 years. There was an earlier Dover Straits earthquake in 1380. They seem to come every 200 years; the last one came in 1950, so the Channel Tunnel should be safe for the time being.

The earthquake quickly entered the scientific and popular culture of the time. Gabriel Harvey wrote a letter to the Edmund Spenser, known as 'the earthquake letter', in which he poked fun at both the popular and the academic explanations for the earthquakes. The servant-poet James Yates noticed that the event fell in Easter week and read some significance into that:

> *Oh sudden motion, and shaking of the earth,*
> *No blustering blastes, the weather calme and milde:*
> *Good Lord the sudden rarenesse of the thing*
> *A sudden feare did bring, to man and childe.*
> *They verily thought, as well in field as Towne,*
> *The earth should sinke, and the houses all fall downe.*
> *Well let us print this present in our heartes,*
> *And call to God, for never neede we more:*
> *Craving of him mercy for our misdeeds.*

The Dover earthquake even helps us to put a date to a

Shakespeare play. In *Romeo and Juliet*, Shakespeare has the Nurse say, 'Tis since the earthquake now eleven years.' This suggests the play was written for performance in 1591.

III
THE ENLIGHTENED WORLD

THE SINKING OF
THE *VASA*

(1628)

IN THE EARLY seventeenth century, the king of Sweden ordered four new galleons to strengthen the fleet of warships he needed to patrol the Baltic Sea. One of these newly commissioned vessels was the big flagship, a bigger ship than any that had yet been built, the *Vasa*. She would be a great fighting ship and also a symbol of the king's power and prestige. The specifications and measurements for the *Vasa* came from the king himself and could not be argued with. The design was similar in concept to that of the *Sovereign of the Seas*, built in 1637. The *Vasa* was built in 1628, with a sturdy hull built out of a huge quantity of northern oak; the building of fleets of ships like the *Vasa* contributed greatly to the deforestation of Europe. Her bow timbers were steamed so that they could be curved; the closely spaced ribs of her hull were clad with triple-laminated oak plank walls that when finished were an astonishing eighteen inches thick. The top of the main mast soared to a height of 190 feet. The rudder was thirty feet tall.

There were the customary decorative carvings, too. Carved and painted gods, demons, kings, knights, warriors, cherubs and mermaids were made in workshops and then mounted on the ship's bow and stern. The work took three years to complete and when she was finished she was both a floating fortress and a work of art.

The *Vasa* was fitted with two gun decks loaded with sixty-four bronze cannon. The king, Gustavus Adolphus, had his initials moulded onto the cannon. The ship also carried a supply of cannon balls, gunpowder, firearms, tools and food – as well as a crew consisting 133 sailors. To counterbalance the huge weight of the cannon, the ship had to carry a great deal of ballast, an estimated 120 tons of rock.

The *Vasa* was setting off on her maiden voyage, brand new, when she sank. She left the city's ship quay on the day of her sailing, 10 August 1628. There was a harmless light breeze blowing from the south-west. She did not set her sails at first, but waited until she reached Sodermalm, the southern edge of the harbour. Then her sails were unfurled. She had sailed for less than one mile when she capsized. She had barely left the little cluster of islands that makes up Stockholm's harbour.

Whether it was the light wind or just a series of minor human mistakes that caused the sinking is hard to tell. Having set sail, her captain ordered a farewell volley to be fired. The cannon were fired in a signal heavy with unconscious irony, and afterwards the gunners failed to close their gun ports. If they had done so, all would have been well. As it was, the ports were left wide open. Then the wind gusted. The sudden squall caused her to heel heavily to port, dipping the square openings of the gun ports on the port side of the hull down below the water line. Water poured in through the open gun ports and she listed further and further to port. Within a few moments the *Vasa* capsized and sank. It was a very similar combination of circumstances that had led to the disastrous loss of the English flagship, the *Mary Rose*, in 1545.

The *Vasa* sank only 300 feet out from the shore in 100 feet of water. The top of her main mast was left sticking diagonally out of the water. The water was clear and there seemed a very good chance that she could be raised. Shortly after the memorial service held for her drowned crew, attempts were made to raise her. An English Royal Engineer, Ian Bulmer, managed to pull the *Vasa* upright so that she was sitting on the seabed on an even keel, but he was unable to make any progress in raising her. After that, there were more attempts, with grappling irons repeatedly thrown down to try to haul the ship up. The grappling irons tore at the lavish carvings, which fell off into the mud. Meanwhile the great ship herself just settled deeper and deeper into the mud.

The disastrous loss of the *Vasa* was a goad to inventors, and experiments were going on all the time with prototype submarines and diving bells. In 1658, a German, Hans Albrecht von Treileben, arrived in Stockholm to offer to use a diving bell. It took him five years to acquire the salvage rights to the wreck of the *Vasa*. Then, in collaboration with a diver, Andreas Peckell, he started retrieving the ship's cannon. Another diver, James Maulde, was first to descend to the *Vasa* in the diving bell. He saw debris on the deck and wooden gun carriages 'in wild confusion'. In the summer of 1664, von Treileben and his team of divers successfully brought up every single gun on the *Vasa*'s upper deck. In 1665, he managed to bring up more guns from the deck below. It was an amazing achievement, given the primitive technology of the time. After that, the *Vasa* was left alone and undisturbed. Even her exact position was forgotten – all knowledge can be lost – and the *Vasa* herself was lost for almost 300 years.

The wreck of the *Vasa* was rediscovered by Anders Franzen in 1956. Franzen's obsession was searching for wrecks, and he had already found some seventeenth-century timber vessels. He had been obsessed with finding the *Vasa* from the age of about twenty, and he did. He researched the accounts of the *Vasa*'s first and last voyage, and found that she had sunk in calm fresh-to-brackish water at the point where the huge Lake Malaren passes through Stockholm in 'Beckholm's udden'. He found what seemed from the description to be the right area, he used a core sampler to find what materials were on the seabed. He eventually, in August 1956, brought to the surface a core of black oak. It was a piece of the *Vasa*. To check, divers from the Naval Diving School went to the spot and the director, Per Edvin, went down first to claim the wreck in the name of the Swedish crown. He reported, 'She was upright, but buried to her original waterline in mud.'

As often happens in the aftermath of this kind of disaster, technology is pushed forward by the particular demands of the situation. A decision was made to lift the *Vasa* out of the water just as she was, move her to a dry dock and excavate her there. This was possible because the *Vasa*'s hull was intact and in a very good state of preservation. The Baltic Sea is brackish water, free of the wood-destroying organism *Teredo navalis*, which is found in open oceans.

Divers started work by drilling six boreholes underneath the keel. The idea was to string hawsers through the tunnels and then raise the hull by attaching the cable ends to two pontoons. Just drilling the boreholes took a year. The two pontoons successfully lifted the ship from the seabed, turned her around and took her to shallower water at Kastellholmen, where she was kept fifty feet under water. Then the hull was carefully repaired so that she could be floated into a dock. The fatal gun ports were sealed with padded watertight covers. Almost incredibly, the repaired ship was indeed able to float the last few hundred feet into a dock though, as if from memory, listing slightly to port.

The *Vasa* is now spectacularly on public display, her hull complete and with ninety-five per cent of her original timber. Only a small amount of reconstruction has been done. The ship and the objects found inside her have given us a detailed picture of everyday life on a ship in the early seventeenth century. In 1959, the *Vasa*'s gigantic figurehead was raised. Made in sections of linden wood, the *Vasa* lion had a deeply carved mane coated with gold leaf. The lion was profoundly evocative and became the salvage project's emblem. The ship itself has become a national monument.

The sinking of the *Vasa*, though a disaster in 1628, is now of great benefit to us because we have a perfect record of ship design. No proper records of naval ship architecture have survived from that period; no models or drawings of ships earlier than 1670 exist. Yet now we have the ship herself, incredibly well preserved.

PLAGUE IN
EUROPE

(1663)

*It was about the beginning of September 1664 that I, among the
rest of my neighbours, heard in ordinary discourse that the plague
was returned again in Holland; for it had been very violent
there, and particularly at Amsterdam and Rotterdam, in the
year 1663, whither, they say, it was brought from Italy, others
from the Levant, among some goods which were brought home by
their Turkey fleet; others said it was brought from Candia
[Heraklion, Crete]; others from Cyprus. It mattered not from
whence it came; but all agreed it was come into Holland again.*

DANIEL DEFOE REPORTED in his *Plague Diary* the reappearance,
actually in 1663, of plague in Europe. It struck the Netherlands
particularly hard. Amsterdam was a city of 200,000 people, and
the death toll of more than 10,000 people in a single year, 1663,
was very heavy; then another 24,000 died in 1664. As with earlier
outbreaks of the plague, the disease was spread from city to city
by traders. From Amsterdam it spread to Brussels and through
much of Flanders. As people travelled from country to country on
business, they took the plague with them. Two Frenchmen
visiting Flanders caught the plague and carried it with them to
London, where they died in Drury Lane.

The English king, Charles II, banned English merchants from
trading with the Dutch, partly to reduce the risk of bringing plague
to England, partly because there was a ferocious trade war going

on between the two countries. But the plague arrived in England anyway and by the early spring of 1665 there was a sharp increase in the number of deaths in London's poorer districts. Curiously the authorities turned a blind eye to it at first. But when spring turned into one of the hottest summers anyone could remember the number of plague deaths soared. There was panic. So many people died of the plague that dead-carts were wheeled along city streets, collecting bodies from houses as they passed and unceremoniously dumping them in common graves or plague pits. The men who wheeled the carts smoked pipes all the time in the mistaken belief that tobacco smoke was an antidote to plague.

The plague flared up in London, a city of 460,000 people, where it reached its peak in 1665. People who were confined to their homes because they were infected marked their doors with a red cross. This was to keep casual callers away and signal that the occupants needed food handed out by the constables. When someone in a particular London house was diagnosed as having the plague, the house was sealed by the authorities until forty days after the victim recovered, or forty days after they died. Sentries were posted at the door to enforce the ruling and make sure that no one left the house until the quarantine period was over. The guard often had to be bribed to allow food to be passed inside. It was no unknown for the occupants of a house to be driven to desperate measures to get out. Some made holes in the walls of their own properties in order to get out unseen. Some lowered nooses from first floor windows, successfully lassoing the guard, who was then hanged.

During this appalling emergency, two-thirds of the inhabitants fled the city in an attempt to avoid catching the plague. The rich aristocrats were inevitably best able to leave the city. Many of them had 'places in the country' to which they could easily retreat. They were soon followed by merchants, clergymen and lawyers. The Inns of Court were deserted. Charles II and his court moved to Hampton Court.

There was a steady ebbing away of London's population. In June, as the death rate rose, the roads were jammed with people trying to leave. The Lord Mayor's response to this was to shut the gates to those who did not produced a certificate of health; obviously the migration was the surest way of transmitting the plague across the whole country. The almost inevitable response was a thriving black market in forged certificates of health.

In spite of these desperate efforts, almost 70,000 Londoners died, and inevitably the refugees were responsible for taking the plague with them to other towns. Several thousand people died in the towns of Norwich, Southampton, Portsmouth and Newcastle. One London family thought they were safe once they reached the village of Yalding in Kent. They were wrong; they died within the week. Even remote villages were not safe. The infected villagers at Eyam in Derbyshire were persuaded by their vicar not to run away and spread the disease to other villages; they heroically agreed to stay and in consequence 259 out of the 292 inhabitants died.

By July more than 1,000 people were dying of plague in London every week. Panic led to hysteria. A rumour was set running that it was cats and dogs that were responsible for spreading plague. The Lord Mayor ordered that all the cats and dogs must be destroyed. In his *Journal of the Plague Years*, Daniel Defoe estimated that as many as 40,000 dogs and 200,000 cats were killed. This pet massacre was pointless and cruel, and of course there was now no check on the real enemy, the rats, now that all the cats were dead.

Another pointless scare was the rumour that plague might be transmitted by letter. Letters received in the provinces from London were treated as if they were contaminated. People tried scraping, heating, soaking, airing and ironing letters in order to decontaminate them. The air of apprehension and unreality is caught by references to plague in Samuel Pepys's diary.

30 April, 1665. Great fears of the Sickenesse here in the City, it being said that two or three houses are already shut up. God preserve us all.

3 May. So to the Change and thence home to dinner; and so out to Gresham College and saw a cat killed with the Duke of Florence's poison.

7 June. This day, much against my Will, I did in Drury-lane see two or three houses marked with a red cross upon the doors, and 'Lord have mercy upon us' write there which was a sad sight to me, being the first of that kind that I ever saw. . . I was forced to buy some roll tobacco and to chew which took away the apprehension.

15 June. The town grows very sickly, and people to be afeared of it, there dying this last week of the plague 112, from 43 the week before.

20 June. This day I inform myself that there died four or five at Westminster of the plague, in one alley over against the Palace-gate.

23 June. The sickness encreasing mightily.

13 July. Above 700 dead of the plague this week.

18 July. I was much troubled this day to hear at Westminster how the officers do bury the dead in the open Tuttle-fields, pretending want of room elsewhere; whereas the New Chapel churchyard was walled at the public charge in the last plague time merely for want of room, and now none but such as are able to pay dear for it can be buried there.

26 July. The Sickenesse is got into our parish this week; and is got indeed everywhere so that I begin to think of setting things in order, both as to soul and body.

31 July. The plague grows mightily upon us, the last week being about 1700 or 1800 [dying] of the plague.

3 August. A maid servant of Mr John Wrights falling sick of the plague, she was removed to an outhouse, and a nurse appointed to look after her who being at once absent, the maid got out and run away. The nurse come knocking, and having no answer, believed she was dead, and went and told Mr Wright; who, and his lady, were in a great strait what to do to get her buried. At last resolved to go to Burntwood hard by and there get people to do it but they would not; so he went home full of trouble, and in the way met the wench walking over the Common, which frighted him worse than before. And was forced to send people to take her; which he did, and they got her into one of the pest coaches and put her into it to carry her to a pest-house.

20 August. After Church to my Inn and ate and drank; and so about seven o'clock by water, got between nine and ten to Queen hive, very dark and I could not get my waterman to go elsewhere for fear of the plague. Thence with a lanthorn, in great fear of meeting dead corpses carrying to be buried.

30 August. Everybody's looks and discourse in the streets is of death and nothing else. The town is like a place distressed and forsaken.

31 August. In the City died this week 7,496, and of them 6,102 of the plague. But it is feared the true number of the dead this week is near 10,000, partly from the poor that cannot be taken notice through the greatness of their number, and partly from the Quakers and others that will not have any bell rung for them.

3 September. Up and put on my coloured silk suit, very fine, and my new periwig, bought a good while since, but darest not wear it because the plague was in Westminster when I bought it. What will be the fashion after the plague is done as to periwigs, for nobody will dare to buy any hair for fear of the infection that it had been cut off the heads of people dead of the plague.

23 November. It continuing to be a great frost (which gives us hope for a perfect cure of the plague).

During the summer of 1665 the death rate increased to a peak of 6,000 a week in August. After that it decreased again, but it was not until February 1666 that Charles II thought it was safe to return to the city. It is not known exactly how many people died, but probably over 100,000 in the London area alone.

The Great Plague of 1665 was the last outbreak of plague to strike London, and the last to sweep through western Europe. It caused incalculable human misery. The painter Rembrandt lost his mistress Henrickje to the plague in 1663. His grief was compounded when his beloved son Titus died in a further outbreak of plague in 1668. Rembrandt did not recover from that, dying himself in 1669. The gradual improvements in living conditions and hygiene in western Europe lowered the risk from that time on, but the disease was still to strike elsewhere; 83,000 people would die in Prague in 1681.

THE GREAT STORM
IN ENGLAND

(1703)

WHEN THE GREAT Storm of October 1987 struck southern England it was a traumatic experience for many people who experienced it (though it must be said that I know of some people who slept soundly through it). Nothing like it had ever happened before – or so most people believed. In fact it was not unprecedented at all. Exactly the same region, southern England, underwent very similar weather conditions in 1703 and one of England's greatest writers wrote a detailed description of it, long since put to one side. It was only after the 1987 experience that people started to research the 1703 storm, to revive the collective memory. Disasters can be forgotten and then recalled again.

Starting on 19 November 1703, and reaching a tremendous climax during the night of 26–27 November, a series of gales swept across southern England, causing enormous damage to property. In the countryside, thousands of trees were uprooted and laid flat and over 400 windmills were reduced to matchwood. In the towns and villages, streets were filled with fallen masonry, broken tiles and chimney pots.

The writer Daniel Defoe witnessed the Great Storm. He wrote, 'No pen could describe it, nor tongue express it, nor thought conceive it unless by one in the extremity of it. Nobody could believe the hundredth part they saw.' It was one of the most violent storms to strike England and Defoe described it as 'a perfect hurricane.' Defoe himself had a narrow escape. He was in a London street, when a chimney toppling from a nearby building crashed into the street beside him. The Bishop of Bath and Wells was not so lucky; he was crushed to death when a falling chimney fell on his bed. At Riddlesworth in Norfolk, Lady Elinor Drury and her niece Mary Fisher were killed as they lay side by side in bed; they too had a chimney stack fall through the roof onto them and kill them outright. One of the memorial stones in the nave at St Peter's Church, Riddlesworth reads: 'In memory of the pious and virtuous Mrs MARY FISHER whose soul tooke her flight to Heaven in ye furious hurricane on November ye 27th 1703.' Queen Anne wisely took shelter that night in a cellar underneath St James's Palace, where she came to no harm.

Although the reason for the storm was not understood at all at the time, it is now thought that the high winds were produced by a deep low-pressure system. The conditions on 26–27 November probably resulted from a low-pressure system moving north-eastwards from South Wales across central England towards the Humber. We know that it had a very steep pressure gradient on its southern flank, as contemporary observers were taking readings from their barometers.

The Great Storm hit the West Country first, and right in its path was the Eddystone lighthouse. Engravings of this extraordinary and rather picturesque structure survive, looking like a cross between Nelson's Column and the Globe Theatre. Its designer, Henry Winstanley, was in the tower and making alterations to it at the time when the storm struck. He had rashly said some weeks earlier that he hoped to be out on the reef 'in the greatest storm that ever blew under the face of heaven', so that he could see what effect the storm would have on his building. Henry Winstanley had his wish.

As the storm advanced across southern England, the roaring of the wind could be heard everywhere. In the countryside, sheds, outhouses, chicken coops, barns and even livestock and people were blown about in the wind. In the New Forest and other wooded areas trees were toppled. On the Isle of Wight, the salty spray from the sea spread an incrustation of salt across the fields that looked like a light fall of snow. As a result the pasturage become inedible to the cattle. Even at Cranbrook, seventeen miles inland, the pastures were rendered inedible by the salt.

In the towns there was extensive damage to buildings. The towns along the English Channel coast 'looked as if the enemy had sackt them and were most miserably torn to pieces.' Water piled into the Bristol Channel by the gales caused a huge flood in the port of Bristol, with water levels ten feet higher than any previous high tide. The sheets of lead on the roof of Westminster Abbey were lifted, 'rolled up like parchment and blown clear of the building' by the wind. Many churches in London lost their spires and towers. Defoe saw 700 ships moored in the Thames 'most crushed together'.

There was significant damage in East Anglia too, where several churches lost their spires, including Stowmarket Church, which had a steeple that had only been up for thirty years. Windmills in the Fens were also damaged, though in a different way. The high winds made the sails spin round so fast that enormous friction was set up; sparks flew and they went up in flames. A noticeable feature of the storm in East Anglia was that the wind speed varied a good deal through time, and from place to place. The levels of damage were equally variable. Cambridge, Stowmarket and the Essex coast suffered severe damage, while Norwich was damaged very little. This was very similar to the pattern of the 1987 storm, which affected the same areas; in the 1987 Great Storm, some farms were wrecked while adjacent farms were completely undamaged.

England was engaged in the War of the Spanish Succession, and fleets of warships were assembled in the Solent, ready to sail against France. The combined effects of high tides, huge waves and hurricane force winds topping 120 mph was to scatter and cripple most of these vessels. The situation was even worse in the anchorage known as 'The Downs', the narrow channel between the infamous Goodwin Sands and the coast of East Kent. On the worst night of the storms, over 100 merchant ships and several warships riding at anchor. Many of these were smashed to pieces or driven onto the sands, and 1,500 sailors lost their lives; some ships were even blown all the way to Sweden. Not a trace remained of Winstanley's tower, nor of Winstanley. Altogether it is estimated that perhaps 10,000 or 15,000 people were killed along the south coast, a startlingly high death toll. Inland there were fewer fatalities; an estimated 100 people lost their lives.

Enormous numbers of houses and other buildings were reduced to ruins. The only good thing about the disaster was that bricklayers, glaziers and tilers were able to make huge amounts of money afterwards from all the repair work that had to be done. There was scarcely a single house in southern England that had not been damaged.

The Great Storm earns its place in history in another way, too. It was the first natural disaster to be reported in a modern journalistic style. The author Daniel Defoe wrote an account of it called *The Storm: or a Collection of Casualties and Disasters*, which was published the following year, 1704. What he did was revolutionary. He placed advertisements in newspapers asking witnesses to write to him, sending their own accounts of what happened where they lived. His new approach was very successful. Many people wrote to him from all over England with their eyewitness accounts, which enabled Defoe to assemble an objective and highly detailed account.

THE EDO EARTHQUAKE AND FIRE

(1703)

TOKYO STANDS ON a site that is prone to earthquakes. It stands at the junction of not two but three of the plates that make up the earth's crust. The Japanese government is aware that it would be better if the capital were located elsewhere, and there is indeed a plan for a new capital on a safer site some distance away to the west. The problem is that, as with the rebuilding of London after the Great Fire, there are always vested property interests that favour the status quo. No one who owns valuable land in the central business district of the capital of a rich country wants the city to be closed down, or for any key functions to be transferred to another location. This geographical inertia explains why Tokyo has remained where it is, ever since Tokugawa Ieyasu chose the site and made it his capital in 1590.

There have been repeated reminders that Tokyo is a bad place to build a city, each in the form of a major earthquake. One of the biggest happened in 1703. On 30 December, there was a major earthquake in Edo (the old name of Tokyo), which upset hearths and lamps, so that fires spread through many parts of the city. Amid the falling buildings and the widespread fires that followed, 200,000 Japanese died. The movement along the plate margin that generated the earthquake generated other changes underground; four years later, Mount Fuji erupted – the last eruption of the volcano in modern times. But in spite of the virtual destruction of Edo, it was rebuilt and twenty years later its population had reached over a million.

The Edo earthquake of 1703 was just one in a sequence of major earthquakes to strike the area. They seem to be separated just widely enough in time for the Japanese to regain confidence in the site of the city. The Edo earthquake and fire would be followed over 200 years later by a disastrous earthquake (and fire) in 1923. This quake, known as the Great Kanto earthquake, destroyed both Tokyo and Yokohama, which had for a long time functioned as the port of Tokyo. It comes as something of a surprise – or shock – to see that the cities were rebuilt in the same place. Although individuals can learn from experience, it seems that whole cities cannot; there is psychological as well as geographical inertia.

THE WRECK OF THE
ASSOCIATION

(1707)

THE *ASSOCIATION* WAS commanded by Sir Cloudesley Shovel, who was born in 1650 and seems to have spelt his own name 'Clowdisley Shovell'. He was able and good-natured and when he went into the Navy he was quickly promoted. In 1674, he served as a lieutenant under Sir John Narborough in the Mediterranean, helping to destroy four men-of-war belonging to pirates at Tripoli. He became captain of the Edgar, was knighted and in 1690 he accompanied William III in convoy across to Ireland. After that he was made a rear-admiral, fought at the Battle of Beachy Head and distinguished himself at the Battle of La Hogue, where he broke through the enemy's line. In 1702, he conveyed the spoils of the French and Spanish fleets home to England from Vigo, after they had been captured by Sir George Rooke. In 1704, Shovel was made commander-in-chief of the British fleets.

Sir Cloudesley Shovel commanded the ships in an attack on the French port of Toulon in 1707. This was unsuccessful. It was when returning home to England from this failure on 22 October 1707 that Sir Cloudesley met his end. He was on board his flagship, the *Association*, and sailing north under full sail when she ran into rocks near the Isles of Scilly. These were the days long before steel hulls and watertight bulkheads; the *Association* was badly holed and those on board one of the other ships in the squadron, the St George, watched helplessly as the flagship sank in less than four minutes. The disaster happened so suddenly and so quickly that everyone on board was drowned.

Sir Cloudesley's body was washed ashore on the beach at Porthellick Cove on the island of St Mary's in the Scilly Isles. It was eventually exhumed and after embalming taken to London for burial in Westminster Abbey.

There is a story that he was still alive when he was washed up on the beach. The local inhabitants were wreckers and, as was their practice, went along the beaches searching for useful jetsam and robbing the corpses of the dead sailors. An old woman found Sir Cloudesley, and must have been very pleased to find such rich pickings. When she realized he was after all not quite dead, she cut off his fingers for the sake of his rings, one of which was set with a big precious stone. Then she buried him alive in the beach sand. The woman confessed to her crime on her deathbed, and a rough stone monument was set up where the body had been buried at Porthellick.

Those who disbelieve this story argue that in the days before refrigeration it would have been essential to bury the body immediately, and this would explain the informal burial. Knowing that a formal burial, possibly a state funeral, would follow, the decision was made to bury the body between high and low water mark to preserve it better. The embalmer reported that the body was that of 'a comely, portly man in full health without any blemishes.' This, it may be argued, proves that his fingers were not cut off for the sake of his rings. On the other hand, the mutilation and the horribly macabre circumstances of Sir Cloudesley's death may have been glossed over to spare the feelings of relatives – or even for the sake of keeping intact an already established and publicized version of the admiral's heroic end.

Another story is that Shovel met his death as a result of a curse. There was a widely held superstition that Psalm 109 had the power of a curse: 'Let his children be fatherless and his wife a widow.' The admiral had a reputation for his hot temper and harsh discipline. He was the sort of commander who expected orders to be blindly obeyed, and if he ordered a course to be sailed, that was what had to happen. This rigidity was a major part of the explanation for his ship, and indeed the entire squadron, sailing at full speed under full sail towards the reef. As it happened, a cabin boy on the *Association* came from Scilly and knew the waters round the Scilly Isles well. He rushed to tell Sir Cloudesley that the squadron was heading towards the infamously dangerous Gilstone Reef. Sir Cloudesley took offence at the cabin boy's impudence, made it clear that he would not be told how to sail his ship. He ordered the boy hanged for his impertinence. As the noose was put round the boy's neck, he cursed Admiral Sir Cloudesley Shovel by uttering this psalm. It was, they later said, this curse that brought about the wreck of the *Association*.

Obviously there is a major problem in believing this colourful story. The incident is supposed to have happened in the hour immediately before the *Association* ran onto the rocks. There were no survivors from the *Association* and therefore no witnesses who could say what happened on board the flagship in the run-up to the disaster. So – how could anybody, after the event, know about the cabin boy's warning or the curse? Whether the curse story is true or not, and I suspect it is not, it may well have been Shovel's pig-headedness as a commander that led to the wreck.

The *Association* and four other ships in the squadron were wrecked on the rocks. In all, between 1,600 and 2,000 men were drowned in the disaster. The accident was one of the biggest peacetime disasters in British history and rightly regarded as a national disaster. Two thousand men, five ships and the commander-in-chief were lost. The *Association* was also carrying a vast amount of treasure. There were chests of gold and silver coin and plate that were put on at Gibraltar by British merchants. There were chests containing British government funds for the war in France. There were chests containing Sir Cloudesley's own cash and still others containing regimental funds and silverware. The financial loss alone was colossal.

Clearly the squadron had sailed northwards onto a reef, a known reef, and therefore Sir Cloudesley must have mis-navigated. The visibility was very poor that day and he and his officers had been unable to navigate by eye. Either he was further to the east or west than he had believed, or the maps were inaccurate and had misled him. In other words he had not been aware of his longitude, or the longitude of the reef. The most important outcome of the disaster was the offer of a huge cash prize for the invention of an instrument that could accurately measure longitude. After a very long struggle, this prize was eventually won by John Harrison, when he invented the ship's chronometer. This invention in turn enabled navigators and explorers to pinpoint locations with far greater accuracy than before. As a result, the maps produced in the later eighteenth and nineteenth centuries were far more accurate than the charts Sir Cloudesley Shovel had been using. It also became possible for ships' captains to navigate their courses more accurately – and safely.

The wreck of the *Association* was discovered on the Gilstone Ledge in 1964 by a diving team led by Roy Graham. The divers found cannon, gold and silver coins and a silver spoon in the disintegrated bow section, though the stern section has yet to be found. The press got hold of the story and divers have flocked to the site to pick over it every year since. In 1969, over 2,000 coins and other artefacts from the wreck were auctioned at Sotheby's. Up to 1,000 more coins are found by divers every year, mostly washed into deep gullies. Most of the gold and silver coins vanished. Three bronze cannon were lifted from the *Association*: a small signal cannon, an early breech loading cannon and a naval stern cannon engraved with the date 1604 – far from up-to-date weaponry.

THE CALCUTTA
DISASTER

(1737)

IN OCTOBER 1737 a very unusual event took place – a large-scale disaster, but of uncertain origin. For a very long time it was assumed that a major earthquake struck Calcutta, but it now looks as if it was a very different kind of disaster.

The duties collector for the British East India Company in Calcutta, Thomas Moore, reported that a storm and flood had destroyed most of the lightly built thatched huts that made up the town of Calcutta, and that 3,000 of its 20,000 inhabitants were dead. There were other reports from the officers of merchant ships, and they indicated that there had been an earthquake and a sea surge of some kind, perhaps a tsunami. This had been responsible for destroying 20,000 ships in Calcutta harbour and killing 300,000 people in the region generally.

It now seems as if the huge death toll of 300,000 may have been a guess, and a very exaggerated guess at that, while the earthquake report was just wrong.

Earthquakes can and do occur on the Ganges Delta, but Calcutta is located no closer than 200 miles from the major plate boundary between India and Eurasia, and it would be unlikely for Calcutta to experience a large earthquake. If the 1737 event really was a major earthquake, resulting from some quirk of local geology, then it would be alarming, as the event would be likely to recur in the future, and Calcutta is now a city of over ten million people.

The nineteenth-century description of the event has both an earthquake and a cyclone involved, with no attempt to distinguish the separate effects of each. If both of those elements were involved, it is more likely that the earthquake was the minor element and the cyclone was the major cause of the damage. Recent rereading of the original reports strongly suggests that the disaster was a cyclone disaster.

One of the earliest accounts came from the *Gentleman's Magazine*, June 1738:

September 30, 1737. There happened a furious Hurricane in the Bay of Bengal, attended with a very heavy Rain which raised 15 inches of Water in six hours, and a violent Earthquake, which threw down an abundance of Houses; and as the Storm reached 60 Leagues [200 miles] up the River Ganges, it is computed that 20,000 Ships, Barks, Sloops, Boats, Canoes, &c, have been cast away. A prodigious Quantity of Cattle of all Sorts, a great many Tygers, and several Rhinoceroses were drowned; even a great many Caymans [Crocodiles] were stifled by the furious Agitation of the waters; and an innumerable Quantity of Birds was beat down into the River by the Storm. Two English ships of 500 Tons were thrown into a Village above 200 Fathom from the bed of the River Ganges, broke to pieces, and all the People drowned pell-mell among the Inhabitants and Cattle. Barks of 60 Tons were blow two leagues up into the Land over the tops of trees. The Water rose in all 40 Foot higher than usual. The English ships drove ashore and broke to Pieces were the Decker, Devonshire *and* Newcastle; *and the* Pelham *is missing.*

A French Ship was drove on shore, and bulged; after the Wind and Waters abated they opened their hatches and took out several Bales of Merchanidize &c, but the Man who was in the Hold to fling the Bales suddenly ceased working; nor by calling could they get a reply; on which they sent down another, but heard nothing of him, which very much added to their fear; so that for some time no one would venture down. At length one more hardy than ye rest went down and became silent and unactive as the two former, to the Astonishment of All. They then agreed by Lights to look down into the Hold, which had a great quantity of water in it; and to their surprise they saw a huge alligator staring as expecting more Prey. It had come in thro' a Hole in the Ship's Side, and 'twas with Difficulty they killed it; when they found the three Men in the Creature's Belly.'

When this account was copied as part of an 'earthquake' disaster account in the 1880s, it was altered in several ways. For example the shaking down of St Anne's Church in Calcutta was added in, a detail that is not in the account in the *Gentleman's Magazine*. Instead, some material from the *London Magazine* of 1739 was used, including a mention that the hurricane happened 'at the mouth of the Ganges' and on a different date, 'the night between 11th and 12th Oct last'.

It is not known where either of the two eighteenth-century accounts originated, but presumably they are eyewitness accounts obtained from passengers or crew members aboard one or more of the merchant ships. There is also an eyewitness account from Sir Francis Russell, a great grandson of Oliver Cromwell, who wrote his account down in December 1737. He emphasized the virulence of a storm on the night of 30 September in the Bay of Bengal, but did not mention an earthquake:

Such a scene of horror as that night was I never saw or heard of. Such Terrible gust of wind like the loudest thunder, and torrents of rain, that I expected every moment the house I live in, which I believe the strongest in the town, would have fallen on my head. The noise was so violent above Stairs, that myself and family was obliged to go down and stay below till morning with poor Mrs Wastell and her children, who fled to our house for Shelter, the doors and windows of hers being burst from the walls. But, Good God, what a Sight was the town and the river in the morning,. Not a ship but the Duke of Dorsett *to be seen in the river where the evening before was above twenty-nine sails of vessels great and small, many being drove ashore, some broke in pieces, and others foundered. And this which is Scarce creditable in a river hardly a mile wide, there was no ebb tide for near 24 hours.*

Our church steeple was blown down as also eight or ten English houses, and numbers belonging to the black Merchants. The whole town looked like a place that had been bombarded by an enemy. Such a havoc did it make that it is impossible to find words to express it. All out beautiful shady roads laid bare, which will not be the like again this twenty years. . . I thank God I have no greater Share of this calamity than what my proportion of refitting the freight ships drove ashore will amount to, which may be five or six thousand rupees. I saved all my fine trees that were blown down by replacing them while the earth was soft.'

Oddly, there were accounts in the French press that explicitly mention earthquakes and hundreds of thousands of fatalities. It is almost as if the different witnesses had witnessed completely different events. One thing is sure, and that is that the destruction of 1737 was the single biggest event to have happened in the history of Calcutta since its foundation, and its effects were evident in the East India records for some years afterwards. Thomas Moore, who was responsible for collecting duties and rents, reported in late October that the ravages of the storm had rendered the native Indian population of Calcutta destitute. He commented that 'hardly twenty Thatch'd houses were standing the next day.' Because of the ruinous and financially ruined state of the town, Moore advised that the collection of revenues should be stopped. He commented, 'what still adds to the Calamity is that by the force of the wind the river overflow'd so much that a great Quantity of Rice was quite spoil'd.' This caused the price of rice to rise. In another report, Moore describes the extensive damage to buildings in Calcutta, all of which is consistent with cyclone damage. In one instance he mentions one of the doors in a town gate as having been 'quite blown out from the wall'.

The mixture of reports, some describing a cyclone, some an earthquake, is puzzling. Could both have happened at once? The cyclone was in itself a very violent event. For an earthquake to be even detectable with all the noise and movement caused by the hurricane force winds, it would have to be a major earthquake; a tremor would not have been noticeable. If a violent earthquake had accompanied the cyclone, it should have damaged the masonry of Fort William and the churches, when they were left undamaged. Conversely all of the damage described is consistent with a cyclone. So, in spite of the fact that the Calcutta disaster of 1737 has repeatedly been referred to as a great earthquake disaster, there was probably no earthquake at all.

THE LISBON
EARTHQUAKE

(1755)

ON ALL SOULS Day, 1 November 1755, the city of Lisbon experienced the worst earthquake in Europe since an earlier quake in the same place, the Lisbon earthquake of 1531. Like Tokyo, Lisbon was a city built in a very unfortunate, badly chosen location on low ground on an estuary close to a plate boundary. The earthquake was triggered by a sideways shift along the boundary between the African and European plates. The epicentre (the point on the land surface directly above the focus of the earthquake) was not in fact in Lisbon but out on the seabed to the west of Gibraltar. Recent photography of the seabed in that area shows that a low vertical cliff was thrown up at the time of the 1755 earthquake, so it produced at least one enduring feature.

The shock waves from this epicentre on the floor of the Atlantic rippled outwards towards Lisbon on the Tagus estuary. It only lasted ten minutes, beginning at about 9.30 in the morning, and consisted of three distinct shocks. The first the people of Lisbon knew of it was a rumbling noise. They said afterwards that it sounded like very heavy traffic in the next street and that it was very frightening. The buildings shook. There was a pause. Then there was a really devastating shock that went on for about two minutes. This one brought down the roofs and walls of houses and shops, the facades of churches and palaces, and all this in the midst of a deafening roar of destruction. The flimsy houses of the poor were shaken down and many were killed when their houses fell in on them and crushed them to death. Then there was another pause, followed by another shock.

After this a dark cloud of suffocating dust settled over the city, the dust of the shattered buildings that had been thrown up into the air. It was like a filthy fog. It had been a clear, bright morning, but it turned into a kind of hellish twilight. After about fifteen minutes the cloud of dust began to settle and people began crawling, confused and bewildered, out of the ruins of their houses.

Inside people's homes lamps, candles, lanterns and hearths were overturned and a thousand fires broke out all over Lisbon, burning down what was left of the centre of the city. This terrible fire, fanned by a north-east wind, burned vigorously and was not finally put out until several days later.

Then, about an hour and a half after the earthquake, came the tsunami. Because the earthquake took place on the seabed, and the seabed on one side of the fault had risen sharply, the sea surface was pushed up. Shock waves travelled outwards through the sea itself, producing a series of big waves that swept up the Tagus estuary. Ships were ripped from their anchors and smashed against one another and against the quays. The earthquake survivors, shaking off some of the dust and looking about them at their ruined city, watched as the waters of the Tagus rocked and rose menacingly. Then three waves up to twenty feet high smashed through the burning remains of the lower town; these drowned many who had survived the earthquake and fire. All the light buildings, sheds, workshops and warehouses along the waterfront were swept away.

There were several aftershocks during the morning, frightening people into thinking that some new disaster was about to follow. One that happened at the same time as the arrival as the tsunami did a lot of damage in the lower town, shattering the church of Santa Catarina on the hill near the river and bringing down the east end of the church of Sao Paulo. A great many people who had lost their homes in the main earthquake were sheltering inside the churches, and they lost their lives there.

Another aftershock came at about midday. Then things began to quieten down. By two o'clock in the afternoon, the Tagus had settled back to normality and boatmen were once more crossing the estuary, but now carrying refugees.

It was a triple disaster – earthquake, fire and tsunami. Within just a few hours, 50,000 people had been killed. The All Souls Day catastrophe deeply shocked the whole of Europe, and caused many to question the existence of a benign God. In a very real sense, the Lisbon earthquake marked a shift in attitudes. It was a psychological plate boundary separating medieval confidence in the wisdom of God from a new and less comfortable world in which people had to look out for themselves.

It was not just Lisbon itself that suffered in the earthquake. A strip along the Tagus about seven miles long and extending northwards about two miles was particularly badly hit. The city of Lisbon was very extensively damaged. Hundreds of ordinary houses and shops were destroyed. More than twenty churches were destroyed. Many of the finer buildings were ruined, too. The headquarters of the Inquisition at the top of the Rossio square was wrecked.

The whole of the lower town was destroyed. The only buildings that remained were those built of stone, so the beautiful icing sugar-white Tower of Belem built in 1520 and the St Jeronimos Monastery built to celebrate the Vasco da Gama voyage remained standing. The old town, the Alfama, was up on higher ground, and more solidly built; as a result it survived far better. The Castle of St George, secure and self-defensive on its hill, was undamaged. The cathedral built in 1150 had already been wrecked by an earthquake in 1344 and rebuilt in 1380; the 1755 earthquake wrecked it again.

Some of the well-built palaces and other public buildings that had stood up to the earthquake were nevertheless destroyed by fire. The palace of the Marques de Lourical was at the northern edge of the area affected by the fire, but it was all destroyed, along with its contents. This one palace will serve as an example of the sort of loss that Lisbon suffered that day in 1755. It housed 200 fine paintings, including works by Correggio, Titian and Rembrandt. They were all destroyed. It housed a splendid library of 18,000 books, 1,000 manuscripts, including a history written by the Emperor Charles V in his own hand, a herbal that had belonged to a fifteenth-century king of Hungary, and a huge collection of maps and charts relating to the great Portuguese voyages of discovery. They were all destroyed.

When the king's palace was burned down in the north-west corner of the present Terreiro do Paco, the losses were on a similar scale. It is believed that as many 70,000 books were destroyed there. When the palace of the dukes of Braganza was burned down at the foot of the Rua Antonio Maria Cordoso, the Braganza family archives were destroyed. The story was repeated at one great palace after another. The scale of the loss to European culture can hardly be guessed at.

The city of Lisbon had turned into a place of nightmares, and a great exodus from its centre started at once. As the ragged procession of people streamed out from the centre, they were joined by refugees from the suburbs. They were in an hysterical state, many of them clutching crucifixes, and images of saints along with a few personal belongings. There were ordinary citizens, the greater part of the city's garrison (only a lieutenant and four soldiers staying at their posts), priests and nuns. Many of the refugees built themselves shacks on higher ground just outside the city, and an informal townscape rather like the shanty towns of the Third World began to develop. The hysterical clutching of images and crucifixes became a significant symptom of the disaster. This was more than just a physical and economic disaster, it was a psychological, emotional and spiritual disaster. The Portuguese at that time were people who depended on icons and religious images and talismans. It was particularly distressing for these superstitious people to know that thousands of them had been lost or destroyed. It must have seemed the most unnatural thing to have happened, and it intensified the general atmosphere of profound pessimism.

Some people refused to leave their homes. Some members of religious orders in particular insisted on staying on in the ruins of their monasteries or convents. Before long the authorities compelled the more useful people out in the camps to return. Technicians, craftsmen and engineers – the people who could help in the long task of reconstruction – were brought back. Many of the shops might be destroyed, but stalls were set up for selling food and other essential items. Replacement houses were erected. About 9,000 wooden houses and shops were built during the six months after the earthquake, which was a real achievement, not least because wood was in very short supply in Lisbon. A town life of a sort was regenerating, but at a much lower cultural level than before.

And now the region was transformed, with the wrecked city ringed by strange new encampments on the hills. When the earthquake struck, the king was staying in a royal residence at Belem, in the lower town. He and his family moved at once into their own squatter settlement, a cluster of tents on open land nearby. There was a general desire to get out into the open air, to live in a hut or a tent rather than a solid building; people didn't trust houses and palaces any more. In due course, a wooden lodge was built for him in the hills north of Belem. Even the king was a refugee.

The situation was prolonged by further threats of disaster. In the days after the big earthquake, there were as many as thirty earth tremors. A week after the big earthquake, early in the morning on 8 November, there was a major earthquake. On 11 and 21 December, there were more powerful shocks. In the August of the following year, it was said that there had been no less than 500 aftershocks.

One positive outcome was that a more spacious street plan could be created on the site of the ruined lower town. The chief minister of Portugal, Sebastio de Carvalho e Mello, was responsible for the rebuilding programme, and he managed to achieve for Lisbon what Sir Christopher Wren had hoped to achieve for London after the Great Fire – he rebuilt to a more spacious and formal plan, with long straight streets and wide avenues, marble pavements, gardens, vistas and big set-piece piazzas. Wide streets made the movement of traffic easier; but they would also act as more effective firebreaks in the event of any future disaster. The western part of Lisbon dates almost entirely from the period after the 1755 earthquake.

Shortly afterwards, Voltaire wrote his pessimistic essay about the Lisbon earthquake, *Customs and the Spirit of Nations*. The Lisbon earthquake was a great natural disaster in which earthquake, fire and tsunami followed one another in remorseless and pitiless succession. It was a demonstration that there was no presiding God looking after human welfare; the human race was incontrovertibly alone in the universe. It was in a sense the dawn of modern humanism, and certainly a landmark in the *Enlightenment*. Voltaire then wrote his masterpiece, *Candide*, a satirical short story ridiculing the philosophy of Leibniz, who appears in it as Dr Pangloss. A world in which the All Souls Day disaster could happen was not the best of all possible worlds. Then, naturally, the first of Voltaire's anti-religious writings appeared.

Nor was Voltaire the only to have his mindset shaken by the earthquake. The poet Pina e Mello wrote a famous earthquake poem, called *Parenesis* (meaning Exhortation), in which he criticized Earth for its fickleness. 'O Earth, you mighty rock-like unassailable thing, is it really credible that one so strong and massive should move in terrifying shudders?' He not only wrote it down, he delivered a passionate speech on the same theme in a convent chapel. He also openly expressed his grievance against God. He was a devout, orthodox Christian of his time, a man who believed in sin, divine punishment. Yet he was so shocked by the Lisbon earthquake that a few days after it happened he addressed God out loud, and asked him if he was just, if he was merciful, if he had any pity. The Lisbon earthquake played an important part in altering the way people thought about the world in which they lived.

IV
THE NINETEENTH-CENTURY WORLD

THE NEW MADRID
EARTHQUAKES

(1811–12)

THE EARTHQUAKES THAT shook the city of New Madrid in Missouri in 1811 and 1812 were startling for many reasons. They were very big earthquakes, with high scores on the Richter scale, and they also happened in the wrong place. Earth tremors or small quakes can happen almost anywhere on the earth's surface; it only takes a settlement of an inch or two along an ancient crack in the rocks to generate a tremor. But the big earthquakes invariably happen along plate margins. The nearest plate boundary to New Madrid runs along the west coast of North America. New Madrid is about as far from a plate boundary as it is possible to be. So the fact that earthquakes of magnitude 8 on the Richter scale happened at new Madrid is in itself worthy of note.

It was in December 1811 that the sequence of earthquake activity started, leading up to the largest earthquake ever recorded in North America. One observer noted 1,874 earthquake shocks between November 1811 and March 1812. The big earthquake is called the New Madrid earthquake because the epicentre was on the major crack known as the New Madrid Fault and New Madrid was the nearest town. Large areas subsided, changing the drainage pattern and forming new lakes; the Mississippi itself changed its course as a result of the changes in the shape of the land surface.

An eye witness, Eliza Brown, wrote a vivid impression of the New Madrid earthquake:

On the 16th of December, 1811, about two o'clock am, we were visited by a violent shock of an earthquake, accompanied by a very awful noise resembling loud but distant thunder, but more hoarse and vibrating, which was followed in a few minutes by the complete saturation of the atmosphere with sulphurious vapour, causing total darkness. The screams of the affrighted inhabitants running to and fro, not knowing where to go – the cries of the fowls and beasts of every species – the cracking of trees falling, and the roaring of the Mississippi – the current of which was retrograde for a few minutes, owing as is supposed, to an irruption in its bed – formed a scene truly horrible.

From that time until about sunrise, a number of lighter shocks occurred; at which time one still more violent than the first took place, with the same accompaniments as the first, and the terror which had been excited in everyone was now doubled. The inhabitants fled in every direction to the country, supposing that there was less danger at a distance from than near to the river.

There were several shocks of a day, but lighter than those already mentioned until the 23rd of January, 1812, when one occurred as violent as the severest of the former ones, accompanied by the same phenomena as the former. From this time until the 4th of February the earth was in continual agitation, visibly waving as a gentle sea. On that day there was another shock, nearly as hard as the preceding ones. Next day four such, and on the 7th about four o'clock am, a concussion took place much more violent than those that had preceded it. The awful darkness of the atmosphere, together with all the other phenomena mentioned formed a scene the description of which would require the most sublimely fanciful imagination.

At first the Mississippi seemed to recede from its banks, and its waters gathered up like a mountain, leaving for a moment many boats, which were here on their way to New Orleans, on bare sand, in which time the poor sailors made their escape from them. It then rising fifteen to twenty-nine feet perpendicularly, and expanding, as it were, at the same moment, the banks were overflowed with the retrograde current, rapid as a torrent – the boats which before had been left on the sand were now torn from their moorings and suddenly driven up a little creek to the distance of a quarter of a mile. The river falling immediately as rapid as it had risen, receded in its banks again with such violence that it took whole groves of cotton-wood trees, which edged its borders. They were broken off with such regularity that persons who had not witnessed the fact would be difficultly persuaded that this has not been the work of art.

A great many fish were left on the banks, being unable to keep pace with the water. The river was literally covered with the wrecks of boats and 'tis said that one was wrecked in which there was a lady and six children, all of whom were lost.

In all the shocks the earth was horribly torn to pieces – the surface of hundreds of acres was, from time to time, covered over by the sand which issued from the fissures which were made in great numbers all over this country, some of which closed up immediately after they had vomited forth their sand and water. In some places there was a substance somewhat resembling coal thrown up with the sand. It is impossible to say what the depths of the fissures were.

The site of this town was evidently settled down at least fifteen feet, and not more than half a mile below the town there does not appear to be any alteration on the bank of the river. But back from the river a small distance, the numerous large ponds or lakes were nearly dried up. The beds of some of them are elevated above their former banks several feet, producing an alteration of ten, fifteen or twenty feet from their original state. And lately is has been discovered that a lake was formed on the opposite side of the Mississippi, in the Indian country, upwards of 100 miles in length, and from one to six miles in width, of the depth of ten to fifty feet. It has communications with the river at *both ends, and it is conjectured that it will not be many years before the Mississippi will pass that way.*

We were constrained by the fear of our houses falling to live twelve or eighteen months, after the first shocks, in little light camps made of boards, but we gradually became callous and returned to our houses again. We still continue to feel slight shocks occasionally. It is seldom indeed that we are more than a week without feeling one, and sometimes three or four a day . . . We begin to hope that ere long they will entirely cease.

A Scottish naturalist called John Bradbury was headed down the Mississippi on 15 December 1811. His boat was tied up for the night just upstream from Chicksaw Bluffs (later to become Memphis) and Bradbury was asleep when 'a most tremendous noise' woke him and the crew up. He wrote, 'All nature seemed running into chaos as wild fowl fled, trees snapped and river banks tumbled into water.'

Bradbury recorded twenty-seven shocks. He was much closer to the epicentre than Eliza Brown. Although the earthquake was named after New Madrid, the main epicentre was sixty-five miles to the south-west, in open country where there were few witnesses, and they were illiterate.

Many in the area thought the end of the world had come, but the earthquakes were really nothing new. The 1811–12 earthquake was really a continuation of the long series of earthquakes reported in 1699, 1776, 1779, 1792 and 1804. A good deal of folklore was generated. The new Madrid earthquake was credited with raising Crowley's Ridge and creating Lake Reelfoot in Tennessee. Yet, despite the earthquake's prominence in the oral history of the region, it had very little long-term effect on its economic or urban development.

But there is good reason to fear future earthquakes in the series. New Madrid and Memphis are substantial cities built now of brick and concrete. They would be very seriously damaged if hit by a magnitude 8.0 earthquake. The whole of downtown Memphis would collapse. The highways and gas pipelines would be ruptured; the levees containing the Mississippi would be broken, flooding up to one-quarter of the state of Arkansas. The loss of life could reach hundreds of thousands.

A business consultant started a scare story, predicting that the next quake was due on 3 December 1990. The public became very alarmed, taking out earthquake insurance policies; some people even left the state. The fateful day passed uneventfully. The next earthquake became the Great Non-Event of 1990. But it did serve the useful purpose of reminding the people of the area that there is a lurking danger of another large-scale and very destructive earthquake in that area – some time in the future.

THE ERUPTION OF
TAMBORA

(1815)

MOUNT TAMBORA IS on the island of Sumbawa in the Sunda Arc, a necklace of volcanic islands forming the southern chain of the Indonesian archipelago. The massive volcano and its extensive slopes form the Sanggar Peninsula, which has the Flores Sea to the north, Saleh Bay to the south and a small island called Mojo to the west.

Tambora stands about 200 miles behind the Sunda Trench, a crease in Earth's crust marking the line where two oceanic crustal plates converge at a rate of three inches per year and one dives (or subducts) under the other. The angle at which the subducting plate dips down into Earth is quite shallow, so the subducting plate is less than 150 miles beneath Tambora. What happens to the subducting plate is that it is heated up and melted; because the molten rock is less dense than the surrounding material huge blobs of it rise up towards the surface, where it is erupted as lava. This process has raised the summit of Mount Tambora to a height of 14,000 feet, which makes it one of the highest peaks in Indonesia.

Thus far, Tambora is a typical volcano in a typical island arc. It is a relatively broad, low, flat volcano, forty miles in diameter at sea level, belonging to the type known as stratovolcanoes. What is truly and awe-inspiringly exceptional about Tambora is the violence with which it erupted in 1815. It had probably been dormant for 5,000 years, and that long period of quiescence may help to explain the violence of the eruption when it finally came. It is a massive volcano, supplied, apparently, from a very large magma chamber, which takes a very time to refill. This very long refill time explains the long time interval between major eruptions. The volcano is nevertheless not very ancient; it is thought to have been building up since 55,000 BC, which implies some very large-scale eruptions in the past. Radiocarbon dating tells us that Tambora erupted in 3910 BC, 3050 BC and AD 740, and the eruptions were all similar in nature.

Not all of the lava has come out of Tambora's big central cone. There are about twenty secondary cones, which release flows of basalt lava.

Before 1815 Tambora had been completely inactive for hundreds of years. The volcano's magma chamber was closed and the magma within it was cooling. There was a period of build-up to the big 1815 eruption. There was an '1812 overture', when the caldera started rumbling and generating a dark cloud. Then, from 1814, the volcano steamed for about six months and there were some small eruptions.

Then on 5 April 1815 there was a medium-sized eruption followed by big explosions that were heard nearly 1,000 miles away. Sir Thomas Raffles noted in his memoirs, 'The first explosions were heard on this Island in the evening of the 5th of April, they were noticed in every quarter, and continued at intervals until the following day. The noise was almost universally attributed to distant cannon; so much so that a detachment of troops were marched from Jakarta in the expectation that a neighbouring post was attacked, and along the coast boats were dispatched in quest of a supposed ship in distress.'

An even bigger eruption occurred on 10–11 April. Those who heard it on Sumatra, over 1,600 miles away, again thought it was gunfire. The explosion reached 7.0 on the Volcanic Explosivity Index, and had four times the energy of the 1883 Krakatoa eruption. The eruption column is estimated to have towered over thirty miles high. When the eruption column collapsed, the debris rushed down the mountain sides as devastating avalanches of hot gas, smoke, ash and lava. As these pyroclastic flows reached the sea, they caused further explosions. Before the eruption, the summit was 14,000 feet high. The summit of the volcano was blasted off, destroying the top 5,000 feet of the mountain, and leaving a large caldera four miles across in its place. The explosions marking the collapse of the caldera were heard 300 miles away.

The Tambora eruption might not have been reported in detail, but for the happy accident that the Rajah of Sangir had a perfect view of it from a vantage point twenty-five miles away. He described three distinct columns of smoke and ash jetting out from close to the summit of Tambora and ascending rapidly into the sky at about seven o'clock in the evening on 10 April. Then the whole mountain turned into a mass of liquid fire [lava], with flames spreading further and further outwards. Then the mountain disappeared from view as the ash started to fall back to the earth all around it. The people of Sangir had to protect themselves from the ash and stones that started raining down on their village. Then they were afflicted by a violent whirlwind, which demolished many lightly built structures in the village. Trees were uprooted, people and livestock were thrown about. The sea rose and swamped the villagers' rice fields, destroying anything in its path. While these winds and tsunamis afflicted Sangir, Tambora itself was fairly quiet. Then, starting at eleven pm and going on for the next twenty-four hours, the air was filled with incredibly loud explosions and lightning flashed inside the eruption column. Streams of lava flowed down the slopes of Tambora to the sea, destroying all the villages.

A volcanic eruption on this scale might have been expected to produce a huge tsunami, but the main force of the eruption was at the mountain's summit, well above sea level. There were tsunami waves, but only between three and ten feet in height.

By 12 April, the eruption was dying down; the explosions were quieter and less frequent. Sangir was smothered in three feet of ash. Then came heavy rains, which mercifully washed some of the ash away, preventing some of the crops from being choked. But it was not until 15 July, three months later, that the explosions finally stopped. On 18 April, Sir Stamford Raffles, the lieutenant-governor of Java, sensed that some terrible disaster had overtaken the area and sent Lieutenant Philips with a shipload of rice and other emergency supplies. It was far worse than Raffles anticipated.

Philips reported in early August: 'On my trip towards the western part of the island, I passed through nearly the whole of Dompo and a considerable part of Bima. The extreme misery to which the inhabitants have been reduced is shocking to behold. There were still on the roadside the remains of several corpses, and the marks of where many others had been interred: the villages almost entirely deserted and the houses fallen down, the inhabitants having dispersed in search of food. Since the eruption a violent diarrhoea has prevailed in Bima, Dompo and Sangir, which has carried off a great number of people. It is supposed by the natives to have been caused by drinking water which has been impregnated by ashes.' Ash covered Lombok, destroying natural vegetation and crops alike, ensuring thousands of deaths by famine.

It had been the most powerful volcanic eruption in recorded history – a great natural spectacle that the Rajah of Sangir was privileged to watch. The great eruption had major repercussions not just locally but globally. There were 1.5 million tons of ash hurled high into the atmosphere, 150 times as much as was erupted by Mount St Helens in 1980. For three days there was total darkness for 300 miles in all directions from Tambora, as the ash blotted out the sun. Ash fell up to 800 miles away. Tambora is only eight degrees south of the equator, so its eruption column would have injected ash into the Krakatoa Easterlies, a stratospheric jet stream blowing from east to west along the equator. These high-level winds in the stratosphere spread the ash all round the world, creating a dust veil that encircled Earth. The dust veil cut out significant amounts of light and heat from the sun, and temperatures all around the world were reduced for the next few years.

Global temperature dropped by three degrees, more in some places. In 1815 the summer temperatures in North America and Europe were only a little lower than usual. By the following year, when the dust had spread all round the world, the effects were more marked. The summer of 1816 was described at the time as 'the year with no summer'. It was cool, overcast and gloomy. The poets Byron and Shelley and their entourage were trapped indoors for much of the summer by the adverse weather – and consequently wrote rather more than they might have done. Mary Shelley, the poet Shelley's young wife, set to work to write *Frankenstein*. It was published in 1818, and was an instant best-seller. Byron's friend John Polidori wrote *The Vampyre*. Byron himself wrote a poem called *Darkness*, the opening lines of which reflect the prevailing gloom of that summer:

I had a dream which was not at all a dream;
The bright sun was extinguish'd and the stars
Did wander darkling in the eternal space,
Rayless, and pathless . . . .

In Great Britain, the low temperatures and heavy falls of rain led to failed harvests. Welsh families in desperation took to the roads, begging for food. There was famine in south-west Ireland because the potato, oats and wheat harvests all failed. In Germany too, the harvests failed and food prices rose sharply; there were demonstrations and riots because no one understood why there were food shortages. There were riots and looting in many cities in Europe.

In the summer of 1816, from Canada to Virginia there were frosts several nights running – in June. Canada experienced very low temperatures that summer. From 6 to 10 June 1816, there was snow twelve inches deep lying on the ground near Quebec City. Heavy snow fell on New York in June and July. Frost killed crops across the Midwest, ruining the harvests. There were frosts in Maine in every month of the year. Farmers would remember that year, without affection, as 'eighteen hundred and froze to death'.

The effects were not limited to Europe and North America. There were catastrophic crop failures in India too, when the monsoon failed. The climatic and environmental effects of Tambora were truly global, and 1816 was the second coldest year (at least in the Northern Hemisphere) since the year 1400. The coldest year of all was 1601, and that was due to the eruption of the Huaynaputina volcano in Peru.

Before the eruption of Tambora, it is believed that around 12,000 people had been living on its slopes. They stood very little chance of surviving, but about a hundred of them did somehow survive. According to conservative estimates between 10,000 and 20,000 people died in the eruption, but there are some estimates that put the overall death toll as high as 92,000 or even 117,000. The higher estimates include people who died as an indirect result, from famine, deprivation, malnutrition, starvation and disease.

Since 1815 there has been more activity. Just four years later there was a small eruption with visible flames and earth tremors. There was another eruption in 1880, but this one was very small scale and the material ejected built a small cone (called Doro Api Toi) up inside the 1815 caldera. Then there was a strong earthquake on 13 January 1909. Its epicentre was very close to Tambora, and therefore probably connected with changes in the magma chamber beneath Tambora. There was another eruption in 1967, but a very small-scale one indeed. It is as if the volcano is gradually settling down again for a long sleep.

The 1815 eruption of Tambora stands out as a major volcanic disaster. It was the largest documented explosion and therefore the loudest noise ever reported as being heard by human beings. Toba was louder, but no one lived to describe it; we only know about Toba from geological evidence.

THE HUSKAR
COLLIERY DISASTER

(1838)

THE HUSKAR COLLIERY, or coal mine, was at Silkstone, Barnsley. It was one of scores of Victorian coal mines scattered across Great Britain's biggest and most productive coalfield, which sprawled across three English counties: Yorkshire, Derbyshire and Nottinghamshire.

The Huskar pit disaster happened on 4 July 1838, which was a hot and sunny day that was startlingly interrupted in the afternoon by a violent thunderstorm that produced both hail and torrential rain. The rain was to play a major part in the disaster that unfolded both above and below ground.

The Huskar pit, owned by Mr Clarke of Noblethorpe, was linked by underground passages to neighbouring Moorend colliery for ventilation purposes. The layout of the Huskar pit was similar to that of many other mines of its day. There was a spinal vertical shaft that was used for bringing coal and miners up to the surface using a lift powered by a steam engine. Radiating from the shaft were galleries leading out more or less horizontally, following the coal seams. There was also another gallery or drift for ventilation purposes, which came out in Nabbs Wood.

The heavy rain that fell between two and four that summer afternoon in 1838 put the boiler out, so there was for the time being no power for bringing the miners up to the surface. A message went down, telling all the miners to make their way to the bottom of the pit, but without giving them any explanation. The implication was that something was wrong, but the miners were left guessing and therefore became alarmed. They feared there might be a fire somewhere. Maybe there was a risk of explosion.

There were children, some of them surprisingly young, working in the Huskar mine – both boys and girls. They decided at first that they would wait. but by this time they had spent nine hours underground. About forty of them decided they would get back to the surface by using the ventilation drift. Acting entirely on their own initiative, and evidently without any adult supervision, they set off. When they reached the bottom of the ventilation drift, they passed through an air door and started to make their way up the drift.

This was when things went disastrously wrong. A stream in Nabbs Wood, swelling into a torrent with the sudden downpour of rain, overflowed into the ventilation drift. The children were swept off their feet and washed back down the passage towards the air door. This was shut, and the water ponded back, filling the passage. Twenty-six children were drowned, mainly the younger ones. Some of the older children managed to find a way out along another passage that led into the neighbouring Moorend pit.

The father of one of the children, James Garnett, went into the ventilation drift after the water had drained out of it along with some other adult miners. In it he found the body of his little daughter. All twenty-six bodies were taken to Thostle Hall, where George Teasdale and another man washed their faces. Then the corpses were taken home in carts.

Among the dead boys were two brothers, George and James Burkinshaw, aged ten and seven, another pair of brothers, Isaac and Abraham Wright, who were aged twelve and eight, and six other little boys aged only eight or nine. The dead girls included Mary Sellars who was ten, Anne Moss who was nine years old and Catherine Garnett, Sarah Jukes and Sarah Newton who were only eight years old.

There was an inquiry, which was held on 18 March 1841 by the

Children's Employment Commission. Benjamin Mellow, the underground steward at four of Mr Clarke's pits, was responsible for supervising the miners – about ninety people altogether. Mellow was in some ways the key witness, who gave away the colliery's attitude towards both the children and the accident.

We have had but one bad accident and that was the 4th July 1838. It had been raining hard during a thunderstorm to such an extent that the water came into the south engine house and the engineer gave the alarm to the banksman, who shouted out incautiously to put the light out and come out of the pit. The children and people were frightened, not knowing what was the matter.

A number of children, either from the fright or from a desire to get a holiday, ran from the shaft towards the pit trail which forms a second outlet, and this, together with the water escaping from the old workings, rushed down the pit trail and met the children who had passed a trapdoor, against which they were driven by the water and being unable to open it, twenty-six were drowned, eleven girls and fifteen boys. The water by the marks it left could not have been above six inches deep in its stream down to the pit trail but rose by the door and there they were drowned. Fourteen had got on before and they had passed sufficiently far to be safe. I am quite sure the stream never overflowed before. No man can prove it. The stream is very small and is dry nine months out of twelve. If the children had remained in the pit or at the shaft, they would have been quite safe. The water never rose anywhere except just where they were drowned.'

Mellow's testimony was designed to vindicate the colliery's management. This was the only accident they had ever had. If the children had stayed where they were, they would have been safe. They only went up the ventilation drift in order to get out of working. There was no mention of their supervisor, no mention of who was responsible for their welfare. Nor was there any suggestion that the stream required management.

Mr Badger, the coroner, held the inquest on the disaster at the Red Lion Inn at Silkstone. The bodies had been viewed at their homes. Joseph Huskar told the court what had happened. 'Eleven of us were together and they all drowned but me. The water swam me down the day hole and through a slit into another bord gate.'

Another witness, William Lamb, said, 'We did not know what we were going out for. We thought it was a fire. The water washed the children down the day hole against a door, through which we had just come, and they were all drowned. If we had stopped at the pit bottom we should have been saved.'

When it had heard all the evidence and the survivors' accounts, the jury returned a verdict of accidental death. Queen Victoria was interested in the disaster, because of the sad loss of so many children, and her interest combined with the pathos of the disaster was a factor in setting up a Royal Commission into the employment of women and children in coal mines.

The disaster was an important step towards the ending of the employment of children in mines, and towards the ending of child labour in Great Britain generally.

A monument to the victims of the disaster was set up in Silkstone churchyard. It is still there and it bears the inscription, 'Take heed, watch and pray, for ye know not when the time is.' It unfortunately goes on to imply that God was responsible for killing the children. 'The Lord sent forth his thunder, lightning, hail and rain, carrying devastation before them, and by a sudden eruption of water into the coal pits of R. C. Clarke Esq., twenty-six beings whose names are recorded here were suddenly summoned to appear before their maker.' The monument bears other dark observations that now look equally inappropriate: 'Boast not thyself of tomorrow,' 'There is but a step between us and death,' and 'Therefore be ye also ready.' The Victorians attempted to present the Huskar disaster as a cautionary tale, a kind of living sermon. But thoughts entirely other than these strike the modern mind, including, 'Who exactly was supervising and looking after these children?' and 'Who took responsibility for them; whose was the duty of care?'

If any good came out of this terrible incident at Huskar, it was that it formed a stepping stone towards the ending of the exploitation of children and towards the modern approach to childhood. Now we see that childhood should be nurtured with as much care as we can muster, and never exploited for commercial gain. We have moved on from sentimental humbug like the Victorian monument at Silkstone to a genuine care for what happens to the young.

LANDSLIDE
IN DORSET

(1839)

IT WAS ON Christmas Day in 1839 that a large section of the Jurassic Coast of Dorset slid into the sea. At Bindon, between Axminster and Lyme Regis, a huge slab of solid limestone had broken away and slid over a layer of clay towards the English Channel. The landslip took forty-five acres of rural England, complete with several cottages, a road, a field of turnips and a wheatfield, and in the space of a few minutes moved them sideways a hundred yards.

Where before Christmas there had been unspectacular level fields, a steep-sided ravine almost a mile long and 300 feet wide had opened up, with walls 160 feet high.

The landslide was described by two of the most eminent scientists of the day. One was Revd William Conybeare, who was Vicar of Axminster, and the other was Revd William Buckland, Professor of Geology at Oxford. Their writings constitute the earliest scientific description of a landslide and the explanations they offered are still considered to be valid. The landslide was also big national news and of great popular interest. People came to see it by land and by paddle steamer. It even had a piece of music written in its honour – *The Landslide Quadrille*. Many engravings and prints were made, illustrating the new landform. Today, now that the chasm is filled with woodland, those prints provide a useful picture of the detail of the land surface.

The Great Chasm became an instant tourist attraction. Local

farmers were able to charge people sixpence each to cross their fields to see it. Queen Victoria came to see the scene of the disaster. One group of visitors, the Foot family, even held a dinner party for their friends in the chasm one summer evening in July 1843. Sketches of the Great Chasm made shortly after it was formed show that as well as the main detached block, called Goat Island, there were several much smaller pieces of rock that had broken away, forming weirdly shaped spikes and pinnacles.

The Dorset coast is noted for its landslides. They commonly happen where a solid and permeable rock layer rests on clay. Rain water passes through the permeable rock, collects in the clay, and the boundary between the two layers becomes lubricated. Then, especially after periods of heavy rain, the solid rock slips over the clay. The Bindon landslide was unusual in that a single very large slab of rock slid intact – and carried human habitations with it. The two cottages were destroyed. It is also unusual in that the slab of rock was moved sideways and tilted slightly towards the sea. Normally in landslips, the movement is rotational, the displaced rock rotating so that its surface tilts back towards the land. The great slab of Goat Island has nevertheless remained in exactly the same position since 1839, still tilting towards the sea.

Two coastguards were standing on Culverhole beach on the night when the disaster happened. They 'observed the sea to be in an extraordinary state of agitation; the beach on which they stood rose and fell; amidst the breakers near the shore something dark appeared to be rising from the bottom of the sea, amidst the deafening roar of crashing rocks.'

Only a month later, there was another landslip at Whitlands, though this was a much smaller affair than the Dowlands Chasm landslide. This landslip, on 3 February 1840, produced a distinctively bumpy and chaotic landscape at the water's edge, known as an undercliff. Viewed from there, the wooded skyline of the mainland can be seen, with the shrub-covered crags of the landslide below, and a deep 'dingle', or valley, form at the bottom.

Although frightening and destructive, landslides can produce excitingly wild landscapes.

Modern research on the landslides along the Dorset coast between Lyme Regis and Axmouth has shown that although the undercliffs appear to be chaotic they consist of fairly regular series of ridges tilted inland and running parallel to the coast. The ridges have been studied, along with the miniature ravines developing in some of the fields, and it seems that Goat Island is really a slab of the mainland that became displaced sideways between sets of tilted ridges both on the seaward side and in the chasm on the landward side.

The rotated ridge in front of the landslide was lifted out of the sea, making a natural breakwater for a small new natural harbour. Both the harbour and its breakwater proved to be short-lived features, though before it was eroded away by the action of the waves it was suggested in Parliament that it might be turned into a port for the British Navy.

THE MAELSTROM

(1841)

A MAELSTROM IS a large, swirling, rotating body of water, a violent whirlpool. Rather oddly, the word seems to have come from the Netherlands, where there are no violent whirlpools, and is made up of two Dutch words, 'malen' (meaning 'to grind') and 'stroom' (meaning 'stream'). The original maelstrom is not in the Netherlands, but Norway. The original phenomenon is the Mokstraumen, which is in the sea off the coast of the Lofoten Islands and close to the southern end of the island group, west of the mainland town of Bodo.

The Moskstraumen is a complex of powerful tidal eddies and whirlpools that develop in a gap or channel between the islands. The development of large whirlpools and standing waves (waves that stay in the same place) happens at other places around the world, especially where strong tidal currents are forced around the tip of a headland sticking out sharply into the sea. There are weakly developed tidal eddies that develop on each side of Selsey Bill in Sussex, for instance. When the tidal current is from the east, the eddy is on the west (lee) side of the Bill; when the current is from the west, the eddy is on the east side. These eddies are several miles across and are not visible from sea level, but they have the effect of combing beach shingle back towards the point of Selsey Bill, which has helped to reduce the rate of erosion there. In other words, tidal eddies can be harmless and even constructive.

The Moskstraumen develops in a fairly shallow channel about three miles across, between the island of Moskenesoya and some small islets off the coast of the island of Mosken. The fairly shallow channel, about 150 feet deep, joins the much deeper Norwegian Sea on the west to the Vestfjord on the east. The Moskstraumen, which is in effect a massive turbulence in the water, forms twice every day at the moment when the tidal current changes direction. The water flowing through the channel is constricted by the islands to north and south, and also by the sharp rise in the seabed from the much deeper water on each side. A significant difference in the level of the sea on each side of the strait develops when the tide turns, and this causes the water to race through in a state of strong turbulence. It is said that the tidal current runs there at about twelve mph, but rather surprisingly as yet no instrumental measurements have been made of the phenomenon. Apparently no one has thought it worthwhile to investigate the phenomenon in detail.

The eddies and whirlpools are quite spectacular, but not as spectacular as they have been made out to be in early descriptions and more recent works of fiction.

The Moskstraumen was first reported as early as the late iron age, by the Greek historian Pytheas. When detailed navigational charts were made, much later, it was marked on with dramatic and exaggerated descriptions. Olaus Magnus, a Swedish bishop, added it to his map Carta marina, drawn in 1539, noted that it was powered by divine force. He said it was stronger than the Charybdis off Sicily. A more down to earth description was included in *The Trumpet of Nordland*, a topographical poem written in 1685 by Petter Dass, a Norwegian priest.

The Moskstraumen, or at any rate some exaggerated descriptions of the Moskstraumen, found its way into mainstream literature through the work of two very high-profile authors, Edgar Allan Poe and Jules Verne. Poe wrote his work *A Descent into the Maelstrom* in 1841. It may well be that Verne read Poe's version of the *Maelstrom*, was inspired by it and so incorporated into his own novel *Twenty Thousand Leagues Under the Sea*. Verne uses the Maelstrom as the setting for his closing scene. Both

Edgar Allan Poe and Jules Verne treat the Maelstrom as if it was a single huge whirlpool, when the Moskstraumen is actually a complex of several whirlpools and eddies.

The Norwegian Maelstrom is an impressive phenomenon, but not as impressive as many writers would have us believe. We have it in our minds as an elemental place of disasters, a place where people, whole shiploads of people, are whirled round and round and sucked to their deaths down a great yawning column like a water-walled gullet. The real Moskstraumen may, over the course of many centuries, have caused some minor boating accidents. It is possible that some lives have been lost there, but it is not the extremely violent, extremely dangerous place that we hold in our minds as an archetype of destructive chaos, a symbol of extreme psychological confusion and disorientation. It is as if the Maelstrom has taken on a much larger-than-life reality of its own inside people's minds, more real than the Moskstraumen.

THE IRISH POTATO FAMINE

(1845)

The Irish potato famine began in September 1845, when the leaves of potato plants turned black, curled up and rotted. It seemed to many people at the time to have been caused by a sinister fog drifting across Ireland, but it was in reality the result of an airborne fungus, *phytophthora infestans*, brought into Europe in the holds of ships sailing from America to England. Winds blowing from the ports of southern England took the fungus across to Ireland. The moist conditions there allowed the fungus to spread quickly; one infected potato plant could infect thousands more plants.

There had been crop failures before – by 1845 there had been sixteen food shortages in Ireland since 1800 – but not on this scale. The freshly dug potatoes at first looked normal, but quickly shriveled and rotted. The British Prime Minister, Sir Robert Peel, set up a Scientific Commission, which reported that more than half of the Irish potato crop, Ireland's main food crop, was likely to be lost as a result of 'wet rot'. The ordinary people of Ireland came up with their own explanations, which ranged from volcanic activity to atmospheric pollution caused by the newly invented railway trains. English clerics came up with the mischievous idea that God had sent the blight to end a cycle of poverty in Ireland that was the result of a misguided dependence on potatoes.

As mass starvation loomed, Peel courageously set about repealing the Corn Laws, protectionist legislation that had been passed in 1815 to maintain a high price for corn. Repealing the Corn Laws would mean that affordable grain could reach the Irish poor. But Peel met strong opposition from the English landowners, who stood to lose large sums of money, and the vehement debate about the Corn Laws overshadowed concern for the plight of the stricken Irish. Previous shortages had been short-lived, and there was an understandable assumption that this one too would be no more than a temporary problem. The relief measures set up and supervised by Charles Trevelyan were totally inadequate. Trevelyan himself was unsuited to the task. He refused to delegate and was often at his desk until three in the morning. This kept him well away from the realities of the famine, which he never saw for himself. In desperation, Peel secretly purchased two shipments of maize from North America for distribution in Ireland, but there were too few mills in Ireland to grind the maize into corn meal. Then the peasants were unable to digest it; unlike potatoes it lacked Vitamin C and resulted in scurvy. The general approach among English officials was that the famine would resolve itself through natural means – a characteristically 'laissez-faire' attitude.

During the first year of the famine, many peasants were able to keep themselves alive by selling livestock, pawning belongings and borrowing from moneylenders. This was an understandable strategy, as the potato crop had never before failed two years running. But this blight was not going to go away; in fact it went on for another three years.

One result of the potato famine was the fall of the Conservative government over the repeal of the Corn Laws. Peel resigned as prime minister in June 1846. Trevelyan unfortunately remained in his post, supervising the famine under the new Whig government of Lord John Russell. Newly empowered, Trevelyan closed the maize depots and stopped further imports of maize, on the grounds that the Irish had to stop depending on the British government; he wanted the Irish to take the initiative for themselves.

Trevelyan was impervious to the letters from Ireland begging him to do something. One Irish priest wrote, 'In many places the wretched people were seated on the fences of their decaying gardens, wringing their hands and wailing bitterly the destruction that had left them foodless.' By September 1846, starvation hit the west of Ireland, where people were completely dependent on the potato crop. The Coastguard Inspector-General, Sir James Dombrain, was so overwhelmed when he saw people starving that he ordered free food handouts. Trevelyan publicly rebuked him for it.

Incredibly, during the famine cash crops of oats were being exported from Irish ports to England. There were food riots in the ports. At Youghal near Cork rioting peasants tried unsuccessfully to seize a shipload of oats. At Dungarvan, British troops opened fire on a crowd, killing two and wounding several more.

The starving Irish were reduced to feeding on wild blackberries, nettles, turnips, old cabbage leaves, seaweed, shellfish, roots, weeds and grass. There were plenty of fish in the sea off the west coast, but they remained out of reach as far as the Irish fishermen were concerned, equipped as they were with inadequate, small, hide-covered boats; many of the fishermen had in any case had to pawn their nets and tackle.

After a hard and cold winter, the Irish peasants were in an even worse state by 1847. They took refuge in futile public works projects. Half a million men, women and children were now at work building stone-paved roads, many of them leading from nowhere to nowhere. Many of the inadequately fed and inadequately clothed workers collapsed or even died of heart failure as they worked on these pointless road-building projects.

The magistrate of Cork visited a badly-affected area and reported what he saw.

I entered some of the hovels, and the scenes which presented themselves were such as no tongue or pen can convey the slightest idea of. In the first, six famished and ghastly skeletons, to all appearances dead, were huddled in a corner on some filthy straw, their sole covering what seemed a ragged horsecloth. I approached with horror, and found by a low moaning they were alive – they were in fever, four children, a woman and what had once been a man . . . Suffice it to say that in a few minutes I was surrounded by at least 200 such phantoms, such frightful spectres as no words can describe, suffering either from famine or from fever. Their demoniac yells are still ringing in my ears, and their horrible images are fixed upon my brain.

In some places, whole families were stricken, and just lay down to die by the roadside, giving in to what became known as 'road fever'. Many died from starvation, but many more died from associated conditions such as dysentery, typhus and famine dropsy. Typhus, known as Black Fever, was spread by body lice, and it killed not only the starving peasants but those who were kind-hearted enough to attend to them in their lice-infested hovels; many doctors, priests and nuns died.

By the early summer of 1847, the British government closed down the public works projects. Trevelyan had been seen to fail, and Russell switched to a more humane policy of keeping people alive. Soup kitchens were set up, though not enough, and the soup was of such a poor quality that it made many people ill.

A new problem was eviction. Many landlords decided to get rid of their poor tenants, often paying them to emigrate. Huge numbers were packed into unregulated and unseaworthy sailing ships heading for North America, often running out of drinking water well before landfall. One ship freshly laden with Irish migrants set sail only to sink minutes later within sight of those who had gone to wave goodbye.

The North American ports were unprepared for the huge influx of immigrants. By the spring of 1847, they were overwhelmed. The Canadian quarantine and medical inspection facilities on

Gross Isle in the St Lawrence River were unable to cope and by June that year a queue of forty ships carrying 14,000 Irish immigrants waited in a line two miles long. Many of the hunger-weakened immigrants were falling ill, catching typhus from fellow passengers. The queue lengthened, as more and more of the immigrants caught typhus. Hundreds of bodies were just dumped over the sides of the ships. Others were taken in small boats to the beach on Gross Isle, and left to crawl on all fours to the hospital. One poor Irish orphan boy walked along the road with some other boys, sat down to rest under a tree and just died there. The Gross Isle fever sheds rapidly turned into death sheds.

The quarantine idea was abandoned and from Gross Isle immigrants were taken to Montreal and Toronto, taking disease and a trail of other problems with them. Of 100,000 Irish people sailing to North America in 1847, one-fifth died of disease or malnutrition.

Many of the survivors walked across the border to live in the United States, attracted by its tradition of hostility to the British. Unfortunately, it also had a long-standing tradition of hostility towards Catholics.

Some Irish refugees crossed the Irish Sea to make a new life in Glasgow, Liverpool and South Wales. Pauper families were allowed to travel free as ballast in empty coal ships. Yet even on these short voyages there were deaths. One crowded steamer arrived in Liverpool with seventy-two dead Irish migrants aboard; they had suffocated below decks when the captain ordered the hatches battened down during a storm.

The effects of these migrations were enormous. Before the famine, Liverpool was a city of 250,000 people; during the first six months of 1847, a wave of 300,000 destitute and starving Irish migrants arrived there, bringing the city to the brink of ruin and causing outbreaks of dysentery and typhus. The British government responded to this by attempting a forced repatriation. Around 15,000 unfortunate Irish people were hauled out of cellars and lodging houses in Liverpool and shipped back to Ireland. Glasgow had a similar experience and attempted a similar solution. The migrants responded by moving deeper into the hinterland of England, Scotland and Wales so that they were harder to find and harder to deport.

Meanwhile, Charles Trevelyan was trying to make the Irish organize and pay for the relief of Irish poverty. The measures, enshrined in a new Poor Law, were strenuous, intrusive and enforced with barbarous severity. Inevitably and justifiably, there was an eruption of anti-British feeling in Ireland and a surge in Irish nationalism. In 1848, the year of revolutions in Europe, a group called 'Young Ireland' organized an armed rebellion, but agents for the British government became aware of the plot and new laws were passed, curtailing civil liberties. A Treason Felony Act made it a crime punishable by transportation to speak against the Crown or Parliament. The seeds of Irish nationalism were sown, seeds that would eventually result in the creation of the Irish Free State in 1921.

Still the famine continued, and 1848 was another potato crop failure year. And still there was no compassion in England for the plight of the Irish. *The Times* thundered, 'In no other country have men talked treason until they are hoarse, and then gone about begging for sympathy from their oppressors. . . and in none have they repeated more humble and piteous [requests for help] to those who they have previously repaid with monstrous ingratitude.' The awful reality was that people in Ireland were reduced to killing and eating dogs, which had themselves fed off human corpses; at least one mother had lost her sanity and eaten her own dead children. Men and boys who had never been in trouble with the law went out of their way to commit crimes in order to be transported to Australia. One teenage convict said, 'Even if I had chains on my legs, I would still have something to eat.'

But the people of Ireland did not simply wait to die. They were on the move. In addition to the thousands who emigrated, thousands more moved around within Ireland. Villages, towns, entire districts were abandoned. Virtually the whole of western Ireland was emptied of people. The disastrous 1848 potato harvest triggered a new wave of emigration to the United States, on ships bound for Boston, New York, Charleston and New Orleans. Altogether nearly a million Irish emigrated to the country – and no welcome awaited them there. They got a rough and contemptuous reception in Boston, a city proud of its descent from English Puritans and now finding itself swamped by 37,000 Irish Catholics. The living conditions in the Irish ghettoes were so poor that the death rate among one to six year olds was sixty per cent; the average life expectancy of adults was just six years after disembarking. New York, being much larger and more cosmopolitan, was better able to absorb the incomers. The influx of 650,000 new people was even so a major demographic jolt.

The large number of immigrants meant that Catholicism came close to being the single largest Christian denomination in the United States, which prompted a severe anti-Catholic backlash from Protestants and a surge of anti-Irish feeling. Advertisements for accommodation and jobs regularly ended with the tag, 'POSITIVELY NO IRISH NEED APPLY.' The Irish potato famine added a significant new thread to American culture. The most remarkable descendant of the famine was President John F. Kennedy, the great-grandson of a County Wexford farmer who had sailed for North America in 1849.

The effects on Ireland were terrible indeed. The country lost nearly one-third of its population. The famine was one of the two greatest natural disasters of the nineteenth century, killing one-and-a-half million people and driving a million to emigrate.

THE WRECK OF THE
BIRKENHEAD

(1852)

THE STORY OF the *Birkenhead* was one that must have been told thousands of times to Victorian and Edwardian schoolboys, as an example to instill all the 'right' values in a boy. What happened aboard the *Birkenhead*, a saga of chivalry, stoicism, self-sacrifice and self-discipline, epitomized all that it meant to be a true Brit in those days.

HMS *Birkenhead*, one of the very first iron-hulled paddle steamers to go into regular service, steamed out of Portsmouth in January 1852, carrying soldiers to fight in the Frontier War in South Africa. The soldiers included Highlanders, Fusiliers, Rifles, Lancers, Green Jackets and others. In command on the Royal Naval vessel was Captain Robert Salmond, whose family had been seagoing people for 300 years. The *Birkenhead* sailed down the English Channel towards the Atlantic, then turned north-west to make a call in southern Ireland. From there, on 17 January, she sailed south for the Cape.

The *Birkenhead* put into Simon's Bay (now Simonstown), just round the Cape of Good Hope from Cape Town, to take on fresh food and water. Then in the late afternoon of 25 February she steamed out into the ocean again with around 634 men, women and children on board. February was winter in England, but late summer in the Cape. The weather was perfect, with a hot sun shining, a blue sky and a calm sea – ideal conditions for a voyage.

Salmond had orders to reach Algoa Bay (now Port Elizabeth)

with all speed. Algoa Bay was over 400 miles away to the east. In the normal way, Salmond might have steered out into open water and headed east in a broad curve. Conscious of the need to get there quickly, he decided to hug the coastline and so shorten the distance. It was a grave error of judgement on his part. He sailed at a steady eight knots, no more than three miles offshore.

In the middle of the night of 25–26 February, the *Birkenhead* got into difficulties. She was heading for a rocky promontory called Danger Point about fifty miles from Simon's Bay, and about halfway between the Cape of Good Hope and Cape Agulhas, the southernmost tip of Africa. Most of the people on board, both passengers and crew, were asleep in their quarters; all in fact except the duty watch. The men on watch scanned the sea ahead for any sign of the breaking water that might indicate a reef, and a sounding of twelve fathoms sounded safe enough. Then, totally without warning, the ship struck a rock. It was a rock that was not on their chart. The steam-powered paddles of the *Birkenhead* had driven her with great force onto the rock, and it ripped right through the hull between the forepeak and the engine room. There was absolutely no chance of floating her off. She had not merely gone aground; she had been torn open and was bound to sink.

The dark water poured into the forward compartment of the lower troop deck. The area was flooded and filled almost instantly, and hundreds of soldiers were drowned as they slept in their hammocks with no possibility of escape. The survivors assembled on deck, some barefooted and in their night clothes, others naked and injured from their struggle to escape from the flooded troop deck.

The senior officer on board the *Birkenhead* was Lieutenant-Colonel Seton of the 74th Royal Highland Fusiliers. He took charge of all the soldiers on board. His first move was to summon the officers and tell them that order and discipline must be maintained.

The captain fired distress rockets, but no one responded. They were too far from any possible help. The captain recognized at once that their situation was utterly hopeless. He ordered the lifeboats to be lowered. This was far from easy, as the lowering gear had not been maintained properly and the mechanisms were gummed up with thick layers of paint. Eventually two cutters and a gig were lowered into the sea. The weather conditions were still very favourable. The night was clear and starry. The seven women and thirteen children on board were rowed away from the wreck towards the shore.

It was in that moment that the great tradition of 'women and children first' was created, and the wreck of the *Birkenhead* would enter a legendary world of British heroism, to say nothing of manners and etiquette.

There were horses on board, and the captain ordered them to be cut loose and thrown overboard; it gave them a thin chance, but at least some chance of saving themselves. It is doubtful whether any of them survived in those shark-infested waters. Then Captain Salmond told the men to save themselves if they could, by jumping into the sea and swimming for the boats. Lieutenant-Colonel Seton was alarmed at this, because he knew it would mean the troops would rush the boats and almost certainly put the lives of the women and children at risk. So he countermanded Captain Salmond's order, drawing his sword and ordering the troops to stay where they were.

The soldiers in Seton's command were inexperienced and likely to be undisciplined. They might have ignored him and rushed for the boats, but they did not. They did exactly as commanded. They stood still, even while the ship, impaled on its rock, broke in two and sank underneath them. It was an extraordinary moment in British naval and military history, this incident that showed men bravely and stoically accepting death – the ultimate act of chivalry and self-sacrifice. The men involved were instantly turned into heroes back in Great Britain and held up as an example to all servicemen for decades to come.

The men did not have to stand about on deck for long waiting for death. The ship sank within twenty-five minutes of hitting the reef. The water was fairly shallow, and after she sank the *Birkenhead*'s topmast and sail stayed above the water. Perhaps fifty men hung onto these pathetic remnants of the ship. Many of the soldiers could not swim, and they drowned quickly. Those who could swim stayed alive longer, but many of them were taken by great white sharks.

When daylight came, a schooner called the *Lioness* arrived to find the lifeboats. After the women and children had been picked up, the Lioness sailed on to the scene of the shipwreck, reaching it in the afternoon. There the surviving men were picked up. The *Birkenhead* had steamed out of Simon's Bay the previous day with 634 people on board. Now only 193 of them were alive.

There was a lot that was far from exemplary, of course. The captain's decision to steam along too close to a rocky coastline that he did not know well was a serious error of professional judgement. The poor maintenance of the ship's life-saving equipment must also be laid at least partly at the captain's door. The serious under-provision of lifeboats was a problem on all nineteenth-century ships, and rather surprisingly no lesson seems to have been learned from the sinking of the *Birkenhead*. And – finally – what was Salmond thinking of when he encouraged hundreds of men to jump into the sea and race one another to the lifeboats? But all of that was set to one side. The story became part of the legend of the British Empire. Rudyard Kipling thought it was wonderful:

> *To stand and be still*
> *To the* Birken'ead *Drill*
> *Is a damn tough bullet to chew.*

STORM ON THE SUN

(1859)

WE TEND TO regard the Sun as dependable and constant. Even when there are overcast days, we know that above the cloud layer it is still shining continuously and constantly. Even though at night the Sun is invisible to us, we know that that is so only because Earth has turned on its axis and the Sun is simply shining on other people. The constancy of the Sun is a given, something we take for granted. What happened in 1859 showed that the Sun is far from constant and reliable, that it can sometimes do very dangerous things, and very unpredictably at that.

On 1 and 2 September 1859, there was a catastrophic storm on the Sun, the most massive storm ever recorded. Many people realized that something significant had happened, because telegraph wires both in Europe and in the United States shorted and stopped functioning.

The Aurora borealis, the Northern Lights, became visible in much lower latitudes than usual. They are normally visible in the night sky inside the Arctic Circle, i.e. north of about sixty-six degrees North. Occasionally they are visible further south: sometimes, but for the cloud cover, we would be able to see them in Great Britain. But during the solar flare of 1859 people were seeing the Northern Lights as far south as Rome, Havana and Hawaii. The Southern Lights, also usually restricted to the Antarctic, were similarly visible over a much larger area. From being the Northern and Southern Lights, these spectacular nocturnal lighting effects had suddenly, though temporarily, become the Everywhere Lights.

What had happened on the Sun was a combination of several events occurring at once. Happening separately they would have been striking enough. Happening together they produced a spectacular space storm.

The Sun is a very large, very massive object. It is a huge incandescent ball 870,000 miles across, and it contains 99.86 percent of the entire mass of the solar system. Its volume could swallow up more than a million Earths. The Sun also radiates a large amount of energy. This varies a little through time, certainly enough to change the earth's climate significantly as it burns a little more or less brightly. A small domestic electric heater radiates one kilowatt. The Sun radiates 383 billion trillion kilowatts. The figure is so large is has little meaning. It is equivalent to the amount of energy of 100 billion tons of TNT exploding every second, but that is very hard to imagine too.

The Sun always gives off an enormous amount of energy, but it does vary through time. The Sun's disc is marbled with a boiling, turbulent texture, with plumes of ejected hot plasma and the distinctive dark sunspots that have been closely observed for 400 years. The Sun's surface is like that all the time: a maelstrom of boiling plasma. Every so often, and it is not possible to predict when, the Sun gives off a tremendous amount of energy in a sudden burst. This is called a solar flare. It is an explosive outburst of very hot, electrified gas. One of these outbursts happened on 1–2 September 1859.

On 28 August, astronomers noticed the development of a lot of sunspots on the surface of the Sun. Sunspots are big disturbances in the Sun's atmosphere, sometimes as big as Jupiter. They are produced by the lines of force within the Sun's magnetic field, so the production of an unusually large number of sunspots meant that there was some major disturbance of the Sun's magnetic field. As the areas of intense magnetization moved around and intertwined, they caused sudden and violent releases of energy. Between 28 August and 2 September astronomers watched several solar flares shoot out from the Sun's surface. It was on 1 September that the biggest of the flares happened. On that day, for about one minute the amount of light produced at the location of the flare was double the Sun's normal brightness, a bright white light that has never been seen before (as far as we know) or since.

During one of these catastrophic events, the Sun can shoot hot plasma in any direction. It would be quite possible, for instance, for the Sun to shoot the plasma out 'backwards', so that we on Earth would not see it and would certainly be unaffected by it. By chance, this very big ejection of plasma on 1 September 1859 pointed towards Earth. Astronomers were able to see it clearly, and eventually the plasma reached Earth. The Sun is 92 million miles away and the plasma ejected from the Sun usually takes three days to travel that distance. The very high-energy flare of 1 September 1859 shot a blob of plasma out so fast that it reached the Earth in only seventeen hours and forty minutes. It was an exceptionally high-speed blast.

The flare was not only moving very fast, it contained within it a magnetic field that was extremely intense and directly opposed to Earth's magnetic field. It overpowered Earth's magnetic field. Earth's magnetic field acts as an invisible cage round the planet, deflecting a great many of the charged particles that stream continuously towards Earth. It is only at the poles, where the magnet field's lines of force bend round and descend towards Earth's surface, that the charged particles from the Sun can reach the lower atmosphere. It is there that the charged particles interact with the particles in the atmosphere to produce the Northern Lights. The 'crashing' of the earth's magnetic field by the solar flare in effect put out of action Earth's defences against excessive bombardment by the Sun. Charged particles were able to reach the lower air in any latitude. This was why the aurora was visible in much lower latitudes.

The collapse of Earth's magnetic field by the Sun's intervention also disrupted the communications system. In 1859, the electric telegraph system was new – it had only been invented a decade or so earlier – and it was not a system that everyone depended upon.

Recent work by NASA scientists has revealed the true intensity of the 1859 solar storm, and also the alarming though perhaps not surprising news that it could happen again. The disruption to modern communications systems and electricity supply grids could be very serious. A minor solar storm in 1994 caused two communications satellites to malfunction, and the radio service throughout Canada was disrupted. There have been other minor solar storms too, which have disrupted television transmissions, electricity supply grids and mobile phone services. A minor storm in 1989, far less powerful than the 1859 storm, caused the electricity supply grid to the whole of Quebec in Canada to go down for nine hours. As a result of this, there were substantial economic losses calculated at hundreds of millions of dollars.

Not only could the events of 1989 and 1994 happen again, they probably will, and so will the much bigger event of 1859. The 1859 solar flare was at least three times more powerful than any other on record. The level of disruption an 1859-scale solar flare would cause can really only be guessed. In 1859, the telegraph was new and the use of electricity itself was new. Now we are dependent on electrical wiring for nearly everything we do. If a big solar flare put all of our satellites, telecommunications and electricity supplies out of action, the consequences would be very serious, and there is nothing we can or conceivably could do to avert it or reduce its impact. It is a future disaster waiting to happen.

THE WRECK OF
THE *LONDON*

(1866)

IT WAS 11 January 1866, and Henry Dennis was expecting to die; he wrote a final letter to his family. The Victorians lived with death. Their children often died in infancy and ailments that we now regard as minor were often sufficient to carry people to their graves. But this was not one of those conventional Victorian deathbed scenes, with a pale-faced consumptive quietly expiring as his anxious family gathered at the bedside. Henry Dennis was a widower with a daughter called Edith. In the American Civil War he had been the first Englishman to employ only non-slave labour on a plantation in the South. That had taken a considerable amount of courage. Now he had to show even more.

He was on a ship, a British steamer called the *London*, crossing the Bay of Biscay in a storm. And the ship was sinking. In his letter he wrote, 'Farewell, father, brother, sisters and my Edith. Ship *London*, Bay of Biscay, Thursday twelve o'clock noon. Reason – Ship over-weighted with cargo, and too slight a house over engine-room all washed away from deck. Bad poop windows. Water broken in – God bless my little orphan.'

Nor was Mr Dennis alone. Around him, other passengers had also resigned themselves to the fact that so much water was coming in that the ship must sink. Indeed, the captain had told them it would. Mr McMillan, a Tasmanian, was travelling homewards and he wrote, 'Dear wife and dear children. May God bless you all! Farewell to this world. Lost in the steamship *London*, bound for Melbourne.' These messages along with messages from four other passengers were found several weeks later in bottles washed up on the beach near Quiberon in Brittany. By then nearly everyone who had been aboard the *London* was dead.

The *London* was an emigrant ship. She had set sail with sixty-nine crew and 220 passengers. Unfortunately she was also carrying cargo, and far too much of it. The ship carried 1,200 tons of iron, 500 tons of coal (fifty tons of that on deck), fourteen tons of machinery and 1,000 tons of merchandise, more than enough to sink her. The deck of the *London* was only three feet six inches above the surface of the water, and then only when there was a flat calm. On 28 December 1865, the *London* started her last voyage, leaving the East India Docks under sail. Most ships of that time were fitted with masts and sails as well as engines so that when appropriate on a long voyage they could eke out their supplies of coal. As the *London* sailed down the Thames, a sailor who watched her pass Purfleet commented, 'It'll be her last voyage, because she is too low in the water; she'll never rise to a stiff sea.' Some pilots at Gravesend, where the ship took on some more unlucky passengers, thought the same. One of the *London*'s own officers was worried; he wrote to his family from Gravesend saying he did not like the ship and feared she would be his coffin.

The weather deteriorated as the ship made her way down the English Channel. By 4 January, when she reached Plymouth, there was a full gale blowing. Fifty-five more passengers boarded at Plymouth. Setting out from Plymouth in improved weather, the *London* headed for the open sea of the Western Approaches. Then the wind got up again, producing some very big waves. Some of the rigging was lost, a broken boom lashed about across the deck and one of the lifeboats was washed away.

The conditions were so bad that the captain, an Australian called John Martin, decided to turn the ship around and take her back to Plymouth. Then a second lifeboat was lost overboard and another boat was destroyed. Coal carried on the deck broke loose, rolled about and became lodged in the scupper holes, the drainage holes around the deck edges; this prevented water from waves breaking over the side from draining back into the sea. Then came the incident that probably sealed the *London*'s fate; on 10 January, the heavy sea smashed the hatch that covered the engine room and poured down inside the ship, putting the furnaces out.

The topsail was set, but it was immediately torn to pieces by the wind. One corner of it was left, and that at least kept the ship running before the wind. The pumps were worked all night by the passengers. One of the passengers was a famous actor of the day, a tragedian called Gustavus V. Brooke; he may have been a celebrity, but now he was hard at work on the pumps with the rest. Other passengers baled with buckets, but the water came in faster they could bale it out and the ship settled gradually lower in the water. At four am on 11 January, the sea smashed away four portholes, letting in even more water.

Not long after that Captain Martin assembled the passengers and crew to tell them that there was no hope of saving the ship. Panic might have broken out. Instead, an air of quiet resignation overwhelmed the ship. There were three clergymen on board and one of them, Revd Daniel Draper, started praying aloud. Some people, hearing about the shipwreck later, thought this was a wonderful moment of profound spirituality, but others saw it differently. A survivor wrote a letter to *The Times* saying that 'if the passengers had exerted themselves more for their own safety and attended less to the pious exhortations of the good clergymen, more would have been saved. The praying paralyzed them.'

There were, indeed, still some lifeboats left, though they were difficult to launch. At ten am, an attempt was made by five of the crew to launch a pinnace, but it capsized; three of the men managed to haul themselves back on board the ship, the other two went into the sea and were rescued with ropes. The sea was very rough, and it was not surprising that most of the passengers thought they were safer on the sinking ship. One woman, Mrs Owen, decided she would take her chance in the pinnace with her young son, but she was persuaded not to go by the captain, who thought she would suffer a lingering death in the pinnace instead of dying quickly in the *London*. It sounds brutal, but Captain Martin meant only to be kind to Mrs Owen. He also argued that it would be improper for her to get into a boat with sailors and a supply of brandy. Another problem was that most of the people on board could not swim. Even sailors usually did not learn to swim; they thought being able to swim would only prolong the agony if they were washed overboard.

In the end, only three passengers boarded the cutter. One was James Wilson. He tried to persuade his friend John Hickman to go too, but Hickman had a wife and four children, and he had to stay with them. Sixteen members of the crew were prepared to take their chance in the cutter. As the small boat pulled away from the *London*, a young woman called out pathetically, 'A thousand guineas if you take me!' But it was too late. The cutter was already pulling away from the sinking ship. The young woman died, along with all the other women and children on board. Fifty passengers on the *London* waved and cheered as the pinnace drew away. The small boat was only 200 feet or so away from the ship when the *London* suddenly tipped up and sank, taking all its waving passengers with it. The last sound the survivors in the cutter heard above the storm was hymn-singing.

The survivors saw two ships in the next day. One failed to spot the cutter, the other could not get close enough to rescue them and gave up. When a third ship appeared, the *Marianople*, the cutter gave chase for five hours before the Italian captain spotted it and took the survivors on board. The eighteen men and a boy – just nineteen survivors – were treated to a rub down, fresh clothes, soup and turkey.

The press coverage of the wreck of the *London* homed in on the severe overloading of the vessel. The idea of load lines had come up before, but the sinking of the *London* gave it a new focus. The main objection was devising rules and regulations that could rationally determine where the load lines should be drawn. The publicity generated by the sinking of the *London* led on to the invention of the famous Plimsoll mark by Samuel Plimsoll, and its enshrinement in law with the Merchant Shipping Act of 1876. The Plimsoll line, which prevents ship owners from overloading their ships, has saved countless lives at sea.

THE PESHTIGO
FIRESTORM

(1871)

THE FIRE THAT swept across north-east Wisconsin in 1871 damaged several small townships, destroying two of them completely, Brussels and Peshtigo. Peshtigo was not far from the north-west shore of Lake Michigan. It was described as a town, but it was really not much more than a prosperous village, making its money on the new railroad that was being built from Milwaukee to the Upper Peninsula of Michigan. There was plenty of work available in the logging industry and in the building industry. Peshtigo could boast the largest wooden-ware factory in the world.

The Peshtigo fire was the deadliest fire in American history, but it was instantly forgotten outside Peshtigo itself. It was over-shadowed at once by the Great Chicago Fire, which coincidentally happened on the same day, 240 miles away. Two hundred and fifty people died in the Chicago Fire, and it was headline news all over the United States. Eight hundred died at Peshtigo, and no one was interested: no one had heard of Peshtigo. Peshtigo was the worse disaster, but Chicago was the better-known place. Our memories of disasters are partial, and conditional.

The night of 8 October 1871, began like any other to the residents of rural Wisconsin. The summer had been a long dry one. Loggers had taken advantage of the dry conditions to clear more land for the railroad. The lumbering activity had, as was characteristic at that time, left big heaps of branches, bark and sawdust scattered through the forest, and the loggers and other settlers had set small fires to get rid of the waste. In the days running up to the Peshtigo fire, smoke billowing from the small 'controlled' fires was so dense that ships in Green Bay (part of Lake Michigan) had to use their foghorns and navigate by compass.

It was common for these small fires to get out of control and spread, and the people working in the timber mills and townships thought nothing of them; they lived with them all the time. This particular fire was different, though. There had been a storm the previous day and in its aftermath there were warm blasts of wind, which would fan the flames up into a firestorm.

It began in the early evening of 8 October. The township's official population was 1,700, but that was probably doubled by the influx of labourers who had recently arrived to work on the railroad. There were also the salesmen, travellers and visitors that you would find in any settlement of the time. Just after eight-thirty that evening there was a dull roaring sound that frightened everyone in Peshtigo. The flames of the forest fire had been whipped up by the strong wind. The fire was racing towards the township.

Fire-fighters set off to deal with the fire as it approached, but they quickly realized that it was futile, threw aside their buckets and returned home to collect their families. They, and many others, set off for the Peshtigo River. When the fire hit the town, the air glowed with burning embers and hot sand and dust, presumably sucked up from the ground by the firestorm.

The Peshtigo fire was described as a 'tornado of fire'. It consumed all available oxygen, sucking air in from outside to supply it, and generating internal winds up to eighty mph. The winds themselves were strong enough to do serious damage, tearing the roofs off houses, pushing trees over, smashing down barns and hen-houses. Houses and rail cars were thrown into the air. Scraps of wood and paper were whirled right across the border into Canada.

The fire swept through Peshtigo at speed. In not much more

than an hour there was nothing left of Peshtigo. The speed of the fire once it was well under way was so great that people had very little chance of escaping from it. Many people were surrounded and trapped by it. The survivors were the ones who took the most radical solution, spending the night standing in lakes, ponds or rivers to get away from the flames. Some of those wading into the Peshtigo River were drowned. Some of those who hid in wells suffocated there; the firestorm burned all the oxygen. But those who stayed in the town all died.

By dawn the next day, when the fire had burned itself out, perhaps half of the people who had been in Peshtigo the previous evening were still alive. Only one house was still standing, and that was only half built. It seems it did not burn because the wood was too green. In total, 1,875 square miles of Wisconsin had been burned. The fire had even jumped the considerable width of Green Bay and burned the Door Peninsula beyond.

News of the Peshtigo disaster took several days to reach the outside world, and there was little interest even then. The Governor of Wisconsin issued a proclamation asking people to divert their gifts of aid from Chicago to Peshtigo and this resulted in the arrival of 155,000 dollars in aid. The survivors rebuilt Peshtigo, and it became a vibrant and successful township once more. Peshtigo has never forgotten its trauma, though, and the Peshtigo Fire Museum was opened in 1963, to make sure that future generations do not forget. Next to it is the Peshtigo Fire Cemetery, which contains the mass grave of several hundred unidentified victims of the fire.

The parish priest for Peshtigo and Marinette, the Revd Peter Pernin, wrote an eyewitness of the event in 1874. Father Pernin lived to the west of the Peshtigo River, normally a five-minute walk to the bridge and dam at the centre of Peshtigo. With the firestorm approaching, walking and breathing were difficult. The air was full of ash, dust and grit, and short of oxygen. Father Pernin walked into town, struggling against the wind and dust, and finding it hard to keep his eyes open in the dusty blast. Several times he found himself breathing noxious gas and instinctively threw himself to the ground, but eventually he reached the town. A terrible deafening noise came from it. Through the wind he could hear neighing horses, falling trees and chimneys, the crackle of fires biting into the wooden houses, but chillingly no sound of humanity whatever. Father Pernin commented, 'People seemed stricken numb by terror.' The most haunting sound of all was the mad tolling of his own church bell, rung by the gusting wind.

There were people everywhere, jostling each other on foot, or mounted on wagons. There was a frenzied exodus, both ways out of town, some going towards Oconto, some towards the river. Father Pernin was sure his choice, to go east, was best. 'Probably it was the same with them. We all hurried blindly on to our fate.' In fact, his was the safer choice, which would take him to the river, the only safe refuge from the fire in the area.

People were already badly affected by inhaling smoke. They had been inhaling it for days as it wafted in from the forest. Carbon monoxide is a common product of burning, and inhaling it even in concentrations as low as one to five per cent can cause functional problems. It becomes harder to distinguish the passage of time accurately, vision is impaired, and muscle co-ordination is poorer. With concentrations above ten per cent, headaches and dizziness set in. Inhaling the carbon monoxide-rich smoke will have made the citizens of Peshtigo less able to make decisions, less able to take action. Crucially, they will have been slowed down. Father Pernin actually mentions observing 'torpor', and that could easily be accounted for by smoke inhalation.

When Father Pernin approached the river, he found he could not reach it. He was pulling a cart laden with the sacred treasures of his church. He could not just drop it and run. He tried again to reach the river and this time succeeded.

The Wisconsin fire burned over a million acres of land, killing 1,500 people. In all, seventeen townships were burned in the fire, but the damage suffered by the town of Peshtigo was the worst. At Peshtigo, as many as 800 people were killed. The fire was a traumatic experience for everyone who lived in Peshtigo. The few objects that survived the firestorm were saved, and they can be seen at the Peshtigo Fire Museum.

THE WRECK OF
THE *ATLANTIC*

(1873)

THE *ATLANTIC* WAS a White Star passenger liner. The White Star Line had a custom of giving its ships names end in '-ic': Britannic, Olympic, Titanic. It was a kind of trademark for the company that distinguished its ships from those of its main rival, Cunard. The Cunarders had names ending in '-ia': *Mauretania, Lusitania, Carpathia*.

Before the loss of the *Titanic*, it was the wreck of the *Atlantic* that was remembered as the worst maritime disaster of all. Unlike the *Titanic*, which went down far out in the ocean, a long way from help, the *Atlantic* ran onto a rock only fifty yards from the coast. The coast was that of Meagher's Island in Halifax, Nova Scotia. Like the *Titanic*, the *Atlantic* went down in April, but 1 April not 15 April. The ship and all of her cargo were lost, along with the lives of 545 people. As the official report later said, it was sad event.

Owned by the Ocean Steam Navigation Company, the *Atlantic* was on a regular White Star route from Liverpool to New York. She was regarded as one of the finest British ocean steamers. She was a 2,376-ton iron steamship built at Belfast in 1871. She was 420 feet long, forty feet in the beam and had 600 horse power engines. By modern standards she was a small ship, but at the time she was considered 'one of the finest ever built'.

She sailed from Liverpool on 20 March, calling in at Queenstown in Ireland on 21 March, and then put out into the

Atlantic. On her last voyage, her captain was James Williams, a qualified and certified 'extra Master', and three of the four mates on board (the ship's officers) also held master's certificates: first officer James Firth, second officer M. Metcalf, fourth officer John Brown. She carried 811 passengers, including thirty-five saloon, and a crew of 141 men, making a total of 957 people on board. At first, the *Atlantic* had good weather and had no difficulty until 26 March, when she steamed into a gale, which went on for three days. Under those conditions she made slow progress, her speed dropping to about seven knots.

On 31 March at noon, the *Atlantic* calculated her position as 460 miles from Sandy Hook. The chief engineer reported that he only had 127 tons of coal left in the bunkers. Captain Williams decided that on the evidence of the barometer the weather was not likely to improve and they were unlikely to have enough coal to get them to New York. So it was sensible for them to change course and put into Halifax instead. At the inquiry, it was agreed that the captain had been right to make that decision.

For the previous three days, the engines had been run on a reduced supply of coal. On the eleventh day of her voyage the ship's bunkers were found to have less than two days' supply of coal left. The conclusion was that the *Atlantic* was not carrying enough coal. If she had carried high-quality coal, the amount loaded, 967 tons, would have been sufficient for a transatlantic crossing, but she was carrying a mixture of high and low quality, and in any case eighty tons were used before she even set sail from Liverpool. Evidently there had been bad judgement concerning the coaling.

If the weather had been fine and the sea calm, if there had been no head winds, the amount of coal she was carrying would have safely taken her to New York, but Captain Williams knew what the weather was likely to be at that time of year. He could not have expected a calm and easy crossing. He ought to have allowed for head winds and gales in his fuelling.

Captain Williams was right, under the circumstances that he had created, to change course for Halifax. He took his position from the Pole Star during the night, and so made efforts to navigate to Halifax. The problem was that although he was steaming north-eastwards, he was being carried further westwards at a rate of more than one mile an hour, because the ship was being carried along by a current of which Williams was unaware.

At midnight the watch was changed. The first and third officers went below to sleep, and the ship was left in the hands of the second and fourth officers. Shortly after midnight Captain Williams retired to his chart room, giving instructions to his servant to call him at two-forty am He told the officers to call him at three am, or if there was a change in the weather, or if they reached the Sambro light, which was the seamark for the port of Halifax. The officers disobeyed Williams in that they did not call him at three as ordered. When the ship struck a rock fifteen minutes after that, Williams was still asleep in his cabin.

Without any warning whatever, the *Atlantic* struck the rock more or less head on at three-fifteen am The ship evidently drove straight onto the rock from the south, for some reason, and the bow stayed fast, locked onto the rock. Within a few minutes hundreds of the passengers and crew had rushed up on deck, but the stern of the ship had swung round to the east and the ship heeled over so that the deck was almost vertical and facing the sea. The waves breaking over the ship washed many of the passengers off the deck and into the sea. It was now impossible to negotiate any of the stairways leading up from the saloon or steerage. The ship quickly filled with water, so those left below decks were trapped and drowned there as the water poured in.

Because of the tilted position of the ship, it was impossible to lower the lifeboats in the normal way. Some of the ship's officers rigged up a rope to enable people to get themselves to shore. But only 'men of strong nerve' were able to save themselves by hauling themselves along the rope, which took them to the rock and then from the rock to the shore. No help arrived from the shore for some time after the accident. Fishermen living in the area eventually realized what had happened and went to the rescue, but by then most of the people who had decided to stay on the deck of the ship had been washed away and drowned. The result was that 545 out of the 957 people on board died. Not a single woman survived the disaster, and only one child, a boy called William Hindley, survived.

As soon as word of the disaster got out, the Canadian government steamer *Lady Head* set off for the wreck site to give assistance. The local community, Terence Bay, did the little that was possible. They buried 277 of the victims in a mass grave at Sandy Cove, overlooking the wreck site, and the local Anglican priest, Revd William Ancient, took a memorial service. The survivors did not want to be a burden to the people of Terence Bay and so they set off on foot – to walk to Halifax.

A tribunal was set up to investigate the cause of the disaster. The tribunal censured the captain for the way he behaved before the disaster, praised him for his energetic efforts to save lives after the ship hit the rock, but noted that by then it was too late. Nothing of any practical value could be done then. His certificate was suspended for two years. The fourth officer, Mr Brown, was reprimanded for his 'want of vigilance' and for disobeying the captain's orders. His certificate was suspended for three months.

The court decided on 18 April 1873 that the disaster was caused by a current running along the Nova Scotia coast, which Captain Williams had not allowed for. The westerly current actually ran more strongly in March and April, and it had a major effect on Williams's navigation. The ship had in effect run into the rocky coastline twelve miles further west of where Captain Williams was steering for, which was Halifax harbour. The ship's officers could have established that they were not where they thought they were if they had been more vigilant. They could have heaved the lead, in other words checked that the water was deep enough to take the *Atlantic*, which needed thirty feet at least to keep afloat. They could also have looked out for land and for lights. If they had been more actively observant, they might have worked out the steamer's actual position and the disaster might have been avoided.

The court also made it its business to make sure that people who had rendered assistance should not be out of pocket. Money was allocated to cover the burial of the bodies.

It is hard to see how Captain Williams thought he was over forty miles from land. The Sambro light and other lighthouses along the Nova Scotia were working properly that night, so the nearness of the coastline must have been apparent. The lights were there to be seen, and the Sambro light should have been visible for some time before the accident. The *Atlantic*'s officers had evidently not been looking out for it properly. Under the circumstances – navigating along an unfamiliar coastline – it would have been sensible to send a crewman up to the masthead to keep lookout.

The loss of the *Atlantic* was a complex disaster. The rock sticking up out of the sea played its part, as did the coastal current and the earlier gales. That much was natural. But the captain did not oversee the coaling of his ship properly before setting off from Liverpool. If the bunkers had been full, and full of high-quality coal, he would not have need to turn back to Halifax, but could have continued to New York. Even after Williams made the decision to put into Halifax, the *Atlantic* and her passengers might still have been safe, if Williams and his officers had been careful in their navigation of the Nova Scotia coastline. But once the *Atlantic* hit the rock, nature took over.

THE TAY BRIDGE
DISASTER

(1879)

THE TAY BRIDGE disaster is probably now best remembered for a very bad and unintentionally entertaining poem written on the subject by William McGonagall. The passage of time has reduced the real horrors of what happened the night when the Tay Bridge collapsed, and we are left with a piece of doggerel. At the time when it happened, the spectacular incident was rightly regarded as a tragedy, a national disaster.

The Tay Bridge was a typical piece of Industrial Revolution engineering, an iron bridge across the one-mile wide Tay estuary in Scotland, designed to carry the railway line to the north. The long and broad estuaries of the Firth of Forth and the Firth of Tay flared out from west to east, and were major barriers to land communication between Edinburgh and the north of Scotland. Diverting by way of Stirling and Perth was adding as much as sixty miles to each northward and southward journey. An alternative was to use the ferries, one across the Forth from Granton to Burntisland, the other across the Tay from Tayport to Broughty Ferry. Using trains and ferries in combination made a travelling time of three hours and twelve minutes to get from Edinburgh to Dundee, a distance of only forty-six miles. And that assumes that everything went according to the timetable. If the weather was very bad, the ferries did not run at all.

The Tay narrows near Dundee to just over one mile wide, which was the obvious choice for a bridging point. Building railway bridges over the two firths would greatly improve communications. It was Thomas Bouch who came up with the idea of a railway bridge over the Tay. Bouch was appointed as manager of the Edinburgh and Northern Railway in 1849. He was twenty-six and initially determined to improve the ferry services. By the following year he had created the world's first roll-on, roll-off ferry, which did much to enhance his reputation, but this was only an interim measure. The real solution to the problem was to build railway bridges. In 1854 the Edinburgh and Northern Railway was taken over by the North British Railway. Bouch tried to persuade his new masters, the directors of the NBR, to build bridges over the Forth and Tay, but they refused, outspokenly declaring it 'the most insane idea ever proposed'.

Eventually they relented and saw that the case for bridges was overwhelming. Bouch had been right, after all. In 1870, a parliamentary Bill was passed enabling the Tay Bridge to be built. Bouch was by this stage an independent consultant and he was given the job of engineering the new bridge. In spite of Bouch's apparent long experience, he lacked a solid grounding in engineering theory. This was a major innovative project; at two miles in length and with eighty-five spans the Tay Bridge was the longest and most elaborate iron structure anywhere in the world and at that time the longest bridge in the world. It was a big project that was beyond Thomas Bouch's capabilities.

The Tay Bridge was completed in February 1878, and by that time everything about it had become Bouch's responsibility. He designed it, oversaw the building work and was now responsible for its maintenance. Like most of his other bridges, the Tay Bridge was made of a lattice of girders supported on slender cast-iron pillars that were braced with wrought iron struts. Bouch's achievement in seeing the project through and creating such an impressive-looking structure led directly to his knighthood.

On the night of 28 December 1879, a gale blew down the Firth of Tay, striking the bridge (and the trains crossing it) at right angles. It is estimated that the winds reached force ten or eleven on the Beaufort scale. The bridge had been in use for a year and a half since its formal opening, but in that time it had become notorious for the way it creaked and groaned in windy weather, so it is clear that the structure was not only moving about in the wind but setting up stresses within its structure as it moved. There were worries about its safety at the time, doubts about its soundness. After the disaster and the inevitable investigation that followed it, it was confirmed that the design and construction of the bridge had been faulty. To make matters worse, the maintenance of the bridge was under the supervision of a man who was unqualified and inexperienced. Every finger pointed at Sir Thomas Bouch.

The 28th of December 1879 started quietly enough. Captain Wright took his ferry, the *Dundee*, across the Firth of Tay in the middle of the day, and noted that the weather was good, the water calm. His four-fifteen pm crossing was also without incident, though he noted that the winds had freshened. An hour later a gale began moving across from the west and Captain Wright observed that the river 'was getting up very fast'. An early evening train arrived at Dundee station at about six pm. Its passengers had had an alarming crossing; their railway carriages had been buffeted by the mounting gale and the sideways force of the wind sent streams of sparks from the wheels.

The mail train left Edinburgh at five-twenty pm, reaching Thornton Junction, twenty-seven miles south of the bridge at 6 pm. The last station before the Tay Bridge was St Fort. There, station staff checked the tickets of the passengers who were intending to go on to Dundee. As the train left St Fort, there were seventy-two passengers on board and three men on the locomotive footplate. By seven-thirteen pm, the doomed train arrived at the Wormit signal station, slowing right down there to check with the signalman that the bridge was clear and safe to cross. Then the driver took the train out onto the bridge, where it was suddenly exposed to the full force of the gale. The signalman went back into his cabin to send the signal 'train entering section' signal to the signalman at the north end of the bridge.

The signalman at the southern end of the bridge watched as the three red tail lights of the train receded into the darkness at seven-fifteen pm, but was puzzled when he suddenly lost sight of the tail lights when it was halfway across. The train had vanished into the night. The train was due to pass the Dundee signal box at seven-nineteen pm. When it did not arrive, the signalman there tried to telegraph the Wormit signal box, but was unable to get through. Obviously the telegraph lines had been broken somewhere on the bridge. James Roberts, the locomotive foreman at the Dundee engine sheds, decided to walk out onto the bridge to see what had happened to the train. The force of the gale was so strong that he could not safely stand up; at times Roberts had to crawl on all fours. Eventually he came to the middle of the bridge, or at least the place where middle of the bridge should have been. The central section of high girders had gone, leaving rails dangling out over the boiling water below.

At about seven-fifteen pm on 28 December 1879, at the height of the storm, the central navigation spans of the bridge had collapsed as the train was crossing, taking the locomotive, six carriages and all the passengers down into the water.

It was the worst and most spectacular structural engineering failure that has ever happened in Great Britain. The Tay Bridge had collapsed under the combined stress of gale-force cross winds and the weight of a train passing over it. The train, its three crewmen and its seventy-two passengers were dropped into the churning waters of the estuary. A steamer was sent to search the area. It was three days before the wreckage of the train was located. There were no survivors. The locomotive was eventually raised, refitted and, almost incredibly, put back into service; it was known among the railwaymen – unofficially – as 'The Diver'.

At the inquiry afterwards, it emerged that it was the failure of the 'high girders' that had led to the collapse of the bridge.

Seventy-two of the bridge's eighty-five spans were carried on spanning girders beneath the level of the railway track and running across more than eighty feet above the water at high tide. It was these spanning girders that were called the 'high girders'.

The inquiry concluded that the bridge fell because of 'the insufficiency of the cross bracing and its fastenings to sustain the force of the gale.' If the piers and the wind bracing had been properly designed and maintained, it was thought that the bridge could have withstood the gale that night, though not with an acceptable margin of safety. Sir Thomas Bouch had not made sufficient allowance for the strength of gale-force winds down the Firth of Tay.

In his design for the Tay Bridge, he had allowed for a maximum wind pressure equivalent to ten pounds per square inch. Interestingly, Bouch was allowing for a pressure equivalent to thirty pounds per square inch in his draft plans for a Forth Bridge in 1866, so it is hard to understand why in his design for the Tay Bridge, built twelve years later, he built in only one-third of the wind-resistance. He must have known that it would not stand up to the wind. In fairness to Bouch, he was not the only one to blame for the disaster. His design and construction method were based on a geological survey that turned out to be significantly incorrect. He was led to believe that the floor of the estuary was made of solid rock, and it was only when the brick-built piers were being raised and started 'going over' that he realized he was building on gravel. He had to change the design at break-neck speed, substituting iron pillars.

At the time of the Tay Bridge disaster, Bouch was still working on his design for the Forth Bridge and had even got as far as laying its foundation stone. Given the catastrophic failure of his earlier bridge and the unequivocal findings of the inquiry, it was not surprising that Bouch had the Forth Bridge project immediately taken away from him and given instead to others: Benjamin Baker and John Fowler. Any hopes Bouch might have had that he would be allowed to rebuild his Tay Bridge were also in vain. A new Tay Bridge, the present one, was built parallel to the old one, and immediately to the west.

In July 1880, it was made clear to Bouch that his services were no longer required by the North British Railway. He was publicly disgraced. He was also in a state of complete breakdown. In August his doctor advised him to take a complete rest. By October Sir Thomas Bouch was dead.

It is hard to resist the temptation to give William McGonagall the last word on the subject. This is how he opened his poem:

> *Beautiful Railway Bridge of the Silv'ry Tay!*
> *Alas! I am very sorry to say*
> *That ninety lives have been taken away*
> *On the last Sabbath day of 1879,*
> *Which will be remember'd for a very long time . . .*

After blaming 'Boreas' or 'the Demon of the air' for the disaster, he ended his poem with these wise words:

> *By telling the world fearlessly and without the least dismay,*
> *That your central girders would not have given way,*
> *At least many sensible men do say,*
> *Had they been supported on each side with buttresses,*
> *At least many men confesses.*
> *For the stronger we our houses do build,*
> *The less chance we have of being killed.*

THE ERUPTION OF KRAKATOA

(1883)

THE ISLAND OF Krakatoa lay on the equator in the Sunda Strait that separates Sumatra and Java. Where the original island had stood, there was now deep water surrounded by a broken ring of islands marking the outer flanks of the original volcanic mountain. This was before the great eruption of 1883. Krakatoa had already destroyed itself once before. At the centre of the little cluster of islands was an island with a large volcano rising to a height of 2,500 feet; it had been built up from the floor of the ancient caldera.

Krakatoa had erupted in 1680; earthquakes were reported from the area and a lot of pumice was ejected from the volcano, but the evidence of this significant activity was quickly covered over by dense vegetation.

A long series of minor earthquakes began in 1877. They marked the stirrings of the mountain as lava began to rise beneath it; the run-up to the big eruption had begun. The situation started to escalate in the early months of 1883, and by May eruptions of ash and pumice had started. Then Krakatoa erupted very violently in a series of explosions on 26–28 August 1883. The most violent of these were the four on the morning of 27 August. This was the greatest volcanic eruption since the bronze age eruption of Santorini. The ancient Santorini eruption was five times more violent than the Krakatoa eruption, but even so the Krakatoa explosion was heard nearly 3,000 miles away, four hours later, at

Rodriguez. It was heard in Bangkok, the Philippines, Sri Lanka and Western and South Australia. Only the Tambora and Santorini eruptions can have rivalled this; no other event is known that can have been heard over such a wide area in the last 10,000 years.

An atmospheric shock wave, called an oscillation, rippled outwards from Krakatoa, travelling to the point on the opposite side of the world from Krakatoa. There it collided with itself, was reflected back again to its point of origin, Krakatoa, where it bounced back again, and so on. The shock wave was observed at some places to pass no less than seven times.

Krakatoa threw out huge amounts of ash. At Batavia, 100 miles away, the sky became dark with the ash. Lamps had to be lit at midday, because it was so dark. The darkness reached as far as Bandung, which was 150 miles away. Krakatoa threw up a tall column of ash that reached right up to the top of the troposphere, the layer of the atmosphere in which we live, way up beyond the altitude of Everest, and on up into the stratosphere. The column reached a height of fifty miles, where it was picked up by a fast-moving, east-west jet stream. From this date on, this jet stream became known as the Krakatoa Easterlies.

The dust travelled westwards at over 60 mph. It soon encircled Earth along the equator to make a huge smoke ring right round the world. It was then spread polewards by other high-altitude winds. The dust affected the entire inhabited world. It was observed from Norway's North Cape to Cape Town near the southern tip of Africa. The pattern was the same as with the Tambora eruption earlier in the nineteenth century. Some of the dust started raining down ten days later up to 3000 miles away, but much of it remained suspended in the upper atmosphere for up to two years. The dust in the atmosphere had the effect of reddening the sunrise and sunset for a year afterwards, and as far away as England. Artists noticed the change and made a point of painting the unusual phenomenon.

The dust from Krakatoa had the visible effect of reddening the sunsets in northern Europe, but it also had the tangible effects of reducing temperatures. After the Krakatoa eruption there was a marked cooling of Earth's atmosphere, which showed up in temperature readings at many weather stations. The values of solar radiation as measured at Montpellier Observatory in the south of France were ten per cent lower than normal for three years following the eruption – a large effect. Although people seem not to have been especially aware of a cooling, the instrumental measurements show that there was; when the temperature graph for the late-nineteenth and early-twentieth centuries is studied it shows a noticeable trough around 1885. It is, even so, difficult to be sure whether this was due to the eruption of Krakatoa or to a coincidental lack of sunspots during that period.

The extreme violence of the eruption emptied the lava chamber beneath the island, leaving a huge, hollow and very hot vault. Unsupported, the chamber collapsed. Cold seawater rushed repeatedly into the hot chamber, turned instantly into steam, and caused the four violent explosive blasts. Because these blasts were on the seabed, huge tsunamis were generated, rippling out from the gaping hole where Krakatoa had stood. The coastal villages on neighbouring islands were engulfed by the tsunamis. There were 163 villages totally destroyed, and 36,000 people were wiped out. Floating pumice was carried hundreds of miles away. The tsunami is known to have reached Cape Horn and was detected even in the English Channel.

After the eruption was over and it was possible to revisit the area, it was clear what had happened. The geography of the area had been transformed. The whole of Krakatoa that had been built within the original crater ring had been blown out. The original caldera had been re-created. Where the volcanic peak had stood, the sea was now over 1,000 feet deep. The surrounding islands and their forests had been buried by ash and rock thrown out from the centre. No living thing remained. The region was sterilized, cauterized, annihilated.

After the big eruption of 1883, Krakatoa was quiet, but from 1927 the area began to reawaken. The area became volcanically active again for a few years and a new cone has gradually been built up, well above sea level, in the middle of the caldera. This is Anak Krakatoa, Child of Krakatoa.

The eruption of Krakatoa was a major event in the history of the Earth. It changed the shape of the Earth's surface radically. It killed an enormous number of people. More than that, it demonstrated that there is a cyclicity to many such events. Remarkable and stupendous though the eruption was, it had clearly happened before, and in the same place. Krakatoa had erupted in the same way in remote antiquity. And one day it will erupt with similar violence again. These are things we need to know.

THE CHARLESTON EARTHQUAKE

(1886)

THE CHARLESTON EARTHQUAKE of 1886 was the most severe earthquake ever to have hit the south-eastern part of the United States. The nearest plate boundaries are on the Pacific coast and the middle of the Atlantic. Charleston in South Carolina is a very long way from either of these boundaries and therefore should be safe from major quakes. In fact, Charleston had absolutely no history of earthquake activity before the major earthquake of 1886, so the event is a very peculiar one.

The town was nevertheless struck by a very violent earthquake in 1886, and the violence may have been intensified by the long period of quiescence beforehand, during which enormous stress had evidently built up inside the Earth. It came at 9.50 in the evening on 31 August and lasted less than a minute, but it was felt as far away as Boston, Chicago, Cuba and Bermuda.

The earthquake was not measured on modern instruments, but it is estimated that it was about magnitude 7.0 on the Richter scale. There were over 300 aftershocks spread over the next thirty-five years. There are still occasional earth tremors that seem to be part of the 1886 earthquake sequence, and altogether there have been about 440 aftershocks. The Charleston earthquake sequence dominates the seismic history of the south-eastern United States.

The earthquake caused an enormous amount of damage. About 2,000 buildings suffered significant damage. The damage was estimated to cost six million dollars, and this at a time when the buildings of the city as a whole were given a total value of twenty-four million dollars. Major damage was done as much as sixty miles away at Tybee Island in Georgia, and some structural damage was reported several hundred miles away in Alabama, Ohio and Kentucky.

It is not absolutely certain how many people were killed: perhaps eighty or a hundred. Most of the damage occurred in an oval area thirty miles by twenty, stretching from Charleston to Jedburg, and centring on Middleton Place, which is assumed to have been the epicentre of the earthquake.

One unusual feature of the earthquake was that in many places the soil liquefied, causing sandblows. The Charleston earthquake was also unusual in occurring in the middle, rather than at the edge of, a tectonic plate. As a result, geologists have made a particular study of it. The quake is believed to have been the result of movement along a very ancient fault, one formed way back in the Jurassic period during the disintegration of the supercontinent Pangaea.

In 1906, in the wake of the San Francisco earthquake, Paul Pinckney wrote that the people of San Francisco had forgotten the Charleston earthquake, and that they should take heart. Charleston had been wrecked by its own earthquake in 1886, yet it had been rebuilt, even finer than before, within the space of four years.

Those who were in Charleston at the time and spent the long, dreadful night with the dead and dying amid the ruins of the proud Southern city have not forgotten, and the memory of its terrible effect at the time and of the sure and steady recovery which followed, comes now as an inspiration and a hope in contemplating the future of this coast.

Though I was just a lad at the time, I vividly recall the sensations of the moment and many heart-rending incidents of that night of terror. In view of the sharp intensity of the shock and its destroying effect, I do not hesitate to assert that the tremblor which wrecked Charleston was more severe than that of April 18 last, and in relative destruction considerably worse.

It was about 9.50 on the evening of August 31, 1886, that the people of Charleston felt the quiverings of the first earthquake shock ever known in that part of the country. They had just returned from worship and not many had retired. The day had been an exceedingly hot one and the evening was unusually sultry, with such a profound stillness in the air that it provoked general remark.

The tremblor came lightly with a gentle vibration of the houses as when a cat trots across the floor; but a very few seconds of this and it began to come in sharp jolts and shocks which grew momentarily more violent until buildings were shaken as toys. Frantic with terror, the people rushed from the houses, and in doing so many lost their lives from falling chimneys or walls. With one mighty wrench, which did most of the damage, the shock passed. It had been accompanied by a low, rumbling noise, unlike anything ever heard before.

No need to tell of the horrors of that moment or of those succeeding. The fact that lighter shocks continued at frequent intervals throughout the long, dreary night kept the nerves of all keyed to such a high tension that it is not strange that several persons lost their reason.

There were no electric lights in those days, and the streets were illuminated with gas. The people gathered in the public parks and squares and there in the dim light brave men and women gave help to the injured and dying. Soon several fires added their horror to the tragedy and much damage was done before they were got under control. It was not until the next day that people began to realize the extent of the calamity that had befallen them. Then it was learned that not a building in the city had escaped injury in greater or less degree. Those of brick and stone suffered most. Many were down, more were roofless, or the walls had fallen out, all chimneys gone, much crockery, plaster and furniture destroyed. St Michael's Church, the pride of the city since 1761, was a wreck, its tall steeple lying in the street.

To add to their dismay the people were cut off from the outer world, all wires being down, and it was not until next day that a courier rode to Summerville, nearly thirty miles away, and gave the world its first news of the disaster. At the same time he brought back the cheering news that the world was not utterly destroyed, as many had believed. The rumors current on the outside were that Charleston and all the coast country had been swept away by a mighty tidal wave and that the Florida peninsula had snapped off from the continent in the general cataclysm and fallen into the sea . . .

Four years later, in 1890, the only visible evidence of the great destruction was seen in the cracks remaining in buildings that were not destroyed. A new and more beautiful, more finished city had sprung up on the ruins of the old in that brief time, and the population had grown to nearly 55,000 with a corresponding increase in wealth and activity.

It will be even so in San Francisco. If anyone thinks there is no resurrection from earthquake effects let him be referred to Charleston for an answer. Thrice in a generation Charleston was nearly obliterated. The Civil War left it in ashes, the earthquake left it in ruins, and a few years later it was visited by a cyclone . . . Yet despite all these disasters her brave people have risen superior to every reverse and are daily growing in wealth and power.

THE YELLOW RIVER CHANGES ITS COURSE AGAIN

(1887)

THE YELLOW RIVER has devastated and destroyed the lands it passes throughout China's long history. One ancient Chinese chronicler recorded that in 2300 BC one Yellow River flood lasted for thirteen years. In 500 BC, the Chinese began reinforcing and raising the river banks in an attempt to stop the river from flooding, but those artificial banks have failed many times over. The building of artificial banks was begun by an engineer called Yu; he was made emperor for his contribution to China's welfare.

The worst flood on the Yellow River occurred in 1887. At Huayankou, near the city of Zhengzhou in Henan province, the river overflowed its banks. Because the plains of north-eastern China are so extensive and level, it was possible for the flood water to inundate a huge area of 50,000 square miles. Eleven cities and hundreds of villages were flooded. Two million people were left homeless. Serious food shortages followed, and in the foul-water conditions disease spread rapidly; as many died in the famine and epidemic as were drowned by the flood water, as is often the way. It is not known for certain how many lost their lives in this great disaster, maybe 900,000, maybe as many as six million altogether.

In an extraordinary and barbaric act of vandalism, Chiang Kai-shek tried to emulate the great flood of 1887. It was a desperate attempt to stop the Japanese invasion of China. In June 1938, Chiang Kai-shek ordered the levees breached by explosives. The resulting flood only slowed the Japanese down a little; it is estimated that something like half a million Chinese died in the flood. It was the ultimate self-inflicted injury.

The periodic natural river floods of the Yellow River – at least 1,500 times since 500 BC – have taken enormous numbers of lives over the centuries. As a result Western observers have named the river 'China's Sorrow'. The 1887 flood killed between one and six million people, the (deliberate) 1938 flood killed half a million; in the 1931 flood the death toll was almost four million. Earlier, in 1332, at least five million people died in a Yellow River flood.

One reason why the Yellow River floods so easily is the very heavy load of yellow-brown silt that it carries. Millions of tons of the silt are deposited in the channel itself, choking it, and causing the water to spill over the banks onto the floodplain. The deposition of silt in the channel and the building of artificial banks up to thirty feet high have together led to the raising of the river well above the plains it passes through. In 1887, the silted river bed was a major factor in causing the flood; there were also several days of heavy rain.

Maybe the massive new Xialangdi Dam Project will hold some of the water (and sediment) back and reduce the danger of destructive flooding in eastern China.

When the 1887 flood waters subsided, the river had resumed its old course. Between 602 BC and AD 1288 the river reached the sea in the Bo Hai Bay near Tientsin. In 1288, the Yellow River flooded and changed course. In 1887, it changed course again.

Whatever the future holds, the 1887 Yellow River flood ranks as one of the worst river floods in human history.

THE JOHNSTOWN FLOOD

(1889)

ON 31 MAY 1889, the collapse of an earthen dam released a huge volume of water, causing a disastrous flood at Johnstown, Pennsylvania. About one-tenth of the town's population, 2,209 people, died in the disaster. Most of them died in the first ten minutes, as a huge wall of water hit the town.

Over the subsequent decades the incident has gathered its own mythology, emphasizing the class struggle between the rich and poor. The South Fork Dam was owned by the South Fork Fishing and Hunting Club, which listed among its members some of the richest people in the United States. Andrew Carnegie and Andrew Mellon were members. The club's members used the Conemaugh Lake, ponded back by the South Fork Dam, as a leisure centre. The wealthy who were using the lake as a recreational facility had their holiday homes built above the lake, and were therefore unaffected when the dam failed and the water poured away down the valley. The poor, living in Johnstown, lived downstream, below the lake, and therefore died.

The South Fork Club was sued for its failure to maintain the dam properly, but the lawsuit yielded no compensation for those who had lost property and family members.

The earth dam had been weakened by several historic factors. The level of the dam had been raised by the addition of quantities of inappropriate materials, including straw and horse manure. There had at one time been drainage pipes to control the flow of excess water around the dam, but they were removed. There was an overflow spillway that was supposed to stop the lake level rising beyond a certain critical level. It was fitted with a grille, intended to stop stocked fish from escaping from the lake. The grille had become so badly blocked with debris that, when the lake overfilled and the excessive weight of water began to weaken the dam, it was impossible to clear it in time to let the excess water through. It was even alleged that there had once been a second overflow spillway, and that it had been removed. Probably all of these factors contributed to the dam's collapse.

The very poor level of maintenance of the dam is surprising, because the club was certainly wealthy enough to carry out checks and routine maintenance. The club was not responsible for building the dam. It had been built by a canal company, and then passed into the ownership of the Pennsylvania Railroad Company before the Hunting Club acquired it. The original earth dam was a harmless ten feet high. By the time of the disaster it had been raised several times and stood a dangerous 100 feet high, and holding back a far greater volume of water than the technology could cope with.

The disaster came during a high-intensity rainstorm. The waters of Lake Conemaugh rose at a rate of a foot an hour as it was overfilled by the inflow from South Fork Creek. The single spillway with its grille completely choked with debris allowed only a trickle of this water through. The lake level rose until, inevitably, water spilled over the top of the dam. By now saturated with water, the centre of the dam gave way, releasing the entire volume of the lake all at once. A wall of water forty feet high surged down the valley at forty mph.

The little towns of South Fork, Mineral Point, Conemaugh and Franklin, along with the company town of Woodvale, were all destroyed before the wall of water hit Johnstown an hour after the dam burst. The flood water was delayed by a number of obstacles, including a stone-built bridge. An hour was long enough for some warnings to get through to Johnstown. Trains blew their whistles.

There were even telegraph warnings. The handful of people in towns with telephones received warnings to evacuate. But the warnings were to no avail. There had been false alarms in the past about the dam, which everyone knew was in a dangerous state.

When the wall of water, loaded with trees, branches and the debris from demolished buildings, reached Johnstown, it came as a big surprise. Most of Johnstown was demolished by the impact. The force of the flood was so strong that it moved railway locomotives a mile down the valley. The water arrived so suddenly and moved so fast that there was no time to react to it, no time to run. Attorney James M. Walters had a lucky escape. He was at home when the water came. He scrambled up onto the roof of his house, which was lifted off its foundations by the wall of water. His house collided with another building, Alma Hall. Walters fell from his roof through a window in Alma Hall, and found that he had been catapulted into his own office. The building was stoutly made, and he was able to take refuge in it along with 200 others. The rest of Walters' family were all killed.

The flood water rafted a huge quantity of debris into downtown Johnstown, where it log-jammed against the buttresses of a stone bridge. Unfortunately the bridge was stoutly built and did not give way. The water ponded back behind this informal dam, creating a huge swirling lake covering much of the lower part of the town. Then, quite extraordinarily, in the middle of the flood an overturned railway carriage started a fire among the debris. A lot of those who had survived the flood died in the flames.

A total of 99 families were completely extinguished in the Johnstown flood. A great many horses also died. The economic cost was very high too. The flood damage cost millions of dollars to repair. Before the flood, Johnstown had been a rapidly growing steel town, a boom town. Afterwards it limped along as a disaster victim, receiving millions of dollars in aid from all over the United States, thanks to the wide newspaper coverage given to the disaster. Clara Burton, who was the founder of the Red Cross, visited Johnstown to set up relief centres for the flood victims. Up until that moment, the Red Cross had mainly interested itself in offering medical care to war wounded. The initiative at Johnstown was a turning point; from then on the Red Cross would enlarge its remit to offer natural disaster relief as well. Another positive development that came out of Johnstown was the initiation of flood control projects by both state and federal governments, including the Army Corps of Engineers.

It took thousands of workers to clear up the chaos following the flood. The debris jammed against the bridge covered more than thirty acres. Finding and identifying the bodies of flood victims was another difficult task. Bodies were found hundreds of miles downstream in the state of Ohio.

THE GALVESTON HURRICANE

(1900)

IN THE DECADES before the hurricane of 1900, Galveston had grown from a small settlement on the coast of Texas into one of the wealthiest cities in the United States. Galveston had a natural deepwater channel, which made it the most important seaport in Texas. At the time when the hurricane struck, Galveston was handling more than seventy per cent of the United State's cotton exports; every year 1,000 ships docked there. Galveston was also developing a role as a seaside resort. Galveston's level beach was considered a safe place from which to bathe in the warm and therapeutic waters of the Gulf of Mexico. Galveston was a city of 42,000 people, a city ahead of its time with many modern facilities. Galveston was the first city in Texas to have electricity and the first to have telephones, and along with this prosperity came a certain complacency.

But Galveston's coastal location and its level beaches were to make it particularly vulnerable to the hurricane, when it struck on 8 September 1900. Even before that, many were aware of the danger, suggesting that a seawall was needed. A quarter of a century before, in 1875, the nearby town of Indianola, which was second to Galveston among the Texas coast ports, had been destroyed by a hurricane. Indianola had been rebuilt. Then there had been a second hurricane at Indianola and the residents had given up and moved away. Some people in Galveston naturally saw what had happened at Indianola as a terrible warning and knew that Galveston, as a flat island with an open coast exposed to the Gulf of Mexico, was in extreme danger. But those who saw this were in a minority, and the seawall did not get built.

It was argued that Galveston had weathered earlier storms and the city had survived. There was no reason to suppose that future storms would be worse than those. The director of the Galveston Weather Bureau, wrote an article for the *Galveston News*, arguing that it was impossible for a powerful hurricane to hit Galveston. These were words he would live to regret, but the result was that the seawall that might have saved thousands of lives was not built. Meanwhile, sand dunes along the seafront were quarried away to raise low-lying areas of the city, removing such natural sea defences as Galveston had.

The hurricane that struck Galveston was first sighted on 27 August, when it was still far out to sea, about 1,000 miles east of the Windward Islands; a ship there reported an area of 'unsettled weather'. On 4 September, the US Weather Bureau's central office in Washington started sending warnings to Galveston that a tropical storm had travelled northwards and reached Cuba; at that stage, the Weather Bureau did not know where the storm was heading. In fact, with the benefit of hindsight, we can see that the storm travelled in an (unusual) almost straight line, along the axes of Jamaica and Cuba, and heading north-westwards towards Galveston, though this could not have been predicted. The skies over the Gulf of Mexico had been cloudless and sunny for several weeks, so the sea water was unusually warm and giving off a lot of water vapour. Hurricanes are powered by water vapour, and it was this factor that strengthened the storm to a lethal level, turning it into a true hurricane.

On 6 September, the storm was reported north of Key West, and the next day there were reports of heavy damage along the Louisiana coast. It was then that the Bureau issued storm warnings for the whole coast, from Pensacola in Florida to Galveston. That day, clouds started to build up at all levels and the Galveston Weather Bureau hoisted its double square flags, signalling a hurricane warning.

One day out from New Orleans, the ship Louisiana was hit by the hurricane; her captain reported winds of 150 mph.

At dawn on the day of the great storm at Galveston, the water level began to rise. The weather still seemed unremarkable, though, and few residents took any notice of the hurricane warning. Few took the opportunity to leave Galveston by way of the bridges across to the mainland.

Isaac Cline, the US Weather Bureau's chief meteorologist in Galveston, noticed that the sea was creeping over the low ends of the island at five am. He watched as the water rose, the barometer fell, the wind grew stronger, and realized that there was a serious danger. According to his own later account, he rode up and down the beach on horseback, urging visitors to return home and residents living within three blocks of the seafront to move back to higher ground, though the highest ground on the island was only nine feet above sea level. Cline's account has been questioned, as no one else remembered him riding up and down. As it happened, even if Cline did give precautionary advice it was pointless, as every part of the island was covered by the flood waters. As Cline wrote later, 'In reality there was no island: just the ocean with houses standing out of the waves which rolled between them.'

The last train to reach Galveston that day left Houston at nine forty-five am. The driver found the tracks awash, and passengers had to transfer to another train on parallel tracks to get into the city. Even so, debris on the track meant that the train could only make slow progress. But passengers on another train, arriving from a different direction, were even less fortunate. Their train, from Beaumont, arrived at Point Bolivar but there was no ferry connection to Galveston by that stage. They were stranded. Ten passengers got off the train and took shelter with residents at Port Bolivar. The eighty-five people who decided to stay on the train were killed when the storm surge overwhelmed their carriages.

Through the day, Cline sent out warnings by telegraph to the Weather Bureau's headquarters in Washington, DC, but by the middle of the afternoon the lines had come down and he was unable to send or receive any more messages. He and Galveston were cut off. Cline's last message, at three-thirty pm, was, 'Gulf rising, water covers streets of about half of city.' Then the lines went dead. He waded home and took refuge with about fifty other people at his house.

At that time little was known about hurricanes and how they worked. His experience that day drove Isaac Cline to devote much of the rest of his life to studying hurricanes. He wanted there to be no repeat of the 1900 disaster. Before the disaster he had rashly dismissed as absurd the idea that such a disaster could happen to Galveston. It was Cline himself who had so publicly campaigned against the seawall; he had in effect been partly responsible for the disaster. He remains a very controversial figure.

The weather instruments Cline was using were less sophisticated and less reliable than modern instruments, and some crucial aspects of the Galveston hurricane were not measured properly simply because the instruments were not functioning at all under the extreme conditions. The Weather Bureau's anemometer (wind meter) measured a wind speed of 100 mph at six o'clock in the evening, but then as the wind speed strengthened it was blown right off the building and gave no more readings at all. The wind speed rose to over 120 mph, probably reaching 140 mph as it piled the sea up into a fifteen-feet high storm surge that covered the island. The Galveston hurricane would today be ranked as a Category 4 storm. Houses fell down as the storm surge rolled over the island, so the water was dense with debris. Survivors described a wall of debris two-storeys high sweeping across towards the bay, destroying everything in its path. Cline's house was one of the buildings knocked down in this surge. A floating jetty broke from its mooring and battered the house until it collapsed. Cline and his family were struggling for their lives all night. The occasional flash of lightning revealed the extent of the destruction all around them.

The eye of the storm, the still centre of the spiral system, passed over Galveston at eight pm. Atmospheric pressure at sea level is normally around 1,000 millibars. The pressure at the centre of this storm is believed to have been about 930 millibars, which is unusually low.

The storm travelled northward, inland. Cut off from its supply of water vapour, the storm quickly weakened. By the time it reached the Great Lakes, the wind speeds were still quite strong – forty mph – but nothing like the winds that had destroyed Galveston. On 12 September, the huge spiral storm was passing over Nova Scotia and out into the North Atlantic, where it turned into a relatively harmless depression.

When the storm finally subsided, the true extent of the damage to Galveston became visible. Nearly every building in the city had been damaged to some extent. The area from First Street to Eighth Street was destroyed, as was the area from the beach to the harbour. The whole area west from Forty-Fifth Street to the edge of the city was destroyed. It was a scene of total desolation. The streets were empty of people, the houses were reduced to heaps of rubble. The corpses buried under that rubble began to decompose, adding an appalling stench to the generally hellish scene. Cline described it as 'one of the most horrible sights that ever a civilized people looked upon.'

Late on 9 September, the railroad manager in Houston reported to the Chief of the US Weather Bureau what he was discovering about Galveston.

First news from Galveston just received by train which could get no closer to the bay shore than six miles where Prairies was strewn with debris and dead bodies. About 200 corpses counted from train. Large steamship stranded two miles inland. Loss of life and property undoubtedly appalling. Weather clear and bright here with gentle south-east wind.

G. L. Vaughan, Manager, Western Union, Houston.

239

Because the telegraph lines were down and the bridges connecting Galveston to the mainland had been destroyed, word of the disaster was slow to reach the outside world. The survivors suffered alone and unaided for many hours. Mid-morning on 9 September, one of the small number of vessels at Galveston to survive the hurricane, the Pherabe, reached Texas City on the west side of Galveston Bay. Six messengers from Galveston were on board, and they made it their business to get to Houston. When they reached the telegraph office there, at three in the morning on 10 September, they sent brief, urgent messages to the Governor of Texas, Joseph D. Sayers, and President McKinley; 'I have been deputized by the Mayor and Citizens' Committee of Galveston to inform you that the city of Galveston is in ruins.' They reported an estimate that 500 people were dead, and their report was believed to be exaggerated.

In fact, it was far worse. More than 3,600 homes were completely destroyed, leaving a wall of debris facing the ocean, as if in mockery of the seawall that might have saved Galveston. A few buildings survived the onslaught of the storm surge, and they were the more solidly built mansions on the Strand. Today they are maintained as tourist attractions.

In response to the news, a workforce was sent off by train from Houston without further delay. The rescuers were astonished to find Galveston completely destroyed. One-fifth of the island's population had been killed. Some had been drowned in the swirling fifteen feet of Gulf water that poured over the island, others had been crushed by collapsing buildings, others died of injuries inflicted by the mass of debris carried in the storm surge. Many of those who died survived the storm itself, but died a lingering death after being trapped under the wreckage of the city for several days. The rescuers could hear the screams of survivors as they walked over the chaos of debris. They had no hope of rescuing all of them. There were so many bodies to dispose of that initially they were loaded onto carts and buried at sea, but the currents brought the bodies back to shore, and another solution was needed. After that huge pyres were started, and the corpses were informally cremated on the spot. There were some terrible incidents where workers had to throw the bodies of their own wives and children onto the pyres; free whiskey was passed out to them.

Between 6,000 and 12,000 people had died in the storm in Galveston and the surrounding area. Somehow 30,000 people had survived in the city but Galveston was in every practical sense destroyed. It would have been quite natural to clear and abandon the site and rebuild in a safer location. Yet the city was rebuilt in the same place. This has often happened, throughout history, the phenomenon of geographical inertia. There are two reasons why settlements tend to be maintained under these circumstances. One is a quirk of human psychology, a kind of bonding or emotional conservatism that makes people hang onto a place that they are familiar with. The other is commercial – that owners of property, especially valuable property in key locations in a city, have a strong vested interest in maintaining (or reconstructing) the status quo. The result is that, around the world, there are many towns and cities which on safety grounds ought to have been abandoned or re-located, but which have been rebuilt on the same spot, sometimes after repeated destruction.

Galveston was rebuilt. A committee of residents was set up to make plans for the new Galveston. Among these plans were the building of a seawall along the Gulf shore and the building of an all-weather bridge to the mainland. The first three miles of the seventeen-feet high seawall were built in 1902. Another improvement was the raising of the land level of the whole city. Along the Gulf coast, the land level was raised sixteen feet. Over 2,000 buildings that survived the hurricane were raised on jacks and the space underneath them was filled with sand from the bay. There was a determination not only to rebuild but to build better and safer. There was also a determination to make the awful experience of the disaster count for something; it was said that if

Galveston could survive the storm it could survive anything. (The last survivor of the Galveston disaster, Mrs Maude Conic, died as recently as 2004.)

The new Galveston has indeed withstood several storms since 1900, but it has to be said that no subsequent storm has so far equalled the intensity of the 1900 hurricane. The 1900 storm has become a benchmark against which other, later, American disasters are compared. Most authorities give 8,000 as the death toll for the Galveston hurricane, which gives it third place in a 'Top Ten' of Atlantic hurricanes, after the Great Hurricane of 1780, in which 22,000 died, and Hurricane Mitch in 1998, in which perhaps as many as 18,000 died. On the other hand, many of those deaths occurred outside the United States, and the Galveston hurricane is still the deadliest hurricane ever to hit the country. Of the purely American storms, the Okeechobee hurricane of 1928 killed about 2,500 people, and hurricane Katrina in 2005 killed 1,600. More people died in this single disaster than have been killed, in total, in the more than 300 hurricanes that have hit the United States subsequently.

Galveston was safer after the 1900 storm, but it never regained its former pre-eminence. It had been seen as a beautiful and prestigious city, the New York of the South. It never really recaptured that image, and oil-rich Houston became the dominant commercial city. The dredging of the Houston Ship Canal in 1909 confirmed that shift in status.

V

THE MODERN WORLD

THE ERUPTION OF
MONT PELÉE

(1902)

AT THE BEGINNING of the twentieth century, the thriving town of St Pierre on Martinique in the West Indies was a favourite haunt of wealthy French holiday-makers. St Pierre was a coastal town, a port, at the foot of a long slope up to the volcanic peak of Mont Pelée. At a distance of several miles, the volcano was nothing to worry about. It was known as 'the bald mountain', because of the way its bare summit rose above the luxuriant tropical forest.

In April 1902, Mont Pelée came to life after fifty years of dormancy with a series of earth tremors and major explosions that went on for several months. Ash began to fall on the town of St Pierre and along with it the overpowering smell of sulphur. Animals and birds sickened and died, poisoned by the gases leaking out of the volcano. The inhabitants of St Pierre themselves began to have difficulty in breathing, and instinctively shut themselves inside their houses to try to avoid inhaling the fumes.

The governor of Martinique visited the town and appointed a commission to assess the situation. It was a strange course of action, when the obvious thing to do was to order the town's immediate evacuation. The commission reported that there was no danger and then the governor concentrated on calming people down and persuading them that they should remain where they were. He had an ulterior motive. An election was coming up, on 10 May, and he was afraid that he would lose his voters. The northern half of the island was by now covered in a mantle of grey ash, and refugees from the north began pouring into St Pierre. The volcano meanwhile rumbled on, releasing more ash and steam.

On 5 May a lahar – mud from a boiling lake on the mountain – swept down the slopes. It destroyed a sugar mill and killed 100 people. Now the people in St Pierre began to panic. When they tried to flee from the city, the governor stationed troops on the road to stop them. Their instinct was to leave St Pierre, and they were right. They were kept in the town by force.

Clouds of incandescent dust soared high in the air. There were also avalanches of hot ash, gas and rock that sped down the mountain side at 200 feet per second. Three days later, disaster came. On the morning of 8 May 1902, one of the billowing 'fiery clouds', a fast-moving layer of lethal hot gas three miles thick, swept down the mountain side towards the town of St Pierre, the capital of Martinique. The temperature of the gas is estimated to have been around 1,000 degrees Celsius (1,800 degrees Fahrenheit). It was hot enough to melt glass, and to kill people instantly.

St Pierre was five miles away from the volcano, which may have seemed a safe distance, but it was totally destroyed even so. All the buildings were demolished and reduced to charred rubble within three minutes by the scalding avalanche, and when would-be rescuers arrived the town was so badly wrecked that they were unable to recognize the street plan. The sea in the harbour boiled and ships were capsized in the churning water. Huge numbers of fish and other marines creatures were scalded to death.

All but two of the inhabitants of St Pierre were killed. Twenty-nine thousand people died instantly that day. It is impossible to explain how one of the survivors lived through the annihilation of St Pierre. Léon Compère-Léandre, a twenty-eight-year-old shoe-maker, was sitting outside on his doorstep when the disaster happened. He described what happened to him. 'All of a sudden I felt a terrible wind blowing, the earth began to tremble and the sky suddenly became dark. I felt my arms and legs burning, also my body. Crazed and almost overcome, I threw myself on a bed, inert and waiting for death.' He had seen everyone around him dying. Then he lost consciousness. When he regained his senses he managed to reach the next village.

The other survivor – there were only two survivors – was a prisoner locked in a dungeon. He was Auguste Ciparis, a twenty-five year old black docker who was under sentence of death and confined in a cell. The tiny window and unusually small and solid door of his cell seem to have saved his life. Ciparis was badly burned, and had to endure the extra suffering of lying in his cell for three days with neither food nor water. But he was eventually found, rescued and reprieved.

The remarkable effects of this eruption show how much energy was released. The avalanche sheared large trees from their roots and drove particles through an iron tank. Some blocks up to twenty feet across were hurled as much as twelve miles from the crater.

THE HEPPNER FLOOD

(1903)

AFTER A VIOLENT rainstorm, a flash flood on the Willow Creek in Oregon caused the deaths of 200 people in the town of Heppner in Morrow County on 14 June 1903. They lie buried in the Heppner cemetery.

Photographs of surprisingly high quality show the flash flood surging towards the town as a deep and fast-flowing sheet of water, pushing trees over as it went. The town, with its stoutly built Palace Hotel, did not look threatened, though the damage inflicted on the town was very great. In fact, the hotel was one of the few buildings to survive; the rest were destroyed.

Morrow County is an area afflicted by thunderstorms yielding very high intensity rainfall (often several inches of rain falling in an hour), and that in turn means that the rivers are prone to rise very high very fast. The town of Heppner itself is in one of those unfortunate locations that attract disaster. It stands at the place where four rivers join together: Hinton Creek, Shobe Creek, Balm Fork and Willow Creek. Of these, Willow Creek is the largest. It has its source in the Blue Mountains seventy miles away, and runs through a narrow valley. Although there is some forest in the headwater area, most of the catchment area is deforested prairie – the sort of landscape that sheds water rapidly when it rains. High-intensity rainfall over the catchments of these rivers inevitably meant that a very large volume of water converged on Heppner.

Heppner was a town that had grown rapidly as a centre trading in wool, cattle and wheat, serving a large area of Oregon. With the arrival of the railway, Heppner's population doubled and by 1900 it boasted two banks, nine saloons and two major hotels. But it was still primarily a market town, and a strong smell of sheep hung about it.

The spring of 1903 was one of the driest in memory. The start of rain on 11 June in a thunderstorm was at first welcome, but the bone-dry ground could not absorb the water, which ran straight off into the streams and rivers, sending a surge down the hitherto dry channel of Willow Creek. 14 June was another hot sultry day. In the afternoon thunderheads began to build up, and at four-thirty the rain started in earnest. Its intensity increased, accompanied by thunder, lightning and hail. The storm was so noisy that people could not hear each other speak; the noise also had the disastrous effect of masking the far more menacing sound of the wall of water and debris as it roared down the Willow Creek valley towards them. It arrived at five o'clock.

A Heppner resident, Cora Phelps, described what it was like.

It began to rain so hard that we had to go in and we watched the storm out of the sitting-room window and the baby had just woke up and I had her in my arms nursing her and Mr and Mrs S and I went upstairs to watch it and pretty soon Bert came up and watched too. Bert started out and I said, 'What are you going to do?' He said 'I am going out to see how bad it is.' He put on his rubber boots and rain coat and went down to the bridge and he said he saw the bridge go and the water came up so fast and he ran back and motioned for us to come and we ran downstairs. When we met him downstairs, the water and mud rushed into our house about two feet deep and I will never forget how cold it was. Bert said 'Give me the baby' for he knew that she was the smallest and most helpless and of course Margaret couldn't walk through it so I picked her up and Bert told us all to go upstairs. I never will forget how thoughtful and brave he

was, and he had so much hope. I never had the least ray of hope,
I thought the world was coming to an end. I just held the baby
in my arms and kneeled on the floor and just prayed and prayed.
It seemed like an hour or two that we were up there but I
suppose it wasn't more than half an hour. So many two-storey
houses went just to kindling.

As Heppner was collapsing around them, two residents had the presence of mind to think of saving other settlements further down the valley. Bruce Kelly said to his friend Leslie Matlock, 'Les, this flood is going to hit Lexington too. Maybe we can save the people at Lexington and the valley below.' They set off on horseback down the Willow Creek Valley by the shortest route, across country, though they were slowed down by having to cut their way through barbed wire fences. They reached Lexington, nine miles away, a short time after the flood waters, and then rode on another eight miles to Ione, shouting warnings to farmers along the way. They reached Ione in time to warn the residents there, and managed to get them all to run up onto higher ground. From there they watched in the evening as the flood ripped through their township. The flood was less intense than at Heppner, but the quick action of Kelly and Matlock certainly saved many lives.

Reports of the Heppner disaster give varying figures for the height of the wall of water. Some say it was six feet high, some fifty feet. Either way, the photographs taken the next day show the devastation that it caused. One reporter wrote:

Scenes at Heppner are indescribable in their gruesomeness, their
anguish, their desolation . . . The silt-laden flood water carried
timber, trees and everything else in their path. The thick mass
acted more like a battering ram or an avalanche than a flood of
liquid. Many homes simply floated off their lots into the flood
waters and careened off to crash into other structures, where

they broke apart, their constituent materials added to the flowing mass.

At the upper end of Heppner, Willow Creek was spanned by a building housing a Chinese laundry. When the flood water arrived, it remained standing for a time, but it was eventually undermined and collapsed; the owner's family and the Chinese workforce were all swept away to their deaths. Further downstream, the Palace Hotel, a solidly built brick structure, resisted the flood water and played a part in diverting it away from the business area of the town. The other hotel, Hotel Heppner, was timber built, and it was destroyed, killing up to fifty guests.

Some people were lucky enough to see the wall of water coming and had time to run up the steep valley sides to safety. Some climbed trees to get out of the reach of the flood water. Most were unable to escape, and were trapped in their houses. A few very lucky people were swept along by the flood and deposited great distances downstream, badly shaken but still alive. Survival was largely a matter of luck, because no one could swim in the flood water. George Conser and his wife rode the flood trapped on the first floor of their house up to their necks in water as it floated through Heppner. Their house was lodged against another house, and then they were able to pull themselves out. Dan Stalter lost his wife and six of his children to the flood, but then was able to escape with his one remaining child; he used a wooden crate as a dinghy and they floated to safety.

When the flood was over, the awful task of finding the bodies and clearing up the debris began. There were very few injuries to deal with, as on the whole the injured perished in the flood: people either died or escaped unscathed. The dead were identified in a temporary morgue, then buried in haste on Cemetery Hill. The weather was hot, so it was imperative to recover and bury corpses as quickly as possible. There was great confusion as a roll call the day after the disaster accounted for only half the population, so there were fears that the death toll was very high. In all, only 257 bodies were recovered, though more may have died, their bodies swept forty-five miles down-valley and dumped in the Columbia River. Martial law was declared to restore order and looters were to be shot on sight.

Many of the survivors left Heppner after the disaster. By 1910, its population was only about half what it had been in 1900. It has since then grown only gradually, and its population is now roughly what it was just before the wall of water arrived.

THE WAIMANGU
GEYSER DISASTER

(1903)

THE WAIMANGU GEYSER eruption of 1903 was an unusual disaster. Geysers are a kind of volcanic eruption, it is true, but on a very limited scale – and often very predictable. Geysers are jets of scalding water and steam. They are the result of ground water seeping down through cracks in the rock until it comes in contact with magma (molten rock) far underground. The water boils, expands and is squirted back up to the surface under enormous pressure. Often the same water goes up and down repeatedly, and often geysers erupt at a particular time interval – hence the name 'Old Faithful' given to one of the Yellowstone geysers. Deaths resulting from geysers are very rare.

One of the visitors to the Rotorua geysers in August 1903 was Mrs Nicholls. She and her three daughters had moved to Auckland from Christchurch just two months before the disaster. They had visited Rotorua before, then gone on a trip to the Pacific Islands. Now Mrs Nicholls was returning to Rotorua with her two older daughters, aged nineteen and twenty. Her husband had owned a big sheep farm in North Canterbury and had recently died.

The Waimangu disaster happened on Sunday 30 August 1903. A press report of the time tells the story under the headline 'The Waimangu horror: how it occurred.'

It appears that thirty-two tourists left on the round trip this morning. One section of the party saw Waimangu, then in eruption, but the geyser only played about 200 feet in height. The other party went by way of Wairoa across the lakes and were late in reaching the geyser. Among them were the two Misses Nicholls, Mr D MacNaughten and Mr Joe Warbrick. At half past three in the afternoon, while this party was near the shelter shed on the hill, a terrific eruption took place. These four were killed and some others injured.

The eruption was seen in Rotorua and must have been stupendous and terrific. The victims were carried in the rush of boiling water nearly a mile in the direction of Lake Rotomahana. It was some time before the bodies were recovered and a considerable portion of their clothing was torn off pointing to the horrible, though mercifully swift, nature of their end.

The eruption is described as the greatest yet witnessed of Waimangu. Those who have seen what this great natural wonder is capable of will know what this means. One man was in close proximity to the geyser when the fatal shot occurred, but succeeded in resisting the force of the water, and escaped being drawn down into the overflow. There seemed to be three shots in quick succession – one straight up and the others spreading. It was doubtless the latter which caught the ill-fated party.

W. A. Constant, who was an eyewitness of the disaster states that no blame was attachable to Guide Warbrick who prior to the eruption begged his brother, the young ladies and MacNaughton to come away from the position they were in as he considered it dangerous. To his brother he remarked, 'If an accident happens you know I will get the sack.' He also told Mrs Nicholls to tell her daughters they were in a dangerous position and urged them to come back. Mrs Nicholls called her daughters by name, requesting them to come away, to which one of them replied, 'Just a moment, mother.' At that moment the geyser went up, and when it subsided the four were gone.

Mrs Nicholls and the guide, Alf Warbrick, were on top of the hill near the shelter shed and the victims were on the brow of a *hill overlooking the overflow. Mr Constant had left the party a minute or two before the accident and had taken a seat on the brow of a hill in front of the shelter shed. MacNaughten's body was found first and the others lower downstream. Mrs Nicholls is almost distracted at the loss of her girls. It is but a few months since her husband died.*

One of the victims, David MacNaughton, was a married man without family, aged thirty, manager of a butcher's shop at Archhil [Auckland]. He was a friend of Warbrick's and was to have returned to Auckland earlier, but wrote that he intended to stay over Sunday to see Waimangu play. Miss Nicholls, aged seventeen, a younger sister of the two young ladies who lost their lives, left for Rotorua by train this morning.

The inquest gave a similar version of the events. The guide, Warbrick, confirmed that he had warned the unfortunate victims, and others, that the place where they were standing was dangerous, and that his warnings had been disregarded. He had told Mrs Nicholls to call her daughters back, but the girls had merely smiled at their mother. He had walked on with Mrs Nicholls assuming that the others would follow, but they did not. He said that when he last saw them they were standing on the brink of the geyser. When the geyser erupted he had to carry Mrs Nicholls out of danger; the others had been swept away.

Another witness, who was actually with the Nicholls girls at the time of the eruption, said that one of them had been anxious to take a photograph. When the geyser erupted he ran, hearing a terrible roar; everything had gone dark; material seemed to cascade down on him as he ran. He acknowledged that if they had taken notice of the guide's warnings they would not have been an accident at all.

The inquest jury brought a verdict of accidental death and affirmed that the guide was blameless.

It was an unusual incident, very small in scale compared with the other disasters in this book, but one bearing its own cautionary tale, its own message. Natural processes have to be respected. Only four people died in the Waimangu disaster, yet the numbers are unimportant. The loss felt by poor Mrs Nicholls must have been overwhelming.

THE SAN FRANCISCO EARTHQUAKE

(1906)

I WITNESSED *A sight I never want to see again. It was dawn and light. I looked up. The air was filled with falling stones. People around me were crushed to death on all sides. All around the huge buildings were shaking and waving. Every moment there were reports like 100 cannons going off at one time. Then streams of fire would shoot out and other reports followed.*

I asked a man standing next to me what happened. Before he could answer a thousand bricks fell on him and he was killed. A woman threw her arms around my neck. I pushed her away and fled. All around me buildings were rocking and flames shooting. As I ran people on all sides were crying, praying and calling for help. I thought the end of the world had come. I met a Catholic priest, and he said, 'We must get to the ferry'. He knew the way, and we rushed down Market Street. Men, women and children were crawling from the debris. Hundreds were rushing down the street and every minute people were felled by debris. At places the streets had cracked and opened. Chasms extended in all directions. I saw a drove of cattle, wild with fright, rushing up Market Street. I crouched beside a swaying building. As they came near they disappeared, seeming to drop out into the earth. When the last had gone I went nearer and found that they had indeed been precipitated into the earth, a wide fissure having swallowed them. I was crazy with fear and the horrible sights.

The great San Francisco earthquake of 1906 is perhaps the best-known earthquake disaster in modern history. It came on 18 April, at five-thirteen in the morning, shaking a large area of central California. Varying estimates of its magnitude have been proposed, but it was probably 7.8 on the Richter scale. There was movement along a 300-mile stretch – an unusually long stretch - of the San Andreas Fault. This is a tear fault; in other words, the land moves sideways rather than up or down, which would be called a normal fault. It was, as is usual on the San Andreas Fault, a right-lateral slip, with the coastal strip moving northwards in relation to the rest of California. The maximum lateral slip along the fault was twenty feet, and that was measured near Olema. It was a very large-scale earth movement and inevitably released a large amount of destructive energy. San Francisco was at the heart of this release of energy and suffered very badly as a result.

A little known feature of the earthquake is that it produced a small and rather unusual tsunami. Ten minutes after the earthquake the sea level in San Francisco Bay fell four inches for about fifteen minutes. After this drawback, one would normally expect the tsunami wave to arrive, but there wasn't one; instead there was just a series of three withdrawals that went on for forty-five minutes. So the San Francisco earthquake produced a kind of 'negative tsunami'.

Large areas of the city were wrecked by the earthquake itself, then incinerated by a great fire – the seventh in the city's history – that raged for four days. An unknown number of people died trapped in the ruins of collapsed tenement buildings. The ground was shaken so energetically in the quake that it liquefied, so that many buildings literally sank into the ground. An eyewitness described some of the initial chaos.

In every direction from the ferry building, flames were seething, and as I stood there, a five-storey building half a block away fell with a crash, and the flames swept clear across Market Street and caught a new fireproof building recently erected. The streets in places had sunk three or four feet. In others, great humps had appeared four or five feet high. The street car tracks were bent and twisted out of shape. Electric wires lay in every direction. Streets on all sides were filled with brick and mortar, buildings either completely collapsed or brick fronts had just dropped completely off. Wagons with horses hitched to them, drivers and all, lying in the streets, all dead, struck and killed by the falling bricks, these mostly the wagons of the produce dealers, who do the greater part of their work at that hour of the morning. Warehouses and large wholesale houses either down, or walls bulging, or else twisted, buildings moved bodily two or three feet out of line and still standing with walls all cracked. The Call building, a twelve-storey skyscraper, stood and looked all right at first glance, but had moved at the base two feet out onto the sidewalk, and the elevators refused to work, all the interior being just twisted out of shape. It afterward burned as I watched it.

Many of the wrecked buildings caught fire and those trapped inside could not be rescued. It is thought that over 3,000 people died altogether as a result of the 1906 earthquake and its after-effects. It caused 500 million dollars' worth of damage, in 1906 dollars.

The earthquake shook the earth's surface over a huge area of 375,000 square miles, half of which was under the Pacific Ocean. The destruction extended 400 miles along the San Andreas Fault from Fresno County to Eureka, and for about twenty-five miles on each side of the fault. All buildings standing on or next to the fault were destroyed, as were many trees. The destruction of trees was most marked near Loma Prieta where the forest looked as if a swathe 200 feet wide had been cut through it.

One eyewitness described what experiencing the earthquake was like:

Of a sudden we had found ourselves staggering and reeling. It was as if the earth was slipping gently from under our feet. Then came the sickening swaying of the earth that threw us flat upon our faces. We struggled to our feet. Then it seemed as though my head were split with the roar that crashed in my ears. Big buildings were crumbling as one might crush a biscuit in one's hand. Ahead of me a great cornice crushed a man as if he were a maggot – a labourer in overalls on his way to the Union Works with a dinner pail on his arm.

One of those who died was the Fire Chief Engineer Dennis Sullivan, who was fatally injured when the dome of the California Theatre toppled onto the fire station where he was living. As a result, Acting Chief Engineer John Dougherty was left to command the fire-fighting operation. Telephone and telegraph communications stopped in San Francisco. A messenger had to be sent to Fort Mason, with orders from General Funston to send all available troops to report to the Hall of Justice. The first troops reported to Mayor Schmitz at seven am and within the hour the rest of the troops were taking up patrol duties. Then, at eight-fourteen am came a major aftershock, which brought down many of the badly damaged buildings and caused widespread panic.

At ten am, the wireless station at San Diego radioed press reports of the disaster at San Francisco to the USS *Chicago*. After getting confirmation from the Mayor of San Diego, Admiral Goodrich ordered his ship to steam at full speed for San Francisco. This was the first time wireless telegraphy was used in a major natural disaster. Half an hour later another ship, the USS *Prebble*, landed a hospital party at San Francisco to aid the wounded and dying, who were gathering at the Harbor Emergency Hospital.

A new fire, known as the Ham and Eggs fire, broke out in Hayes Street, quickly spreading to destroy an area of the city that included the Mechanics' Pavilion and City Hall. The Winchester Hotel caught fire at Third and Stevenson Streets, collapsing at eleven am. Troops from Fort Miley, the 25th and 64th Companies Coast Artillery, arrived in the city at 11.30. Not long after that, two earthquakes struck Los Angeles, ten minutes apart, just as crowds were gathering around bulletin boards to read the latest telegraph dispatches from San Francisco. Thousands of people in Los Angeles were sent running in panic.

The spread of the Ham and Eggs fire led to the evacuation of Mechanics' Pavilion, Grove and Larkin at about noon. Mechanics' Pavilion caught fire at 1 pm. At the same time, St Mary's Hospital on First Street was given up to the fire; its patients were taken to Oakland by ferry. Prisoners were moved out of the city prison to Alcatraz. The whole Financial District behind the Hall of Justice was now in flames. In a desperate attempt to stop the fire spreading, the dynamiting of buildings started at 2.30 pm. By this stage 750 seriously injured people were being treated at various hospitals. The city morgue and the police pistol range were used to store corpses; now that they were full, bodies were informally buried by the police in Portsmouth Square.

The fires presented the firefighters and would-be rescuers with some terrible choices to make. One witness described such a scene. 'When the fire caught the Windsor Hotel at Fifth and Market Street there were three men on the roof, and it was impossible to get them down. Rather than see the crazed men fall in with the roof and be roasted alive, the military officer directed his men to shoot them, which they did in the presence of 5,000 people.' Another witness saw a policeman facing the same dilemma. 'The most terrible thing I saw was the futile struggle of a policeman and others to rescue a man who was pinned down in burning wreckage. The helpless man watched it in silence till the fire began burning his feet. Then he screamed and begged to be killed. The policeman took his name and address and shot him through the head.'

It became clear that the call for huge numbers of troops to ensure law and order was entirely necessary. When appointing a

Committee of Fifty at three pm, the mayor announced that upholding the law was a major priority. 'Let it be given out that three men have already been shot down without mercy for looting. Let it also be understood that the order has been given to all soldiers and policemen to do likewise without hesitation in the cases of any and all miscreants who may seek to take advantage of the city's awful misfortune.'

At eight pm, Mayor Schmitz was confident that a fair part of downtown San Francisco could be saved. Then an arsonist set fire to the Delmonico Restaurant in the Alcazar Theatre Building, and that fire spread rapidly into Downtown and Nob Hill, in spite of the efforts of firefighters to stop it. General Funston sent a telegram to the War Department at eight-forty pm, asking for thousands of tents and as much in the way of food as possible; Funston estimated that 1,000 people had died. At four am the Secretary of War ordered 200,000 rations and the tents Funston asked for to be sent to San Francisco from the Vancouver Barracks and a variety of other army posts.

At two in the morning on 19 April, Governor Pardee arrived in Oakland. He was three hours late because the railway track had foundered in the marshes during the earthquake. The fires burned on through the night, the St Francis Hotel catching fire at two-thirty am.

That evening, at six pm, the USS *Chicago* steamed into San Francisco Bay. Still the fires were burning, now reaching Van Ness Avenue. Troops under Colonel Morris tried to create a fire break by dynamiting mansions along the avenue.

At dawn on 20 April, two days after the earthquake, the fire was still burning. At the lower end of Van Ness Avenue, just eighteen men from the USS *Chicago* supervised the rescue of 20,000 people who were fleeing from the Great Fire. It was a huge operation, the largest peacetime evacuation by sea in history; only the Dunkirk evacuation in the Second World War was larger in scale.

At 8.30 pm General Funston wired the War Department to report on the spread of the fire. He said that Fort Mason had been saved, and that some looters had been shot. He also commented that there were few casualties in the better-off parts of the city, and that most of the casualties were in the poorer districts.

On 21 April, a statue of President McKinley that had been commissioned from the sculptor Haig Patigian for the city of Arcata was found among the debris of a destroyed foundry; several workmen rescued it from the rubble, dragging it out into the street for safety. Still the fire raged on, though it was halted in Mission Street by the determined efforts of 3,000 volunteers and a few firefighters, who fought the blaze with brooms, knapsacks and a trickle of water from a hydrant.

The fires raged for three days and nights continuously before they burned themselves out. By the time the fires were out, they had destroyed 490 blocks of the city, ruined a total of 25,000 buildings and made over 250,000 people homeless.

On 22 April, Father Ricard wrote in the San Jose Mercury, 'The earthquake period is gone. At the most a succession of minor shocks may be felt and that's all. People should fearlessly go to work, repair mischief down and sleep quietly at night. Seismometry is in its infancy and those therefore who venture out with predictions of future earthquakes ought to be arrested as disturbers of the peace.' The following day Governor Pardee was starting to talk more optimistically; 'The work of rebuilding San Francisco has commenced, and I expect to see the great metropolis replaced on a much grander scale than ever before.' The Dowager Empress of China offered to send a personal contribution towards the relief of the San Francisco victims, but President Theodore Roosevelt ungraciously refused it accept it, along with donations from other foreign countries.

The San Francisco earthquake is rightly remembered as a major disaster. It lasted only a minute, but in all 3,000 people died and about 225,000 people were injured. It was also a landmark in the scientific understanding of earthquakes. The sheer length of the rupture, 300 miles from San Juan Bautista to the triple fault junction of Cape Mendocino, was something new to geologists. The significance of the large offset of the San Andreas Fault dawned on geologists little by little, and played its part in helping them to make the great imaginative leap into plate tectonics in the 1960s. Analyzing the displacements in 1906 led to the development of the elastic-rebound theory of earthquakes in 1910, which is still the main model for understanding earthquakes. Today, the main significance of the earthquake lies in the role that it played in the Great Leap Forward in our understanding of Earth.

THE TUNGUSKA FIREBALL

(1908)

AT SEVEN-SEVENTEEN IN the morning on 30 June 1908, there was a very unusual event in Siberia. It was a huge explosion in the air above the forest seventy miles north of Vanavara and it is still not known for certain what caused it. It happened about halfway across the Russian Federation, on the latitude of Helsinki, specifically on the Tunguska River and it is sometimes known as the Tunguska Event, or the Great Siberian Explosion.

A commonly held and now often repeated view is that the explosion was the airburst of a meteorite or a comet about four miles above the earth's surface. The energy of the blast is estimated to have been equivalent to ten or fifteen megatons of TNT, on a level with the most powerful nuclear bomb ever detonated by the United States. Whatever the cause of this massive, high-energy explosion, it was very fortunate that it happened in a virtually uninhabited region. There was, it is believed, only one human casualty. The natural environment suffered a terrific impact. Sixty million trees were knocked flat over an area of 830 square miles. Fires burned in the devastated forest for weeks. Ash and powdered tundra vegetation were sucked up into the sky by a fiery vortex to be carried all around the world by upper air winds.

The Tunguska event stands as a warning of the dangers the planet faces from collision with interplanetary debris of one sort or another. Collision with quite small objects can have devastating effects. In recent decades, there has been a great deal of speculation about the possibility of the Earth colliding with a comet, a large meteorite or even an asteroid. The odds are that such a collision will happen from time to time, but infrequently. When such a collision does happen, there are likely to be huge impacts on global ecology, and this has been a favoured explanation for periodic mass extinctions visible in the geological record. For many people, Tunguska is a glimpse of doomsday.

There were a few Russian settlers living in the hill country to the north-west of Lake Baikal, along with a small number of native people, the Tungus. What they saw, that early morning in June was a 'pipe', or cylinder, of piercingly bright bluish light almost as bright as the sun moving diagonally across the sky, down towards Earth. It left a brilliant tail perhaps 500 miles long. About ten minutes after this sighting, as the body approached the ground, the bright body seemed to smudge, as one eye witness described it. There was a flash and a gigantic billowing of black smoke. The object disintegrated in a rapid series of cataclysmic explosions lasting in all perhaps only half a second, but because the object was travelling so fast this shattering took place over a distance of about ten miles. There was a loud knocking sound like a short burst of gunfire. On the ground people heard repeated bursts of this noise, which came at increasingly long intervals; it was as if great rocks were falling to the ground. All the buildings in the area were shaken by these impacts. At the same time the black cloud 'began emitting flames of uncertain shapes'.

The people in the area were understandably panic-stricken by these frightening and totally inexplicable phenomena. Some of the women cried, thinking the end of the world had come. Eyewitnesses who were close to the explosion said the sound source moved across the sky with each barrage, travelling from the east towards the north. The sounds were accompanied by a shock wave that was powerful enough to knock people over and break windows hundreds of miles away. Most of the witnesses reported the sounds and the shock waves, not the sight of the explosion. It may be significant that different witnesses gave different sequences of events and attributed different spans of time to the events.

Even though the explosion happened in the sky, and about four miles up at that, it shook the ground. It was picked up at seismic stations across Eurasia. The powerful shock waves that passed through the air were strong enough to be picked up in Great Britain on the recently invented barographs. The explosion had other effects too, some that are hard to explain. For several weeks afterwards the skies glowed at night, and sufficiently brightly for people to be able to read by the light. It was reported in the *New York Times* on 3 July 1908 that 'remarkable lights' had been seen in the northern sky for two successive nights. Scientists mistakenly jumped to the conclusion that these were the Northern Lights, produced by solar radiation. The newspaper nevertheless noted that similar lighting effects were reported after the Krakatoa eruption twenty-five years earlier, implying a terrestrial origin. The optical fireworks and light nights were even commoner in Siberia. Dust from the explosion was suspended in the air between twenty-five and forty miles up, and it was this that caused high-level cloud to light up in an unusual way; a phenomenon sometimes called 'noctiluscence'. Associated with this dust, observatories in the United States measured a decrease in the transparency of the atmosphere that lasted for several months.

The area was remote and inaccessible, and it was a long time before scientists reached it. By then, of course, the trail of evidence was running cold. Eyewitness accounts were collected, but more than twenty years later. One of the witness accounts came from Semen Semenov, who was interviewed during the expedition to Tunguska led by Leonid Kulik in 1930.

At breakfast time I was sitting in the house at Vananara trading post [forty miles north of the explosion], facing north . . . I suddenly saw that directly to the north, over Onkoul's Tunguska road, the sky spilt in two and fire appeared high and wide over the forest [Semenov indicated an altitude of fifty degrees up]. The split in the sky grew larger and the entire northern side was covered with fire. At that moment I became so hot that I couldn't bear it, as if my shirt was on fire; from the northern side, where the fire was, came strong heat. I wanted to tear off my shirt and throw it down, but then the sky closed and a strong thump sounded, and I was thrown a few yards. I lost my senses for a moment, but then my wife ran out and led me to the house. After that such noise came, as if rocks were falling or cannons were firing, the earth shook and when I was on the ground, I pressed my head down, fearing rocks would smash it. When the sky opened up, hot wind raced between the houses, like from cannons. Later we saw that many windows were shattered, and in the barn a part of the iron lock snapped.

In 1926, an eyewitness description was recorded from a Shanyagir tribesman. He described the exploding object as 'mighty bright, as if there was a second sun'. He also described a series of five separate explosions, like thunderclaps; the fourth and fifth were quieter, as if coming from further away.

Some witnesses heard only two explosions; others as many as ten, each coming about fifteen minutes after the last; others described 'fifty to sixty salvoes at short equal intervals, which got progressively weaker'. In the part of the sky where most of the thumps were heard, 'a kind of ashen cloud was seen near the horizon which kept getting smaller and more transparent, and by about two or three o'clock in the afternoon it had completely disappeared. What people heard and saw depended on how close they were to the event.

It is thought that the people who were nearest were some reindeer herders who were sleeping in tents in several encampments about twenty miles from the explosion. They were blown up into the air and knocked senseless. When they regained consciousness they heard a great deal of noise and saw the forest burning around them; much of it was devastated. The ground shook and they heard a prolonged roaring sound. Many of the herders' reindeer ran off and were lost. One old man was blown forty feet up into a tree and later died of his injuries, apparently the only human casualty of this unique disaster. But Vasiliy Dzhenkoul's reindeer were instantly incinerated – a herd over 600 strong; his tepees, stores, furs and hunting dogs were also reduced to ashes.

One of many peculiarities surrounding the Tunguska event was the apparent lack of curiosity shown by scientists. Obviously the Tunguska area was remote and difficult to reach – but not impossible. If there were any expeditions by scientists before 1920, all record of them has been lost, which is indeed possible, given the chaotic conditions of the First World War, the Russian Revolution and the Civil War. One explanation that has been suggested is that the shaman headman of the Evenks, the native people of the Tungus, proclaimed the area enchanted and sealed it off from the outside world. The Evenks were, it was said, afraid of further angering the gods who had inflicted the 1908 explosion on them. The first known expedition was the 1921 expedition of Leonid Kulik, who braved the mosquito swarms and visited the Tunguska River basin as part of a survey for the Soviet Academy of Sciences. Kulik deduced from the accounts he was given by the local people that the event had been caused by the impact of a giant meteorite. He persuaded the government to provide funds for a full-scale expedition to Tunguska, based on the expectation that it would be found to be rich in iron from the meteorite; the salvaged iron, he argued, would more than cover the cost of the expedition.

The iron-hunting expedition reached Tunguska in 1927. Kulik was surprised to find that there was no impact crater. Instead he found only an area of scorched trees about thirty miles across. A few that had stood exactly beneath the explosion were, rather unexpectedly, still standing upright, but with their branches and bark stripped down. Those further out were flattened radially outwards from the centre. There were three more expeditions in the following ten years. Kulik thought at one point he had found the crater in a boggy depression, but after laboriously draining the bog he found tree stumps at the bottom, ruling it out as an impact crater. In 1938, Kulik managed to arrange aerial photography of the area; this too showed no sign of a crater. There are indeed numerous small circular depressions in the area, but these are easily explained as pingoes, which are formed by thawing ice lenses all over the Arctic. The 1992 expedition also failed to find a crater, though exploring the area thoroughly on foot had become more dangerous because of the presence of displaced bears and wolves.

The evolving technologies of the 1950s and 1960s produced further and highly significant information about Tunguska. When they sieved soil samples, visiting scientists discovered microscopic glass balls containing high proportions of nickel and iridium. These are minerals found in high concentrations in meteorites, and indicated an extraterrestrial origin. More eyewitness accounts were collected, as late as 1959, which was over fifty years after the event, and some of these revealed significant new facts. The local people claimed that they suffered badly from boils after the explosion and that whole families had died. The medical scientist on the expedition attributed this to a smallpox epidemic. Although the skin complaints and the deaths might have been produced by radiation, the scientists found no raised levels of radiation in the Tunguska landscape.

Among scientists, the favoured explanation is that a meteorite entered the Earth's atmosphere and exploded before reaching the ground. Meteorites fly into the atmosphere every day, as Earth travels around its orbit and collides with interplanetary debris. These random lumps of rock travel in at speeds of over six miles per second. The heat generated by the compression of the air in front of the meteorite is enormous. Most meteorites are small, and burn up harmlessly in the stratosphere – or explode. Closer monitoring of the atmosphere in recent decades shows that these explosions, or airbursts, are quite common. A large meteorite would produce a large explosion. A boulder thirty feet across can produce an explosion as powerful as the atom bomb dropped on Hiroshima (twenty kilotons). Explosions like these occur up in the stratosphere more than once a year. Events like Tunguska are much rarer, possibly once in 300 years, and they are in the megaton range. The Tunguska explosion was on the energy level of perhaps sixty atom bombs, closer in scale to a hydrogen bomb.

Many rocky objects of different sizes circle the Sun. The Tunguska object was one of the larger of these objects to collide with Earth. Significant near-collisions like Tunguska happen once a century, and of those three-quarters happen over the oceans. Of those that happen over the continents, three-quarters will be over unpopulated areas. Another significant feature of the phenomenon is one that we have seen before; it has a positive skew – in other words, the larger the event, the less frequent it is.

In the 1990s an American satellite noted an explosion smaller than Tunguska over the Pacific. Earlier, in 1972, an object weighing 1,000 tons skimmed the Earth's atmosphere over Wyoming, like a pebble bouncing across a pond. It was photographed by tourists and also detected by satellites. If it had approached the atmosphere at a steeper angle, nearer the thirty degrees of the Tunguska object, it could have caused an explosion over Canada on the scale of the Hiroshima bomb. The consequences of such an event in a nervous Cold-War setting are not hard to imagine; a full-scale retaliatory nuclear attack on the Soviet Union might have been launched.

The strange radial destruction pattern created in the forest was reproduced in H-bomb tests in the 1950s and 1960s, and is the result of the shock waves produced by an explosion. Trees directly under the blast are stripped down by blast waves moving vertically downwards; trees further out are swept flat, because the shock wave is moving nearly horizontally. Experiments carried out on model forests suggest that the meteorite came down at an angle of thirty degrees from the south-east – and exploded in mid-air. The pattern of tree fall suggests to some scientists that there are four minor 'epicentres' within the larger radial pattern, each with its own radial pattern. This strongly suggests that the four secondary radial patterns might have been formed by the separate explosions.

Another theory about the Tunguska object is that it was an asteroid or comet. The British astronomer Fred Whipple thought a small comet was likely. Because comets are composed mainly of dust and ice, they could completely vaporize as they passed through the atmosphere, leaving no obvious trace and no crater. The comet theory is supported by the 'skyglows' seen across Europe for several evenings after the explosions. These could be explained by dust dispersed by the comet across the stratosphere. Furthermore, soil samples from the area show that it is rich in cometary material. It has been suggested that the object was a chunk of the Comet Encke, which produces the Beta Taurid meteor shower. The Tunguska event coincided with a peak in that shower.

A recent Italian expedition to Tunguska examined the resin of trees knocked over by the explosion. Particles of calcium, iron-nickel, silicates, cobalt-wolfram and lead were all found in the resin, and these are minerals that are found in certain asteroids.

On the other hand, a comet ought to have disintegrated long before reaching the lower atmosphere, whereas the Tunguska object had fallen to between four and five miles of the ground before exploding. A dense and rocky object perhaps 200 feet across seems more likely, and an asteroid has been proposed as more likely than a comet.

There is no shortage of alternative theories, and this is largely a reflection of the poor understanding of meteorite behaviour in the early twentieth century; people have looked around for alternatives. There was also an unhelpful secretiveness about

Tunguska during the Cold War, which fuelled speculation in the West that something far more significant and sinister was involved than a mere meteorite. A bewildering range of theories is available. Maybe it was an explosion of methane gas emitted from the earth. Maybe it was a small black hole passing through the earth (though this would have entailed an exit explosion as the black hole came out the other side). Maybe it was annihilation of a chunk of antimatter falling from space. Maybe it was a comet acting as a natural H-bomb.

The idea that it was an exploding alien spacecraft originated in a science fiction story written by Alexander Kazantsev in 1946; the pilot of his Martian spaceship was looking for a supply of fresh water from Lake Baikal. Kazantsev's story was for some unaccountable reason taken seriously in the West, leading to some enthusiasts referring to Tunguska as the Russian Roswell. (The Roswell UFO incident was a purported crash of an unidentified flying object in Roswell, New Mexico.) Some Russian scientists have encouraged this view. Coincidentally, the Tunguska site is down-range from the Baikonur Cosmodrome and, after many space projects, it has been repeatedly contaminated by space debris raining down on it. The discovery of bits of this wreckage may have fuelled the Roswell comparison.

Evidence from the 1992 expedition gives some support to the idea that some kind of nuclear explosion was involved. Following the explosion in 1908 there was accelerated plant growth just underneath where the explosion happened and that accelerated growth has continued now for a century. There was also an increase in the number of biological mutations, not just at the epicentre but along the whole 500-mile trajectory of the object.

There is probably a catastrophic explosion on the Tunguska scale over land about every 1,800 years, and over a populated area only once in 3,600 years. In other words, in the period of recorded history there could only have been one or two such events. If the Tunguska event had happened over a city, 500,000 people would have died. The fact that the event happened in an almost empty region was only by chance. As it was, the disaster was primarily a disaster for the landscape and ecology of the Tunguska region. The area has been set aside as a national reserve for a twenty-year period, to allow more scientific research into this extraordinary and very alarming event.

THE YANGTZE
FLOOD

(1911)

IN A COUNTRY of great rivers, the Yangtze is one of the greatest. It is the longest river in China, the third longest in the world, after the Amazon and Nile, and the third largest in the world in terms of volume, after the Amazon and Congo. The Yangtze deposits rich layers of soil in its lower course, but causes destructive large-scale flooding in its middle reach. The Yangtze River has very long documented history of flooding. During the course of the 2,200 years from the start of the Han Dynasty until the end of the Qing Dynasty in 1911, there were 214 recorded floods. On average, the Yangtze has flooded once every ten years. In the twentieth century, there were five major floods.

The flood of 1911 was one of the biggest flood in modern times. It was in effect a double flood, involving not just the Yangtze but the Han River as well. The exact death toll is not known, but it is believed that hundreds of thousands of people lost their lives. In 1931, the Yangtze flooded again, inundating 7.5 million acres of agricultural land, destroying 108 million houses and taking 145,000 lives. Only three years after that, in 1935, there was yet another catastrophic flood, in which 142,000 people died.

In 1954, a Yangtze flood submerged 100 million acres of farmland, disrupting the lives of eighteen million people, and causing 30,000 deaths. The main railway line through the area was closed for three months.

A serious flood in 1996 was followed by a much bigger flood in

1998. The 1998 flood destroyed five million houses, inundated forty-five million acres of farmland, caused 3,656 deaths and disrupted the lives of 290 million people. The economic cost of the 1998 flood was thirty billion dollars, even though in purely hydrological terms it was a less severe flood than the 1954 event. What had happened was that China had undergone significant economic development. Each successive flood on the Yangtze was going to cost China more and more money. If a flood of 1954 proportions happened today, it would cause ten times as much damage as it did in 1954 – in economic terms.

It was the huge loss of property, food and human lives in this twentieth-century sequence that led directly on to the design of the Three Gorges Project. This involved building a massive dam to create an enormous lake. The reservoir is intended to reduce the danger of flooding further downstream. The negative impacts of the project are enormous, though; something such as 40,000 acres of food-producing land have been lost under the water, as well as numerous settlements. 1,130,000 people have had to move from their homes, and the dislocation has accelerated an undesirable drift of population from countryside to cities like Shanghai. The forced migrations involved have caused major emotional and psychological problems for those who have had to leave their villages and see them swallowed up by the reservoir.

There is a huge price to pay for controlling river floods. On the other hand, we must not forget the long history of flooding, and that the 1998 Yangtze flood killed 3,000 people and forced the (temporary) evacuation of almost fourteen million people.

THE SINKING OF
THE *TITANIC*

(1912)

AT THE TIME of her maiden voyage, the *Titanic* was the largest ship
in the world – apart from her almost identical twin sister ship, the
Olympic. The two passenger liners were built side by side at the
famous Belfast shipyards of Harland & Wolf for the White Star
Line. The White Star Line was in hot competition with Cunard
and other companies for the prestigious transatlantic crossings.

The *Titanic* was given plenty of gloss in her luxury fittings, and
in her advance publicity. It was said that White Star had spared
no expense in fitting her out, but behind the scenes there had
been a great deal of cheese-paring to keep the cost down, and
some of that cheese-paring was to cost hundreds of lives.
Although she could have been fitted with enough lifeboats for
everyone on board, and that was what the lifeboat contractor, Mr
Welin, advised, White Star saw this as an area where money could
be saved. Instead of stacking four lifeboats beside each pair of
davits (cranes for lowering lifeboats), White Star's executives
decided to place just one. Part of the executive's thinking on this
issue revolved around the watertight compartments. By fitting
numerous vertical bulkheads at intervals along the hull, they were
spending a good deal of money on making the *Titanic* unsinkable;
the ship was in herself a huge lifeboat. The executives may also
have thought that have all those lifeboats cluttering the decks
might send the wrong message to the passengers. Instead of
reassuring they might cause alarm.

On 10 April 1912, the great ship steamed slowly out of Southampton on the first leg of her maiden voyage. She crossed the English Channel first, to pick up more passengers at Cherbourg, then stopped at Cork to pick up some steerage passengers. One of the things that stood out about the *Titanic*'s first and last voyage, was her passenger list. At one end of the social scale, she was carrying half a dozen of the world's richest men; at the other, she was carrying some poverty-stricken migrants desperate to escape from poverty in Europe and find a better life in the New World. It was a complete cross section of society, a sort of floating metropolis.

Four days into the Atlantic crossing, with only another day to go, the ship was steaming at full speed through an icefield when she scraped an iceberg, which buckled, dented and twisted the plates for a long distance along her starboard side. Here again was a piece of irony. The lookouts in the crow's nest halfway up the forward mast did not have binoculars. There were binoculars on board, but the White Star Line did not give the crew enough time to familiarize themselves with the layout of the ship or its equipment before the voyage; and once the voyage had started there was no time. If the lookout had been supplied with binoculars he would almost certainly have seen the iceberg sooner, the order to turn the ship to avoid the collision would have been given sooner and the ship would have missed the iceberg altogether.

The avoiding action presented the side of the ship to the iceberg, which was the most dangerous thing of all to do. If the ship had hit the iceberg head on, obviously the lookout and the duty watch would have had many serious questions to answer, but only the foremost watertight compartment would have been flooded, and the *Titanic* would have remained afloat. As it was, several compartments were punctured and water poured into all of them. Exploration of the wreck has shown that there was not an open tear 200 feet long as was thought for a long time, but a lot of small punctures and leaks. The fact that the ship remained afloat for so long is explained by the slow leaking of several of the compartments. It is possible that if the ship had been fitted with more efficient pumps she might have been kept afloat for many hours, possibly long enough for her to reach New York, certainly long enough for the *Carpathia* to reach her and take the people off.

As it was, the forward compartments filled with water, and as they sank lower the water poured over the top of each bulkhead into the compartment behind. The ship's bow sank slowly under the water and the stern lifted slowly into the air. The lifeboats were lowered, some of them half-empty, and sent well away from the ship.

Meanwhile the captain, Captain Smith, ordered distress rockets to be fired, trying to attract the attention of a ship he could see, stopped, not many miles away. The other ship was almost certainly the *Californian*. Her radio operator had not long before started to send a message to the *Titanic*, to warn her about the ice, but unfortunately he opened in a rather chatty style and Phillips, the *Titanic's* chief radio operator, interrupted him. Evans opened with, 'Say old man we are surrounded by ice and stopped – ' But then Phillips told him to shut up as he was busy. Evans did as he was told and, at eleven-thirty pm, he listened in on the *Titanic*, as passengers' telegrams to New York were pouring out. Evans stopped eavesdropping and turned in at eleven thirty-five pm, just five minutes before the collision. If Evans had carried on listening for fifteen minutes, he would have picked up *Titanic's* first calls for help.

Other members of the *Californian's* crew saw the *Titanic* sailing along in the distance, though without recognizing who she was. Third Officer Groves saw her at eleven-forty pm and also saw that she had stopped, so he saw her just a minute or two after the collision. He thought he saw her lights go out, which is odd, because we know that the *Titanic's* lights stayed on for at least another hour. It may be that once the *Titanic* stopped steaming westwards across the Atlantic her sinking bow section was gradually turned by the current so that at a certain point the crew of the *Californian* were looking at her end-on and were no longer able to see the huge array of lights along her side. Captain Lord, the skipper of the *Californian*, took it into his head that the big ship was not a passenger steamer. Grove disagreed and said she was. Second Officer Stone, who came on duty at midnight, saw the distant lights of the mystery ship. He thought she was about five miles away. At twelve forty-five am, Stone saw the first of *Titanic*'s white distress rockets go up. He thought it was a shooting star. Then he saw four more, decided they were after all rockets, but did not make the obvious inference that the big steamer was in serious trouble. Stone spoke to Lord, who had gone to his cabin, through the speaking tube. He wasn't interested.

For whatever reason, Captain Lord of the *Californian* was not going to the aid of the *Titanic*. In the aftermath of the sinking, Lord denied that it was his ship that the *Titanic*'s officers could see, but his own evidence and that of his crew showed that they had watched the lights and distress rockets of the sinking liner. And if Lord, Stone and Groves were able to see the *Titanic*, the officers on the bridge of the *Titanic* could just as easily have seen the *Californian*. They were the only two ships in the area at the time. If the *Californian* had gone to *Titanic*'s aid, no one who had survived the initial collision need have died that night.

As the *Titanic* tipped up at a steeper and steeper angle, the passengers and crew gathering in the stern began to fall down, either onto the ship itself or into the sea.

The ship was lit up by its own lights from the bridge to the stern until very near the end, so the whole appalling spectacle was watched by the people in the boats. One American youth who managed to reach a lifeboat, Jack Thayer, said, 'We could see groups of the almost fifteen hundred people still aboard, clinging in clusters or bunches, like swarming bees; only to fall in masses, pairs or singly, as the great after part of the ship, two hundred and fifty feet of it, rose into the sky, till it reached a sixty-five or seventy degree angle.' Many people must have been killed in these falls. The strain amidships made the vessel bend and crack. The bow section finally broke away and sank, leaving the still buoyant stern section to settle back in the water for a few minutes until it too gradually filled with water and sank.

Captain Smith had tried to raise the attention of the *Californian*, with no result. His radio operators managed to raise a Cunard liner, the *Carpathia*, but she was too far away to reach the *Titanic* before she sank. The *Carpathia* reached the scene of the sinking at dawn, by which time all the people in the water were long dead, and some of those in the lifeboats had also died of hypothermia. Only 705 survivors were lifted aboard the *Carpathia*. They were in various states of shock. As one of the women said, 'We have watched our husbands die.'

If Captain Lord had steamed, even very slowly, to the *Titanic*'s aid, he could have reached her in half an hour and rescued everyone on board. The iceberg may have sunk the *Titanic*, but there were human factors that made the incident into a disaster. Lord's failure to go to the *Titanic*'s aid was responsible for the deaths of 1,500 people. But others were to blame too. The White Star executives, headed by Bruce Ismay, decided not to fit the ship with the sixty-four lifeboats recommended by Welin but a mere sixteen. It may have been Bruce Ismay who was to blame for the *Titanic*'s excessive speed. A conversation between Ismay and Captain Smith was overheard by a passenger in the dining room. Ismay was making it clear that he wanted *Titanic* to arrive in New York sooner rather than later. Smith himself would have needed little encouragement to steam at full pelt through the icefield. He looked like a safe pair of hands, but he was a risk-taker, a danger-ous driver. There had been several near misses in harbour with this ship or that, even with the *Titanic* on leaving port. He was a captain who liked to sail in style, make a big entrance or a swaggering exit. He steamed in and out of harbours far too fast. On the fatal night, he was going too fast in relation to the conditions – as usual. Whatever we say in criticism of Captain Lord, he at least had the sense to heave to when there was a lot of ice about, whereas Captain Smith sailed full steam ahead into the iceberg.

The effects and aftershocks of the *Titanic* disaster went on reverberating through the twentieth century. Safety procedures were overhauled. Lifeboat drills became mandatory on all voyages; from that time on, passengers and crew have always had to attend one lifeboat drill to make sure that everyone knows the way to the boat deck in an emergency. Inevitably the Board of Trade's rules on the provision of lifeboats were changed; from that time on, there had on every ship to be enough space in the lifeboats for everyone on board.

The *Titanic* disaster was presented by the popular press of the time as another epic tale of Anglo-Saxon heroism, just like the Birkenhead. The newspapers initially crowed that all the women and children had been saved; but they hadn't. The first-class women and children had been saved, but very few women and children travelling steerage class had been allowed anywhere near the lifeboats – they had been locked below decks until the last lifeboat had gone – and they had died. As time wore on, and the formal inquiries got under way, more and more stories of cowardice, inhumanity and folly emerged. Bruce Ismay was disgraced when it emerged that he had pulled rank in order to step into a lifeboat. There was evidently a lot wrong with the ship of fools that was western civilization. If the *Titanic* was a floating metropolis, a microcosm of western society, there was much to be remedied. Reaction to the *Titanic* disaster was an early shaking of the bars of nineteenth century complacency. It had begun with the suffragette movement and would soon be followed by the wrenching social changes brought about by the First World War. But certainly from 1912 on, the class system was perforated and slowly sinking.

Many of the survivors were pursued over the years for their versions of what had happened. Elizabeth Shutes was one of those who wrote down her reminiscence. She was a forty-year-old governess to Margaret Graham, a nineteen-year-old young woman who was traveling with her parents. Elizabeth was sitting in a first-class cabin with Margaret when they both felt the ship shuddering at its brush with the iceberg. At first Elizabeth believes the ship must be safe, but then becomes alarmed.

Suddenly a queer quivering ran under me, apparently the whole length of the ship. Startled by the very strangeness of the shivering motion, I sprang to the floor. With too perfect a trust in that mighty vessel I again lay down. Some one knocked at my door, and the voice of a friend said, 'Come quickly to my cabin; an iceberg has just passed our window. I know we have just struck one.'

No confusion, no noise of any kind, one could believe no danger imminent. Our stewardess came and said she could learn nothing. Looking out into the companionway I saw heads appearing asking questions from half-closed doors. All sepulchrally still, no excitement. I sat down again. My friend was by the time dressed; still her daughter and I talked on, Margaret pretending to eat a sandwich. Her hand shook so that the bread kept parting company from the chicken. Then I saw that she was frightened, and for the first time I was too, but why get dressed, as no one had given the slightest hint of any possible danger? An officer's cap passed the door. I asked. 'Is there an accident or danger of any kind?' 'None, so far as I know', was his courteous answer, spoken quietly and most kindly. This same officer then entered a cabin a little distance down the companionway and, by this time distrustful of everything, I listened intently, and distinctly heard, 'We can keep the water out for a while.' Then, and not until then, did I realize the horrro of an accident at sea. Now it was too late to dress; no time for a waist, but a coat and skirt were soon on; slippers were quicker than shoes; the stewardess put on our life-preservers, and we were just ready when Mr Roebling came to tell us he would take us to our friend's mother, who was waiting above.

No laughing throng, but on either side [of the stairs] stand quietly, bravely, the stewards, all equipped with the white, ghostly life-preservers. Always the thing one tries not to see even crossing a ferry. Now only pale faces, each form strapped about with those white bars. So gruesome a scene. We passed on. The awful goodbyes. The quiet look of hope in the brave men's eyes as the wives were put into the lifeboats. Nothing escaped one at this fearful moment. We left from the sun deck, seventy-five above the water. Mr Case and Mr Roebling, brave American men, saw us to the lifeboat, made no effort to save themselves, but stepped back on deck. Later they went to an honoured grave.

Our lifeboat, with thirty-six in it, began lowering into the sea. This was done amid the greatest confusion. Rough seamen all giving different orders. No officer aboard. As only one side of the ropes worked, the lifeboat at one time was in such a position that it seemed we must capsize in mid-air. At last the ropes worked together, and we drew nearer and nearer the black oily water. The first touch of our lifeboat on that black sea came to me as a last goodbye to life, and so we put off – a tiny boat on a great sea – rowed away from what had been a safe home for five days.

The first wish on the part of all was to stay near the Titanic. We all felt so much safer near the ship. Surely such a vessel could not sink. I thought the danger must be exaggerated, and we could all be taken aboard again. But surely the outline of that great, good ship was growing less. The bow of the boat was getting black. Light after light was disappearing, and now those rough seamen put to their oars and we were told to hunt under seats, any place, anywhere, for a lantern, a light of any kind. Every place was empty. There was no water – no stimulant of any kind. Not a biscuit – nothing to keep us alive, had we drifted long . . .

Sitting by me in the lifeboat were a mother and daughter. The mother had left a husband on the Titanic, *and the daughter a father and husband, and while we were near the other boats those two stricken women would call out a name and ask, 'Are you there?' 'No' would come back the awful answer, but these brave women never lost courage, forgot their own sorrow, telling me to sit close to them to keep warm. The life-preservers helped to keep us warm, but the night was bitter cold, and it grew colder and colder, and just before dawn, the coldest, darkest hour of all, no help seemed possible.*

The stars slowly disappeared. In their place came the faint pink glow of another day. Then I heard, 'A light, a ship.' I could not, would not look while there was a bit of doubt. All night long I had heard, 'A light!' Each time it proved to be one of our lifeboats, someone lighting a piece of paper, and now I could not believe. Someone found a newspaper; it was lighted and held up. Then I looked and saw a ship. A ship bright with lights; strong and steady she waited, and we were to be saved. A straw hat was offered, it would burn longer. That same ship that had come to save us might run us down. But no; she is still. The two, the ship and the dawn, came together, a living painting.

THE MOUNT KATMAI ERUPTION

(1912)

THE MOUNT KATMAI eruption on the Alaskan Peninsula was the biggest eruption of the twentieth century in North America, on a bigger scale than the Mont Pelée eruption, and ten times bigger than the 1980 eruption of Mount St Helens. It was a very violent eruption with a Volcanic Explosivity Index (VEI) of six. The ash flows from Katmai partly filled a valley close to the crater. It was fortunate that there were no large settlements in the vicinity; if there had been, thousands of people might have been killed. In fact, it is useful to imagine what the effect would have been if Katmai had been on Manhattan Island. The whole of Greater New York would have been covered in between ten and fifteen feet of ash. Even far-off Philadelphia would have been covered with a foot of ash, and plunged in total darkness for three days. Washington and Buffalo would have been coated with one-quarter of an inch of ash. The deafening roar of the explosive eruption would have been heard in Atlanta and St Louis. The fumes would have been smelt in Jamaica. As it was, this colossal eruption happened safely in an almost completely uninhabited wilderness.

The eruption of the Novarupta volcano dramatically changed the physical geography of the Katmai area. As is usual with major volcanic eruptions, the eruption itself was preceded by a sequence of earthquakes. The several days of premonitory earthquakes prompted fishermen to evacuate a fishing camp twenty miles to the south of Katmai. Then Novarupta violently exploded with what is called a Plinian eruption, in other words throwing up an ash column like the one thrown up by Vesuvius in AD 79; vast quantities of red-hot pumice and ash were thrown out of Novarupta and cracks in the rock opened around it.

The people of Kodiak, 100 miles away, were among the first Alaskans to observe and experience the eruption. A heavy blanket of ash fell on the town, which created a great deal of fear and concern about what was to follow; no one knew where the ash had come from. It was six-thirty pm on 6 June, at the start of what should have been a long, light summer evening, and yet the town had been plunged into total darkness. At the same time, lightning struck Kodiak's radio station. The station went up in flames and there was no further contact with the outside world.

Following the eruption of the ash column, a huge sheet of lava poured fifteen miles across the landscape, destroying all the vegetation; trees were snapped off and reduced to charcoal by blasts of scalding gases. The pyroclastic flows consisted of eleven cubic miles of lava, and they filled the valley next to Novarupta; this would become the valley with all the steam vents that is now known as the Valley of Ten Thousand Smokes. The eruption of ash, pumice and gas from the main vent of Novarupta went on for several days, creating a haze that darkened the sky over most of the Northern Hemisphere. At Kodiak, close to Katmai, people could not see a lighted lantern held only two feet away.

The 1912 eruption of Katmai eruption, the largest in North America in the twentieth century, continued for three days, 6-8 June 1912, and in that short space of time over seven cubic miles of material were ejected. After the main eruption ended, the main inner vent was plugged by a lava dome, in itself a large-scale landscape feature 1,300 feet across and more than 200 feet high. The main vent of Novarupta is well preserved, in spite of the formation of a caldera. It seems that the magma chamber was complicated in shape and consisted of a system of interconnected fissures and caverns. The emptying of the magma chamber via the Novarupta vent led Mount Katmai, about seven miles away, to collapse into the magma chamber beneath it, forming a caldera, a large depression now partly filled by a lake. The Katmai caldera is one of the most complicated and chaotic volcanic landscapes on the planet; it is still, almost a century afterwards, a scene of incredible desolation.

As the third day of the eruption began, the people in Kodiak was still living in a volcanic night. Ash went on falling on the town and there were frequent earthquakes. In the afternoon, Captain Perry of the US Revenue Cutter *Manning* decided it would be best to evacuate the residents of Kodiak. He was apprehensive that in the darkness he might lose his way; there was only a narrow navigable channel out of the harbour. Even so, he thought the risk of going aground was preferable to staying in Kodiak, which could face destruction. Several hundred Kodiak residents embarked on the *Manning*. It was uncomfortable, but it seemed the safest option; everyone thought of Pompeii. In fact the main eruption sequence was almost over and Kodiak was spared destruction. Once the ash was cleared, life in Kodiak quickly returned to normal.

Comparisons have been made between the Katmai eruption of 1912 and the bronze age eruption of Santorini. Although the two eruptions were similar in size and scale, there were important differences. Katmai took place on dry land, with the Novarupta vent located about 3,000 feet above sea level, whereas at Santorini the eruption was at sea level, with the sea itself playing a major role. The Santorini eruption also completely annihilated the pre-existing central volcanic cones and vents, whereas at Katmai the Novarupta survived the caldera collapse. There were more than forty pyroclastic flows in the Minoan eruption, only one big one at Katmai, the flow that filled the Valley of Ten Thousand Smokes.

When the eruption ended, the full effects of the cataclysm were plain to see. Over forty square miles of what had been green and vegetated landscape were buried under volcanic debris, which in places lay as much as 700 feet deep, giving an idea of the huge scale of the eruption. The acid rain caused by the eruption made people's clothes disintegrate far away at Vancouver in Canada. In the Ukak and Knife Creek valleys, a lot of cracks opened up in the volcanic deposits, releasing columns of gas and steam from the heated groundwater. These steam emissions continued long after the eruption was over. Robert Griggs explored the area in 1916 for the National Geographic Society, and he was amazed at the otherworldly landscape, riddled by thousands of steam vents. It was Griggs who named it The Valley of Ten Thousand Smokes. A huge quantity of ash was ejected by Katmai, a total of seven cubic miles of it, all thrown out in the space of only three days. The ash was deposited in a layer at least half an inch thick across an area of 46,000 square miles; thinner sprinklings covered an even bigger area.

The area is an incredible wilderness and has become the largest of the national monuments of the United States. It has not been a quiet place since the big eruption of 1912. There were minor eruptions of uncertain location in 1914, 1920, 1921, 1929 and 1931, and these are thought to have been at Katmai.

Clouds of fine ash from the eruption travelled around the world, reducing the value of solar radiation measured in Algeria by twenty per cent. This was the last major ash eruption until the Pinatubo eruption, and from 1912 onwards global atmospheric temperatures were to drift upwards. There were minor ash eruptions (Mount Spurr near Anchorage in Alaska in 1953, Kamchatka in 1956), but these had little effect. The eruptions of Mount Trident near Katmai in 1963 and Agung on Bali, also in 1963, may have contributed to a marked global cooling phase in the mid-1960s. The Agung eruption sent ash right across the Pacific Ocean, darkening the skies of Colorado with a dust veil fifteen miles up several months later.

The eruption of Katmai in 1912 was a great natural cataclysm that traumatized and transformed the landscape. If it had

ABOVE: *A skeleton encased in volcanic ash. This person was one of the victims of the eruption of Mount Vesuvius, which buried the Roman city of Herculaneum in AD 79.*

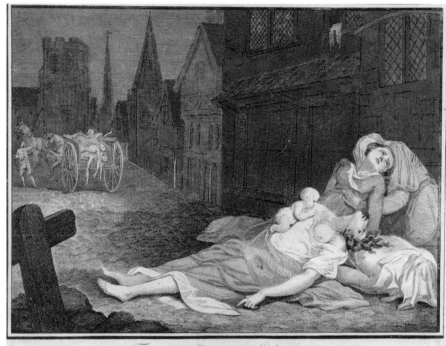

The Dreadful Plague in London, 1665.

ABOVE: *An etching of the dreadful plague in London in 1665. A family lies dead and dying in the street while a cart carries away corpses of those who have already succumbed to the plague.*

VIEW OF THE TAY BRIDGE BEFORE THE ACCIDENT.

VIEW OF THE TERRIBLE RAILWAY ACCIDENT AT TAY BRIDGE ON DEC. 28.

ABOVE: *December 28 1879 – The original Tay Railway Bridge before a section collapsed whilst a train was crossing it.*

BELOW: *The scene of the disaster, showing the locomotive plunging into the Firth of Tay estuary. About seventy-five passengers were killed.*

From an etching in the 'Christian Herald and Signs of Our Times'

ABOVE: *April 14 1912: Survivors of the* Titanic *disaster nearing the* Carpathia, *in a lifeboat. The arrow points to Joseph Bruce Ismay, chairman of the White Star Line.*

ABOVE: *October 21 1966: Rescue workers continue their search for victims of the Aberfan disaster, in South Wales, where 190 people lost their lives after part of the village school was engulfed by a giant coal slag heap.*

ABOVE: *Rescue workers use cranes in the search for survivors in the remains of a collapsed building in Mexico City. An earthquake registering 8.1 on the Richter scale hit central Mexico on September 19 1985 causing damage to about 500 buildings in Mexico City and killing over 8,000 people.*

ABOVE: *26 December 2004: Disaster struck just after dawn as a huge earthquake in Indonesia sent tsunamis crashing westwards, sweeping men, women and children out to sea. Although initial estimates have put the worldwide death toll at over 275,000 with thousands of others missing, recent analysis compiled lists a total of 229,866 people lost, including 186,983 dead and 42,883 still missing.*

ABOVE: *Eighty-year-old Yang Changdi shows the devastation from the drought on August 28, 2006 at Shuangshi Town, Chongqing, China. At least 14 million people and 15 million livestock are suffering from a shortage of drinking water as continuous droughts and searing heat ravage western China. The hardest hit area is Chongqing Municipality in Southwest China, which is being plagued by its severest drought in fifty years. It has had no rain for more than seventy consecutive days and two-thirds of the rivers have dried up.*

happened anywhere near a city, the eruption was certainly powerful enough to destroy and bury it – in fact just as the bronze age eruption of Santorini had done. It was very fortunate that the 1912 eruption happened in a remote location on the Alaska Peninsula, in a deserted region far from any major centre of population. Not one person was killed.

THE SPANISH FLU PANDEMIC

(1918-19)

THE INFLUENZA EPIDEMIC of 1918–19 was responsible for more deaths than the First World War. The death toll from this influenza outbreak was between twenty and a hundred million. It is thought to have been the most destructive and devastating epidemic in the history of the world, including the infamous Black Death in the fourteenth century. More people died of influenza in one year of Spanish flu than in four years of the Black Death between 1347 and 1351.

The virulent strain of influenza was nicknamed 'Spanish flu' or 'La Grippe', but its effects went far beyond the frontiers of Spain or France. It was a global disaster. The reason why it was so lethal is that it was a new strain of influenza. A population can develop a resistance to a strain of influenza, but that takes time. Just like any other species, human beings are very vulnerable to new strains of viruses.

In the autumn of 1918, the First World War was drawing to a close as the influenza outbreak began. Initially it seemed no more serious than the common cold; then people failed to recover from it. Today, when people contract influenza they expect to recover, but the Spanish flu had a mortality rate between two and three per cent. Another peculiarity of the Spanish flu was its sheer speed and virulence. People literally dropped in the streets and died soon afterwards. It was said that four women played bridge together late into the night, and by morning three of them were dead. Other stories told of people falling ill on their way to work and dying before nightfall. The epidemic acquired its own folklore – and even its own children's skipping rhyme.

> *I had a little bird:*
> *Its name was Enza.*
> *I opened the window,*
> *And in flew Enza.*

Doctors treating the illness commented that their patients developed an extreme form of pneumonia, struggling for air until they suffocated.

Many diseases produce higher casualties among the very young or the very old, those who are naturally vulnerable. The Spanish flu virus was unusual in producing the highest casualties among young adults. It spread and spread for two years, infecting one-fifth of the world's population. Twenty-eight per cent of all Americans contracted the virus. Of the American soldiers who died in Europe, only half fell to enemy fire, the other half to influenza. The task of defeating the Germans gave way to a desperate attempt to fight the virus; emergency field hospitals were set up to treat stricken soldiers.

The Spanish flu pandemic had serious demographic effects; the average life span in the United States was reduced by ten years. It spread from country to country, affecting every continent. In India the death rate was unusually high at five per cent. The First World War is believed to have played a major part in the spread of the influenza, with its large-scale and long-distance movements of troops. Its actual origin was unknown, but there was endless speculation about it. One explanation circulated among the British and Americans was that the pandemic was a fiendish weapon of biological warfare dreamed up by the Germans. Many thought it was a direct result of the general air pollution involved in the fighting: smoke, fumes and chlorine. Climatic and racial explanations were explored. One positive result of the pandemic was that it accelerated the new science of immunology; there was enormous pressure to produce a vaccine against the deadly virus.

It is probable that the Spanish flu had its ultimate origins in the Far East, and more specifically in China. The virus acquired its name from the early appearance of the virus in Spain and the large number of casualties there; as many as eight million people died in Spain in May 1918. But it appeared even earlier at Fort Riley in Kansas, where forty-eight soldiers died of it, and then in other US military camps. Instead of containing the outbreak at Fort Riley, as would probably have happened in peacetime, infected soldiers from Fort Riley were shipped to Europe to fight. That troop movement was intended to help the Allies to win the war, but it also infected the whole of Europe.

It is also probable that it represented a genetic shift of the influenza virus. Recently the virus has been reconstructed from the body tissue of a dead soldier and the characteristics of its genes are being analyzed. Obviously we need to understand what this mysterious illness really was and how it developed, in order to deal with any future outbreak. It looks from the pattern of incidence as if not enough was done to acknowledge or respond to the virus during the first few months, and that this negligence led to the spread of the virus all around the world. In the midst of the horrors of the First World War, it was easy to overlook an outbreak of influenza; there seemed to be more serious matters to worry about. But failing to deal with the early cases in the spring meant that by the autumn there were huge increases in the numbers of reported cases as the winter weather set in.

The ending of the war brought about a large-scale return home of troops and there was a large-scale explosion of influenza. In October 1918, 200,000 Americans died. The strain on the medical profession was enormous. In the United States, the Red Cross recruited many more volunteers to fight the epidemic, pleading with businesses to allow workers to have a day off so that they could serve a night shift in the hospitals. There was a shortage of coffins and gravediggers.

One-quarter of the people in the United States caught the virus, including President Woodrow Wilson, while he was negotiating the Treaty of Versailles in early 1919. But the timing of the pandemic, at the close of the Great War, also had some benefits. It was a moment when nationalism was very strongly felt and people were ready to accept government authority; they were prepared to obey instructions from public health departments and accept restrictions. In the United States, public gatherings of all kinds, even in bars and saloons, were banned. Handshakes became illegal. Funerals were not allowed to go on for more than fifteen minutes. There was some high-profile flouting of the regulations, such as the organization of a rally of 200,000 people to sell war bonds in San Francisco. The authorities advised against it, but it went ahead and there were 12,000 deaths from 'the Spanish Lady', possibly as a result of that gathering. But on the whole people accepted the extraordinary restrictions. They were also conditioned to face a new emergency calmly, without panic. The war had given developments in science and technology a high profile and created a range of more flexible social attitudes. But there was also a resurgence of sheer old-fashioned super-stition; one recommended remedy was to tie a red ribbon around your right arm.

In recent years, scientists have re-examined the Spanish flu pandemic and concluded that it was a form of avian influenza, similar to the recent bird flu outbreak in the Far East. The virus in other words jumped from birds to people. The key stage is for the flu virus to attach itself to cells in which it can breed. To do this it uses molecules called Haemaglutinins (HA) to bind to receptors on the cell surface. Human and bird virus HAs interact with different cell receptors, so bird viruses usually cannot infect people. But recent analysis of the 1918 virus shows that only tiny changes in its HA structure were needed to turn it from a bird virus to a human virus, and those changes were all that were needed to allow the virus to cause the devastating human pandemic.

This is an interesting proposition, and worrying in its implication that the current avian flu outbreak could, unless it is contained, wipe out huge numbers of people. With modern air travel and much greater mobility generally, viruses can be spread very quickly all around the world, even faster than in 1918. It is unfortunately still impossible to prevent viruses from crossing from one species to another, but at least an awareness of the mechanism may alert people to what is happening earlier in any future outbreak. Apart from its obviously horrific death toll, perhaps the most alarming aspects of the Spanish flu pandemic were the suddenness of the outbreak and the speed with which it was able to spread. In just one year, this latter-day plague – because that is what it was – had swept right around the world, scything down as many as fifty million people; it became, in that short space of time, the greatest natural disaster of the twentieth century.

THE HAIG PIT DISASTER

(1922)

IT WAS FIVE AM on 5 September 1922 at the Haig Pit, Whitehaven, a coal mine in the small Cumbrian coalfield in north-west England. The man in charge of the Six Quarters Seam that day was William Weightman, and he was just starting his shift. His report book revealed that gas had been noticed in the previous few days in one area of the mine, the North District, but when Weightman went to check it seemed to be clear. The men went to work as usual. At seven am, a shot firer called Brewster went down and made his way to the North District to join Weightman.

Then, just before nine am, the Banksman, Alexander Pitblade, saw a cloud of dust erupting from the Number Four Shaft. Robert Steel, the agent, was informed. Steel called the Mines Rescue and then set off for the Haig Pit with Mr Cook the Inspector of Mines to find out what had happened. Clearly there had been an explosion.

When the explosion happened, a rope splicer called Trevaskis and Millar, the under-manager, were underground and standing near the compressor house. They were knocked over by the blast, which came from the North District. Trevaskis broke some ribs. Millar was unhurt and went to see what had happened. He came across the first dead body, a nineteen year old called Thomas Telford, who had been thrown with great force against the side wall of the drift (one of the narrow low-roofed horizontal passages in the mine). Over in the South-west District, the miners knew there had been an explosion and made their way out to safety. When Steel, Cook and others arrived, they heard Millar shouting for help. They found him almost unconscious about 360 feet along the drift and dragged him back. The search was resumed, and a hewer called William Carter was found dying under empty tubs that had been derailed.

Cook and Steel continued to the Six Quarters Junction. The air there was full of what was called afterdamp, which consisted mainly of carbon monoxide, and a white vapour. Cook and Steel came to the conclusion that everyone in the area close to the explosion must be dead. Millar, Steel and Brodie were all taken back up to the surface suffering from the effects of the poisonous fumes and taken to hospital. There were to be no further attempts at rescue until the air in the mine was improved. Trevaskis was also brought out and gradually recovered in bed at home; a reporter from the local newspaper visited him for an eyewitness account of the disaster but was unable to get anything coherent out of him.

By the afternoon, the air was breathable and the rescue team moved in, recovering dead bodies and making repairs as they went. There was still carbon monoxide in the air and many of the rescuers had to be helped back to the surface, some unconscious. By the following morning, twenty-five bodies had been recovered. There were more men in the mine, but their bodies were buried under roof falls, and they were not brought out for another four days.

The scene at the pithead was the usual one at mine disasters. There were clusters of relatives, waiting for news. There were women with babies in their arms and small children clinging to their skirts, women with taut, anxious faces, fathers waiting quietly for news of sons. In an outbuilding at the pit, the dead were laid out for identification. Relatives, many of them women, were ushered in to look at the bodies to see whether they could identify husbands, fathers, brothers. It was his father who identified the body of Thomas Telford. Efforts were made to spare the feelings of relatives by making the dead look as respectable as possible, but with some of the injuries that was difficult. Thomas Corlett was identifiable only by his trousers and belt; his face was unrecognizable.

Several of the victims of the pit disaster came from Thwaiteville, a poor little colony of army huts where the colliery employees lived. The sense of loss there was overwhelming.

The inquest was opened in the power house at the pit, with the bodies kept in the cellars below. The dead were formally identified by name. The verdict was that the victims had been killed by carbon monoxide poisoning, burns, shock or 'violence of the explosion'. In all, thirty-nine men had died.

At a point along the drift known as Moore's Place, Weightman and Brewster had evidently ignited a 'shot', a small controlled explosion to loosen the coal at a coal face to make the job of hewing the coal easier, and this had released a pocket of gas. The gas had ignited, causing a much bigger explosion. Questions were raised at the inquiry about the powerful emission of firedamp (methane, the natural gas released from the coal seam) that was found leaking from the fissure at Moore's Place. Had Weightman and Brewster taken an unnecessary risk at a dangerous coalface? On balance it was thought that the two men would not have fired shots into a coal face if they had any suspicion that there was a pocket of methane behind it. They were just unlucky.

A boy called Joyce had a very lucky escape. He happened to be using the telephone in a manhole on the main road (one of the drifts or galleries in the mine), at the moment when the blast of the explosion ripped past him. If he had been out in the drift he would certainly have died. A Mayor's Fund was set up to help to 'place the relatives beyond the reach of poverty'. Money poured in from all over Great Britain. A woman in Scotland who had lost her two sons in the First World War sent a letter and twenty shillings (one pound), because her dead sons had the same names as the two McCreadie brothers who died in the explosion, Gordon and Robert. The McCreadie boys' father George also died in the disaster, so there was one poor woman living in a hut in Thwaiteville who had to cope with the loss of a husband and two sons, and somehow carry on supporting five surviving children.

THE GREAT KANTO EARTHQUAKE

(1923)

JAPAN HAS A long history of earthquake disasters. It sits right on the edge of one tectonic plate, while another, on the Pacific Ocean side, dips underneath it, scraping against its under side and generating earthquakes as it does so. There are many earth tremors every year. Occasionally there is a large earthquake. Very large earthquakes are very infrequent. The one that struck in 1923 was one of the most destructive earthquakes Japan has ever experienced.

Just two minutes before midday on 1 September 1923, an earthquake struck Honshu, the main island of Japan. It was a very violent earthquake, measuring between 7.9 and 8.4 on the Richter scale, and its epicentre was close enough to the big industrial cities of Tokyo and Yokohama to do great damage. The epicentre was in Sagami Bay, just to the south-west of Tokyo Bay. The initial shock was followed by hundreds of much smaller after-shocks, and one big aftershock, during the following few days.

The Great Kanto earthquake, named after the district of Japan that includes Tokyo, was by no means the biggest earthquake to strike Japan, but it struck a particularly sensitive area where the population density was very high. The total population of the area affected by the earthquake was two million. The death toll was therefore inevitably very high; an estimated 142,000 people died. Of these, 104,000 are known to have died, and the rest were missing after the disaster. The economic cost was very high too, because the main business and industrial districts of Tokyo were destroyed.

In 1923, thousands of Japanese homes had open fires for heating, gas ranges for cooking, and the houses themselves, if of traditional design, were made of wood and paper. As buildings collapsed, they caught fire. The chemicals used in the industrial district and explosions at a munitions factory naturally created further fires. Tokyo's firefighters were well-trained and prepared, but the pace at which the fire spread made it impossible for them to keep up with it. Their task was made even harder by the fracturing of most of the water mains, which meant there was no water for the firefighter's hoses.

The fire burned fiercely, fanned by strong winds, consuming all the available oxygen and flammable materials. Where it burned most ferociously, no living thing survived the intense heat and the lack of oxygen. The hot air rose in strong updrafts, generating tornadoes. The fire left thousands of people homeless. In Tokyo, fires in the Honjo and Fukagawa districts cut 40,000 people off, surrounded them like a predatory beast and closed in. They fled to an open space at Rikugun Homjo Hifukushu, which looked large enough to give them a safe refuge. But the fire was burning so fiercely that even there they were engulfed by the firestorm; a cyclone of superheated air swept through the area, incinerating them all where they stood.

The actual earth movement itself did a significant amount of damage. Houses were demolished by it; some large fissures in the ground were opened up; roads and railways were displaced by several yards; the statue of the Great Buddha at Kamakura was shunted off its foundations. But the fire that followed did far more damage. Natural gas pipelines were disrupted and the leaking gas caught fire. Domestic fires and cooking ranges created hundreds of small fires, which quickly spread across the densely packed cities of Tokyo and Yokohama.

The Kanto earthquake proved to be a disaster on the grand

scale. It lasted a mere six minutes, but in that time an incredible amount of damage was done: the fires it initiated went on for much longer. Of the twelve million people living in the Kanto district, over two million lost their homes, 52,000 were injured and 104,000 are known for certain to have been killed; another 37,000 were unaccounted for and it must be assumed that they too died. In the two main cities, the damage was on an appalling scale. In Tokyo, seventy-one per cent of the people lost their homes to the earthquake and fire; in Yokohama eighty-six per cent The damage to property was estimated to be five billion (1923) US dollars. The scale of destruction was extremely severe in the residential areas that were built in traditional style, mainly of wood. There were public parks and open areas, but they were very small by comparison with the open spaces in British cities. As a result there were no real firebreaks, and no refuges where people go to escape from the fire. Some people did find safety. Those who gathered in the grounds of the Russian Orthodox Cathedral in Kanda survived, as did the church itself.

In the rural areas, there was more open space and it was easier for people to get away from falling buildings. It was also harder for fires to spread. In consequence, fewer buildings were destroyed and fewer people were killed. Altogether only 12,000 died in the rural areas. But there were other hazards in the countryside. In the hills and mountains of western Kanagawa prefecture, several landslides triggered by the earthquake swept houses away and caused 800 deaths. At the railway station at the village of Nebukawa, west of Odawara, a landslide on the mountain side pushed a passing train with over 100 people on board down into the sea – along with the railway station and the village.

The earthquake, with its epicentre in Sagami Bay, shook the seabed and within minutes tsunamis reached the coast of Honshu, hitting the shores of Sagami Bay, Boso Peninsula and the Izu Islands. The tsunamis were up to thirty feet high, big enough to do serious damage. About 100 people were killed along Yui-gahama beach and another fifty were swept to their death on the Enoshima causeway.

The task of rebuilding after the Great Kanto earthquake was a huge one, yet it went at enormous speed. Unfortunately, the extensive damage was not seen as an opportunity to rebuild more spaciously, with adequate firebreaks and refuges. The pre-existing pattern of the narrow streets was reproduced. The high-density buildings were replaced. Even the same flammable materials were used. The Tokyo authorities built a new city that was just as vulnerable to earthquake disaster as the old. What was not foreseen was that the Second World War would intervene and that enemy bombers would reproduce artificially many of the effects of the Great Kanto earthquake.

THE TRI-STATE
TORNADO

(1925)

ONE OF THE worst tornadoes of the twentieth century hit Ellington, Missouri, on 18 March 1925. It was in the middle of the day, at 1 pm, that the tornado started. It began with trees rocking and swaying until branches snapped off, and it became gradually more severe.

A tornado is a column of air in the lower atmosphere that rotates at very high speed. The bottom touches the ground, where it sucks up dust and debris like a powerful vacuum cleaner, while the top is connected to the base of a big storm cloud. Tornadoes come in a variety of shapes. Some are thin and snake-like; some are funnel or cone shaped; some are ill-defined, in effect shapeless. Usually the base of the tornado is surrounded by a cloud of dust. The rotating winds are usually 80–110 mph. Usually the destruction path is about 250 feet across and only a few miles long. Occasionally, a tornado exceeds these expectations, and the tornado that struck the Midwest in March 1925 certainly did that.

The Tri-state tornado set records in US history for wind speed and for the length of its destruction path. It was not just Ellington that suffered: the tornado crossed fourteen counties in three states, though Illinois suffered most. The tornado travelled in a straight line for 183 miles of its 219-mile path, from west-south-west to east-north-east. It followed a low ridge across the land-scape, on which a series of mining towns stood.

The very long destruction path, 219 miles, has been questioned by some modern climatologists, who wonder if the so-called Tri-state tornado (ie it affected three states in the United States) was one tornado or several separate tornadoes. They argue that without a modern damage survey, which would link the damage pattern into a continuous line it is not possible to be sure that it was a single tornado. If they are right and the Tri-state tornado was more than one tornado, the longest destruction known modern-day destruction path was 160 miles in north-east Carolina on 22 November 1992. It seems to me that it is fair to assume that it was a single tornado; there was so much damage reported along a single straight line, and the description of the tornado's character was fairly consistent – especially its speed.

A tornado has two speeds: one is the speed with which the column of wind rotates around its axis, and the other is the speed at which the whole system moves across the landscape. With a hurricane, the rotating wind may be 150 mph, while the weather system as a whole advances at 10 mph, slow enough to cycle away from it. This tornado moved across the land at a dangerous 62 mph (on average), which meant that there was very little warning of its approach and very little prospect of getting away from it.

The line of mining towns looked like the tornado's targets. Between the towns of Gorham and Murphysboro, the tornado shifted along at a record speed of 73 mph. Often a tornado has a well-defined central funnel, visible because of the dust sucked up from ground level, but this one had no clearly defined funnel. Rather oddly, in spite of this lack of visual definition, for at least half of its length the width of the destruction path was very uniform at just under one mile across.

The tornado's career began at 1 o'clock, when it touched down three miles west of Ellington, Missouri. After damaging some trees, it killed a farmer. The ill-defined funnel was very wide, really the width of two tornadoes, and it had the strength of two tornadoes. When it hit the town of Annapolis it brought a downpour of rain. Tornadoes are sometimes accompanied by heavy rain, sometimes not, and this tornado was intermittent: the rain switched on and off. It also hit two miles south of another town, Leadanna. Two people were killed and seventy-five were injured in the Annapolis–Leadanna area; 500,000 dollars' worth of damage was done. The tornado passed through Iron and Madison Counties, but no one was injured there.

Five miles south of Fredericktown, the damage done by the high winds was intensified by an added heavy downpour of rain. Once the tornado left the Ozark Hills and moved out across the agricultural plains of Bollinger and Perry Counties, the tornado started injuring and killing more people. Five miles outside Altenburg in Perry County, a child was killed at a rural school. Thirty-two children were injured at two schools in Bollinger County. Altogether thirteen people died in Missouri.

The level of destruction peaked in the state of Illinois. Thirty-four people died at Gorham, seven of them students in the school, as virtually the entire town was destroyed. The tornado was not just a spiralling cone of air: there was a lot of debris in it as well. People who are caught outside in tornadoes are hit by all this flying debris, and the injuries they suffer are terrible. Even the toughest farmers in the Midwest are frightened of tornadoes. Being indoors is safer, but tornadoes can easily demolish the traditional wooden houses, and many are injured or killed when their houses collapse on them.

At Murphysboro, 234 people died. This is the largest number of people to have been killed in one settlement by a tornado in American history. Surprisingly, twenty-five of these deaths were in three different schools, all built of brick and stone. Unfortunately, they were not reinforced with steel frames. As in an earthquake, when an unreinforced brick building is rocked, shaken or vibrated by a tornado, the mortar bond is broken and the walls turn into a heap of bricks. The children who died at the three schools in Murphysboro were buried and crushed under falling brick walls.

At the town of Desoto, another sixty-nine people died, thirty-three of them at the school. Parrish too was destroyed, and twenty-two of its inhabitants were killed. At West Frankfort, 800 miners were trapped 500 feet down a mine shaft when the tornado hit and cut off their electricity supply. Fortunately there was a narrow escape tunnel. When they eventually got out, they found that most of their homes had been demolished by the tornado. Some of them found that their wives and children were dead: 127 died and 450 were injured there. The farmers of Hamilton and White county, like farmers everywhere, were normally very good at sensing the approach of bad weather, but this time they were caught out. The tornado's forward movement was so fast that there was no chance of forecasting the tornado from the ground. The farmers were taken completely by surprise as the tornado bore down on them like a speeding car.

Still the tornado had no visible funnel, which made it identifiable (to anyone) as a tornado. At some points the funnel form did exist, but it was impossible to see it clearly because of the chaotic cloud of debris and dust around it. It just appeared over the horizon as an anonymous blurred boiling mass of clouds. In Indiana, it was occasionally possible to see several funnels at once, still within the one-mile wide destruction path. The structure of this tornado must have been incredibly complex. Over seventy people were killed in Indiana. In the town of Griffin, 150 houses were destroyed and children died on their way home from school. There was more destruction out in the countryside between Griffin and Princeton, where eighty-five farms were laid waste. Half of Princeton was destroyed.

The tornado of March 1925 was one of the most violent and most destructive tornadoes in American history. It happened at a time of year that normally marks the start of what is called the tornado season, from March to November. They have a tendency to happen in the afternoons or early evenings, mainly because it is the sun heating the ground that generates the convection currents that build the cumulo-nimbus clouds above the tornadoes. The afternoon occurrence of this big tornado was therefore also typical.

One of the problems with tornadoes is to do with our perception of them. They are spectacular, and therefore attract enormous attention. As a result, they sometimes attract some over-enthusiastic and sometimes sensational journalism. This can result in what are called 'weather wars', in which competing radio and TV stations, or local newspapers, try to outbid one another in their reporting, especially in the Great Plains of the Midwest. The major tornado described here was genuinely destructive, as we can see from the alarming death tolls at town after town, but all too often the significance of a tornado is exaggerated in the press. The chances of being killed by a tornado, if you live in North America, are twelve million to one; in other words, there is very little likelihood of being killed.

THE GROS VENTRE
LANDSLIDE

(1925)

IT IS HARD to think of a simpler type of natural disaster than a landslide. A steep slope becomes unstable, either because of undercutting at its toe by an erosion process like wave attack, or because it becomes saturated after a long period of rain. Then gravity takes over and the slope fails. The material the slope is made of collapses and creates a gentler, more stable slope. Landslides are much commoner in wild and sparsely settled mountain country, though just occasionally they happen in towns.

The Gros Ventre Wilderness is part of the Bridger-Teton National Forest in Wyoming, USA. It contains the site of the Gros Ventre landslide, about seven miles east of Jackson Hole Valley and the Grand Teton National Park.

The landslide, which happened on 23 June 1925, following several weeks of heavy rain, formed a huge natural dam more than 200 feet high and 1,200 feet wide across the Gros Ventre Valley. Water ponded back behind the barrier to form a new lake, called Lower Slide Lake. The landslide involved the collapse of fifty million cubic yards of rock, which slid down the steep north slope of Sheep Mountain to the bottom of the valley, and crossed the path of the Gros Ventre River. The slope failure left a huge semicircular scar 600 feet high on the north side of Sheep Mountain. The momentum of the landslide was so great that it continued up the valley side opposite for a distance of 300 feet.

The natural dam across the river was only made of loose

material, and two years later, on 16 May 1927, part of the dam collapsed. This released a huge amount of water stored in Lower Slide Lake, and flooded the valley for at least twenty-five miles to a depth of six feet. This second disaster was in its way more catastrophic than the landslide, because it destroyed the small town of Kelly six miles away and six people were killed there.

The landslide was a major landscape event in its own right. It is the largest landslide known in American history, and one of the largest mass movement events apart from those produced by volcanic eruptions. Slide Lake is now much smaller than before the 1927 flood, but still an important tourist attraction for fishing and boating. The landslide has been partially overgrown by the surrounding forest, but it is still a very obvious landform and can be seen from many viewpoints in the Jackson Hole Valley.

THE ERUPTION OF MAUNA LOA

(1926)

MAUNA LOA IS an active shield volcano in the Hawaiian Islands, one of the five volcanoes that make up the island of Hawaii itself. Mauna Loa has the distinction of being the biggest mountain on the planet, with a volume of 18,000 cubic miles and built up from the ocean floor. The Hawaiian volcanoes are noted for their quiet, harmless eruptions. The basic lava flows long distances before solidifying, so the slopes are gentle and the vents are usually left clear; there are no destructively violent explosions.

On 10 April 1926, the Mauna Loa volcano erupted, after an hour of warning earthquakes. The eruption started at the summit, but gradually migrated down towards a rift zone on the south-west side. The initial eruption fissure extended three miles along this crack, ejecting flows of silvery pahoehoe lava south-westwards towards Hilea. The opening phase of the eruption was witnessed by Edwin Wingate, a geographer who happened to be mapping the volcano for the US Geological Survey.

The eruption continued for three days, when a set of earthquakes marked the start of a change in activity. The focus of the eruption was shifting further down the south-west rift zone. On 14 April, three vents formed at an altitude of 8,000 feet, just to the east of the vents created in the 1919 eruption. The fissure was now several miles long and it began to look as if the massive lava flows would head for the settlement of Waiohinu. One of them did indeed advance towards Waiohinu but only slowly, and it stopped on 24 April before reaching it. Another lava flow moved rapidly towards the sea at Hoopuloa, and there on 18 April it destroyed a tiny village consisting of twelve houses and a church. That flow stopped on 19 April. Another parallel flow advanced along the side of it, still fed by lava pouring out of the six-mile long fissure.

The main lava eruption sequence was over by 26 April, though smoke and fumes continued to pour from the lower vents for another week. The eruption had added 150 million cubic yards of lava to the island of Hawaii, reshaping over thirteen square miles of landscape.

Mauna Loa was very active between 1850 and 1950. Lava from the volcano's south-west rift flowed all the way to the ocean in 1868, 1877, 1919, 1926 and 1950. Eruptions in 1916 and 1907 threatened south Kona, and in the 1907 eruption a lava flow cut across the road. These eruptions caused only a small amount of disruption, but if they were repeated today they would cause much more severe dislocation because communications would be interrupted.

This part of the island has steep slopes, encouraging the lava to flow fast. In 1926, the lava flows took about four days to reach the sea, but in 1950, one flow reached the sea within three hours. Today, Mauna Loa is monitored with a set of seismometers, and the changing shape of the volcano is measured to detect the shifting lava as it wells up inside it. This is a volcano that is well worth monitoring because it is very active. The rest periods between eruptions are usually less than eight years, so the current quietness of the volcano is uncharacteristic.

Mauna Loa's latest eruption came in 1984. Although the volcano has caused no fatalities, the eruptions of 1926 and 1950 did destroy small settlements.

Mauna Loa has been an active volcano for 700,000 years and its peak probably emerged above the waves of the Pacific about 400,000 years ago. The lava of which it is made comes from an unusually active plume. This is a column of molten rock rising slowly through Earth's mantle that has been responsible for creating the Hawaiian Islands – and the long chain of seamounts (extinct volcanoes on the ocean floor) that runs across the ocean floor all the way to Asia. The slow westward crawl of the Pacific Plate will in time carry Mauna Loa away from the plume. Some time in the next half million years, Mauna Loa will become extinct and quietly descend beneath the waves.

THE MISSISSIPPI FLOODS

(1927)

THE MISSISSIPPI FLOODS of 1927 had their beginnings in the summer of 1926, when the central basin of the Mississippi was pounded by heavy rain. By the autumn, the river's major feeders in the states of Iowa and Kansas were already filled to capacity. On New Year's Day in 1927, the Cumberland River at Nashville overtopped its levees. The Mississippi overtopped or broke through its levees in 145 places, flooding 27,000 square miles to a depth of thirty feet.

The flooding affected the states of Kentucky, Louisiana, Mississippi, Tennessee, Arkansas and Illinois. It was Arkansas that was worst affected, with fourteen per cent of its territory going under water. By May in 1927, the lower reach of the Mississippi, below Memphis, was so badly affected that the entire Mississippi floodplain was under water, a huge tract of land sixty miles wide.

Further downstream, where more tributaries added yet more water, there were fears that New Orleans would disappear under water as the flood peak reached the city. Dynamite was used to breach the levee at Caernarvon, Louisiana, upstream from New Orleans, deliberately releasing a colossal volume of water out onto the floodplain. At 250,000 cubic feet per second, this outflow from the Mississippi was itself the equivalent of a mighty river. The effect was, as intended, that the level of the Mississippi as it reached New Orleans was significantly lower, although by chance the levees gave way at several other points without the help of dynamite. The city did experience flooding, but not the catastrophic level of flooding that it would otherwise have had.

The 1927 floods caused damage to property that cost more than 400 million dollars. They also took the lives of about 300 people and left 637,000 people homeless.

Herbert Hoover was Secretary of Commerce at the time, and it was he who took charge of the relief effort. It was partly this high-profile role in a national emergency that led to Hoover's election as President of the United States. It also helped Huey Long to become Governor of Louisiana. The outcomes of disasters can be highly unpredictable.

By August 1927, the flood waters were going down. The human effects were huge: 700,000 people had been evacuated, including 330,000 black Americans who were moved to 154 relief camps. In one particularly unpleasant incident, 13,000 black evacuees at Greenville were collected from low-lying farms on the floodplain and taken to the crest of a levee (a high point on the floodplain), where they were left stranded for days without food or clean water; meanwhile, white evacuees were collected in boats and taken to safety. The racial discrimination inherent in the relief effort was very marked. Many black people were held at gunpoint and treated as slave labour during the flood-relief effort. The terrible situation in the refugee camps was described in several reports, but Herbert Hoover took trouble to ensure that these reports did not reach the press. He promised that the question of civil rights reform would be addressed after the presidential election. He did not keep this promise, and black American leaders such as Robert Moton campaigned to shift the loyalties of black Americans away from Hoover and the Republicans to Roosevelt and the Democrats. Hoover lost the black vote, and failed in his bid for re-election. So the backwash from the flood that propelled Hoover to the White House also helped to flush him out again four years later.

Another result of the flooding was to accelerate the Great

Migration of black Americans from the South to the cities of the North. Displaced from their homes in the South for up to six months, millions of Southern black people decided to make a new life for themselves in the cities of the North – especially Chicago. The disaster had its effect on literature, folklore and music, too; the blues musicians of the Delta wrote melancholy songs about the Mississippi flood.

THE COLLAPSE OF THE SAN FRANCIS DAM

(1928)

THE SAN FRANCIS Dam was a concrete-arched dam built in 1924–26 to create a large reservoir near Los Angeles in California. The dam was designed by William Mulholland of the Los Angeles Department of Water and Power. It was only two years old when, at a few minutes to midnight on 12 March in 1928, the San Francis Dam collapsed.

Mulholland was a self-taught Irish civil engineer. He had designed and built the Los Angeles viaduct, which at 235 miles long was the longest aqueduct in the world, bringing water from the Owens Valley to Los Angeles. By 1920, LA's water needs were outgrowing the viaduct, and several small reservoirs were created in 1921, but it was plain that a large reservoir was needed to meet the city's growing needs. For many years, Mulholland had had his eye on the San Francisquito Canyon site, thirty miles north of Los Angeles.

Unfortunately Mulholland had little understanding of geology, but his choice of site was supported by expert advice from two reputable professional geologists. Neither John Branner nor Carl Grunsky could find fault with the San Francisquito location, which was ironic, because it was on a significant line of geological weakness, the San Francisquito fault, which was active and prone to earthquakes. Modern geologists would have argued strenuously against Mulholland's choice of site.

In 1924, construction work began quietly, in the hope that

farmers in the area who depended on the river for water would not notice and by the time they did it would be too late to stop the project. The new dam was given an anglicized name, San Francis, and was designed to stand 175 feet high. During the early stages of construction it was decided to raise it by ten feet in order to increase its capacity. Then, when the dam was half finished, Mulholland decided to raise it by another ten feet; a wing dyke 590 feet long and fifteen feet high had to be built along a low ridge on the west side to stop the reservoir from overflowing there. Mulholland raised the dam by twenty feet without widening its base, and it was this oversight that made the finished dam unstable.

In 1927, residents of the Owens Valley who were fighting the so-called water wars blew up the Los Angeles Aqueduct several times. Threats were made against the new San Francis Dam, though no attempt was made to dynamite it. In the end the dam was sabotaged by its own design. Cracks appeared in the dam in 1926, even before the reservoir had filled. Mulholland inspected the cracks and declared that they were not significant.

On 7 March 1928, the reservoir was full for the first time. The dam-keeper, Tony Harnischfeger, reported some leaks in the dam to Mulholland, but Mulholland again insisted that they were not serious and the cracks were sealed with pitch. The dam structure was clearly unstable and about to collapse. Another factor in the disaster was the building of a new road along the eastern abutment, which was on the site of an ancient landslide, about which neither Mulholland nor any of the professional geologists of his day knew. The blasting associated with this road building could have loosened – and reactivated – the ancient landslide. It is possible for landslides to be reactivated after tens of thousands of years.

The dam collapsed for two main reasons; Mulholland's unsound dam design, which was too high for the width of its base, and the instability of the ancient landslide. Alarmingly, it has subsequently been discovered that over a hundred other dams in the United States have been built on or against ancient landslides. A third and minor factor was the composition of the dam. The concrete was made with too little water and was therefore brittle. The gravel used included pieces of clay. The gravel was dug directly out of the creek bed, not washed, and so included 'great chunks of clay'.

The dam was not revetted on its upstream side, so it gradually became completely saturated. The sheer weight of the water in the reservoir was enough to lift the dam slightly. This caused networks of cracks to open. The weight of the water could then simply push the dam over and down the valley. On the morning of 12 March, Harnischfeger found another new leak and was anxious that it might indicate that the dam was weakening. He was right. Mulholland again expressed his view that there was nothing to worry about, though his son Perry saw it and thought it looked serious. It was only twelve hours later that the dam finally disintegrated. There were no surviving eye-witnesses, but a man standing half a mile away felt a strange shaking of the ground and the sound of 'crashing, falling blocks'. What he heard was the sound of heavy chunks of concrete falling from the dam.

A flood wave 125 feet high swept down the valley. The first to die were Tony Harnishfeger and his wife, who were seen anxiously inspecting the dam with lanterns half an hour before the disaster, presumably alerted by the sound of leaking water or cracking concrete. Mrs Harnischfeger's body was found wedged between two blocks of concrete just below the dam.

Twelve and a half billion gallons of water rushed through the collapsing dam, down the San Francisquito Canyon, destroying the concrete walls of the hydroelectric power station and everything else in the floor of the valley. The flood wave passed into the Santa Clarita Valley. The towns of Castaic Junction, Fillmore, Bardsdale and Santa Paula were hit especially hard by the flood water. After that the wall of water rushed on to reach the sea near Ventura, about fifty miles from the dam. When it reached the ocean it was still fifteen feet high and nearly a mile wide.

There were some remarkable stories of survival and loss, which found their way into the local newspapers. The *Fillmore American* carried one such story under the headline, 'Shot his Way Out Thru Roof of House Saved by Sycamores.'

Frank Maier and his wife and three children, residing on a ranch below the Bardsdale bridge, had a remarkable escape. As the waters swirled in around them, they made their way to the attic. Here Frank shot a hole through the roof, through which he passed his wife and two of the children to the roof. As he was about to follow them with his son, the house began to move, it was caught in a little circle of sycamore trees, where it rocked from side to side, without turning over or being carried away. The house floated, like a leaky boat, the mark showing that there had never been more than eighteen inches of water in it, when it dropped back to the ground.

It is not known exactly how many died. The official body count given in August 1928 was 385, but each year after that more bodies were discovered, right up to the 1950s. One was even found, deep underground, near Newhall in 1992. The likely total death toll was between 400 and 500. There were 900 buildings destroyed, 300 houses damaged and 24,000 acres of agricultural land were devastated.

It was the second worst disaster in the history of California. Only the San Francisco earthquake of 1906 killed more people. It is perhaps surprising that it is so little known and so unpublicized.

Mulholland willingly accepted responsibility for the disaster. He was devastated by it; photos of him at the scene surveying the damage the day after the disaster show him in a state of shock. Everyone was so ready to blame him that the circumstances of the disaster were not properly investigated. When Mulholland was put on trial for manslaughter, he hinted that he believed that sabotage was involved. Public opinion was scathing. One uncompromising headline ran, 'Blame Mulholland for Dam Structure'. The *Fillmore American* raged against those who were responsible for building the dam.

> *The story of the breaking dam has greeted your eyes from scores of newspaper pages. How the big $2,500,000 dam, built on the insecure foundation of a great city's greed for what did not belong to it, crumbled as the result of faulty designing and hasty construction. Engineer Grunsky was right. That great dam built in the centre of the canyon, with light-flung wings to the soft earth of the mountains, was 'an old woman's apron'. And the strings broke and the result was a hell of swirling waters that took life after life, until its fury was stayed in the waters of the sea.'*

Mulholland's dam was never rebuilt. The central section of the dam remained in position, but after a young man exploring the ruins fell to his death two months later this remnant was dynamited away. All that is left now are a few chunks of weathered grey concrete and remnants of the handrail that ran along the top of the dam.

THE OKEECHOBEE HURRICANE

(1928)

HURRICANE SAN FELIPE Segundo, or the Okeechobee Hurricane, was an unusually fierce and destructive hurricane that struck the Caribbean and Florida in September 1928. The Okeechobee Hurricane has the distinction of being the first Atlantic hurricane on record to have reached Category 5, the highest possible rating on the hurricane scale. It still remains the only Category 5 storm to have struck Puerto Rico.

Okeechobee was first spotted by an American vessel 900 miles east of Guadeloupe, on 10 September. At the time, this was the most easterly 'sighting' of a hurricane to be reported by ship's radio. It is likely that the hurricane formed four days before this between the coast of Africa and the Cape Verde Islands. As it approached the Caribbean, the storm intensified to a Category 3 hurricane, passing over Guadeloupe on 12 September. The air pressure at the centre of the storm was measured at 931 millibars, which is extremely low, and helps to explain why the wind speeds were so high. The lowest air pressure recorded in an American hurricane is 892 millibars in the 'Labor Day' Hurricane of 1935. Winds of 160 mph were measured using a cup wind meter in Puerto Rico, and that was three hours before the storm peak was reached; the meter was destroyed by the hurricane before the highest speeds could be measured.

Puerto Rico suffered the fullest force of the hurricane. The islanders were warned of the storm's approach well in advance by radio and they were well prepared; that is why there were so few fatalities. The death toll was only 312 and not a single ship was lost in the seas around Puerto Rico. By contrast, Hurricane San Ciriaco in 1889 killed around 3,000 people, even though it was a weaker storm. Even so, the Okeechobee Hurricane inflicted catastrophic damage to property on Puerto Rico and several hundred thousand people were made homeless. In Puerto Rico, the storm is remembered as the San Felipe Hurricane because the eye of the hurricane arrived on the feast day of St Philip. The 'Segundo' was added because there had been another destructive hurricane, fifty-two years earlier, which had also arrived on St Philip's feast day. The hurricane was unusually large, with an estimated diameter of about 230 miles, which meant that places passed over by it were subjected by high winds for an unusually long time – eighteen hours on Puerto Rico. Although the wind speed inside the hurricane may have topped 170 mph, the spiral storm itself was moving over the sea, island-hopping, at only about thirteen mph.

As well as Puerto Rico, the hurricane affected the Leeward Islands, the Bahamas and Florida, causing devastation as it tracked north-westwards. Up to 1,200 people were killed in Guadeloupe. In Puerto Rico, over 300 were killed and hundreds of thousands of people were left without homes.

When the storm reached the US mainland in southern Florida on the evening of 16 September, it was still a Category 4 hurricane, striking the coast with winds of 150 mph. As in Puerto Rico, the residents were warned and prepared. At Palm Beach, there were only twenty-six fatalities, in spite of the combination of high winds and a storm surge ten feet high. The residents of the low-lying ground next to Lake Okeechobee were also warned of the approach of the hurricane and they evacuated the area, but when it did not arrive at the expected time they returned to their homes and were caught there when the storm arrived late. The eye of the hurricane passed directly over Lake Okeechobee. Here the hurricane did something very unusual as the eye approached: it produced a storm surge in a lake. The storm surge raised in Lake Okeechobee was sufficient to breach the embankment that edged the southern shore of the lake. An area extending across hundreds of square miles on the southern shores of the lake was flooded with lake water up to twenty feet deep. As the eye crossed the lake, the winds went into reverse, piling the water against the northern shore and causing major flooding there, too. In all, 2,500 people were killed. The level of damage in Florida was very severe. It has been estimated that the same storm occurring today might cause damage costing almost nineteen billion dollars. On the other hand, the embankments around Lake Okeechobee have been replaced with larger barriers, which reduces the probability that the same level of flooding would occur again.

When the hurricane had passed, it became clear that well-built houses fitted with shutters had scarcely been damaged at all. The same observation was made following the Miami hurricane of 1926. One important and enduring effect of the 1928 Okeechobee Hurricane was the improvement of building regulations through-out southern Florida. As a result, later hurricanes of similar strength, like the Fort Lauderdale hurricane of 1947, caused far less damage.

After causing mayhem around the shores of Lake Okeechobee, the hurricane veered to the north and north-east through Florida, crossing Georgia and the Carolinas. After that it weakened and merged with a mid-latitude low-pressure system at Toronto on 20 September.

Altogether, the Okeechobee Hurricane killed over 4,075 people and caused 100 million dollars' worth of damage. This makes it the second most lethal natural disaster in the history of North America, after the Galveston hurricane of 1900.

THE NEWFOUNDLAND SUBMARINE LANDSLIDE

(1929)

A LANDSLIDE WAS detected on the seafloor off the coast of Newfoundland in 1929. This was the first time such an event happened – and was recognized for being what it was. Given that such a thing happened in 1929 in the North Atlantic, it must have happened a lot of times through the course of history and prehistory without our being aware of it. It was a new process, a new type of event, a new type of disaster, and yet people gave it very little thought at the time.

What happened in 1929 was that an enormous slab of sediment about 1,000 miles long slid off the edge of the continental shelf, down the steep continental slope in a shallow broad flow and into the deep ocean basin beyond. As the sediment started moving, it mixed with the bottom layers of the ocean, which meant that it was able to move as a fluid. This huge mass of liquidized sediment plunged down into the deep ocean at fifty mph, immediately to the west of the wreck of the *Titanic*. If the landslide had extended a little further to the east, the wreck of the *Titanic* would have been buried under the sediment, and therefore probably eluded discovery.

The landslide flowed across several transatlantic telegraph cables, major lines of communication between Europe and North America. It snapped them off one by one. The locations of the cables were precisely known, so the exact timing of the disconnection of the cables made it possible to work out that the speed of the landslide was 50 mph. The disconnection of the cables was a major inconvenience because it disrupted communication, but it did at least alert people to the fact that something significant had happened on the ocean floor, which otherwise no one would have known about.

A landslide happening at the bottom of the sea might seem like something about which we need not worry too much. But that is not so. The things that happen in remote and inaccessible places on this planet have a way of affecting us, sometimes directly, more often indirectly. The Newfoundland seabed landslide displaced so much ocean water that it generated a tsunami. We tend to think of tsunamis as being caused by earthquakes on the seabed, but they can also be caused by major landslides on the seabed. The landslide-generated tsunami in 1929 was given no publicity whatever at the time. This was because it affected the coastline of Newfoundland and Nova Scotia, which were very sparsely populated, so very few people actually saw the tsunami. The Newfoundland tsunami was nevertheless a major phenomenon; it was forty feet high and it killed thirty people. For a long time people did not connect the tsunami with the landslide, but it is clear now that the landslide was responsible for the tsunami, and that connection, as in all the other landscape processes we have stumbled upon, is highly significant. It is unravelling all these cause-and-effect relationships that leads to an understanding of how the planet as a whole works.

The Newfoundland landslide was a big event, but it was still only one-tenth of the size of the biggest of the Storegga landslides.

The biggest and most dangerous landslide tsunamis in the world are generated on the flanks of oceanic volcanic islands. There the landslides begin on land and end up in the sea. They are hybrids, not entirely land animals, not entirely sea creatures, but passing from one to the other like amphibians. Volcanic islands are particularly vulnerable, because they often have unstable steep slopes built up of lava and loose ash – and they are relatively prone to being jolted and vibrated by earthquakes. The movement of magma up from below, in the run-up to an eruption also has the effect of making the volcano expand and develop networks of cracks in its flanks.

There are two places in the world where future landslide tsunamis are likely to happen. There have been recent and ongoing movements on the flanks of volcanic islands in both the Hawaiian group and the Canary Islands. The recent shifts in the land surface on the sides of the Kilauea volcano in Hawaii have to be watched carefully by volcanologists. The release of huge volumes of rock and ash from the flanks of Hawaiian volcanoes has certainly happened in the past. There are tsunami deposits at the alarming altitude of 1,200 feet above sea level on the flanks of the Kohala volcano on Hawaii. This is evidence of a massive landslide into the sea from the neighbouring volcano of Mauna Loa.

A very similar watch is being kept on the precipitously steep western flank of the Cumbre Vieja volcano on La Palma in the Canary Islands. There are huge volumes of rock there, perched precariously above the North Atlantic, waiting to crash down the mountain side when the volcano next erupts and fall into the sea.

Luckily such large-scale landslides are rare. Luckily large-scale landslide tsunamis are rare, too. But, as with other large-scale and infrequent events, when they happen they are catastrophic in the extreme. The western flank of the Cumbre Vieja volcano comprises a mass of rock that is about one-third of the volume of the largest of the Storegga landslides. If and when it collapses into the sea, it could have catastrophic effects. It could break loose next year, or in 1,000 years. But when it does, it is likely to generate a colossal landslide tsunami, a tsunami that will dwarf any wave seen in historic times. The landslide will generate waves up to 300 feet high that will scour the coasts of the Canary Islands. They will race westwards across to New York, and they will still be 100 feet high when they get there. The damage such waves will do to a great low-lying metropolis such as New York can only be imagined, especially when the warning to evacuate the city will be minimal. The waves could even reach the Caribbean and the English Channel, where they would still be twenty feet high. Tsunami waves on this scale – far bigger than those generated in the Indian Ocean Boxing Day disaster – would cause hundreds of thousands of deaths, wreck thousands of homes and businesses, and inflict incalculable economic damage. It is hard to see what we can do to prepare ourselves, or our towns and cities, for the eventuality of a mega-tsunami.

THE R101
DISASTER

(1930)

PLANS FOR BUILDING the R101 airship were proposed in 1924 as part of an Imperial Airship Scheme. The airship was to be able to carry 200 troops or five fighter planes; it was in effect to be a flying aircraft carrier. From the start it was realized that the eventual airship would need to be large, a vessel of eight million cubic feet, but the project would start with two prototypes, working models of five million cubic feet. One was to be contracted out to a private company and the other was to be built at Cardington (the Royal Airship Workshops in Bedfordshire). The first, the R100, was built by the Airship Guarantee Company at Howden in Yorkshire. The second, the ill-fated R101, was built at Cardington.

The R101 was to have many innovative features and these caused delays, but building work started in 1926. The biggest airship in the world up to that time was the *Graf Zeppelin*, which was based on the earlier design of the LZ126, and the R101 was to be much bigger than the *Graf Zeppelin*. The R101 was completed in October 1929. She was a disappointment in trials, in that she did not have as much lifting power as anticipated. The designers decided to let out the bracing wires that held in the gas cells so that the overall volume of the ship and its lifting capacity could be increased. Further trials showed that this was not enough. Something more radical was needed to increase the lifting capacity. In the winter of 1929–1930, the airship was cut in half so that an extra gas bag could be inserted in the middle, increasing the length from 735 feet to 777 feet and raising the volume to five and a half million cubic feet. She could now fly at speeds up to 71 mph.

Hugo Eckener visited Cardington in the *Graf Zeppelin* to see the new airship and was impressed; he considered that he was looking at an exceptional new breed of airship. Confidence in the R101 was regained, and bigger airships, R102 and R103, were planned as a result. Ideas were in the air for commercial operations as well as military. Transatlantic passengers were keen to use the new airships; one offered £20,000 for a flight to new York in 1931.

There were some adverse comments. The R101 was often described as flying too low. The response was that commercial airships flying long range had to fly at low altitude and the ship was designed to do this. The most economical flights, the ones that gave the best financial return, were those that flew at an altitude of 1,500 feet. It was also argued that this was more interesting for passengers, because it gave the best views of the land and sea they were travelling over. The Zeppelin Company adopted a similar policy with the LZ129-Hindenburg, which regularly flew at 1,500-4,000 feet.

The R101 was regarded as a flying hotel, and a rather smart hotel at that. There were open promenades and public spaces, which are certainly not available on modern aircraft. The big British airships were the first to use the interiors of the ship rather than a gondola based on the balloon gondola for passenger accommodation. The *Graf Zeppelin* could only accommodate twenty passengers in an elongated gondola attached to the underside of the hull. The R100 and R101 were the first airships to make use of the interior space, which made it possible to create two decks that could accommodate a smoking room that seated twenty and a dining room that seated sixty. The promenades showed off the spectacular views of the passing landscapes and seascapes to best advantage. It is not surprising that these beautiful, graceful airships were seen as luxurious. The facilities, comfort and service compared well with what was on offer on the transatlantic liners.

The big problem was the airships' lifting capacity. The extra gas bag had been added to the R101 by the spring of 1930, giving another fifty tons of lift. There was pressure to have the airship ready to fly the Air Minister, Lord Thompson, to Karachi in September 1930. There was too much wind, and the R101 had to stay in its shed until 1 October. She was brought out at 6.30 in the morning. At the same time, her sister ship, the R100, was walked out of the shed next door and put into the R101's place, where it was planned to cut her in half and insert a new gas bag just like the R101. It was to be the R100's last outing; after the R101 disaster the R100 had no future. Meanwhile the R101 went on her final trial flight, starting at 4.30 pm. She slipped her mooring mast and left Cardington to head south for London. In central London, she turned east and followed the Thames down to the sea, spending the night out over the North Sea. The flying conditions were described as perfect and the atmosphere on board was quiet and serene. The quietness and smoothness of airship travel were the big advantages over conventional aeroplanes and ships.

A cooler in the forward starboard engine failed, so it was not possible to fly the ship at full speed. Even so, the new airship was handling so well that the decision was made to cut the trial short and return to Cardington, where she arrived at nine in the morning on 2 October after flying for seventeen hours in perfect flying conditions. She had not, in other words, been tested under any adverse weather conditions; no one knew how she might behave in a strong wind, or in turbulence. In a conference that evening, it was decided that it was necessary to carry out a trial at full speed in poor weather conditions before the flight to India was attempted. But the crew and engineers were under pressure. Lord Thompson was saying, 'You mustn't allow my natural impatience or anxiety to start to influence you in any way. You must use your considered judgment.' But it was also made very clear to the decision makers that Lord Thompson needed to go to India and return to England in time for an Imperial Conference on 20 October 1930. They really had very little choice but to go along with the flight to Karachi with the Air Minister on board – without the further trial that they needed.

There were two days of preparation before the R101's final flight. A meteorological officer provided information on likely weather and his advice guided the route selected. The ship had not been flown under adverse conditions, and this trip was not the right occasion to try them. On the morning of 4 October, it was reported that the weather over northern France was deteriorating; it was getting cloudy and the wind was picking up. Even so, they decided that the ship would leave in the early evening. There were more weather forecasts, indicating one that the weather in northern France would deteriorate during the evening. It was decided that the predicted weather was not severe enough to justify cancelling the voyage. The passengers and their luggage were loaded on board.

The R101 left its mast at Cardington at six twenty-four pm on 4 October in darkness and drizzle, with searchlight from the mooring mast and the lights along the promenade deck lighting her up against the dark sky. The ship was loaded with passengers, crew, luggage and fuel. She was too heavy to make it safely to Egypt, so four tons of ballast were dropped to enable her to gain height. The old problem of the ship's weak lifting capacity was rearing its head again.

The R101 first (and entirely unnecessarily) headed west to show itself to the town of Bedford before heading south-east for London. There was a sense in which the new ship was not merely being shown off, she was on a kind of royal progress. She was flying at her chosen cruising height of 1,500 feet, which happened to be just below the cloud base that day. At eight o'clock in the evening, the ship reached London. Then a wireless message from the ship declared, 'Course now set for Paris. Intend to proceed via Paris, Tours, Toulouse and Narbonne.'

At nine forty-seven pm the R101 radioed, 'Crossing coast in the vicinity of Hastings. It is raining hard and there is a strong south-westerly wind. Cloud base is at 1,500 feet.' There was a review of the course so far. 'Gradually increasing height so as to avoid high land. Ship is behaving well and we have already begun to recover water ballast.' This was done by way of special catchments along the top of the envelope; they could catch rainwater that would compensate the fuel that was consumed during the flight. If the crew had decided to take on ballast, they cannot at that stage have thought the ship was too heavy to stay up.

At eleven thirty-six pm, after a two-hour Channel crossing, the R101 reached the French coast at Pointe de St Quentin. There was a stiff thirty-five mph wind. This was a crossing that one of the officers, Squadron Leader Johnson, knew well. He had flown it many times before. The R101 was now flying rather low, at an altitude of about 800 feet. First Officer Atherstone took over the elevator wheel and ordered the coxswain not to fly below 1,000 feet. There was at this stage nothing to indicate any anxiety on board. A lengthy radio message was sent from fifteen miles south-west of Abbeville to Cardington giving technical details of the flight so far, and then a vivid description of the pleasantness life on board: 'After an excellent supper our distinguished passengers smoked a final cigar and having sighted the French coast have now gone to bed to rest after the excitement of their leave-taking. All essential services are functioning satisfactorily. Crew have settled down to watch-keeping routine.'

After that, the R101 sent out occasional directional signals The last signal of all from the R101 was at one fifty-two in the morning, a simple acknowledgement of an incoming signal. Then nothing. At two o'clock, there was a change of watch as usual, and still nothing was reported to be wrong with the ship. If anything had been noted, the captain would certainly have reported it back to base; he was reporting absolutely everything back to base. At the inquiry, Engineer Leech confirmed that that was the situation. He was off duty and having a smoke in the smoking room between one and two in the morning, when Captain Irwin came in and spoke to him and the Chief Engineer. The captain only commented that the engines continued to run well. Later Leech went and inspected all the engines, then went back to the smoking room.

At two in the morning, the R101 reached the French town of Beauvais, passing to the east. There is some evidence that now the airship was getting into difficulties with gusts of wind. Witnesses on the ground suggested that the promenade lights disappeared because the ship was rolling badly, but it is more likely that they just went behind the low cloud. At two am the ship made a long and fairly steep ninety second dive, steep enough to make the crew lose their balance and make the furniture in the smoking room slide about. This was probably caused by the continuous rain soaking the envelope skin over the nose and causing a tear. The gas bags at the nose were then exposed to the elements and were damaged by the rain and wind. The loss of gas at the nose of the ship would have been enough to make the ship very difficult to handle. Unbalanced like this, she would been hard to steer.

The R101 was also heading straight for the notorious Beauvais ridge, an escarpment that was already well known to airmen as an extremely dangerous place for its gusts of wind and unpredictable turbulence. The loss of gas at the nose probably coincided with a sudden downward gust of wind. The dive, at about eighteen degrees, must have alarmed the crew, and they would have made every effort to correct it. They did in fact manage to steady the ship. They flew the ship at a nose-up angle of three degrees for half a minute, but the elevator was up as high as it would go, so it was obvious that there had been a serious loss of gas from the bow and that the ship was nose-heavy.

At this point the Captain ordered all engines to reduce speed. Bells were rung to rouse all the crew. Chief Coxswain Hunt passed Disley, the wireless operator, and said, 'We're down, lads.' Hunt was one of the most experienced airship crew members, and his remark made it clear, at the time and at the inquiry, that it was obvious that the ship could not stay in the air any longer and that preparations were being made for an emergency landing. At that moment the airship began a second dive. She was now only 530 feet above the ground and given that she was 777 feet long this was a very dangerous position to be in; any minor movement could bring her to the ground. One of the crew was ordered to release the emergency ballast and was on his way to do this when he felt the ship enter its second dive.

Almost immediately the nose hit the ground, but very gently as the ship was only moving at thirteen mph. The ship bounced forwards about sixty feet and settled on the ground. The only mark left on the ground was a shallow groove nine feet long made by the nose cone. It was, by all accounts, a very good emergency landing. But then fire broke out. This probably happened because one of the engines was twisted on impact and the hot engine came in contact with the gas escaping from the already damaged gas bags. There were explosions and the outer casing of the airship instantly went up in flames.

Of all of those on board the R101, only eight were able to escape. Leech, who was still sitting in the smoking room when the airship landed, was able to escape through the broken wooden walls of the smoking room. He was then able to push through the cloth envelope and get out. Disley, the wireless operator, was asleep in his bunk but woke up when the ship went into her first dive. He was warned of the impending landing, started to turn off electrical switches, guessing that there was a risk of fire breaking out; when the ship landed, like Leech, he was able to force his way out through the outer envelope. The four engineers were in their four separate engine cars, which were outside the hull, so they were able to climb out relatively easily. Two other crewman, Radcliffe and Church, worked their way out of the blazing wreck but died later of their injuries.

Two of the survivors noticed, as they ran away from the wreck, that though the cover was burning there was virtually nothing left of the cover on the top of the ship at the rear end. The elevator was visibly still in its full up position, showing that the crew had gone on trying to keep the ship up to the end.

In the aftermath of the tragedy, a medium called Eileen Garrett was holding a séance at the National Laboratory of Psychical Research, when the proceedings were interrupted by the spirit of the dead captain of the R101. Among other things, he said, 'Too short trials. No one knew the ship properly. Weather bad long flight. Fabric all waterlogged and ship's nose is down. Impossible to rise. Cannot trim. Almost scraped the roofs of Achy. At enquiry it will be found that the superstructure had no resilience and had far too much weight.' Charlton, one of the engineers responsible for building the R101, was astounded by it. He said the dead captain's 'testimony' contained over forty highly technical and confidential details of what happened on the last flight; nobody present at the séance could have got hold of that information by normal means. Whatever went on at the séance, the words of the dead captain were treated as hot news in Great Britain.

The loss of the R101 was seen as a national disaster, as indeed it was. The British public were staggered by the appalling news. The bodies of the victims were taken by train to be loaded aboard HMS *Tempest* for transport to Dover. From there they were taken by special train to London. They were given a formal lying-in-state in Westminster Hall, where people filed past the coffins. A memorial service was given in St Paul's Cathedral. Finally the forty-eight victims of the R101 disaster were buried in a special grave at Cardington, where a memorial still dominates the little church.

The wreck of the R101 was left where it landed for several

months, on the hillside at Allonne just south-east of Beauvais, its forward half resting in a patch of woodland. People went to see the collapsed skeleton of the burned-out airship. Scrap contractors salvaged the metal. The Zeppelin company bought the aluminium from the wreckage, and it is quite possible that this was used to build the most famous airship of all, the *Hindenburg*.

The causes of the R101 disaster were partly human error. Airship technology was new, untried, experimental. With hindsight it is clear that the R101 did not have enough lifting power, a problem that was recognized at the time. With hindsight we can see that the airship should have been given trials in wet and windy weather, but her engineers knew that at the time. Political pressure was partly to blame. If the Air Minister's trip to Karachi had not been a part of the scenario, the R101 might have been more thoroughly tested before taking on passengers. But natural forces also played their part in the R101 disaster: the wind, the rain, the unpredictable turbulence over the Beauvais ridge and, above all else, gravity.

An important outcome of the disaster was that the future of airships was less certain. The more spectacular destruction of the *Hindenburg* at its mooring mast clinched it. The loss of these two airships meant that people simply didn't want them any more. It was a great loss, because they were smoother, quieter and more fuel-efficient than conventional aircraft and more flexible than ships, simply because they could cross land or water with equal ease. The two disasters, the loss of the R101 and the loss of the *Hindenburg*, meant that a whole line of evolution in transport technology became extinct.

THE YELLOW RIVER FLOOD

(1931)

THE REASONS WHY the Yellow River has suffered so badly from flooding are not hard to find. A typical small English stream has a flow of perhaps ten cubic feet per second, which means that at the point where the flow is measured a cube of water just over two feet across goes by every second. The average flow over the course of a year on the Yellow River is 92,556 cubic feet per second; from July to October the flow is even higher, at 102,888 cubic feet per second.

The lower course of the Yellow River has no valley, just an open expanse of level plain, so when the river overflows its banks it covers an enormous area. The problems are compounded by the high population density. People have always been attracted to the fertile soils of the floodplain, and now over 100 million people live along its banks. Another factor is the high volume of silt carried along by the river. In fact over half of the volume of the river is silt. This has a tendency to choke the river, raising its bed and increasing the likelihood of flooding.

When the Yellow River flooded in 1931, 34,000 square miles of the plain were completely inundated, and another 8,100 square miles were partially submerged.

The Yellow River, China's sorrow, had flooded repeatedly through the centuries, but rarely if ever as severely as in 1931. The great flood of 1931 was responsible for the deaths of no less than 3,700,000 people. If we use its death toll as a measure, this was the worst natural disaster in the documented history of the world, apart from the pandemics. Given that there were far fewer people in prehistory and that population densities were lower, it is very unlikely that the human death toll in any prehistoric natural disaster took more lives than the Yellow River flood of 1931.

If the Yellow River flood were not a great enough disaster for China to bear, the Yangtze flooded catastrophically only a few weeks afterwards.

The 1931 flood was the last natural flood disaster of this severity on the Yellow River. Two years later the Yellow River flooded again, rather less severely, and 18,000 people died. The 1938 Yellow River flood caused enormous numbers of casualties, but it was not a natural disaster. The Chinese Kuomintang forces deliberately breached the river's levees in an attempt to block the advance of the Japanese army during the Second Sino-Japanese War. This man-made flood caused one million deaths, making it the third worst flood disaster in recorded history, not just on the Yellow River, but in the world.

THE SANRIKU EARTHQUAKE AND TSUNAMI

(1933)

THE 8.1 MAGNITUDE earthquake at Sanriku in Japan in March 1933 generated a tsunami that caused enormous damage. Because there was an earlier earthquake-and-tsunami disaster, in 1896, the 1933 disaster is sometimes referred to as the Showa disaster; the earlier one is referred to as the Meiji disaster. This is a classic case of a disaster repeating itself at the same location. Sanriku is close to the Japan Trench, where the Pacific Plate dives under the continental plate that makes up north-eastern Asia. The Meiji earthquake was generated by friction between these two plates. The Showa earthquake was generated on a normal (up and down) fault within the Pacific Plate itself.

The Meiji earthquake caused 26,360 deaths, whereas the Showa earthquake caused only 3,064 deaths, even though the earth movement was more energetic. One reason for the contrast is that the Meiji earthquake happened in the evening of the Boys' Festival, a special day in the lunar calendar, and many people had gathered indoors for parties. This preoccupation with festivities seriously delayed the evacuation and raised the death toll. By 1933, some lessons had been learned from the Meiji Sanriku disaster and the evacuation was achieved more efficiently.

The Showa earthquake cracked the walls of buildings and triggered landslides. It was followed by a very big aftershock three hours later. Then there was a long series of smaller aftershocks, as many as seventy-seven spread through a period of six months.

The Meiji tsunami was more than 100 feet high, whereas the Showa tsunami was rather lower, seventy feet high. By the time the Showa earthquake happened, a modern system for measuring tsunamis had been set up, so the Showa tsunami is often used as a benchmark for tsunami studies. The studies show that the shape of the coastline has a big effect on the size of the tsunami. Where there are V-shaped sea inlets flanked by hills, such as those that are found on a ria coastline, the tsunamis are amplified. It has also emerged that the first tsunami to arrive is not necessarily the largest, so even if the first wave seems harmless an immediate evacuation response is essential. Tsunamis can be generated by any earthquake in the Pacific Basin larger than magnitude six on the Richter Scale.

The 1933 tsunami disaster led to a number of responses. Instructions for Tsunami Disaster Prevention were published immediately afterwards. The large-scale damage along the Sanriku coastline led to resettlement in higher locations, at Yoshihama, Tanohama, Ryori and Aikawa. A sea wall has been built and areas of forest planted; woodland can help to brake the flow of a tsunami. Some areas have been designated tsunami prevention areas, which raises awareness, and certain roads have been designated tsunami evacuation roads, so that there are well-defined escape routes. A tsunami warning system is in place.

Some seabed earthquakes generate tsunamis that travel right across the Pacific. Large-scale though it was, the Showa earthquake of 1933 did not generate a tsunami that had noticeable effects elsewhere in the Pacific. This may be because it happened in an area where there is marked vertical subduction along the Japan Trench, in other words the Pacific Plate was bent sharply downwards into the mantle, and so less of the earthquake energy was transmitted sideways.

THE DUST BOWL DROUGHT

(1934, 1936 AND 1939)

THE SO-CALLED Dust Bowl drought affected a huge area of North America, not just the dry western plains that were known as the Dust Bowl, but much of the rest of the United States as well. The drought was an ongoing problem that came in three waves, in 1934, 1936 and 1939. The worst affected regions, such was the High Plains, experienced very dry conditions more or less continuously for eight long years.

As early as 1931, severe drought had begun to hit the Midwest and the southern Plains. The crops died, the soil turned to dust and the winds blew them up into dust storms. Some farmers lost their soil; others further east had their fields, outbuildings and fences buried under drifts of dust. It was disastrous for all of them. In 1932 there were more dust storms; fourteen were counted and the following year that would rise to thirty-eight. When Franklin D. Roosevelt took office as president in 1933, he saw that the United States was in serious economic straits. He declared a four-day bank holiday, during which time Congress passed an Emergency Banking Act. This stabilized the banking system and restored public confidence in it by demonstrating a measure of state supervision.

In 1934, the dust storms that had affected the Dust Bowl area so badly in 1933 spread outwards. By now the drought had become the worst in American history, affecting twenty-seven states and over seventy-five per cent of the country. A Bankruptcy Act was passed, to restrict the power of the banks to dispossess farmers who were in distress and unable to pay bills. A Grazing Act was passed, allowing 140 million acres of federally-owned land to be used as grazing land; the idea was to try to reverse the damage that had been done by ploughing up grazing land. It was clear now that the great plough-up had been very destructive. The Grazing Acts was able to halt the deterioration of the landscape, but it could not undo damage already done. In December 1934, it was announced that thirty-five million acres of farmland had been destroyed as far as the production of crops was concerned, and 100 million acres had lost all their topsoil. A further 125 million acres were rapidly losing their topsoil. The Dust Bowl had become a national disaster.

In January 1935, a Drought Relief Service was set up to co-ordinate relief work. One government initiative was to buy unfit, undernourished and unsaleable cattle from farmers and so save them from bankruptcy. This was a godsend to many poor farmers. In April, Roosevelt presided over an Emergency Relief Appropriation Act, which authorized drought relief and the creation of alternative jobs for dispossessed farmers. The worst Dust Bowl dust storm came in April, prompting the US Congress to declare soil erosion a national menace and announce the creation of The Soil Conservation Service under Hugh Bennett. Farmers were to be given cash rewards for following newly recommended procedures such as crop rotation and strip cropping. By the end of the year, 850 million tons of soil had blown off the southern Plains. Plans were in hand to buy up more than two million acres and retire it from cultivation.

In 1936, the Los Angeles police chief ordered officers at the borders of Arizona and Oregon to keep 'undesirables' out of California; these were agricultural refugees from the Dust Bowl. In March, Roosevelt launched his Shelterbelt Project. This entailed large-scale tree planting across the Great Plains as a means of reducing wind speeds and reducing soil erosion. This ambitious project involved planting red cedar and green ash along the fenced boundaries between properties, but there were problems in organizing the funding for it. The other soil conservation technique, such as strip cropping and contour ploughing, proved very successful, though, and there was already a sixty-five per cent reduction in the amount of soil blowing about in the wind.

It was not until late in 1939 that the rains finally came, bringing the long drought to an end.

The Dust Bowl drought was a natural disaster induced by a period of low rainfall, but it was also worsened by inappropriate land management.

The interior of North America is a rain shadow area. Far from the sea, the rain-bearing winds have lost most of their moisture before they reach the Prairies and High Plains. The prevailing wind is from the west, and that has to cross the Rockies before reaching the Prairies. The lifting of the air over the Rockies cools and causes a lot of the water vapour in the air to condense, so there is heavy rain (or snow) over the Rockies, but very little on the eastern flanks. So, the interior of North America is a low-rainfall area, sometimes described by climatologists as sub-humid, though the western parts might qualify as semi-arid.

But the Dust Bowl drought was drier than normal because conditions in the Pacific and Atlantic Oceans were abnormal. Research done over fifty years after the drought has revealed what happened, by using computer models. The unusually dry conditions in the Dust Bowl drought were created by cooler than normal conditions in the tropical Pacific Ocean and warmer than normal conditions in the tropical Atlantic. These changes caused major shifts in weather patterns in and around North America. In particular, they reduced the normal supply of moisture from southerly winds entering the Prairies from the Gulf of Mexico. This in turn reduced the rainfall throughout the Prairies.

The normal situation is for a high-pressure cell over the Azores to send air outwards in a great clockwise spiral, with winds passing westwards across the warm tropical Atlantic, into the Caribbean, veering northwards across the Gulf of Mexico and into the Prairies. When they arrive there, it is usually with enough moisture from the warm oceans to supply a moderate amount of rain, certainly enough to grow grass and cereal crops. Under the abnormal conditions of the 1930s, the same winds passed further to the south, continued westwards across the Caribbean, and missed out the Prairies.

This discovery of the mechanism behind the Dust Bowl drought came about because of concerns surrounding El Niño. What is emerging from this research is the crucial inter-dependence of one region upon others. The patterns geographers are assembling may help in the prediction of another Dust Bowl drought.

The Prairies are very extensive, large enough to have significant climatic variations within them. Towards the Mississippi Valley the conditions are more humid; this was the area where the natural grass cover grew tall. Towards the Rockies the conditions are drier; here the natural grass cover was short and patchy. The long-grass prairie was settled for farming in the nineteenth century. In the decade or so before the Dust Bowl drought, conditions in the short-grass prairie were moister. This tempted people to farm it like the long-grass prairie. Instead of leaving it as rough grazing, large areas were ploughed for arable farming.

The farmers were also goaded into ploughing by the Depression. The national economic crisis of the Great Depression had created serious financial difficulties for the farmers. To try to compensate for the losses, they decided to step up their crop production; they were trying to offset lower prices by producing more grain. As the economic situation worsened, they had to keep increasing production. This meant more and more ploughing.

The great plough-up turned out to be a big mistake, as the moister episode in the 1920s was only temporary. When the drier conditions set in, the ploughed soil of the short-grass prairie completely dried out, turned to dust and was blown away by the wind. In fact, it was lifted by the wind into enormous clouds of sand and dust that were so dense and deep that the sun was blotted out for several days at a time. They were described as 'black blizzards'.

The situation had been made worse by another phenomenon caused by the Rockies. The mountains were responsible for creating the rain shadow effect, and thus the low rainfall in the Prairies. They were also responsible for producing the Chinook wind. The lapse rate is a well-known phenomenon: the fact that temperature drops at a regular rate as you walk up a mountain, or go up in a balloon. The air cools as it rises and expands, and that is why mountain peaks sometimes have snow on them. What is less well-known is the other side of this coin: that air warms up as it descends. So the westerly winds that blow over the Rocky Mountains cool down and drop their rain on the west-facing flanks of the Rockies, but then warm up and absorb water as they pass down the eastern flanks. In the Prairies, these westerly winds are felt as warm and drying winds. The native North Americans called these winds Chinook or 'snow-eaters', because they quickly melted the winter snow falling in the Prairies and brought an early spring.

It was these same Chinook winds that helped to desiccate the short-grass prairie, turn the soil to dust and carry it away.

Large areas of the newly ploughed arable land were stripped bare of their soil as it was carried away by the wind. The agricultural communities of the Great Plains were ruined by this sudden change in their fortunes. There was emergency financial aid from the state, but many farmers were forced to sell up. One in ten farms on the Great Plains changed hands.

After the Dust Bowl disaster was over, it became clear that many factors had contributed to it. It also became clear that what was needed was a far better understanding of the way the physical processes and people interacted. There were academics and other specialists studying weather, climate, soils and plants. There were still more academics and specialists studying agriculture, economics and politics. What was needed was a new breed of researchers, who would be both academic and pragmatic, to study the interrelationships among all of these. This was where the discipline of geography made a great step forward. Instead of studying, in a rather sterile way, what was where, geographers moved towards ecology, towards seeing all the things that happen not only in a particular region but in the world as a whole – in a holistic way. Everything, after all, is connected to everything else.

One major practical development that came in the wake of the Dust Bowl drought was the devising of scientific methods for exploiting the agricultural landscape. Contour ploughing (ploughing systematically along the slopes, not up and down them) was introduced to reduce the effects of soil erosion; it slowed down the rate at which soil particles moved down the slope. New cultivation methods were introduced that were more appropriate to a dry-land or semi-arid ecosystem. In fact, the new concept of a semi-arid ecosystem dates from this period. Geographers had been familiar with the idea of deserts, as well as woodland, grassland and other ecosystems, but semi-arid and sub-humid landscapes had been on the edges of academic studies. Increasingly, these transitional landscapes would be given more and more attention. A few decades later, when famine broke out in the Sahel, the semi-desert fringe of the Sahara would similarly focus attention on transitional environments.

As a result of this revolution in perception, and the consequent changes in land management, later droughts in the same area have had far less destructive effects. The Dust Bowl drought was a terrible experience for all those involved, but it did in the end yield some major benefits to mankind.

THE LOSS OF THE
HINDENBURG

(1937)

THE AIRSHIP LZ129, better known as the *Hindenburg*, was a German-built Zeppelin. She and her sister ship, the LZ130 *Graf Zeppelin II*, were the biggest aircraft ever built. She was named after the German president. Originally the plan was to name her the *Adolf Hitler*, but the director of the Zeppelin company, Hugo Eckener, disapproved of the Nazis and prevented it.

The huge airship was just over 800 feet long, 135 feet wide and contained seven million cubic feet of gas held in sixteen separate bags. She was powered by four Daimler-Benz diesel engines, which gave her a top speed of 84 mph. She was very, very big. She was longer than three Boeing 747s end to end. There were cabins on board for fifty passengers, increased to seventy in 1937, and there was a crew of sixty-one. To improve the airship's aerodynamics, the passengers' quarters were contained inside the cigar-shaped hull, not a gondola slung underneath.

The airship's hull was given a skin of cotton coated with cellulose acetate butyrate and aluminium powder. This may have been a fatal choice of ingredients, because they were also ingredients for rocket fuel. Initially the intention was to use helium as the lift gas, but the United States had placed a restriction on the supply of helium and this persuaded the Germans to use hydrogen instead. Helium is non-flammable; hydrogen is flammable. At this point the seeds of the disasters were sown. The Germans had used hydrogen as a lifting gas before and were confident that with a variety of safety measures in place, the *Hindenburg* would not explode or catch fire. The strange coating applied to the airship's skin was designed to stop electric sparks. In fact, the German designers were so confident that they included a smoking room in the passengers' quarters; they increased the air pressure in it so that hydrogen could not leak into it.

The *Hindenburg* was built in 1936, when it made its first flight on 4 March. A ticket from New Jersey to Germany cost 400 dollars, which was a huge sum of money at a time of economic depression. Only the rich could afford to fly in the *Hindenburg*. They even had at their disposal a specially made Blüthner grand piano – made of aluminium. It was the first flying grand piano, but it was quickly decommissioned to save weight.

The *Hindenburg*'s first year in service was a great success. She flew over 190,000 miles, carried 2,800 passengers and 160 tons of cargo. She did seventeen round trips across the Atlantic Ocean and seven to Brazil. In May and June 1936, the *Hindenburg* twice flew over Great Britain, possibly on a spying mission. An airship was an ideal vehicle for high-precision air photography. The first year in service was such a triumph that the Zeppelin company began planning the expansion of its transatlantic service, and building more Zeppelins.

It was on 6 May 1937, while she was in her second year of service, that the *Hindenburg* was destroyed by fire as she was landing at Lakehurst Naval Air Station at Manchester, New Jersey. The airship had just arrived at her mooring mast and the mooring ropes were thrown down to the ground. At that moment flames appeared near the tail and rapidly spread forward along the whole length of the hull. Within seconds the whole of the skin was either aflame or in tatters and the hydrogen inside ignited. The entire airship was a gigantic fireball, gradually collapsing onto the airfield. It all happened incredibly quickly. From the moment when the flames first appeared to the total destruction of the airship on the ground took only thirty-seven seconds. In the circumstances, it is amazing that anyone survived.

Thirty-six people, one-third of the people she was carrying, were killed in the accident. Thirteen of the thirty-six passengers and twenty-two of the sixty-one crew died. One member of the ground crew died, too: Allen Hagaman. The film footage shows the airship as a gigantic fireball, and its is easy to assume from this that the victims were burned to death, but in fact most deaths resulted from people jumping from the airship. The passengers who kept their nerve and stayed aboard while it gently settled to the ground escaped. The hydrogen-filled hull looked lethal, but twice as many people died when the USS *Akron* crashed, and that was helium-filled.

The cause of the fire has still not been agreed. Given the political tensions of the time, sabotage was a favourite explanation. Hugo Eckener, the former head of the Zeppelin company, thought sabotage was most likely, but he later changed his mind. The FBI disagreed; it was certainly the case that ordinary people saw Zeppelins as symbols of the power of Hitler's Germany, but the FBI knew that the Zeppelin executives were anti-Hitler and that they had refused to name the ship after Hitler. On the other hand, the *Hindenburg*'s commander, Max Pruss, supported the sabotage theory. Several books have been written in attempts to identify the saboteur; some favour a Zionist agent, others name Eric Spehl, a member of the *Hindenburg*'s crew who died in the disaster. Another suspect was Joseph Spah, who survived the disaster, though his German shepherd dog did not. The FBI investigated Spah and could find nothing incriminating about him. Some have proposed that Hitler ordered the destruction of the *Hindenburg* as revenge against Eckener. Although this may seem too mad to be true, we should perhaps not forget that Stalin had it in mind to order the assassination of John Wayne for his political views and he was only talked out of it by Khrushchev.

The problem with the sabotage theories is that there is no firm evidence of any kind. The theorists in some cases fall back on the idea of an establishment conspiracy to conceal the evidence, which is an argumentative position that leads absolutely nowhere.

Lightning has been blamed for the accident. A. J. Dessler, former director of the NASA Space Flight Center, pointed out that the *Hindenburg* is known to have been struck by lightning a number of times. This does not start fires when the airship is in mid-air, because the hydrogen is not mixed with oxygen. On the other hand, when preparing to land, airships often released hydrogen in order to make a descent. If the *Hindenburg* was venting hydrogen and lightning struck at that moment, it could have ignited the mixture of hydrogen and oxygen. Dessler reminds us that there was an airship saying from those times: 'Never blow off gas during a thunderstorm.'

An alternative theory about the burning of the *Hindenburg* is that a spark was caused by the build-up of static electricity between the airship and the ground. There is a well-argued case for this. The passage of the wet Zeppelin went through a weather front, where it picked up a high electrical charge. The wet mooring lines would have been highly conductive. The moment the wet mooring lines tied to the airship frame touched the ground the airship would have earthed; a massive discharge of electricity passed between the airship and the ground. It is a tenable theory, and there is some corroboration for it. Witnesses saw a glow like St Elmo's fire along the tail of the airship immediately before the flames appeared.

The *Hindenburg*'s skin was coated with a flammable finish. When the mooring line earthed the hull, electricity passing through the line could have set fire to the skin. The hydrogen caught fire later, after the skin had burned through. This can be clearly seen on the archive film. Remarkably, some pieces of the *Hindenburg* have survived to the present day. The destruction of the airship was recognized as an historic event. Inevitably, people collected remnants of the airship as mementoes. The radio operator's chair survived intact and is on display at the Frontiers of Flight Museum on Love Field Airport at Dallas. Pieces of the huge cotton envelope were scattered all over the Lakeworth field and these were easy for people to pick up and take away. One researcher, Dr Bain, believed that people were too ready to blame the hydrogen for the fire, and that it was the treated cotton that was the real culprit. Bain looked through German archives and found that German scientists had concluded in the 1930s that the paint on the canvas was the cause of the fire. The widow of one of the German scientists confirmed that the German government hushed up the outcome of the investigation because it was politically embarrassing. Bain concluded his own very persuasive investigation by acquiring a piece of the *Hindenburg*'s coated skin and igniting it. It burned very readily indeed, just like the *Hindenburg* as a whole.

There are many more theories, too. Some of them involve fuel leaks, as a sixteen year old witness said that he could smell fuel just before the fire. Other theories involve design defects in the structure. It has been claimed that the film of the burning airship reveals how fragile the frame of the hull was, buckling and bending very easily. The ship had also had any number of minor accidents, some of which had been hushed up in the interest of German national pride; even the Zeppelin executives did not want to annoy Dr Goebbels. The ship's fin had been damaged on one occasion because she had been made to fly at full speed in windy conditions, simply so that some good propaganda film could be made. It seems the *Hindenburg* was not regularly or thoroughly inspected, and so it was likely to be faulty. This turbulent history could be the background for any number of theories involving mechanical, electrical or structural failures.

The incident was a great tragedy, not just for the people who died, but for the whole technology of airships. With the loss of the *Hindenburg*, there was no future for airships. One reason why the disaster made such a huge impact was that it was a very public and melodramatic disaster, witnessed by scores of journalists, photographers, film-makers and radio reporters. There has rarely been such intensive media coverage of a disaster actually happening. There are photographs and film of the pale skeleton of the R101 (*see* pages 321–28) lying on the hillside outside Beauvais, but not of the

R101 diving out of the sky and going up in a fireball. And that is why the *Hindenburg* disaster made a much greater impression on people, at the time and subsequently, than the R101 disaster.

A particular feature of the media coverage was the highly emotional and necessarily impromptu radio report recorded during the disaster by Herbert Morrison. His intensely personal response on the edge of tears to the events he was watching made an immediate impact on those who heard it, and those who have gone on hearing it ever since. 'Oh, the humanity!' His audiotape report, only semi-coherent and full of empathy for the suffering he imagined he was witnessing was later dubbed onto the newsreel film footage of the airship falling in flames, and ever since then people – people of the television age – have assumed that the words and images were always together. Quite unintentionally, the event marked the beginning of a new age in news reporting, and a far more immediate and visceral one.

There had been other airship accidents before the *Hindenburg*, but most of these had been caused by poor weather and most had involved British or American airships. Zeppelin were proud of their track record in terms of safety. The *Hindenburg*'s predecessor, the *Graf Zeppelin*, had flown more than a million miles without an accident, including making the first airship circumnavigation of the world. No passenger had ever been injured on a Zeppelin – until the *Hindenburg*. The *Hindenburg* disaster changed everything. Suddenly the faith of the public in airships evaporated. If the disaster had been reported, as with the R101 disaster, maybe the airships would have survived. But the spectacular newsreel film footage and Morrison's passionate commentary ensured that the public reaction was one of profound shock.

As it happened, a viable alternative had appeared at exactly the right moment in the shape of Pan American Airways. International air travel was now available, and it was conveniently fast for people with business to do. The Pan American planes flew much faster than the Hindenburg's top speed of 80 mph.

THE PARICUTIN ERUPTION

(1943)

PARICUTIN IS A volcano that lies 200 miles to the west of Mexico City. It is the newest of 1,400 volcanic vents in the Michoacán-Guanajuato volcanic field, which is a basalt lava plateau spattered with cones, small shield volcanoes and lava domes. What is particularly unusual about Paricutin is that scientists have been able to watch the entire process of the building of this volcano from its very beginning. Some volcanoes are very ancient. Paricutin is very new. It was born in 1943, and it takes its name from the village that once stood where the volcano now stands.

Three weeks before the new volcano made its first appearance, people living in Paricutin village heard rumbling noises that they thought sounded like thunder, but they were puzzled because the skies were cloudless. The noises were actually caused by earthquakes deep underneath Paricutin, representing the lava forcing its way towards the surface. Then, on 20 February 1943, a farmer called Dionisio Pulido and his wife Paula were burning shrubs encroaching on their cornfield when they saw the ground in front of them swell up like a great blister and split open to form a fissure eight feet across. There was a hissing sound as smoke and stinking fumes of hydrogen sulphide came from the fissure. This sinister blister in the Pulidos' cornfield would within a matter of a few hours become a small volcano. It would bury their farm and their village under a new mountain.

Dionisio Pulido described what happened.

At 4 pm I left my wife to set fire to a pile of branches, when I noticed that a crack, which was situated on one of the knolls on my farm, had opened . . . and I saw that it was a kind of fissure that had a depth of only half a metre. I set about igniting the branches again when I felt a thunderclap, the trees trembled, and I turned to speak to Paula. It was then I saw how the ground swelled and raised itself two-and-a-half metres high, and a kind of smoke began to rise up. Immediately more smoke began to rise with a hiss or whistle, loud and continuous, and there was a smell of sulphur.

I then became very frightened and I tried to unyoke one of the ox teams. I was so stunned I hardly knew what to do – or what to think – and I couldn't find my wife, or my son, or my animals. At last I came to my senses and I remembered the sacred Lord of the Miracles. I shouted out, 'Blessed Lord of the Miracles, you brought me into this world! Now save me!' I looked into the fissure where the smoke was rising and my fear disappeared for the first time. I ran to see if I could save my family, my friends and my oxen, but I could not see them and I thought they must have taken the oxen to the spring for water. I saw that there was no water in the spring, and thought the water had gone because of the fissure. I was very frightened and I mounted my mare and galloped to Paricutin where I found my wife and son and friends waiting for me. They had been afraid that I was dead and that they would never see me again.

The Paludos were right to run away from the fissure. It instantly became the main eruption vent. Within twenty-four hours a steep-sided cone 150 feet high stood on the site. Within a week it risen to a height of 300 feet. As the coarser material fell onto the growing cone, finer material, ash, rained down on the village of Paricutin. In March, the eruption became more energetic. There were eruption columns several miles high and there were occasional explosions like heavy artillery fire separated by periods of silence.

As the houses and the church in Paricutin became increasingly buried under volcanic debris, it was clear that the village was doomed. On 12 June its fate was sealed, when a lobe of lava began to crawl towards it. On 13 June, people began to leave. The larger village of San Juan Parangaricutiro, a little further from the volcano, would be evacuated a few months afterwards. By the following summer, most of the two villages were smothered in ash and lava. The church at the larger village seemed to resist burial, but finally all that remained of it – and all that remained of San Juan - were its two white towers standing proudly above a wilderness of dark lava.

That was at the height of the eruption sequence, in the summer of 1945, when Paricutin was ejecting 116,000 tons of material every day. About 16,000 tons of that was water, in vapour form, and the rest was lava. Paricutin's lava was acidic, which meant that it solidified almost on contact with the air. As a result, the lava did not flow like the basic lavas of the Hawaiian volcanoes. The sides of the new Mexican volcano were very steep, making it look like a huge slag heap, and the eruption was very explosive.

When the eruption sequence finally came to an end in 1952, the new mountain had reached the impressive height of 1,300 feet. The building of the Paricutin cone between 1943 and 1952 was the first time geologists were able to watch the process of the creation of a volcano in its entirety. The knowledge they gained was a very important addition to geological science, adding enormously to our understanding of volcanoes generally.

The Paricutin eruption was unusually long, with several phases spread across a period of nine years. After two years of mostly pyroclastic activity (the eruption of blocks of very hot but solidified lava), Paricutin switched to ejecting liquid lava from the cone's base for the next seven years. No one was actually killed directly by the Paricutin eruption, but three died when they were struck by lightning generated by the pyroclastic eruptions. The residents of the two lost villages were traumatized by their experience, and of course they had to abandon their homes and their fields for ever to the volcano.

THE ALEUTIAN EARTHQUAKE

(1946)

EARLY IN THE morning of 1 April 1946, a powerful earthquake (magnitude 7.4 on the Richter scale) shook the seabed off the Aleutian Islands in the North Pacific. Its epicentre was ninety miles south of Unimak Island, which is one of the islands in the chain of islands running in an arc between Asia and North America.

During this large-scale earthquake, a large chunk of the seabed lifted along the fault where the earthquake focus was. It was this lifting that generated the tsunami. As the seabed jerked upward, the water column above it was also pushed up; naturally this generated a set of concentric waves that sped away from the earthquake epicentre. The tsunami spread out across the entire Pacific Ocean basin.

The most detailed accounts of the 1946 tsunami come from Scotch Cap on Unimak Island, and the Hawaiian Islands. It seems that the phenomenon of wave refraction – the bending of the waves so they wrap themselves around islands – led to the Aleutian Islands taking the brunt of the tsunami. They acted like a natural breakwater and the coast of Alaska was relatively unaffected. Meanwhile, at Scotch Cap on Unimak Island the tsunami was enormous.

It was forty-eight minutes after the earthquake out in the Aleutian Trench that the tsunami struck the Unimak coastline at Scotch Cap, its south-western tip. It was 100 feet high and it completely annihilated the US Coast Guard lighthouse that had just been built there. All five men crewing the lighthouse were killed. As the wave broke over the coastline, it surged up over the cliffs, reaching 135 feet above sea level.

The total destruction of the Scotch Cap Coast Guard station meant that there was no possibility of sending any radio warning to Hawaii; no one was left alive to send it. So, when the first of several tsunamis arrived in the Hawaiian Islands, the people there were caught completely unprepared, even though five hours had elapsed since the earthquake. The first of the waves reached Hawaii at seven in the morning, causing widespread devastation along the coastline. There was severe damage at Hilo, on the main island of Hawaii; the whole of the Hilo waterfront was destroyed. In spite of the enormous distance the waves travelled, they were still as much as fifty-five feet high on Hawaii, thirty-six feet high on O'ahu and thirty-three feet high on Maui.

As is usual with tsunamis, these pushed vast quantities of water well inland, and flooded low-lying areas up to half a mile from the sea. Altogether 159 people were killed by the tsunami in Hawaii.

The tsunami reached the west coast of the United States, where Taholah in Washington state was hit by a surge five feet high, which caused damage to some of the boats in Taholah harbour. In Coo's Bay in Oregon, a tsunami ten feet high was experienced. Muir Beach and Half Moon Bay were hit by a wave over thirteen feet high, causing damage to both boats and waterfront. At Santa Cruz, waves ten feet high were responsible for drowning one person. The tsunami was small but nevertheless noticeable at Santa Barbara and in the Los Angeles area. There were even reports of fishing vessels being damaged as far south as Chile.

The tsunami reached the other side of the Pacific as well. Waves as high as thirty feet reached The Marquesas Islands in Polynesia.

THE ERUPTION OF
MOUNT HEKLA

(1947)

MOUNT HEKLA IS one of the most active volcanoes in Iceland. It has erupted intermittently through the centuries – sixteen times since 1104. These eruptions always have major local effects and often significant effects further afield. Located a few hundred miles from Northern Europe, the volcano is in a position to have adverse effects on its climate.

Recent research on Hekla has shown that it is supplied by a magma reservoir just four miles below the surface, which may come as a surprise to those who imagine that lava comes from the centre of the earth. In fact, most volcanic eruptions are fed by lava that been melted down fairly near the earth's surface. Hekla stands at a very significant location, on one edge of the rift that crosses Iceland. Since its formation, tens of millions years ago, Iceland has grown gradually wider and wider as it has repeatedly split open down the middle (north-east to south-west), the fissures sealed with the lava of successive volcanic eruptions. The eruptions of Hekla are a sign that Iceland continues to expand.

When Hekla erupted in 1947 it was the first eruption since 1913, when explosive eruptions produced lava flows just to the east of the mountain, at Mundafit and Lambafit.

At 6.41 am on 29 March 1947, without any warning a huge cloud of smoke and steam rose from Hekla to a height of nineteen miles. This great tower of cloud was built in the space of just ten minutes. It was a typical prelude to a Hekla eruption; the 1991 eruption began in exactly the same way. Within half an hour, lava started to well up from the fissure, pouring over the south-east slopes of the volcano. Huge volumes of lava poured out: 126,000 cubic feet of lava every second. By the evening of 29 March, lava was pouring from both ends of the fissure. The heat from the molten rock melted snow and ice fields on the western slope, causing floods and more huge clouds of steam.

By the second day of the eruption, no fewer than eight separate eruption columns could be seen. At the lower end of the fissure a crater had formed, and from it poured a great river of lava. This new crater was named Hraungigur, or Lava Crater. Two more craters had been formed, one on the south-west slope called Axlargigur and another on the summit called Toppgigur. This was all developing on the second day of the eruption, which was to continue not only into April, but until the April of the following year. Mount Hekla had by then grown in height by 184 feet to a total height above sea level of 4,930 feet.

Hekla's recorded history shows that it erupts, on average, every fifty-five years. The second half of the twentieth century showed a significant stepping-up of activity. The eruption in January 1991 was the third eruption in only twenty years.

THE MISSISSIPPI
FLOOD

(1947)

IN EARLY JULY 1947, a high flood peak passed down the Mississippi. It was the highest flood peak for 103 years.

The city of St Louis escaped serious damage, but waterfront towns further downstream, such as Grand Tower in Illinois, were still in grave danger. The authorities in Grand Tower had been reinforcing their inadequate levee against rising river levels for three months before the flood peak arrived. The residents worked shoulder to shoulder carrying the sandbags to levee, while their children used toy spades to fill the bags for them. By the end of June it was clear the town was going to be flooded. People took what furniture they could upstairs and ferried their animals up to the high ground near the cemetery. They knew it was going to be a 'duck drownder'. The river broke through the weak levee in one place after another. One resident recalled, 'Then I heard a boy hollerin', and I seen it was all over. We started runnin' and the water was right at our heels.' They ran for the high ground, encouraging everyone to run with them. One old lady, Lula Packwell, said she was danged if she'd leave, but the water pouring into her living room changed her mind.

By the following day, 600 out of the 1,000 people who lived at Grand Tower were crouching in tents on the one-block square of high ground, or perched in the two churches, surrounded by dangerously deep water. They were taken supplies each morning by the Coast Guard boat; they were even rowed in a new film to

361

watch each night. The residents knew that Grand Tower had to have a new levee, or they would have to evacuate for good.

As the flood waters receded up and down the Mississippi Valley, 48,000 flood refugees returned to their wrecked homes. Their houses stank of river mud and their livestock had been drowned. After forty days of flooding across five states, the long process of cleaning up and economic and psychological recovery began.

The cost of the flood was equivalent to the amount spent on flood prevention over the previous fifteen years. Congress had cut spending on flood control, and the governors of ten states met to insist that Congress put the money back. What was most significant about the 1947 flood on the Mississippi was that a relatively small number of people died – only sixteen – but the property damage was very severe – 850 million dollars. This was to mark the beginning of a trend that would continue for the next half century.

THE RIVER THAMES FLOOD

(1947)

THREE MONTHS BEFORE the big Mississippi flood, there had been disastrous flooding in Gret Britain, too. There, heavy rains in March had melted earlier heavy snowfalls and been unable to soak away because the ground remained frozen. Rivers overflowed their banks on a grand scale in what was to be the benchmark flood of the twentieth century for most British rivers. The River Thames flood in March 1947 is still remembered for the inundation of 2,000 homes in Maidenhead, Windsor and Eton. The Deputy Ranger of Windsor Great Park said the water ran off the park as if off a slate roof. This produced local floods in streams such as the Bourne Brook, which overflowed and swept through houses two days before the main flood peak passing down the Thames reached Windsor. Worst of all, there was no warning. Steam trains were used to evacuate the boys from Eton College. Flooded roads made food deliveries difficult, although one baker specialized in delivering by boat, hurling loaves through open bedroom windows; his aim eventually became quite good.

Serious though it was in 1947, if a flood of the same magnitude were to be repeated today its impact would be far more severe. In spite of the creation of Planning Services in the late 1940s, there has been ongoing urban development on the Thames floodplain, and indeed on many other floodplains in Great Britain. The problem is that many settlements were founded on valley-side river terraces and as they grew almost inevitably they extended down onto adjacent floodplains. It still goes on. Just in the Maidenhead and

Windsor reach of the Thames, 700 commercial units and 4,800 homes would be awash in a '1947' flood, bringing serious hardship, misery and trauma to over 12,500 people. The M4 motorway, designed and built since 1947, would also be submerged, causing serious disruption. The economic cost of a recurrence of the 1947 flood would be in the region of forty million pounds.

It was said in a report on the 1947 flood that it would have taken three River Thames channels to contain the volume of water shed by its catchment area that March. There would have no possibility of containing that volume of water within the channel. A Mississippi levee-style solution would have been useless. It would also be impossible to solve the problem by deepening and widening the Thames to create that extra capacity.

Post-1947, British engineers and hydrologists have tried to find acceptable solutions to the problem of flooding, while trying to conserve the flora and fauna. The Windsor and Eton Flood Alleviation Scheme, built 1996–2001, fifty years after the 1947 flood, is a good example of an integrated flood scheme. It gives the Thames a second channel, the Flood Relief Channel, which branches off the natural river in north Maidenhead and rejoins it seven miles away, downstream of Windsor. The flood Relief Channel in effect doubles the bankfull capacity of the River Thames, and allows flood water to bypass Windsor. When not in use, the Flood Relief Channel looks very like a natural river, about fifteen feet deep with a trapezium-shaped cross section, and with restored wetland habitats along its banks.

New building has nevertheless been allowed to take place on the floodplain. The cheapest and most sensible solution would be to recognize that the river needs its floodplain as space to store its excess discharge – that is the floodplain's function – and undertake the staged demolition of all building developments on floodplains. This strategy is known as managed retreat. Although those of us who have undertaken research on river floods know it is the only sustainable long-term solution, both authorities and communities are resisting it.

DESERTIFICATION
IN AFRICA

(1950–)

THE HOT DESERTS of the world were formed by natural processes over long periods. They are mainly regions of very low rainfall and high evaporation, and they have existed quite independently of human activity. There is geological evidence, such as the Old Red Sandstone, that there were hot deserts in the distant past, long before the human race had evolved. In the last century or so, it is evident that deserts have expanded, and there has been a lot of discussion among geographers about the reason for this. Some experts believe the expansion of deserts (desertification) may be mainly due to natural processes, others believe that human activities such as overgrazing are behind it. A particular problem is that the areas where desertification has happened and is happening are transitional areas on the desert edge, zones where things are very delicately balanced and there is often a mosaic of micro-environments. Small changes in rainfall patterns or land use management can have large-scale effects. They are also areas people are tempted to try to colonize; very few people would attempt to live in the Sahara, but there are thousands of people attempting to live in the Sahel, the desert-edge zone along its southern edge.

In the Sahel, people can easily push the environment over the edge. Too many people living in an area, with too many livestock, can inflict high levels of damage. Excessive trampling by animal hoofs can destroy the grass cover and change the nature of the soil, compacting it, making it impervious to water and increasing erosion when there is a thunderstorm; the trampling also powders the soil and exposes it to wind erosion. People need firewood for cooking, and that leads to the destruction of shrubs and trees, whose root systems help to hold the soil in place.

The 1950s brought the first real awareness that the deserts were expanding. This is not to say that desertification itself started in 1950, only that people became conscious of it; in fact, it seems to have been going on for 1,000 years. The word 'desertification' appears to have been coined by a French ecologist in 1949. Since then the process of desertification has been noticed, observed, mapped and studied in many parts of the world. The advent of remote sensing by satellite from the 1970s onwards, especially Landsat, has made it possible to map environmental change much more accurately than ever before.

Whether this is a natural or a man-made disaster is very hard to unravel. Desertification produced by human agency is likely to lead to a reduction in the amount of water in the regional water cycle and therefore to a change in local climate. On the other hand, a reduction in rainfall is likely to lead to desertification. It can be difficult to see what is causing the desert to spread. In some situations the process of desertification may be dramatic. The town of Nouakchott, the capital of Mauretania, is besieged by sand dunes from the Sahara Desert. This is a haunting image, but it is in fact rarely seen. There are very few places where the sand seas of the Sahara are invading non-desert areas.

Rainfall measurements can confirm that some phases of desertification appear to be natural in origin. There was, for instance, a severe drought in the Sahel of West Africa beginning in 1968. Over 100,000 people died. Over twelve million cattle died. Social and political organization from village to national level fell apart. It was a great disaster, but it is still not clear whether the scale of the losses were due mainly to the low rainfall or to inappropriate land management. Some people argue that the disaster was due to an economic and a political failure. A very telling satellite photograph taken in the 1970s shows a brown and barren landscape in Niger, but within it is a green rectangle, the Ekrafane Ranch, where scientific land management was able to overcome the natural problems of the drought.

It was in the 1950s that the first efforts were made to publicize desertification. The United Nations Educational, Scientific and Cultural Organization (UNESCO) launched a major ten-year campaign of Scientific Research on Arid Lands in 1951. The catastrophic drought of 1968–1973 in the African Sahel drew attention to the seriousness of the situation in countries such as Mauritania, Senegal, Mali, Upper Volta, Niger and Chad. An International Conference on Desertification was held in Nairobi in 1977.

AVALANCHES
IN THE ALPS

(1951)

HEAVY RAIN EARLY in 1951 caused a whole series of avalanches at different places in the Alps. The Swiss resort of Andermatt experienced as many as six avalanches in the space of an hour, and they killed thirteen people. Among this crop of Alpine avalanches was one that killed 240 people and trapped 45,000. This was the worst known avalanche disaster in modern times.

The history of avalanches goes back a long way. As Hannibal was crossing the Alps in 218 BC, he lost horses and elephants and 18,000 men in avalanches. In 1440 an avalanche fell on Davos, destroying two houses and killing eleven people; another avalanche at Davos in 1606 killed 100. In 1518, an avalanche fell on the Swiss village of Leukerbad killing sixty-one people and destroying the entire village. The so-called Rodi avalanche of 4 September 1618 buried the Swiss village of Plurs and all 1,500 of its residents, apart from four people who happened to be away from the village at the time; the total death toll in the Rodi avalanche was 2,427.

In an avalanche on 19 March 1775, in the Stura Valley in the Italian Alps, several members of a family were buried alive in a stable, with their livestock, for thirty-seven days. The forty-five-year-old Maria Anna Rocha, her sister-in-law, her thirteen-year-old daughter and six-year-old son were trapped in the stable behind their house when fifty feet of compacted snow buried the whole farm. The men of the family were not at home at the time and it was just assumed that the entire family had been killed, so no attempt was made to rescue them. The stable roof eventually gave way under the enormous weight of the snow, which confined the four people in a space twelve feet long, eight feet wide and five feet high. All the livestock died except for two goats. After twelve days the little boy died. The women were driven mad by the constant sound of dripping water and the awful stench of decomposing bodies. Then, on 24 April, the spring thaw exposed the roof of the shed. The men returned at this time, with the intention of digging out the bodies for burial and were amazed to find the two women and the girl still alive. The girl did not appear to have been seriously affected by the ordeal, but the sister-in-law had lost the power of speech and Maria Anna Rocha had lost all her hair.

An avalanche destroyed the Swiss village of Biel in 1869, killing twenty-seven. A series of avalanches in the Italian and Austrian Alps killed as many as 10,000 soldiers in the space of twenty-four hours on 13 December 1916. A barracks in the Marmolada Hills was destroyed, killing 250 soldiers. In total, over 60,000 Italian and Austrian soldiers were lost in avalanches during fighting in mountain passes during the First World War. Some of the avalanches were deliberately set off by enemy bombs. According to one report, 3,000 Austrians died in just two days. As an officer commented, 'The mountains in winter are more dangerous than the Italians.'

The winter of 1950–51 was an unusual one, with an incredibly large number of avalanches – 649 in the space of only three months. It was known as the Winter of Terror. The meeting of warm moist air from the Atlantic Ocean and cold air from the Arctic produced first heavy snow and then heavy rain in the Alps. There were many incidents all over the Alps, but Austria seems to have suffered the most damage, with thousands of acres of forest destroyed and over 100 people killed, but the death toll in Switzerland was only slightly lower.

Research into managing avalanches began in 1938 with the founding of a Swiss Federal Institute for Snow and Avalanche Research. The timing was significant. The Swiss expected a German invasion, anticipated having to fight in the mountains and did not want to repeat the experience of the Austrian and Italian armies in the First World War. The average death toll is quite low, with twenty-five people dying per year in Switzerland as a result of avalanches; many of these fatalities are off-piste skiers. But when 100 died in the winter of 1950–51, research into avalanches accelerated.

The people of the mountain villages already knew which places were most likely to suffer from avalanches and which routes down the mountain side the avalanches would follow. Often these routes are given names. The modern research phase collates this knowledge, maps it and identifies methods of controlling avalanches and. defending settlements that are at particular risk. Local authorities have also used the hazard maps in a number of ways; to develop plans for evacuating areas in an emergency, to ensure that houses are designed to withstand avalanches, and to provide avalanche barriers.

There is now a more scientific understanding of the way in which avalanches start. Expert observers can identify dangerous cracks in snowfields on high mountain sides and forecast avalanches. In the winter of 1999, they watched as cracks several miles long and up to twenty-five feet deep opened in the snowfields along the crests of valley sides. This was obviously going to be a very big avalanche once the packed snow broke free. When snow falls in small quantities it has virtually no weight, but when a large volume of it is packed together it can weigh tens of thousands of tons, move at 100 mph and exert pressures of five tons per square foot. Most conventionally designed houses will collapse when hit with that force. So will trees, which means that forests will not protect a valley floor village from a big avalanche, though they may act as a brake on the smaller avalanches.

The dynamics of avalanche movement are complex, because some of the material is solid or semi-solid and rolls or flows down the slope, and some of it is an airborne cloud of particles. An avalanche does not move like a landslide or a flood, where all of the moving material is in contact with the ground. Another problem in prediction is that avalanches pick up extra snow on their way down the mountain, and the faster the avalanche travels the more snow it picks up. Ignoring this cumulative addition, which is called entrainment, has led people in the past to build some avalanche barriers and deflectors too low. Immediately after the 1951 avalanches, scientists began working on theoretical models for avalanche behaviour. Among the first to emerge was the model proposed by the Swiss physicist Adolf Voellmy in 1955.

FLOODING IN NORTHERN ITALY

(1951)

HEAVY RAINS IN the Alps the autumn of 1951 swelled the River Po and its tributaries. The Po, the largest river in Italy, rose and overflowed its banks in November, leading to widespread flooding in the North Italian Plain. The flood was unusually severe from the Po's confluence with the River Ticino to the sea. This was because the flood peaks travelling down the many separate Alpine tributaries of the River Po just happened to arrive in the main river at the same time, creating a catastrophically high flood peak in the lower Po, the largest ever recorded for the river. The intensity of the rainfall was also unusually high – over one inch in a day, and eight inches in a week – and there was no possibility of the ground absorbing that amount of water.

There was also, as so often with river floods, a man-made component in the disaster. There had been a long history of river bank engineering works along the Po. In particular, there were levees built to prevent flooding along the middle reach of the river. These reduced the river's ability to shed excess water for storage on the floodplain (which is what they were designed for) but they also had the inadvertent effect of increasing the size of the flood peaks further downstream in the lower valley. Human interference actually produced more serious flooding in the lower reaches of the Po. This is a story that is repeated in the valleys of many rivers in more economically developed countries, where so-called 'flood prevention' measures have frequently made flooding worse.

Over 220 billion cubic feet of water poured out onto the North Italian Plain. Farmhouses disintegrated under the onslaught of the flood waters, 30,000 cattle were drowned and 150 people lost their lives. Lorry-loads of flood refugees arrived in the city of Milan.

The flood disaster was intensified by a storm surge in the Adriatic. The wind was blowing strongly from the east, piling the waters of the Adriatic up against the mouth of the Po. This caused the flood waters that would normally have emptied into the sea to back up and inundate large areas of the plain.

American and British seaplanes and helicopters were sent in to help rescue people, and 150,000 were evacuated. Of those, 20,000 people made homeless by the flooding were forced to queue for food at army field kitchens and sleep under very crowded conditions in schools and churches. A few people resisted rescue, standing on patches of dry high ground. Around them, in the flood water, bobbed branches, furniture and even coffins eroded from graveyards. A lorry loaded with refugees was swept off the road by a great jet of water spurting from a bursting river embankment. Thirty-three of its forty passengers were drowned.

The flood disaster was economically catastrophic. The plain had been the main food-producing region of Italy and it was to be months before it was back in production again. Repairing the damage cost the equivalent of one-quarter of Italy's annual income. It was the worst flood in Italy for 100 years.

THE LYNMOUTH
FLOOD DISASTER

(1952)

IN THE EARLY evening of 15 August 1952, a wall of water swept without warning through the small town of Lynmouth on the North Devon coast, killing thirty-four people.

The water had fallen on Exmoor just four miles away to the south, where a summer storm produced very high intensity rainfall that lasted all day. More than nine inches of rain fell on Exmoor that day. It would have been impossible for any land surface to absorb this amount of water, so a proportion would be bound to run off into streams and rivers. The situation was made worse by the dense and impermeable nature of the rocks, and the fact that the valley sides were very steep. There was a contemporary rumour that the disaster was caused by a government-authorized rain-making experiment that went wrong. The *Sunday Times* eventually found evidence in declassified secret files that at the height of the Cold War the British Ministry of Defence was indeed experimenting with techniques for creating heavy rain with a view to flooding enemy trenches and immobilizing tanks in the event of a Russian invasion. There is, even so, no reason to connect this with the Lynmouth disaster, which can be fully explained in terms of the weather conditions reported at the time. The rain-making experiments seem to have taken place far away downwind, in East Anglia.

As the storm water flowed in sheets one or two inches thick off the moors and into the streams and rivers, it picked up speed. The streams turned quickly into torrents that were able to uproot trees and dislodge boulders; they were able to use these as battering rams to smash culverts and bridges. Once the water reached a speed of fifteen feet per second it was able to move a boulder three feet across. It seems the speed must have reached a speed of thirty feet per second to account for the boulder weighing more than seven tons that was later found dumped in the basement of a hotel in Lynmouth. The biggest boulder moved during the flood was 350 cubic feet in size, and that was transported by the West Lyn.

Very large volumes of water arrived in several streams converging on Lynmouth, including the East Lyn and the West Lyn, as well as Farley Water and Hoaroak Water, which joined the already swollen East Lyn at Watersmeet, a picturesque spot not far from the town. Usually in storms the flood peaks of the East and West Lyn are out of phase with each other; on this occasion they coincided. From their confluence a raging torrent sped through Lynmouth, giving no warning whatever of its approach.

One alarming aspect of the flood was the way it repeatedly surged. There was not just one flood peak, but several. It is thought that this was caused by bridges and culverts in the catchment area becoming blocked with trees, branches and boulders, ponding back the water for a while to create temporary reservoirs, followed by dam-bursts releasing all the debris and water at once.

Tom Denham, owner of the Lyndale Hotel, said his cellars had flooded before in previous storms, so at first he was not too worried. 'About half- past nine there was a tremendous roar. The West Lyn had broken its banks and pushed against the side of the hotel, bringing with it thousands of tons of rock and debris in its course. It carried away the chapel opposite and a fruit shop. Three people in the fruit shop were against the lounge windows of the hotel. We managed to pull them through in the nick of time. I then ordered everyone to go to the second floor, where they huddled in the corridors for safety. In all we had sixty people in the hotel that night.' Mr Watson of Catford was staying at the hotel with his family and described the same scene; 'From seven o'clock last night the waters rose rapidly and at nine o'clock it was just like an avalanche coming through our hotel, bringing down boulders from the hills and breaking down walls, doors and windows. Within half an hour the guests had evacuated the ground floor. In another ten minutes. the second floor was covered, and then we made for the top floor where we spent the night.' Another hotel guest, Arthur Brooks, described the rescue of the people from the fruit shop. 'We were looking out when we saw three people being washed out to sea. We managed to get a hold of them and brought them through the window. By the morning, boulders were piled twenty feet high outside that window.'

A flood of this magnitude had not happened for a very long time, so several generations of Lynmouth residents had confidently built right up to the river banks. There was nowhere for the storm water to go except straight through the houses. The wall of water, twenty feet high, wrecked ninety-three buildings and destroyed twenty-eight bridges. Four bridges on the main road were washed away.

One of the fishermen, Ken Oxenholme, saw that Lynmouth High Street was flooded, so he ran through the woods to reach his wife and child, who were staying in a caravan on the inland edge of the town. He said, 'As we watched, we saw a row of cottages near the river, in the flashes of lightning, because it was dark by this time, fold up like a pack of cards and swept out with the river with the agonizing screams of some of the local inhabitants who I knew very well.'

All the Exmoor valleys have V-shaped cross sections with steep sides and bottoms that are so narrow that that there is scarcely room for a road, let alone a settlement, beside the river. Lynmouth is the only place where a settlement in the valley bottom has been attempted, and there only by building on the river bed itself – an extremely dangerous thing to have done. The settlement developed out into the river channel itself, both confining and diverting it. During the flood, the river reverted to its natural path and attempting to re-establish its original wider channel, demolishing the houses that stood in its way. It simply reclaimed for itself the boulder beds that were part of its original channel.

As the storm water subsided, the village was evacuated so that troops and council workers could clear the buildings that had been ruined or rendered dangerous by the flood. There was no water, gas or electricity supply to the town and all the boats in the harbour were washed out to sea. Twelve bodies were recovered quite quickly, the rest were found later.

The whole of Exmoor was affected by the freak storm and the flooding it produced. There was considerable damage in the valleys of the Barle, Exe, Heddon and Bray, but the worst effects were felt at Lynmouth. This was far from being a flood on the grand scale – nothing to compare with the major floods on the Mississippi or the Yellow River – but its impact was considerable. The emotional and psychological aspects of the drama filled the newspapers for days afterwards. The *Western Morning News* carried the story under the headline 'Unparalleled scene of destruction'; 'Superlatives are too puny to describe the calamity which has befallen Lynmouth and Barbrook. Deaths on a wartime scale, destruction at Barbrook worse than in the heaviest blitz, hundreds of residents and visitors ruined and destitute – the story stuns the human mind.'

The reconstruction of Lynmouth was done carefully to ensure that sufficient space was left for a future storm discharge to reach the sea without going through any houses. Some of the recommendations made in the Dobbie Report on the disaster were never implemented. No dams were constructed to trap boulders further up the valleys. No flood relief channel was built. But a wide open space was left at the river mouth, the bridge spans were all enlarged, and the capacity of the East and West Lyn channels was increased so that they could accommodate a peak discharge of 23,000 cubic feet per second, which is the rate at which water was pouring through Lynmouth at the height of the flood.

From the disaster, geomorphologists learned a great deal about the way landscapes can develop in jumps. Views about landscape development seem to flip backwards and forwards between uniformitarianism (processes operating continuously at a steady rate through time) and catastrophism (change by infrequent upheavals). Studying the Lynmouth disaster gave evidence in favour of catastrophism. An enormous amount of work was done by water acting on the North Devon landscape in a single day and night; in places the river channel was cut down twelve feet. The morning after the disaster, people were amazed to see hundreds of trees, weighted down by boulders locked into the root systems, standing half a mile out to sea with their branches sticking up out of the water. This fantastic floating forest showed the scale of the overnight change to the landscape.

One thing that startled geomorphologists was that such a catastrophic flood could be generated in such a small catchment area – just thirty-nine square miles. The flood disaster has been very closely studied and a far greater understanding of the mechanics of river floods and their relationship to other environmental factors has been reached. One factor that emerged as crucially important was the role of rainfall patterns over a period. There was a very heavy fall of rain on 15 August 1952, but there had been a significant amount of rain on each of the fourteen days running up to that day. This antecedent rainfall played a big part in saturating the landscape before the big storm. Because Exmoor was totally waterlogged, it refused the extra water poured onto it on 15 August; all of it poured off into the rivers.

Immediately after the flood, there was plenty of evidence of the catastrophe left in the landscape – erosional scars, flood channels, piles of boulders – but nearly all of that evidence has subsequently been eroded away or concealed by subsequent small-scale river activity. This has made geomorphologists realize that catastrophic events do not always leave clear and indelible imprints on the landscape, and that many such events must have passed away out of memory. As for the Lynmouth disaster itself, there are few people now, fifty years on, who can still remember it. The result of this collective memory failure is that we can be caught out over and over again.

In fact, during the research phase following the Lynmouth disaster, geomorphologists found evidence, in the form of alternate layers of loam, gravel and boulders, of past floods that were even bigger than the 1952 flood. The 1952 flood eroded the river bed and exposed some huge boulders that could only have been transported by a very large discharge of water. Unfortunately it was not possible to discover the dates of these earlier floods. We know from a contemporary account that there was a devastating flood in 1770. 'The river at Lynmouth by the late rain rose to such a degree as was never known by the memory of man now living, which brought down great rocks of several tons each, and choked up the harbour. And also carried away the foundation under the Kay [Quay?] on that side of the river six foot down and ninety foot long, and some places two foot under the Kay, which stands now in great danger of falling.' An even more destructive flood was reported in 1607, but it sounds as if this was a tidal surge or even a tsunami, a flood from the sea, not a flood from the moors.

The 1952 Lynmouth disaster made people who were living in what they thought were safe settlements in a rich and well-organized state realize that they were, after all, still very vulnerable to violent acts of nature, even if they were infrequent. It also made many people stop to consider whether the design of settlements really took sufficient heed of natural hazards, especially those with a long return period. It may be that the Lynmouth flood was a 'once in 200 years' flood, and it opened a debate about the desirability of designing towns and individual structures to cope with events that are very unlikely to happen for the next two or three generations. Because of the delicate balance between cost and risk, it is a debate that still continues.

SEA FLOODS ON THE EAST COAST OF ENGLAND

(1953)

JANUARY 1953 SAW some of the most serious coastal flooding in north-west Europe in modern times. The so-called 'East Coast' floods affected the low-lying coastline of Lincolnshire, East Anglia and the Thames Estuary. The floods continued across the southern North Sea into the Netherlands, where the losses were significantly greater. A peculiarity of this disaster is that at the time it was treated as a lot of separate and very local disasters; with today's media coverage, it would almost certainly be treated as a great national or indeed international disaster.

The floods of 1953 were by no means the first time the low-lying coasts of south-east England were flooded by the sea. They had happened many times before. As early as AD 38, 10,000 people were drowned along the same coastline. In 1099, the *Anglo-Saxon Chronicle* tells of a flood of 'such a height and did so much damage, as no man remembered before.' Thousands of people were drowned, as far south as Kent. In 1236, the Thames overflowed its banks in London, when river water was backed up by high tides. 'In the Palace of Westminster men did row wherries.' The Fenland towns were flooded. Many were drowned; 'about a hundred bodies were committed in one day.' In 1287, the Norfolk coast was flooded – 'parts which no age past times had recorded to have been covered by water' – and 500 people were lost. A coastal flood stretching from the Humber to the Thames in 1570 drowned 20,000 sheep and cattle. In 1663, Samuel Pepys described another London flood; 'the Greatest tide that ever was. . . all Whitehall having been drowned.' In 1897, after serious sea floods in Norfolk, Suffolk, Essex and the Thames estuary, pleas were made for flood defence to be made a national rather than a local issue. The 1953 East Coast floods therefore came, like so many other disasters, with a history.

On the morning of Saturday 31 January 1953, the Dutch flood-warning system issued a warning of 'rather high tides', though this was not co-ordinated with British weather warnings. An hour or so later the Meteorological Office at Dunstable warned that 'exceptionally strong winds' were expected, though there was no mention of flooding. By noon the centre of the strong low pressure system responsible for all the problems that were to follow had moved to the east of Scotland, the atmospheric pressure dropping to 966 millibars.

The strong winds were severe enough to build waves in the Irish Sea powerful enough to capsize the ferry Princess Victoria. She sank at one forty-five pm, drowning nearly everyone on board. By five pm, waves twenty feet high were crashing into the Lincolnshire coastline, tearing down thirty miles of sea defences; forty-one people were drowned. By six pm, the sea defences were breached at Mablethorpe, Saltfleet and Sutton, and at several points along the north Norfolk coast, too. At six-fifteen pm, it was high tide at King's Lynn. As the Dutch had predicted it was unusually high; in fact, it was eight feet higher than expected, and the flooding at King's Lynn drowned eight people. A few minutes later sixty-six people died when sea defences at Heacham and Snettisham were broken through. At seven twenty-seven pm the Hunstanton to King's Lynn train collided with a floating bungalow.

By eight pm, Force 12 winds were recorded at Felixstowe. At nine pm, sea water poured into the town of Great Yarmouth, drowning ten people. An hour later the Lincolnshire Police issued a statement saying that there were no casualties and the situation was 'in hand'; probably the intention was to prevent panic, and the tendency to understate and keep a traditionally British stiff upper lip was a major characteristic of this disaster, which was much larger in scale than the authorities or the media were ready to reveal.

At midnight, a storm surge six feet high inundated part of the port of Harwich in Essex, drowning eight people. The unusually high tide now reached the Thames Estuary, flooding Canvey Island, drowning fifty-eight people and making over 11,000 people homeless. At one am on Sunday 1 February, the sea wall at Felixstowe broke, drowning forty. Many of the survivors climbed onto the rooftops to escape the rising water. People living at Jaywick in Essex also had to climb onto their roofs to get out of the flood water; thirty-seven drowned there.

The cause of the disaster was a storm surge. The low-pressure system moving across Scotland towards Denmark generated strong north winds that piled water towards the southern end of the North Sea. This coincided with and exaggerated the high tide. The low-pressure system also played a part in lifting the surface of the North Sea slightly. The overall effect was to pull the sea level as much as nine feet above the normal high tide level, allowing the sea to spill over sea defences. The powerful waves generated by the strong north wind also did a lot of damage to sea walls.

There was a human element in the disaster as well. In spite of the existence of telephone, radio and television, information about the developing situation was not passed to the relevant communities, who were – at every location – taken by surprise when the storm surge arrived. Flood defence was organized at a very local level by the many separate river boards, and they had no system for coordinating information. There was an almost complete failure of communication.

It is difficult to arrive at a total death toll, because at the time the disaster was treated as a lot of separate incidents. The death

toll for the East Coast flood is often given as 307, but to this should really be added the loss of 224 people on the *Princess Victoria* in the Irish Sea, the ferry that sank in the same storm. The sea floods of 1953 were the worst national peacetime disaster to affect Great Britain. It came as a great shock and it had a number of significant effects. The Waverley Committee was set up to investigate the causes of the disaster and explore ways of preventing a repetition. Millions of pounds were spent during the years that followed on developing flood warning systems and on rebuilding sea walls. It led directly on to the building of the Thames Barrier, the world's largest movable flood barrier, to stop a storm surge from entering London. The Met Office was given the job of supplying a twenty-four-hour forecast of tidal surges.

These specific outcomes led on to the formation in 1989 of a National Rivers Authority, whose job it became to oversee and co-ordinate river flood defences, and then to the creation in 1996 of the Environment Agency, which has overall responsibility for dealing with all flood defences.

SEA FLOODS IN THE
NETHERLANDS

(1953)

As ALONG THE coast of south-eastern England, the Dutch coastline had a long history of flooding associated by storm surges. The most famous sea floods were the St Elisabeth Flood of 1421 and the All Saints' Day Flood of 1570. These both caused enormous amounts of damage and thousands of deaths.

The 1953 flood disaster in the Netherlands was a continuation of the one that affected the east coast of England. On the night of 31 January–1 February, hurricane-force onshore winds from the north-west exaggerating a high tide pushed sea water right over the artificial coastal embankments and into huge expanses of low-lying land beyond. The Dutch had built an elaborate system of protecting embankments (dykes), but the 1953 storm conclusively showed that they were completely inadequate to the task of keeping out the sea. A very large area was submerged, both on the mainland and out in the islands. Large parts of South Holland, Zeeland and North Brabant were submerged. Altogether 5,500 square miles of land, and nine per cent of the country's agricultural land, went under water that night.

At Cadzand, the sea overtopped the dyke. At Kruiningen, it was able to sweep through the gates of the ferry dock, which had been left open. The Kruiningen Polder, an area of six square miles, was flooded very quickly. At Rotterdam, new records were set for the height of flood waters. Parts of Rotterdam-South on the island of Ysselmonde were inundated when the water came over the quays. One unfortunate person was drowned while sleeping in a cellar there. The dykes were broken through on the island of Roozenburg and at Wolphaartsdijk and Ossenisse. Reigerspolder and areas of South Beveland were submerged.

The scale of the Dutch disaster was enormous – far greater than the East Coast floods in England. Thirty miles of dykes were destroyed, and another 100 miles of dykes damaged. There were also 47,000 houses damaged or destroyed, 72,000 people evacuated, 10,000 cattle drowned and 1,835 people lost their lives. The statistics alone give an idea of the magnitude of the disaster.

The piling up of sea water at the southern end of the North Sea was made even more dangerous by the physical shape of the North Sea basin. The coasts of England to the west and Denmark, Germany, Holland and Belgium to the east converge on the Straits of Dover. As the water was pushed southwards by the depression, it was forced into a smaller and smaller space, causing the sea level to rise higher and higher. The result was that at two am on 1 February the storm surge was one foot high in Northumberland, three feet high at Holderness, six feet high along the East Anglian coast, and nine feet high on the Dutch coast.

The coast of the Netherlands took the full force of the storm, suffering winds at Force nine or ten for twenty hours without ceasing. The wind maintained the water at the high-tide level and on 1 February there was no ebb tide at all. The waves were powerful enough to start destroying the stoutly made sea walls. The sea walls were strongly revetted on the seaward side, but not on the inland side. As the sea poured through and over the walls, it attacked them on the landward side – pulling them apart by suction. Long stretches of the dykes were destroyed. The dykes at Kruiningen and Oude-Tonge were the first to break, then many more followed, along a stretch of coast over 100 miles long.

There was one redeeming feature of the disaster, and that was the timing of the storm surge, which came three hours before the arrival of the spring tide. If the two had coincided, the flooding would have been even worse.

People woke up in the night to the sound of rushing water and found themselves trapped in their homes. Some houses collapsed under the force of the water. As the winds dropped, some people tried to save themselves by making for higher ground, while others climbed out onto their roofs. There were individual rescue initiatives, as villagers set off in boats to look for people who were stranded. As in England, the communications system was disrupted, and the seriousness of their predicament was unknown to the outside world; as a result, it was some time before an organized rescue operation was mounted.

There was a second flood on the afternoon of 1 February, and this one killed even more people than the first. The dykes were already breached, so sea water was able to pour straight into the polders. Houses that survived the first onslaught succumbed to the second. Livestock and people were swept away by the flood water. As one sea wall and dyke after another collapsed, just one dyke remained along the River Yssel to protect the three million people living in the provinces of North and South Holland from the rising waters of the North Sea. This was the Schielandse Hoge Zeedijk. For some time this major embankment prevented the flood water from invading Holland. There was one section of this dyke, called the Groenendijk, that was not revetted with stone, and was therefore very vulnerable to collapse under the great weight of water pressing against it. At the height of the storm, teams of volunteers worked hard to reinforce it.

It was to no avail. In the end, at 5.30 in the morning of 1 February, the Groenendijk collapsed and sea water surged through the breach, flooding the province of South Holland. In an act of sheer desperation, one local mayor, the mayor of Nieuwerkerk, commandeered a river ship called *The Two Brothers* and ordered it to be sailed into the hole in the dyke in order to seal it up. The captain, Arie Evegroen, feared that his ship might go right through the breach in the dyke and dive down into the polder beyond, so he took a rowing boat with him. But the mayor's extraordinary idea turned out to be a complete success. The ship sailed into the hole in the dyke, lodged itself there and plugged the hole, stopping any further water escaping into the polders. Without *The Two Brothers*, the death toll would have been much higher.

It was not until Monday 2 February that large-scale relief began to get under way. Helicopters flew over the disaster area and dropped sandbags and food supplies. Mass evacuation was organized and by the evening of 3 February the worst of the disaster was over. There were still some people who were stranded, but they would be rescued soon.

Communications were a major problem, just as they were in Great Britain that night. There were local radio stations, but none of them broadcast at night. There were weather stations, but many of the smaller stations only operated in the daytime. The flood came not only at night, but on a Saturday night, which was a night when many people who might have been on a night duty were having a night off.

In consequence of these unfortunate circumstances, the flood and severe weather warnings that were transmitted did not penetrate the affected areas. Because people did not receive warnings, they were completely unprepared when the flooding came. And once the flooding started, the telephone networks were disrupted. There was an heroic attempt by amateur radio operators to set up a voluntary emergency radio network, and this ran radio communications for ten days and nights continuously. These amateurs were the only people who kept contact between the flooded areas and the outside world.

It was the worst sea-flood disaster in the Netherlands for 300 years. The impact of the double storm surge in Holland was enormous. In total, 1,835 people were drowned in the flood – along with 200,000 cattle, horses and pigs – 72,000 people had to be evacuated, and 3,000 houses were destroyed and another 40,000 were damaged. Huge areas of the polders, over four million acres, were contaminated by the salt water and they would take several years to regain their fertility. It is estimated that Holland lost nearly ten percent of its arable land. The sea defences were badly eroded, with 100 separate breaches totalling many miles in length. The total cost of the damage was 300 million dollars. Nine months had passed before the last breach in the dykes had been closed.

This was the first flood disaster in the Netherlands to be photographed, and it was photographed and filmed on a grand scale. Journalists, film-makers and photographers from all over the world arrived in large numbers to make their own record of what had happened. One of the photographers wrote in a book called *The Disaster*, 'In the hours during which the disaster took place, no photographs were made at all; it was dark and, besides, people had other things on their minds. Most photographs of the disaster were taken after the storm had died down and the water was therefore a lot less wild.' This is often the way; the photographs we see are usually the aftermath of disaster rather than the disaster itself.

As a direct result of the disaster, the Dutch government launched an expensive new programme of sea defences that would cost 650 million dollars. This Delta Project would create a new set of barriers along a stretch of coast in the south-west twenty-five miles long. They would have three separate lines of defence, poetically named 'watchers' (the stout outer sea wall), 'sleepers' (lighter walls built further inland) and 'dreamers' (smaller barriers around individual farms). The dreamers were in effect a modern version of the ancient terps, the artificial mounds built by the earliest inhabitants of the Netherlands. The Delta Project was one of the most ambitious flood-prevention projects ever attempted anywhere; it took from 1955 until 1997 to complete. There were delays because of opposition from conservationists who wanted to preserve the distinctive wildlife habitats of the several estuaries that make up the Rhine Delta. Major river floods in 1993 and 1995 nudged the authorities into overriding the objections from the conservationists.

THE MALPASSET DAM DISASTER

(1959)

THE NAME OF the dam, 'Malpasset', sounds the same as the French phrase *mal passer*, meaning 'to go wrong', which is exactly what the Malpasset Dam did. The Malpasset Dam was an arch dam on the Reyran River in the south of France, designed by qualified French engineers to supply domestic and irrigation water to the region. It was only five years old, a graceful sweeping curve of concrete 740 feet across and 200 feet high that looked the embodiment of modern technology. But it was only twenty-two feet thick at its base, tapering to a mere five feet at the top. The French engineers who designed it boasted that it was the world's thinnest dam. It was a very unfortunate boast. The dam was wafer-thin and just too weak to support the great weight of water behind it.

Upvalley from the Malpasset Dam, the River Reyran was ponded back to form a lake six miles long, one mile wide and 200 feet deep. Downvalley and five miles from the perilously fragile dam was the small Riviera town of Fréjus, where 14,000 people lived. Ironically they liked to call their town the Pompeii of Provence, not because it was doomed to be overwhelmed by catastrophe but because it was rich in Roman remains. Fréjus had been founded in 49 BC by Julius Caesar, and it was at Fréjus that some of the galleys were built that defeated Antony and Cleopatra at the Battle of Actium in 31 BC.

Some weeks before the dam collapsed, ominous cracking

noises had been heard coming from inside the structure. There were some minor leaks, too. The Malpasset Dam was beginning to disintegrate.

In the last week of November 1959, there were five days of continuous rain that threatened to overfill the reservoir, which was rising alarmingly. As much as five inches of rain fell in the twenty-four hours immediately before the dam failed. This brought the water level in the reservoir to within eleven inches of the top of the dam. As the rain went on falling and the reservoir level went on rising, the dam's caretaker, André Ferraud, decided he had to let some water out but the authorities refused to allow him to do this. He did this in spite of the engineers' warning him not to do this for fear that the overflow could undermine the foundations of the highway that was being built very close to the dam. In fact, according to one theory about the disaster, the real threat may have been the other way around; it may have been explosions connected with the road-building project that caused the dam to crack. Another theory is that a geological fault, a crack in the rock passing under the dam, may have fatally weakened it. Whatever actually caused the dam to fail, Ferraud was in no doubt that the dam was overstrained by being so full and he wanted to lower the level of the water to reduce the pressure on the dam wall. In the early evening of 2 December, Ferraud decided to open the dam's sluice gates a little, against direct orders from above. At six o'clock, he opened the water release valves. Water started to drain down, but only at a rate of 360 cubic feet per second, and this unfortunately was not fast enough to release the pressure in time.

Whatever the exact reason, just three hours after he had opened the sluices, André Ferraud felt 'a terrible cracking' underneath him. It was the dam breaking up. He grabbed his child, and with his wife he ran for higher ground.

Moments later, at nine-thirteen pm, the Malpasset Dam collapsed like a smashed pot, releasing the entire reservoir behind it. A wall of water 125 feet high rushed down the valley at a speed of fifty mph, pushing trees, houses, cars and people before it towards the sea. It swept through and destroyed two small villages, Malpasset and Bozon, as well as the site of the new highway just 600 feet away from the dam. When the water reached Fréjus, twenty minutes after the dam failed, it still formed a threatening wall ten feet high. This may not sound very high or very dangerous, but it is worth remembering that it is quite possible for an able-bodied adult to be knocked over and drowned by a fast-moving sheet of water that is only two feet deep. It spared the old Roman part of the town, but submerged the densely populated western part. Many minor roads were destroyed as the water surged towards the sea. Hundreds of buildings were damaged or destroyed; at least 421 people died (and maybe as many as 510) and 2,600 were made homeless by the disaster.

It was not until the following morning that an organized rescue operation got under way. That operation was impeded by the flood damage. A long slick of mud coated the valley between the broken ruin of the dam and the sea. The main highway from Paris to Nice and Cannes was blocked by a tangle of trees and wrecked houses, and a one-mile stretch of the main railway between Paris and the Riviera was ripped away. Meanwhile, virtually nothing of the dam was left standing. Only a few blocks remained in place on one side. Pieces of the crumbled dam were spread down the valley by the flood waters and chunks of it can still be found today.

EARTHQUAKE IN CHILE

(1960)

THE EPICENTRE OF the 1960 Chilean earthquake, which happened at just after ten o'clock in the morning on 22 May 1960, was 100 miles off the coast of Chile. It was a shallow earthquake, originating no more than 200 feet below the floor of the Pacific Ocean. It was generated along the Peru-Chile Trench, where the Nazca Plate dives underneath the South American Plate. Movement along this boundary is continual and intermittent earthquakes are bound to keep on happening.

The earthquake was a very powerful one, though its force varied from place to place. The nearest big towns, Valdivia and Puerto Montt, suffered severe damage and the lower town at Puerto Montt was hit with tremendous violence. The town of Concepción was also seriously damaged. Relatively few people were killed – far fewer than was at first feared – because there was a sequence of foreshocks that were strong enough to bring people out of buildings and into the streets. The main quake came while people were still outside. As a result, the houses and business premises that fell down were mainly empty. The early press reports guessed that as many as 10,000 people had been killed, but it seems likely that the death toll was only one-quarter of that figure. There were few human fatalities, but the property damage was considerable, running to 550 million dollars. More than 58,000 houses were totally destroyed in this disaster. The government of Chile estimated that two million people were made homeless.

The earthquake also transformed the landscape. It altered the shape of the coastline. It also triggered huge rockfalls and landslides high in the Andes Mountains. Some of these were large enough to divert major rivers or dam them to create new though possibly temporary lakes. One of these new lakes was created on the Rio San Pedro, the river flowing out of Lake Rinihue. The coastline at Puerto Montt sank as a result of the earth movement and a strip along the coast was flooded with ocean water. The earthquake triggered a volcanic eruption, too; the volcano Puyehue erupted on 24 May, less than forty-eight hours after the main shock.

Tsunamis were generated by the seabed earthquake, waves that rippled out at a speed of 200 mph, travelling right across the Pacific Ocean to reach the Hawaiian Islands, the Philippines and Japan. Along the coast of Chile, the tsunami caused havoc, drowning at least 1,200 people. When it reached Hawaii and Japan, many hours later, it caused more deaths.

The arrival of the tsunami along the Hawaiian beaches was fairly quiet, but it still killed sixty-one people and injured forty-three. But the third wave in the tsunami sequence was funneled into Hilo Bay, which exaggerated its height, so that it reached twenty feet and caused the flooding of about 600 acres. Twenty-three million dollars' worth of damage was done in Hilo Bay by this wave, and all of the Hawaiian deaths were concentrated in that area. Only structures built of steel or reinforced concrete were left standing in Hilo Bay, and even they were gutted. A ten-ton tractor was swept away. Huge boulders from a rock groyne were thrown 500 feet inland.

On Maui, most of the damage was on the north coast, around Kahului. Half a dozen houses and a warehouse were destroyed. The tsunami floated a church off its foundations and moved it twenty feet. Other islands in the Hawaiian group, such as Kauai and Oahu, escaped serious damage. A beach house was destroyed on the island of Lanai. On the whole, on this occasion the Pacific tsunami warning system worked well.

The tsunami crossed the entire width of the Pacific to ravage the east coast of the Japanese island of Honshu. Because of the tsunami 100 people were killed, 855 were injured, eighty-five were unaccounted for, and 1,678 homes were destroyed – and this with the benefit of an early warning system.

The tsunami rippled northwards, too, and arrived in San Francisco Bay on the morning of 23 May, around fifteen hours after the seabed earthquake. A tsunami wave about five feet high washed along the coast of California, and was observed at that height at a number of places, such as Stenson beach and Santa Barbara; over long distances along the Pacific coast it was lower, at about three feet high. This may not sound high, but tsunami waves are very broad and contain enormous volumes of water. It caused more than a million dollars' worth of damage in Los Angeles and Long Beach harbours. It is estimated that as many as 300 small boats were torn from their moorings and set adrift, and about thirty of them were sunk. These included a seventy-five-foot yacht, which was smashed into the piers of a bridge, seriously damaging them. The capsizing of boats meant spillage of petrol, with the consequent risk of fire. At the Yacht Center, 235 landing stages were lost; 110 more were destroyed at the Colonial Yacht Anchorage and Cerritos Yacht Anchorage. These losses cost 300,000 dollars.

Raymond Stuart, a skin diver, went missing, presumed drowned, at Cabrillo Beach. The strong currents associated with the tsunami undermined pilings and foundations of various installations. A coastguard landing stage with the tide gauge mounted on it was washed four miles out to sea, but it was rescued. The scale of damage at Los Angeles and Long Beach was out of all proportion to the height of the wave.

At San Diego, it was a similar story. A ferry laden with passengers was smashed into the dock at Coronado, knocking out eight piles. Another ferry was washed a mile off course and swept, out of control, into a flotilla of destroyers riding at anchor. A dredger was smashed into the concrete piles of the Mission Bay

Bridge, ripping out a section sixty feet wide. A bait barge swept along by the wave smashed eight landing stages at the Seaforth Landing before breaking in half and foundering.

At Santa Monica, during the draw-down before the tsunami, the water level fell so low that the base of the breakwater was almost exposed. One tsunami surge swept over 300 feet up the beach, flooding a car park next to the Pacific Coast Highway.

At Santa Barbara an oil exploration barge broke adrift and repeatedly slammed into a new dredger. This caused over 10,000 dollars' worth of damage. As much again was lost when forty small boats were set adrift there.

Overall, the earthquake and tsunami caused 550 million dollars' worth of damage in Chile, twenty-four million in Hawaii, fifty million in Japan and between 500,000 and one million in the United States. The death toll was around 1,000 in Chile, sixty-one in Hawaii, 199 in Japan and a handful in the United States, but it is important to note that widely different figures are available in different published sources; the total death toll is given as 2,231, 3,000 or 5,700. Estimates of property damage are similarly varied, but the outstanding feature of the disaster is how widespread the damage to coastal property was, as a result of the tsunami, all around the Pacific margin.

The 1960 Chile earthquake was not the most spectacular earthquake of all time. It did not shake down whole cities, although Valdivia and Puerto Montt suffered very serious damage. It did not cause enormous changes to the landscape, although it did trigger landslides. It not kill tens of thousands of people, although there was serious loss of life in the tsunami that followed. But it was, in its way, the greatest earthquake of all. It was the highest-energy earthquake in history to be caught on tape and measured, and measured in terms of the amount of energy released it was a very big earthquake indeed. It was initially measured at 8.6 on the Richter scale but was later more accurately calibrated to 9.5, which makes it one of the most violent events of the twentieth century.

THE HUBBARDS HILL LANDSLIPS

(1962)

THE PROBLEMS ENGLISH civil engineers encountered when they were building the Sevenoaks bypass in Great Britain in 1962 did not involve any sudden deaths, nor did they produce any large-scale natural spectacle. The disaster was interfering with the landscape without having any idea what the outcome would be. The Sevenoaks bypass finds its way into these pages because what happened during its construction changed the way in which local authorities, planners and engineers approached building projects from that time onwards. Perceptions of landscape and landscape management changed. An important lesson was learned.

Both Sevenoaks and the nearby town of Tonbridge in Kent suffered from serious traffic congestion and a scheme was devised to create a kind of double bypass. The A21 would loop around the western and southern edges of Sevenoaks, and then continue south-eastwards to skirt the western edge of Tonbridge. The first stretch of the road ran southwards up the gentle dip slop of the Lower Greensand, and then swung south-east to cut diagonally across the steeper scarp slope of the Greensand, between Sevenoaks and the village of Sevenoaks Weald, before turning south across the clay country of the Weald of Kent.

The problems began when road construction began on the steep scarp slope. It looked harmless enough, a patchwork of well-established meadows used for cattle pasture, separated by centuries-old hedgerows. It was a classic English pastoral landscape. The problem was that with the added weight of the new roadway and a new concrete bridge to carry the minor road down from Sevenoaks to Sevenoaks Weald (Hubbards Hill), the landscape started to move. The pasture was very hummocky, and the bumps were ancient mudflows. Under Arctic conditions 11,000 years ago, these five mudflows were unvegetated tongues of mud. In antiquity, they had slowly slid under gravity and the influence of repeated freezing and thawing down the 7-10 degree slope about 400 yards towards the clay vale below. They flowed on top of an older sheet of mud that had flowed down the hill around 18,000 years ago. They in turn flowed out on top of an even older sheet of mud that had flowed out as much as two miles in front of the escarpment and solidified there in a previous cold stage, perhaps 200,000 years ago. Under modern climatic conditions, dried out and covered with grass and trees, these ancient landslips were immobile. But they were only inactive so long as they were left alone.

It was as if the civil engineering works woke a sleeping dragon. The half-built road and the footings for the bridge were in place, when the hill slope started to move again. The old landslides were reactivated. Although the land surface appeared to be stable, it was only conditionally stable, only stable so long as people did not interfere with it. Work on the project had to stop immediately. The road was re-routed 100 feet or so further to the south, so that it no longer crossed the fossil landslips, and work resumed. A considerable amount of time and money was wasted as result.

It seems that the engineers responsible for surveying the area had noticed that it was bumpy but had not interpreted the bumpiness in a meaningful way. At this stage, civil engineering works such as road and bridge building had to be preceded by geological surveys. It was usual, for instance, to commission a geologist to make a series of boreholes to find out whether the rock layers would stand the weight of the proposed structure. It was not normal practice to commission a geomorphologist, someone who understands landscape processes. A geomorphologist would have understood the significance of the bumps – and that they could be reactivated. Landslips, whether small or large, may be reactivated after hundreds or even tens of thousands of years of inactivity.

At Sevenoaks Weald, it was and still is difficult to appreciate on the ground the true shape of the lobes, but it is easy to do so on high-quality air photographs. In fact, air photographs were used, but they were taken under inappropriate conditions. They were taken at midday in August 1961, in other words when the sun was very high in the sky to the south and the detailed micro-relief of the south-facing hill slope was drowned out by the saturating sunlight. If the photographs had been taken, say, on a December afternoon, the lobes would have stood out sharply; as it was, they went undetected.

One positive outcome of the Sevenoaks bypass episode was that a more thorough investigation of the geomorphology of the area began, and in the 1970s a whole range of landforms created under cold conditions in the last two or three cold stages of the Ice Age was discovered and mapped. Another positive outcome is that geomorphologists are regularly hired as consultants for building projects, though still not as often as they should be. A negative outcome was that the re-routing of the bypass to the south took it across the site of a fine old timber-framed farmhouse dating from the sixteenth century. In the hurry to move the road-building project forward, this building was unceremoniously demolished. And so we lost Panthurst Farm.

The irony is that the local people knew about the lobes. One of the landowners, Colonel Rogers of Riverhill House, reported that one of his fields actually developed a hummocky surface in the 1920s, so the lobes were then already on the move. The local farm labourers who worked in those fields, my grandfather among them, knew about the sleeping hummocks on the hill, and knew that the road would move – but of course nobody thought to ask them.

THE VAJONT DAM
DISASTER

(1963)

THE VAJONT DAM disaster was very different from the Malpasset Dam disaster of only a decade earlier. Instead of the dam collapsing, a freak wave overtopped it. Put simply, the Vajont Dam disaster is a classic case of what happens when engineers and geologists fail to understand the significance of the landscape processes that are staring them in the face. What happened is that while the reservoir was being filled a colossal block of rock detached itself from one side of the valley and slid down into the lake at high speed. This slab of mountain side displaced a huge volume of water, which lapped over the top of the dam and swept down the valley below the dam.

Vajont is in the Italian Alps, about seventy miles north of Venice, and its dam was part of Italy's post-war development programme to supply cheap hydroelectricity to the expanding cities of Milan, Modena and Turin. The site had been proposed in the 1920s, but work on the site did not start until 1956 and the dam was not completed until 1960. Its design was a graceful doubly curved arch, in other words, curved in plan and curved in profile as well. The Vajont Dam stood 800 feet high, making it the tallest thin-arch dam in the world. It was 500 feet across, a very large and imposing structure.

The dam was built into a deep and narrow gorge. The walls of this gorge are in places almost vertical, and developed in rather weak Jurassic and Cretaceous rocks that included layers of clay.

Any combination of permable rocks and layers of clay is likely to be unstable, even on moderate slopes. Given that erosion by rivers and glaciers had left this valley with very steep sides, this was obviously a profoundly unstable landscape – not a good place to build a very large structure like a dam, and certainly not a good place to put a huge reservoir.

In the light of what happened, it seems extraordinary that the engineers who designed the dam were fully aware of the geology of the Vajont Valley, and even knew of an ancient landslide on the north side, just above the dam site. During the filling of the reservoir in 1960, the south valley side started to move. In March, there was a small landslide. The engineers went on filling the reservoir. By October, when the reservoir was 500 feet deep, the creeping movement of the valley side was accelerating. It was now moving at a rate of two inches a day. Even more significantly, a great long crack over a mile long opened up, showing that the next landslide was going to be very big. On 4 November, by which time the reservoir had been allowed to fill to a depth of 550 feet, a huge block of rock about 270 million cubic yards detached itself from the south valley side and slid down into the lake at high speed, about 100 feet per second.

The dam's engineers now had clear evidence of the dangers of the site and as a precaution they lowered the lake level from 600 feet to 400 feet. Nature was giving the dam's designers a demonstration of what this particular landscape did. Lines of weakness were visible along the mountainside all around the site of the 1960 landslide. The engineers could see that there was going to be another landslide, but were unable to see how they prevent it. It was clearly impossible to pin the impending landslide into position; it was also impossible to seal the whole mountain side in with a concrete revetment. The engineers decided that even when the big landslide fell into the reservoir, the reduced-capacity reservoir would still be useful. They also believed that by raising the water level in careful stages they could control the landslide. In this they were seriously over-optimistic.

By February 1962, the lake level was raised back up to its previous highest level. Then it was taken down again before raising it to 700 feet in June 1963. The big landslide was all the time creeping gradually down the slope. The thin clay layers within the valley side were becoming saturated by the rising lake water.

The catastrophic collapse happened at 10.40 pm on 9 October 1963. Against the engineers' expectations, the entire mass of the landslide slid 1,500 feet northwards, and at very high speed. The engineers seem to have hoped the huge mass of rock would creep down into the water. Instead, it shot down at 100 feet per second. The landslide completely blocked the gorge to a depth of 1,200 feet. The landslide lasted forty-five seconds and generated a colossal wave that rushed up the opposite valley side and destroyed the village of Casso, which was 800 feet above the level of the lake.

A very large volume of water was involved in this destructive wave, and the phenomenon is aptly known as a landslide tsunami. The volume of water in this wave is estimated to have been one thousand million cubic feet. The huge landslide tsunami wave, 750 feet high, spilt over the dam and swept down the valley below. Five villages below the dam were totally destroyed: Longarone, Pirago, Fae, Villanova and Rivalta. About 2,500 people died in the Vajont dam disaster. In the village of Longarone, ninety-four per cent of the inhabitants were killed. The next day, survivors from the villages stood on bridges in the valley of the Piave River, fishing in the river with poles, in a desperate attempt to retrieve the bodies of both people and livestock. The Piave valley itself was scoured snow-white by the tsunami wave. It was a strange transformation of the landscape. For days afterwards the survivors wandered about in bewilderment, trying to adjust, and trying to find their dead, hoping they would not be washed all the way to the Adriatic, 100 miles away down-river. The relatives of the dead began the lengthy process of litigation, sensing that the landslide tsunami was a man-made disaster. They were right, though the proprietors of the dam took the position that it was an entirely natural phenomenon.

Since the catastrophic landslide, a great deal of geomorphological research has been undertaken to pinpoint its causes. The thin layers of clay in the mountain side seem to have played a crucial role, because the sliding took place along these clay layers, which are less than five inches thick, but sufficient to lubricate the rock layers on top of them. The mountain sides were indeed prone to landslides, and the scar of the ancient landslide on the north side of the valley shows that landslides have occurred naturally and unaided in the area. On the other hand, the careful process of filling, drawing-down and refilling of the reservoir shows that the dam's engineers understood fully that saturation by the reservoir water had a great deal to do with the landslides in 1960 and 1963. Controversy still continues as to whether the big landslide was a brand-new landslide or a reactivated ancient landslide.

Remarkably, the dam itself remained undamaged by the wave and it is still standing today. The deadly dam and its killer reservoir remain in use, generating hydroelectricity, and one can only feel pity for the people who have to go on living in the valley down below.

THE ANCHORAGE EARTHQUAKE AND TSUNAMI

(1964)

THE ALASKAN EARTHQUAKE, often known as the Anchorage earthquake, happened on Good Friday, 1964. At 5.36 pm on 27 March the big earthquake struck. The magnitude of the Anchorage earthquake was 8.7, the biggest earthquake that has ever been recorded in North America. Often in earthquakes the ground shakes for a few seconds; in this earthquake, it went on shaking for five minutes.

The epicentre was between the settlements of Anchorage and Valdez, in Prince William Sound, seventy-five miles east of Anchorage itself. It was caused by the release of frictional pressure along the subduction zone where the Pacific Plate plunges beneath the North American Plate. It was a shallow-seated earthquake, with a focus sixteen miles down.

The sea floor off the Alaskan coast suddenly jolted up, creating a 400 mph tsunami that killed 122 people; the earthquake itself killed only nine. The tsunami raced off across the North Pacific, reaching Hawaii and Crescent City in California, where ten people were killed.

The violent shaking of the ground caused sand and soil layers in some places to liquefy. Where this liquefaction happened underneath buildings, the buildings sank into the ground, which then resolidified. The liquefaction in turn helped to produce landslides and avalanches. Some of these landslides occurred at

Anchorage, at Turnagain Heights, when steep slopes made of soft clay collapsed, destroying seventy-five houses.

Another phenomenon that earthquakes can produce in enclosed bodies of water, such as lakes, is the seiche. This is a back and forth sloshing of water. The Anchorage earthquake caused seiches in lakes, rivers and sheltered harbours, as far away as the Gulf coast of Texas and Louisiana. The earthquake caused landslides, and when they crashed down into the sea these too created waves, in some places up to 100 feet high.

Property damage, mostly at Anchorage itself, totalled 311 million dollars. The Penney Company building had a facade consisting of concrete panels five inches thick. These broke away and fell out into the street, killing a woman who was driving past and a young man who was crouching in the street. Several schools in Anchorage were destroyed, but luckily the schools were empty because of the Good Friday holiday. The concrete control tower at the airport fell over, killing the air traffic controller. The town's infrastructure was badly disrupted, with water, sewer and gas pipes broken and telephone and electricity lines disconnected.

There was serious damage at Valdez too, 120 miles to the east of Anchorage. A freighter called the *Chena* was unloading at the quayside at Valdez when a wave (whether a tsunami or a seiche) lifted the ship thirty feet. The *Chena* broke free and was able to move out safely into the bay, but twenty-eight people on the quay were killed. Many houses and commercial buildings along the waterfront at Valdez were wrecked. The residents at Valdez felt the ground move in waves three feet high. Later on in the evening, tsunami waves coinciding with a rising tide flooded large areas of Valdez. The waves kept coming at half hour intervals until two in the morning.

At Seward, an oil port eighty miles south of Anchorage, a section of the waterfront was shaken loose by the earthquake and slid into Resurrection Bay. This set off a local tsunami, which caused a great deal of damage. About twenty minutes after this local tsunami, the first wave of the main tsunami from Prince William Sound arrived. The earthquake and tsunamis together seriously damaged the oil installations. Pipes were split open and whole storage tanks erupted in flames. A sheet of fire spread across the harbour. Twelve people died at Seward.

Kodiak Island was not damaged very much by the main earthquake itself, but the tsunami caused havoc. Fishermen in the harbour at St Paul noticed a long, gentle swell followed by a sudden ebbing of the water. The water went on and on receding until the entire fleet of 160 fishing boats was sitting on the bottom of the harbour. Then a series of gigantic waves hit the harbour, starting at six-twenty pm. Canning factories on the waterfront were totally destroyed.

The tsunamis were truly colossal. The largest wave reported was one that surged into Shoup Bay, Valdez Inlet; it was 200 feet high. By the time the tsunamis reached San Francisco Bay, they were still seven feet high, and quite high enough to tear boats and floating docks from their moorings and damage docks and piers. It was the most destructive tsunami so far experienced on the west coast of North America, causing 106 deaths and eighty-four million dollars' worth of damage.

There were major changes to the coastal landscape. The release of pent-up compression in the earth's crust meant that after the quake some areas that had been gradually pushed up were now suddenly lower; large areas around Portage were eight feet lower, which drowned and killed a large area of forest. Other areas that had been depressed before the earthquake were afterwards hoisted up in the air. Some areas east of Kodiak are as much as thirty feet higher than they were, creating a raised beach and stranded cliffline.

People who lived through those experiences never forgot them. One eighteen-year-old girl later reminisced:

My sister Kathy was sixteen. We got off the school bus and walked the mile and a half of our homestead road to our cabin on Longmere Lake. I fixed our dinner and was doing the dishes when the quake hit. I remember the water in the sink stood up sideways and then fell back again. We didn't have doors on the kitchen cupboards and things started falling out all around me. My sister started to become hysterical so I held onto her and told her we were going outside. I opened the door. The trees were lying on the ground one minute and upright the next, then back down again. Then the lake started to crack open and the mud from the bottom shot many feet up into the air. It looked like the cracks were headed straight for us, so we huddled in the doorway until the shaking finally quit. I didn't think it would ever stop, it felt like forever . . . To this day, any earth shake brings back all the vivid details, and the fear.

Many people affected by disasters are permanently scarred by them. One of the Anchorage survivors said:

Nearly forty years later (and in another state) I had an 'earthquake flashback'. I was in a pharmacy, which had antique pharmaceutical bottles on display. There was a demolition and construction project under way across the street. Some heavy equipment was rumbling and all those display bottles were vibrating and clinking. It felt and sounded like an earthquake. I had to leave.

Most of the 115 (Alaskan) deaths in the 1964 Anchorage earthquake were due to the tsunamis, which are a constant danger along the south coast of Alaska. The 1964 earthquake alerted both state and federal authorities to the need to set up an effective early-warning system for tsunamis. As a direct result, the West Coast & Alaska Tsunami Warning System was set up three years later at Palmer.

THE ABERFAN
DISASTER

(1966)

THE CHILDREN RETURNED to their classrooms after singing *All Things Bright and Beautiful* at their morning assembly at Pantglas Junior School in the South Welsh mining village of Aberfan. It was 9.15 on the morning of Friday 21 October 1966, a foggy morning with poor visibility down in the village but sunny up on the slag heaps at the back.

The coal mines had been producing coal for a century. They had also been producing a great deal of waste rock, which was dumped on huge slag heaps. Many of these were steep-sided and most were completely unvegetated. They were clearly unstable and many local people, including the local council, had expressed anxiety about the safety of the slag heaps as they grew larger and extended closer to the settlement. The slag heap nearest to Aberfan was trebly unstable. It was not only steep-sided and free of anchoring vegetation; it was built across a spring, which lubricated the debris from inside the heap.

A tipping gang saw the landslide start, but were unable to raise the alarm because their telephone cable had been stolen. In fact, the slide happened so fast that a phone warning would have done no good anyway. In the village itself, no one saw anything at all, partly because of the fog, partly because the slag came down behind the houses, out of sight from the road. But everyone heard the noise. One little girl who was at the school later remembered it. 'It was a tremendous rumbling sound and all the school went dead. You could hear a pin drop. Everyone just froze in their seats. I just managed to get up and I reached the end of my desk when the sound got louder and nearer, until I could see the black out of the window. I can't remember any more but I woke up to find that a horrible nightmare had just begun in front of my eyes.'

The loose black coal slag had surged in a continuous landslide right over the school and twenty neighbouring houses before it came to a halt. Then it went very quiet. One boy who was trapped in the debris recalled that 'in that silence you couldn't hear a bird or a child.'

In those few moments 144 people died, and 116 of them were junior school children. Roughly half of the children at the Pantglas Junior School were killed along with five of their teachers.

The people of the area were desperate to help. Many came from surrounding villages carrying shovels and tried to help in the rescue, but the untrained rescuers simply got in the way. In the two hours following the landslide some children were dug out alive by the trained rescue teams, but no one living was dug out after eleven am. The digging went on for a week, until all the bodies had been recovered. The acute distress of the small, close-knit community can only be imagined.

A tribunal was set up to investigate the causes of the disaster, chaired by Sir Herbert Davies, a barrister. Emotions ran high, and there were accusations that warnings about the tip's instability had been brushed aside by coal board officials. What emerged was that there had been local anxiety about the stability of the tip for a long time. The Chairman of the National Coal Board, Lord Robens, claimed that the NCB had not known about the existence of a spring underneath the tip, but it turned out that this was untrue. Lord Robens finally admitted that the coal board had been negligent, but he publicly refused to offer his resignation.

The Report, published in August 1967, said the Aberfan disaster was 'a terrifying tale of bungling ineptitude by many men charged with tasks for which they were totally unfitted, of failure to heed clear warnings, and of total lack of direction from above. Not villains but decent men, led astray by foolishness or by ignorance or by both in combination, are responsible for what happened at Aberfan.' The Report concluded unflinchingly, 'Blame for the disaster rests upon the National Coal Board.' The local council and the National Union of Mineworkers were exonerated; they had had no choice but to accept the assurances of the NCB that everything was under control. Nobody faced criminal proceedings, but those responsible for the disaster had to live with the knowledge of their responsibility for the deaths of the children of Aberfan for the rest of their lives.

THE ARNO FLOOD

(1966)

THE CITY OF Florence has been flooded by the River Arno several times in its history. The Arno is a flashy and unpredictable river. It can switch from being an almost dry river bed to flood conditions in a few days, following high-intensity rainfall. The river rises in the Apennines, and at the point where it leaves the mountains its discharge varies enormously, from twenty cubic feet to 125,000 cubic feet per second.

One outcome of the 1966 flood was the building of dams upstream from Florence to regulate the flow of the river and prevent a repeat of the 1966 catastrophe.

The high-intensity rainfall across southern Europe in the autumn of 1966 produced flooding in several countries. In Yugoslavia, Austria, Switzerland and Italy, 150 people lost their lives in the flooding. The flood of 4–5 November 1966 on the Arno produced a flow of 130,000 cubic feet per second in Florence. It was at two-thirty in the morning that the flood peak started to roll towards the city at thirty-six mph. A nightwatchman called Romeldo Cesaroni cycled across the city to wake up the shopkeepers on the Ponte Vecchio, the famous old bridge over the Arno with shops built along its parapets. The shopkeepers were able to reach their shops just in time to save their gold and silver jewellery before the flood water arrived.

The flood water swept into the main square of Florence at four o'clock in the morning. Three hours later the city was cut off from the rest of Italy. The flood broke open oil tanks, and this pollution was later to do serious damage to art treasures. When the waters finally began to fall, they left behind 600,000 tons of filthy debris and 1,400 works of art damaged beyond repair. The muddy, oil-contaminated water did not reach the main galleries on the second floor of the Uffizi, but it did pour into its store rooms, damaging 1,000 medieval and Renaissance paintings and sculptures. Perhaps the most serious single loss in the flood was Cimabue's painting of the Crucifixion. Frescoes painted by Botticelli, Martini and Uccello were destroyed. Bronze panels from Pisano's Baptistry doors were ripped away by the flood water. Many historic scientific instruments and musical instruments were lost as well as two million books.

The loss of so much of Italy's artistic and cultural heritage was extremely distressing to the people of Florence, but so too was the lack of warning that the flood was coming. The authorities apparently did not want to alarm people in the middle of the night. But previous generations of Tuscans too must bear some of the responsibility for this destructive flood. Ever since the earliest settlement of the region, the slopes of the hills and mountains have been progressively stripped of their natural vegetation, which contributed greatly to the Arno's very flashy regime. Nor had any measures been taken to install flood-regulating reservoirs.

One outcome of the Arno flood was an enormous amount of restoration work on the hundreds of damaged works of art. Umberto Baldini, the director of conservation at the Uffizi Gallery, took a leading role in organizing the restoration work, not just at the Uffizi but everywhere else in Florence. He worked with other experts to devise new techniques, including removing entire frescoes from church walls in order to protect them from the damaging salts that were seeping through the masonry behind the paint layer. Restorers working on Donatello's sculpture of Mary Magdalene made the discovery that her knee-length dark hair had once been covered in gold leaf. The huge restoration project led on in the 1980s to Baldini's project to clean and restore the Masaccio frescoes in the Carmine Church in Florence, so that these wonderful images can now be seen virtually as they were when first painted.

THE *TORREY CANYON* OIL SPILL

(1967)

GREAT BRITAIN FACED the worst pollution disaster of the twentieth century when a huge oil tanker called the *Torrey Canyon* ran onto a reef between Land's End and the Isles of Scilly. It happened on 18 March 1967. The tanker was one of the largest of its time, 975 feet long, and she was fully laden with a cargo of 117,000 tons of crude oil from Kuwait. The ship was heading for the large natural harbour of Milford Haven on the coast of South Wales. She was nearly at her destination when she ran aground. The jagged rocks tore open the ship's hull as she rode over them, and the thick black oil began to leak out.

To begin with, it looked as the *Torrey Canyon* might be re-floated, but two days after running onto the rocks she broke her back and even more oil flooded out of the two halves of the ship.

The crude oil went on leaking out of the wrecked ship for a week afterwards, creating a huge layer of black floating on the sea, covering 260 square miles. In an attempt to ignite the oil before it left the ship, Royal Air Force bombers dropped huge amounts of explosives on the wreck on 28 and 29 March. This had little effect, and by then a huge area of the British Channel was covered with an oil slick. Seabirds diving into the sea to catch fish were fatally coated in the oil. When the oil reached the land, it coated the beaches, and 145 miles of the Cornish coastline were polluted with oil. Brittany and the Channel Islands were similarly affected. It had become an international disaster.

The immediate effects were catastrophic. A great deal of seashore wildlife was killed – it is estimated that 25,000 birds died in Cornwall alone. There were also fears that the beaches in all three areas would be polluted for several summers and ruin the tourist industry. Yet the beaches were clean within three or four months. This was partly due to the cleaning up operation organized by the various local authorities concerned, and also partly due to natural processes. Some of the oil decomposed, some of it dried out and was reduced to small hard pellets that became lost in the beach sand; some of it was broken up by the energy of the waves. It has been a continuing surprise that oil slicks have not had the overwhelmingly destructive effects on shorelines that was anticipated.

One effect of the *Torrey Canyon* disaster was that many questions were asked about ships flying flags of convenience. The *Torrey Canyon* was registered in Liberia, a very common convenience flag. Questions were also asked about the quality of seamanship on the bridges of these very large vessels.

THE PERU
EARTHQUAKE

(1970)

THE BIG EARTHQUAKE that struck Peru in 1970 was, according to the US Geological Survey, 'the most destructive historic earthquake in the western hemisphere.' There are records of earthquakes in Peru as early as 1619, and this was the most violent earthquake since that date.

A World Cup football match was being broadcast, so a great many people were indoors watching the match on television. About twenty minutes after kick-off, the seabed off the Peruvian coast shifted and sent shock waves to north, east and south, devastating 600 miles of the South American coast. The epicentre was not far out to sea off the fishing port of Chimbote, where seventy per cent of the buildings were destroyed and thousands of people were killed. A pervasive, shocked silence spread over all the ruined towns and villages.

Up in the Andes, the snow and ice capping the summit of Mount Huascaran collapsed, creating massive avalanches and landslides that tumbled down the valleys at 200 mph. A ski resort called Yungay disappeared under the landslide, along with part of the neighbouring settlement of Ranrahirca. Of the inhabitants of the town of Yungay, only the ninety-two who had run up onto Cemetery Hill at the edge of the town survived; an unscathed statue of Christ spread its arms as if in dismay at the scene of devastation below. Several villages in the same valley were similarly wiped out.

Many of the remote mountain settlements suffered particularly badly because it was very difficult to get assistance to them from outside. The roads were buried, and freezing rain made the task of rescue even harder. Many thousands of poor people were stranded for several days with neither food nor water outside the wreckage of their villages. They saw themselves as victims of 'the giant's hand', as they called it. Some set off for the nearest towns, where they found the townspeople in the same desperate state. Those who stayed in their villages hid their children and injured relatives from the rescue workers, out of a deep distrust of strangers.

Five days after the earthquake, rescue workers at Chimbote were still digging bodies out of the ruined houses. Gradually, the process of clearance and rebuilding got under way, and interest in the World Cup revived, but the great earthquake had left 50,000 people dead and 800,000 homeless.

THE BHOLA
CYCLONE

(1970)

ON 13 NOVEMBER 1970, Bangladesh (then still called East Pakistan) was struck by a violent tropical cyclone. It has been given the name Bhola cyclone. It deserves a special name as it was the most lethal cyclone or hurricane of all time. It killed 500,000 people.

Like all the cyclones that strike Bangladesh, the Bhola cyclone had its beginnings out in the Bay of Bengal, somewhere east of Sri Lanka, curving northwards until it reached the Ganges Delta. The strong winds, more than 120 mph, piled the water up in front of the cyclone as it approached the Delta coast. By the time the storm surge reached the coast it was twenty feet high, driving a huge amount of sea water across the low-lying and densely populated Delta.

The cyclone and the storm surge made landfall in the early hours of the morning, and many people were drowned in their sleep. The official figures were that 500,000 died, but another 100,000 were unaccounted for, and some unofficial sources put the death toll even higher than that. There is no question that this was one of the worst disasters of all time, bearing comparison with the Tangshan earthquake of 1976 and the Indian Ocean tsunami of 2004. In the chaotic circumstances of each of these major disasters it may be that we will never know for certain which of these three was the deadliest.

The greatest loss of life was in the low-lying islands of the

Ganges Delta south of Dhaka. The island of Bhola was particularly badly hit. Over 100,000 people died there, and the towns of Tazmuddin and Charfasson were destroyed. The town of Chittagong was also badly damaged.

The movement of the Bhola cyclone was monitored by weather satellites, and successive photographs clearly showed that a major cyclone was heading for the Ganges Delta. The Americans duly passed the severe weather warning on to the government of Pakistan, based in Karachi, the chief city of West Pakistan. There had for some time been serious political tensions between the two halves of Pakistan, which had been created as a Muslim state at the time of Indian independence. For whatever reason, the severe weather warning passed by the Americans to Karachi was not passed on to Dhaka. As a result, the people living out on the Ganges Delta were given no warning of the approaching storm surge, and that is why the death toll was so high.

The people of East Pakistan were understandably incensed by this failure of communication, which they saw as a willful betrayal by West Pakistan, and a full-scale civil war was launched in the spring of 1971, a war of liberation. The Indian government quickly intervened as warplanes flew across Indian airspace. East Pakistan was given its independence, and its new identity as Bangladesh.

THE HEIMAEY ERUPTION

(1973)

IN THE MIDDLE of the night of 22–23 January 1973, an old
Icelandic farmer was woken up by a noise outside his house.
When he looked out he saw a great fissure running right across
his farm, with red-hot lava fountains spouting from it. This was
the start of a spectacular eruption sequence. The one-mile long
fissure was in the hills to the east of the little port of Heimaey in
the Vestmann Islands, just south of Iceland. There had been very
little warning that a major volcanic eruption was about to start:
just a few mild earthquakes beginning at ten o'clock the previous
evening, the strongest of them coming at 1.40 in the morning, just
fifteen minutes before the eruption started.

People in Heimaey had gone to bed just as usual the evening
before the eruption, and all the fishing boats were in the harbour
as there had been a force 12 gale that day. Then the police
received a phone call to say that an eruption had started not far
above and to the east of Kirkjubaer (Church Farm) at the very
eastern edge of the town. The police drove there to find the
eruption fissure opening up all the way to the sea to the north and
to Helgafell, an existing volcano, to the south. The lava fountains
were so close together that they formed a continuous curtain of
fire. The starting-point for the eruption eventually became the site
of the new volcano's main crater. The new volcano was given the
name Eldfell.

Lava started running down the hill side from the fissure and started to build out into the sea. The police returned to the town and used their sirens to wake people up. Within two hours everyone was outside and streaming down to the harbour with warm clothing and a few belongings. They were evacuated by boat in relays. The town council decided that the only safe thing to do was to evacuate the entire town, apart from 200 people who stayed behind to carry out essential work.

As the lava spilling into the sea solidified to form a huge natural pier, there were fears that the harbour entrance would be completely sealed off by it. If the fissure opened any further to the south, it could close the airfield too. During the night 300 people, mostly the elderly and the sick, were flown to Reykjavik. Altogether about 5,000 people were evacuated on that first night, most of them by boat. The whole operation went remarkably smoothly and without mishap, largely because people did not panic.

During the next few days, ash rained down thickly onto the roofs of Heimaey. The workforce tried initially to sweep the ash off, but they were unable to keep pace with the continuous accumulation. By 31 January, a week after the eruption began, the ash had accumulated in layers up to twelve feet thick on some of the roofs. The houses in the eastern part of Heimaey were buried one by one under the layers of ash and lava. Many of them collapsed under the weight. It began to look as if the lava flows were going to engulf the town completely and destroy it. The emergency task force decided to attempt the impossible, and divert the lava. The Vestmann Islands fire brigade started installing hoses on 6 February and pumping cold sea water onto the edge of the lava flow. This solidified the edge of the flow and created a solid rock barrier which prevented the lava from going any further in that direction. The lava was instead diverted into the sea, adding about one square mile of land to the island.

On 20 February, the newly built volcano split apart. The first 'vagabond', a colossal slab of rock weighing millions of tons, floated away on the lava flow, and headed for Heimaey harbour at a speed of seventy-five feet per hour.

On 22 March, an increase in the flow of lava towards the west and north-west caused it to overtop one of the artificial lava dams protecting the town, and it looked once again as if Heimaey would be destroyed in the eruption. It unexpectedly stopped at 5 am on 23 March, but only after burying seventy houses under lava. On 25 March, the lava advanced 200 yards and consumed another forty-one houses. On 26 March, the volcano split open again, and another 'vagabond' was released, floating off to the north at about thjrty feet an hour. By 1 April, the lava edge reached its final position. The volcano went on erupting, but the lava flows did not encroach any further on Heimaey. The imaginative attempt to save the town by training fire hoses and pumping more than five million tons of sea water onto the advancing lava had succeeded. On 3 June, the authorities declared that the eruption was over. It had gone on for an exhausting five months.

The Heimaey eruption had ejected 7,500 million cubic feet of lava and ash, and by the end of it the brand new volcano, Eldfell, had been built to a height of 700 feet. Remarkably, the port of Heimaey had survived the eruption. About half of its 800 houses were either destroyed or badly damaged. By 1975, most of the ash smothering the town had been cleared away, some of it used to make roads, enlarge the airstrips and make foundations for the new houses. Two-thirds of the evacuated islanders returned to Heimaey, giving it a post-eruption population of 3,500, compared with the 5,300 before. Today, Heimaey has grown back to its original size. The survival of Heimaey is an incredible story of human resilience and determination.

THE INDUS FLOOD

(1973)

HIGH-INTENSITY RAINFALL caused the River Indus to overflow its banks for ten days in August 1973. Flood waters up to twenty feet deep covered the fields of lowland Pakistan, destroying the cotton crop and the wheat harvest. Towns, too, were inundated. The hardest hit region was the Punjab, where 70,000 cattle and 300 people died – and over 250,000 homes were destroyed.

Pakistan was not a rich country and the effect of this flood, and the other river floods that preceded it, was to weaken its economy. Since Pakistan, initially called West Pakistan, became independent in 1947, it has suffered ten severe floods (in 1950, 1955, 1956, 1973, 1975, 1976, 1978, 1988, 1992 and 1995) costing a total of four billion US dollars and taking nearly 8,000 lives.

The Indus floods are the result of several different mechanisms, but they usually operate in late summer and the main cause is the heavy monsoon rain, which is exaggerated as the south-west winds rise over the Himalayas. In the upper and middle Indus basin, the flooding is mainly caused by major tributaries such as the Jhelum and Chenab. Sometimes melting snow can produce flooding earlier in the summer. Heat waves may cause catas-trophic bursting of glacial lakes, of which there are over 2,000 in the Indus basin. Higher temperatures in recent years make these glacial lake outburst floods more likely to happen. Yet another mechanism is the collapse of temporary natural dams created by landslides or shifting glaciers up in the mountains.

Political instability prevented the development of any flood prevention strategy. But the devastation caused by the big floods of 1973 and 1975 jolted the government of Pakistan into devising a unified national approach to the problem of river floods. The Federal Flood Commission was created in 1977 to prepare flood protection plans for the whole of Pakistan, and a National Flood Protection Plan was produced the following year.

CYCLONE TRACY

(1974)

IN AUSTRALIA, 1974 opened with Cyclone Wanda bringing heavy rain to the city of Brisbane and ended with Cyclone Tracy bringing devastation to the city of Darwin. On the global scale, Tracy was not a big tropical storm. It had a radius of only thirty miles and its central low pressure was not especially intense. But the winds it generated were unusually strong, and they did a great deal of damage.

Tracy had its origins as a mild low-pressure system in the Arafura Sea on 20 December. As it moved gradually south-westwards it passed Bathurst Island on 23 December and intensified. Then the cyclone turned sharply towards the east-south-east and headed straight for Darwin. It hit the city early on Christmas morning.

Severe weather warnings were broadcast but people took little notice of them, partly because Darwin had not experienced a severe cyclone for a very long time, and partly because it was Christmas Eve and they were preoccupied with preparing for Christmas. As a result, a great many people living in Darwin were caught completely unprepared for the cyclone. The combination of very strong winds and the inappropriately flimsy design of a lot of the houses meant that there was wholesale destruction. It probably would have made little difference if the entire population of Darwin had spent the whole of Christmas Eve preparing for the cyclone.

As it was, forty-nine people in Darwin were killed by Cyclone Tracy; another sixteen people died at sea. Most of the buildings were completely destroyed. Those that were not were severely damaged. A lot of the communication links were knocked out by the cyclone, but enough were left in place for the people of Darwin to be able to contact the outside world. A relief operation was under way at once. An airlift was organized using both military and civilian aircraft, though many people chose to drive away from Darwin. Within the space of a few weeks, Darwin was virtually empty. Three-quarters of its residents had gone.

Darwin had not had a severe cyclone for a long time, but cyclones were a well-established part of Darwin's climate regime. The town had been hit hard by a cyclone in March 1937, and before that in January 1897. There was really no excuse for building flimsy, lightweight housing that could not stand up to a cyclone when the place had that kind of history. One major effect of Cyclone Tracy was that it made the authorities take action, if belatedly, to change the building regulations. More attention was also given to the social aspects of planning, to disaster management. In the weeks following Cyclone Tracy, Darwin looked like a ghost town, a town that was so badly damaged that it could never recover. But it did. The city was rebuilt. Now that Australia's economy has positively oriented itself to interact with the rapidly developing countries of South-East Asia, Darwin has become a dynamic gateway to Asia.

US TORNADO SWARM

(1974)

Tornadoes are a normal feature of the weather pattern of the American Midwest. There are around 1000 tornadoes a year in the United States as a whole, and they cause an average of eighty deaths and 1,500 injuries.

A tornado is a very small diameter low-pressure system that extends down to the ground from the base of a thundercloud. It is a kind of miniature hurricane, consisting of a violently rotating column of air. These twisters are visible and easily recognizable because of all the dust and debris they suck up from the ground and spin around in a great funnel-shaped vortex. With their 250 mph winds they cause tremendous destruction along narrow corridors of the landscape. Because the centre of the tornado has very low atmospheric pressure, it can cause buildings to explode as it passes, just by the difference in air pressure. Tornado damage paths are often fifty miles long but only one mile wide. Tornadoes vary enormously in size and intensity. Small tornadoes are quite common in England, especially during hot summers. They are measured on the Fujita Tornado Damage Scale, which runs from Category F0 (causing light damage) to F5 (causing incredible damage).

On 3–4 April 1974, there was a super outbreak of tornadoes in the United States. There were 148 tornadoes affecting eleven states on just those two days, associated with severe thunderstorms. In the super outbreak 330 people were killed and 5,484 were injured.

In 1974, a tornado could only be remotely detected as a green blip on a radar screen and forecasters waited for a sighting before issuing a minimal warning. After the 1974 super outbreak, which caused catastrophic damage, there was a 4.5 billion-dollar investment in weather forecasting. As a result, it is now possible to see storms evolving and give an eleven minute warning before a tornado actually forms. Super outbreaks like the one in 1974 will happen again, but now there is greater awareness, understanding – and preparation.

HURRICANE FIFI

(1974)

HURRICANE FIFI (OR Fifi-Orlene) was a North Atlantic hurricane that made its landfall in Belize. Twisted in response to Earth's rotation, the hurricane tracks normally curve towards the north, taking them towards the Gulf coast of the United States. Fifi was one of the few Atlantic storms to continue in a straight line, tracking westwards and crossing into the Pacific Ocean. On its way it caused 3.7 billion dollars' worth of damage and killed 8,000 people. It was in every way one of the costliest hurricanes in history.

Like many hurricanes, it started in a small way as an Atlantic storm off the coast of West Africa and moved westwards towards the Caribbean, where it became a fully developed hurricane on 17 September. It passed south of Jamaica and Cuba and reached Belize on 19 September. On reaching the Pacific Ocean, it (at last) veered northwards and headed for the Gulf of California. By this stage it had weakened, interacted with a depression and changed its identity to Orlene. After running parallel with the coast of Mexico for a while, it turned and made landfall again, south-east of Culiacan, on 23 September.

Fifi produced exceptionally heavy rainfall in Honduras. In the north-east of Honduras, twenty-four inches of rain fell in thirty-six hours. This swelled the rivers, caused widespread flooding, which in turn caused enormous damage to poor villages, towns and banana plantations. Half of the subsistence crops and ninety-five per cent of the commercial banana crops were destroyed in the flooding. Enormous numbers of fishing vessels were destroyed, too. The towns of Omoa, Choloma and Trujillo were severely damaged. The valley of the River Ulua turned into a lake twenty miles wide for several days after Fifi passed across. Nearly all of the 8,000 deaths connected with Fifi were the result of the flooding. Fifi was the third or fourth deadliest Atlantic hurricane in recorded history; only Mitch (in 1998) and the Great Hurricane of 1780 are known to have killed more people but it may have been slightly eclipsed by Galveston (in 1900).

The hurricane was such an appalling disaster that it was agreed that the name Fifi would never be used again for any future Atlantic hurricane.

THE SHOEPAC LAKE SINKHOLES

(1976)

ONE OF THE most interesting characteristics of limestone scenery (sometimes called karst scenery) is the networks of caves and underground streams that lie beneath them. Initially, when a limestone landscape is formed, the streams run over the surface, but as the water dissolves the limestone in its channel, especially along the cracks or joints in the rock, more and more of the water finds its way underground. Out of sight inside the rock, the underground stream opens up caverns, often in lines or chains. Eventually, a cavern may become too big for the walls to support its roof and the roof collapses. This then causes subsidence above and creates a collapse feature on the land surface. This is called a sinkhole, or doline.

The sinkholes in Michigan are not just round, they are exactly circular. This is a common characteristic of solution pits and solution pipes all over the world. It is nevertheless uncanny to look down from the air and see holes in the ground that are so precisely geometric in shape.

The accessibility of the underground drainage system varies a lot. In some areas, it is possible for potholers to abseil down sinkholes and use them as an access route to the cave systems. In the Pennines in Great Britain, this is a popular pastime. But the Michigan sinkholes are less accessible because of the layer of glacial sediment that rests like a carpet on top of the limestone. There are some tall stories about the sinks and the caves below.

In the early twentieth century, it was said that lumbermen tried to float logs down the North Branch of the Thunder Bay River at Mystery Valley, but the logs stopped at the large sinkhole in the valley, and plugged it. The river water ponded back and flooded the valley. A diversion dam was built to take the logs around the sinkhole at Sunken Lake. Maybe it happened, maybe not. Another story is that loggers would ride into the sinkholes on their logs, and reappear in Misery Bay on Lake Huron, twenty-three miles away, still smoking their pipes!

Out in open country, for instance in farmland, the sudden appearance of a bowl-shaped or cone-shaped crater may not look like a major problem, but in a built-up area it may be catastrophic. Houses may collapse without warning. Roads may suddenly become impassable.

One area that has many of these sinkholes is fifteen miles north of Atlanta in Michigan, an area known as Presque Isle County. The bedrock there is limestone that has been dissolved away by stream and rainwater to form networks of caves and sinks. One of the sinks is 100 feet deep and full of water; this is Shoepac Lake. Most of the sinks are circular, between eighty and 100 feet deep and with quite steep sides.

From the human point of view, sinks create many problems. When they are formed, they destroy any structure built on the site. In Michigan, there have been some spectacular house collapses, where an originally level ground surface has collapsed in a series of concentric rings. The result is something that looks very like tornado damage. Subsidence may not sound very violent, but the results can be dramatic and costly. A house demolished when a sink forms under it cannot be rebuilt.

After they have formed, they become highways for the transit of water from above ground to below ground, and the passage of water can cause the sink to go on developing, enlarging, perhaps turning into a swallow-hole, which literally swallows a stream. They may turn into lakes, such as Devil's Lake north of Alpena and Long Lakes in northern Alpena and southern Presque Isle counties. They also become sites of potential contamination of groundwater, because any materials deposited on the land surface in or near the sink, such as agricultural fertilizer or livestock dung, are taken down to be added to the groundwater.

Sinks are destructive, intrusive, yet fascinating landscape features. The Michigan Karst Conservancy is trying to preserve some sinks, purely for their scientific interest and curiosity value – and to ensure that the public have access to them. In 1993, the Stevens Twin Sinks Preserve was set up, a small nature reserve that contains two sinks separated by a narrow saddle-ridge. They are 200 feet across and 85 feet deep.

The Bruski Sink very inconveniently opened across a road, and this too has recently been made part of the Preserve. The Bruski Sink was used for many years for fly-tipping (illegal dumping of rubbish), but is now being cleaned up.

There is no early warning of subsidence, but there is a pattern to the distribution of sinkholes. They normally occur in lines, just as the underground caves occur in lines along lines of weakness in the limestone, and this 'lineation' can be seen in the layout of the Twin and Bruski sinkholes. So it would be unwise to build a house, or indeed anything at all, on the same alignment as a row of sinkholes. Unfortunately, when buying property, most people do not consider landscape processes, and agents and surveyors are not obliged to advise on or investigate problems of this kind.

In 1976, there was active subsidence at the eastern edge of Shoepac Lake, which confirms that the collapse of the sinkhole, or sinkholes, beneath the lake is still developing. The ongoing development of the Shoepac doline was confirmed in 1994, when some more of the land surface collapsed at the eastern edge in line with a row of at least five more sinkholes running away to the east. The karst landscape of Michigan is a dynamically developing landscape, which makes it harder to live in, harder to use. What we learn from the sinkhole landscape and its intermittent collapses is that the landscapes we live on are actively changing, sometimes smoothly and continuously, sometimes in startling jumps – and right under our feet.

THE WAURIKA
TORNADO

(1976)

APART FROM CUMULUS clouds, the sort that even very young children can draw, tornadoes are probably the easiest type of weather to identify. They are usually snake-like lines or broad-topped funnels descending from thunderclouds to the ground. But they can undergo some interesting transformations. If they pass over water, instead of sucking up dust they suck up the fresh or seawater from below, and spray it out like a garden sprinkler. This is a waterspout. If they pass over a bare rocky surface, where there is nothing to suck up, they can become invisible. Where, as in the Great Plains of the United States, they pass over a reddish-brown soil, they can become red. If they pass through snow-covered terrain in mountain country, they can turn a brilliant white. If they pass over a nursery full of red roses, they can turn pink with the ripped-off petals. In the sunset, they take on the many colours of the setting sun.

The Waurika tornado, which struck the town of Waurika in Oklahoma on 30 May 1976, was repeatedly photographed. The images show vividly how tornadoes can undergo these transformations. Some of the photographs were taken at the same time, from different places by different people. What a tornado looks like can vary a great deal according to the lighting conditions. Looking at the Waurika tornado with the light behind you made it show up light against a dark grey sky. Looking at the same tornado from the opposite side made it show up black against a bright sky. The appearance of a tornado is very different according to whether it is front-lit or back-lit.

What is likely to remain impossible to photograph or see is the centre of the tornado. But there is mounting evidence from Doppler radar images that tornadoes have clear, calm centres. This makes them very similar in structure to the much larger hurricanes, which have long been known to have well developed eyes – circular central areas of very low pressure where there is little or no wind. So the centre of a tornado is a narrow column of still air. Obviously surviving tornado eyewitnesses are unable, in the chaos of such a fast-moving and traumatic experience, to appreciate this.

THE TANGSHAN EARTHQUAKE

(1976)

THE TANGSHAN EARTHQUAKE, which hit China on 28 July 1976, was one of the most violent earthquakes of the last century or so. In terms of the loss of life it is without equal. But it is also a remarkable event in another way. Because of the nature of the political regime in China at that time, information about the earthquake and its consequences was not shared with the outside world. Seismographs around the world picked up the outer ripples of the Tangshan earthquake, and scientists were able to infer from these that a major earthquake had happened – and where – but the scale of the destruction could not really be inferred. The Chinese government saw to it that the true level of China's suffering was hidden. It was almost as if it was ashamed that such a terrible calamity had befallen China. It was only many years later, after a change of regime, that the scale of the Tangshan earthquake and its appalling death toll leaked out to the outside world.

The epicentre of the earthquake was near the industrial city of Tangshan, where one million people lived. The earthquake, registering 8.2 on the Richter scale, struck at three forty-two am and lasted for just fifteen seconds. About fifteen hours later there was an aftershock, which was a major earthquake in its own right, with a magnitude of 7.1, and taking more lives. According to official Chinese statistics, 242,419 people were killed by the earthquake, though some outside sources put the death toll much higher. Another 164,000 people were seriously injured.

Many residents of Tangshan said they saw unusual lights, 'earthquake lights', the night before the earthquake. Water in a well in a village outside Tangshan rose and fell three times during the day before the earthquake. Many animals behaved abnormally. A thousand hens refused to eat and went wild; dogs barked unceasingly; goldfish jumped out of their bowls.

In one area close to Tangshan, there had been an official warning two years earlier that an earthquake would strike. There was an organized programme of education and preparation, and when monitoring stations detected changes in the groundwater, implying that the quake was imminent, schools started conducting lessons outdoors. As a result of this careful preparation, only one person died there during the earthquake – and he died of a heart attack. In Tangshan itself, there was no such preparation, and the timing of the quake, in the middle of the night when people were sound asleep, meant that there was a slow response when it struck. The city was believed, wrongly, not to be at risk from severe earthquakes, and its buildings were not designed to withstand them.

An area of about sixteen square miles in Tangshan was completely wrecked. Seventy-eight per cent of the factories and other industrial buildings were destroyed. Ninety-three per cent of the housing was destroyed. It amounted to an almost total destruction of the city. A few buildings were damaged as far afield as Beijing, which lay 100 miles from the earthquake epicentre. To put the Tangshan earthquake in context, its 242,000 official death toll was slightly higher than the Aleppo earthquake in Syria in 1138, in which 230,000 died, but lower than the Indian Ocean earthquake of 2004, in which 287,00 died. China has nevertheless suffered very badly from great earthquakes. Three out of five of the deadliest earthquakes in the world in the last 1,000 years have occurred in China – the Shensi earthquake of 1556, the Gansu earthquake of 1920 and the Tangshan earthquake of 1976. In those three disasters combined, at least 1,280,000,000 people were killed. Put differently, one-and-a-quarter billion people. That figure of course accepts the official Chinese statistics for Tangshan, and some sources suggest that the death toll at Tangshan was more in the region of 726,000, though that would still be lower than the death toll in the Shensi earthquake.

The Chinese government refused offers of aid from foreign countries, and its relief efforts were widely condemned as inadequate. The Chinese government was also criticized strongly for failing to take appropriate action on the warnings given by geologists. Perceptions of the disaster were very different within China, where it was seen as part of an ongoing 'Curse of 1976'. Just before the earthquake came the death of Zhou Enlai; just after it came the death of Mao Zedong. Both men were prominent leaders of the Communist Party of China. The political fallout did much to bring the Cultural Revolution in China to an end. The earthquake led, indirectly, to regime change. Rebuilding work began straight away in the city of Tangshan, which has now been completely rebuilt as the Brave City of China.

THE BIG THOMPSON CANYON FLASH FLOOD

(1976)

A RAINSTORM in Colorado caused a flash flood along a twenty-five mile long stretch of the Big Thompson Canyon in 1976. On 31 July, a wall of flood water twenty feet high swept through the canyon and 145 people lost their lives. The flood happened at the peak of the tourist season in the state of Colorado. Several thousand people had escaped from the heat of the cities to this popular camping area north-west of Denver. By the end of the fateful afternoon, there were about 3,000 people in the canyon enjoying the scenery.

The landscape was barren, with little soil or vegetation to absorb water, and very steep valley walls that shed storm rain very rapidly. It was as if the physical landscape was designed to produce disastrous flash floods. The tourist trade encouraged the development of houses and eating places, and Highway 34 stretched along the length of the canyon.

A thunderstorm started to drop heavy rain in the Rockies at about six o'clock in the evening. The storm remained stationary for over three hours, dumping a huge amount of water into the Big Thompson Canyon. Eight inches of rain fell in a single hour. The river, normally a placid stream only two feet deep, was transformed into a torrent twenty feet deep, pushing boulders ten feet across in front of it. Hit by this wall of water and rock, buildings, cars and tourists had little chance of surviving. Highway 34 was flooded, so the only escape route was up the walls of the canyon; for most people this meant that they were totally trapped.

In just two hours, the Big Thompson Canyon flood killed 145 people, including six whose bodies were never recovered. There were 418 buildings and 152 businesses destroyed. One positive outcome of the disaster was that new regulations were introduced throughout the United States, restricting building developments along river sides in canyons. Another was the setting up of early-warning systems for flash floods, especially in tourist areas.

THE IZU
EARTHQUAKE

(1978)

THE IZU EARTHQUAKE, measuring 7.0 on the Richter scale, struck Sagami Bay in Japan on 14 January 1978. The area worst affected was about ten miles across, causing extensive damage on the central Izu peninsula. The epicentre of the earthquake was on the seabed off the southern tip of Izu Peninsula.

There had been dozens of foreshocks the day before the main quake, including several of magnitude 3, and these made it possible for the authorities to give credible warnings of an impending major earthquake. There were several aftershocks, the largest of them measuring 5.8 on the Richter scale and striking an hour after the main shock. The biggest aftershock caused severe damage in the mountains of the western part of the peninsula.

Most of the major hazards were to do with slope failure. Unstable steep slopes including sea cliffs, mountain sides and road embankments collapsed when they were shaken to produce landslides, especially along the fault lines where the rocks were displaced in the earthquake. The displacement of the rocks extended for about three miles. The vertical displacement reached a maximum of two feet, the horizontal displacement a maximum of one foot. There was large-scale damage to many concrete retaining walls, simply because of the poor load-bearing capacity of the ground underneath, especially when shaken. There was also a miniature tsunami two feet high.

Altogether, thirty people died and 134 houses collapsed.

Damage to roads, bridges and water pipes was common throughout the area. The relatively low death toll showed that the Japanese were prepared for the disaster and were able to minimize its impact. Most of the damage from this earthquake was due to landslides, and it is clear from the landscape of the peninsula that landslides are an integral part of the region's personality.

THE *AMOCO CADIZ* OIL SPILL

(1978)

IN MARCH 1978, the oil tanker *Amoco Cadiz* came to grief in almost exactly the same way as the *Torrey Canyon* eleven years earlier, and with the same effects. The tanker belonged to the American-owned company Amoco International Oil Co. She was making her way from the Gulf to the port of Rotterdam, when she lost her steering gear in heavy sea. The huge ship was out of control. Attempts were made to get her under tow, but the weather conditions were too severe and she drifted onto the rocks. She broke her back in the same way as the *Torrey Canyon*, allowing her oil to flood out into the sea.

The captain of the *Amoco Cadiz* was later strongly criticized for delaying his request for help. Had he used the radio to get help when he first got into difficulties the ship might have been safely towed into port.

The oil slick from the wrecked tanker washed onto the beaches on the French side of the English Channel. The French authorities had developed contingency plans to deal with oil spillages of up to 30,000 tons. The problem was that the *Amoco Cadiz*, a very big tanker, was carrying 223,000 tons of crude oil. The efforts of the beach cleaners who arrived to clean up the French beaches were initially very ineffectual indeed, and the people of Brittany were furious at what they saw as the inadequacy of the whole operation. To be fair, there was an enormous length of coastline to clean up. The oil coated about 250 miles of shoreline.

The oil settled on the beaches as a stodgy black mousse, and it was too thick to be siphoned up and piped away. The authorities refused to use detergents on the oil because that in turn would poison fish and oyster beds. The solution was Operation Teaspoon. The oil looked like chocolate mousse, and it was physically scooped up, small amounts at a time, almost with teaspoons. Up to 8,000 people were on the French beaches every day, scarping up the oil by hand and putting it in drums to take away for burial. After that the rocks were sprayed.

The authorities were strongly criticized for their approach at the time, but in time they were vindicated. Although 22,000 seabirds unavoidably died in the disaster, there was very little long-term impact on wildlife, and that was because those responsible for organizing the clean-up had had the self-restraint to avoid using chemicals on a big scale.

THE ERUPTION OF MOUNT ST HELENS

(1980)

THE ERUPTION OF Mount St Helens in May 1980 was by no means the biggest in the last 200 years, but it occupies a key high-profile position in history because it is the most thoroughly studied volcanic eruption of modern times. It also brought about a revolution in public awareness of the dangers of volcanic activity. The perception of the average American before 1980 was that there was no serious danger from volcanoes in the American Northwest, yet geologists were acutely aware of the mounting danger.

Along the Cascade Range there are fifteen active volcanoes. Prior to 1980, the last to erupt had been Mount Lassen (1914-17). In the mid-1970s, geologists thought that Mount Baker in Washington might be the next to erupt. In 1978, geologists at the USGS converged on Mount St Helens as the likeliest to erupt next. Dwight Crandell and Don Millineaux drew attention to the volcano's young age – less than 37,000 years old - and the fact that it has been much more active over the last 4,000 years. The Mount St Helens eruptions are quite frequent; since the middle ages Mount St Helens has erupted once every century, and it was 130 years since it had last erupted. That was worrying, because it implied that the eruption was overdue and therefore likely to be particularly violent. Mount St Helens has a history of violent pyroclastic eruptions. Its character is different from other Cascade volcanoes, which typically do not erupt explosively.

Months before the catastrophic eruption actually happened,

the US Geological Survey set up a base of operations at Vancouver, Washington, for monitoring developments at Mount St Helens. Seismometers were fitted to detect earth movements on and around the mountain. The first indications that the volcano was stirring came on 20 March, when it was shaken by a 4.2 magnitude earthquake. Three days later there was another big earthquake under the volcano, followed by swarms of smaller earthquakes every fifteen minutes, as the molten rock made its way towards the surface. On 25 March, a light aircraft flew over the volcano, and it reported new fractures opening up on the surface of the glacier and several avalanches and rockfalls.

On 27 March, there was a loud explosion and a dense column of ash and steam shot up to a height of 6,000 feet. This was hard to detect as the area was engulfed in thick cloud, but when the cloud cleared, a brand-new crater about 250 feet across was visible on the volcano's summit and the snow around it was covered by a layer of dark ash. The eruption had begun. There were several more small similar eruptions in April and early May. The steam that was jetting off was the groundwater heated by a rising tongue of molten lava rising up the volcano's throat.

On 27 March, two huge cracks opened on the north side of the summit of Mt St Helens, extending 4,000 feet down the mountain side, and the area between them swelled out to make a bulge that grew bigger and bigger during the following month. By the time of the big eruption, it had swelled out 300 feet and was expanding at a rate of six feet every day.

Then, at 8.32 am on 18 May, there was a big earthquake as the lava edged nearer the surface and cracked open the volcano. The whole northern slope of the mountain over the bulge collapsed, sliding down. This removed a great weight from the pressurized lava and hot groundwater underneath, and the superheated water converted instantaneously to steam. The blast flashed sideways through the landslide, devastating an area twenty miles across. Unlike most disasters, all of this was captured on film.

One of the USGS volcanologists, David Johnston, was encamped on Coldwater Ridge, a few miles to the north of the volcano. When the climatic eruption happened, Johnston sent a radio message in great excitement, 'Vancouver, Vancouver, this is it!' The scale of the eruption was such that a few minutes later Johnston was dead. Fifty-six other people also died. Two other geologists, Keith and Dorothy Stoffel, happened to be flying in a light aircraft over the mountain as it erupted. They watched as one of the biggest landslides ever recorded demolished the north side of the volcano, releasing an explosive sideways eruption out towards the north, towards Spirit Lake and Coldwater Ridge (now renamed Johnston Ridge in David Johnston's memory). The cloud of smoke and ash billowed and expanded, threatening to engulf the aircraft, but the Stoffels managed to escape by turning south, out of the path of the ash cloud.

The eruption flattened millions of Douglas fir trees across a huge fan-shaped area. Debris lined the lake bed of Spirit Lake with over 200 feet of sediment, displacing the water and doubling the lake's area. A huge amount of ash and rock landed in the North Fork of the Toulle River, filling the valley for fifteen miles with a rocky and chaotic deposit.

Immediately after the sideways blast, an eruption column rose rapidly from the summit. In ten minutes, it reached a height of fifteen miles, where high-altitude winds carried the ash away to the east. This Plinian eruption went on all day. Ash fell from the umbrella-shaped ash cloud across the Great Plains and further afield. There were fears that the ash veil might spoil the European summer, but the deflection of most of the energy sideways ensured that relatively little ash reached the troposphere. There was no 'Tambora effect', no year without a summer.

The shape of the mountain was changed out of recognition. The landslide, the sideways blast and the Plinian eruption column combined to create a huge amphitheatre on the mountain's northern flank, a hole two miles across.

The release of gases from the volcano meant that the viscous lava could begin to rise through the central vent from 12 June onwards, to form a lava dome at the centre of the amphitheatre. The sticky lava solidified immediately on contact with the air, plugging the vent. Pressure from below blew it apart; in all, the lava dome was built up three times, the first two being destroyed on 22 July and 18 October 1980.

Our understanding of the nature of volcanic eruptions made enormous advances as a result of the Mount St Helens eruption sequence. Some of what happened was accurately predicted by geologists, but they had not reckoned on the volcano erupting sideways. For some reason, they did not realize the significance of the bulging mountain side. The circular area that was evacuated immediately before the eruption turned out to be the wrong area, because the main force of the blast was directed northwards instead of upwards. As a result of this miscalculation, the death toll was higher than anticipated.

THE PENLEE
LIFEBOAT DISASTER

(1981)

ON 19 DECEMBER 1981, a small Dublin-registered cargo ship called the *Union Star* was on her maiden voyage from IJmuiden in the Netherlands to Arklow in Ireland. She was carrying a cargo of fertilizer. The *Union Star* carried a crew of five, including the captain, Henry Morton. Morton had his wife, Dawn, and their two teenage daughters on board; they were travelling as a family, because it was Christmas.

The problems began in earnest when the *Union Star* was about eight miles east of Wolf Rock, off the south coast of Cornwall. These are dangerous waters, and the *Union Star* was unlucky enough to develop an engine problem. Assistance was offered by a tug, the *Noord Holland*, under a salvage contract. Morton was not the first captain to turn down such an offer. A salvage offer is a kind of holding to ransom, and Morton turned it down because he was reluctant to pay an open-ended sum for salvage. On the other hand, as things turned out, it would have been better for everyone involved if he had agreed. He was not to know how badly things would end that day.

The *Union Star*'s fuel supply became contaminated by seawater and the weather worsened. Morton released a distress signal to the coastguard at Falmouth. By this stage, the winds had reached eighty mph with gusts up to ninety-five mph – hurricane force. With her serious engine problem, the *Union Star* was completely at the mercy of the wind and waves. She was gradually driven towards the rocky coastline at Boscawen Cove, near Lamorna. The Sea King helicopter from RNAS Culdrose was unable to lift any of those on board the *Union Star* to safety.

Then the Penlee lifeboat was launched. She was a forty-seven feet long, wooden Watson class lifeboat named *Solomon Browne*. The seas were so violent that the lifeboat was in difficulty from the launch. Her crew, eight men from the village of Mousehole, were all experienced seamen. Twelve men had responded to the call out. Eight were chosen with care. The weather conditions were so appalling and the dangers so great that only one man from each family was allowed to go. The crew knew, from before the launch, how great the risks were.

The *Union Star* was driven by the wind very close to the cliffs. The lifeboat coxswain, Trevelyan Richards, made several attempt before succeeding in getting alongside the *Union Star*. The sea was so rough that the lifeboat was twice thrown up onto the *Union Star*'s deck and once slammed against the ship's side. Incredibly, in spite of mountainous waves more than fifty feet high, the crew of the *Solomon Browne* managed to get four of the people from the wheelhouse of the *Union Star* into the lifeboat. Then the lifeboat was forced to turn away from the ship, for its own safety.

The lifeboat crew then made a fatal error in deciding to go back to rescue the rest of the crew. No more was seen or heard of the *Solomon Browne*. The last radio message from her was, 'We've got four men off, hang on, we have got four at the moment. There's two left on board.' After that the radio went dead.

It is not clear exactly what happened to the Penlee lifeboat in those final seconds. She may have been thrown up and right over the *Union Star* by a big wave. She may have been smashed against the side of the freighter. She may have been raked by one of the many rocks in the cove.

The Sennen Cove lifeboat was launched in attempt to find and rescue the Penlee lifeboat, but It was physically impossible for her to get round Land's End to reach the scene of the disaster. The lifeboat from St Mary's in the Scilly Isles made the voyage to the mainland to search for survivors. The Lizard lifeboat also went to sea, sustaining structural damage in the mountainous seas – some of the waves were sixty feet high.

Both the *Union Star* and the *Solomon Browne* were total losses. Everyone on board both vessels was lost. The launching of the *Solomon Browne* was an amazingly courageous act, but it could not have succeeded. Eight bodies were eventually found, four from the *Union Star*, four from the *Solomon Browne*. Fragments of the lifeboat were found along the shore.

The crew of the *Solomon Browne* were William Trevelyan Richards (56), Charles Greenhaugh (46), John Blewitt (43), Nigel Brockman (43), James Madron (35), Barrie Torrie (33), Kevin Smith (23) and Gary Wallis (23). The coxswain, Trevelyan Richards, was awarded the Royal National Lifeboat Institution's Gold Medal, and each of the crew members the Bronze Medal.

The action of the Penlee lifeboat crew aroused universal admiration in Great Britain, and led to a large-scale public appeal for the benefit of the village of Mousehole; it raised more than three million pounds.

There was an inquiry into the disaster in 1982, which concluded that no one was to blame for the disaster. It was entirely due to unusually savage weather conditions. There were, even so, some changes to legislation relating to salvage. From then on, it became possible for a coastguard to override a captain's decision; if a captain turned down an offer of assistance on financial grounds, the coastguard could authorize it anyway.

At the time of writing, Nigel Brockman's son Neil is coxswain of the Penlee lifeboat. He was one of the twelve men who volunteered back in 1981 but was sent home by Richards. The current Penlee lifeboat is of a superior design to the one destroyed in the disaster, and it is stationed at Newlyn. The old lifeboat house at Penlee Point stands empty as a memorial to its heroic 1981 crew.

THE AIDS
EPIDEMIC

(1981–)

AIDS STANDS FOR Acquired Immune Deficiency Syndrome. It is not so much a disease as a collection of symptoms that people display when their immune system is damaged by a specific virus, the human immunodeficiency virus, usually shortened to HIV. In the early stages, there are no symptoms. In the late stages people suffer from weakening infections and tumours. There are now treatments that can slow down the progress of HIV and AIDS, but there is as yet no known cure.

The virus is transmitted from one person to another through the direct contact of a mucous membrane (or the bloodstream itself) with a body fluid containing the virus. The commonest ways in which the virus is passed from one person to another are during sex, by a transfusion of infected blood, or by the use of contaminated hypodermic needles.

AIDS was only identified in 1981, when five homosexual men in Los Angeles were diagnosed as having it, but it may have been in existence for much longer. It is hard to be sure where the virus came from, but it is thought that it came from Africa in the mid-twentieth century and may somehow have made a cross-species leap, rather like Spanish influenza or bird flu. One 1990s theory that the virus came from chimpanzees has now been discredited. The earliest known occurrence of the virus was in central Africa in 1959. Because the disease can be transmitted in several different ways, and there are no immediate symptoms, it spread rapidly in the 1980s.

451

AIDS has become a pandemic and there are probably as many as 40 million people globally who have the virus. In 2006, it was estimated that more than 25 million people have died of AIDS since it was first recognized as a condition on 5 June 1981. In one year alone, 2005, between two-and-a-half and three million people died, of whom half a million were children who had inherited AIDS from their mothers. This death toll makes it one of the deadliest epidemics in human history. In many regions of the Third World, HIV-AIDS has spread through whole populations, laying up huge demographic, economic and psychological problems for the future.

The death toll in itself has caused untold human misery. But there is another problem with AIDS – and that is the terrible stigma that is connected with it, partly because of its association with illicit extra-marital sexual activity, partly because of the overwhelming fear that people have of catching it. The association of AIDS with male homosexuals was a serious setback to the gay liberation movement, and there was an increase in homophobia. The initial identification of the condition led to the name GRID, Gay-Related Immune Deficiency, but quite early on it became apparent to medics that half of the victims were not gay men at all, so the name was changed. The public perception is nevertheless still that AIDS is a 'gay plague' and some newspaper journalists still unhelpfully use this inappropriate phrase.

BUSH FIRES IN AUSTRALIA

(1983)

IN THE LONG, hot, dry summers of southern Australia, bush and forest fires are an annual problem. An older generation of 'bush dwellers', living in small communities of around 250 people, can vividly remember the 'Black Friday' on 1983, when bush fires ravaged the state of Victoria. Seventy-one people were killed.

The fire happened on 16 February 1983, at the height of the summer, and temperatures had soared to record levels. The region had also become thoroughly dried after three continuous years of drought conditions. The landscape of desiccated shrubland and grassland between the cities and the semi-desert of the outback was ripe for fire and the authorities knew it. There was an extra factor, too. Bush fires are seen a destructive, though they are part of the natural ecosystem. It is probably firing from time to time that has actually created the bush, and that without the periodic fires the whole area would be forested. The dry season is a natural part of the climatic regime, and lightning strikes in thunderstorms are too. People, equally naturally, do not want fires sweeping across the landscape near their towns and cities, so efforts are made to prevent fires from starting, and when they do start they are put out. The result is there now tend to be longer time intervals between fires. That allows more twigs and fallen leaves to accumulate and the litter layer detains the fire, when it eventually arrives, much longer in each place, making it burn hotter. So, human interference may have made the situation worse.

There were daily warnings of fire hazard. An extensive fire in the bush was an ecological disaster in itself, but because there were townships adjacent to it there was the added danger that residential areas would go up in flames too. And a single spark was all that was needed.

Fire broke out in several places at once, on the afternoon of an intensely hot day when the temperatures reached fofty-three degrees Celsius. The general conditions certainly made the outbreak of fires likely, but it is still not known what, in the end, actually ignited them. Some suspected that people were to blame. A casually dropped cigarette end would be enough. Others thought strong winds had snapped overhead power lines, and that sparks from these started the fire.

Three fires broke out on the outskirts of the city of Adelaide and another four started outside the city of Melbourne. The shrubland in some places developed into full-scale woodland, with tall eucalyptus trees. The oil-filled leaves of the eucalyptus trees were intensely flammable, turning the gum trees into spectacular fireballs.

The fire swept across to a small town east of Melbourne, Cockatoo. The firestorm was by now forty feet high, with huge golden fireballs flying towards the town. People naturally tried to get away from the fire. They got into their cars and drove as fast as they could, but the fire was sweeping forwards at 100 mph and they had no chance of escape. They were swallowed up by the fire, dying instantly in the holocaust. Twenty-nine people died at Cockatoo. But some people survived. Among them was a family who dived into a water tank and crouched in the water; as the fire raged all around them the water rose almost to boiling point, but they survived. In the schoolhouse, which was built of brick and therefore resisted the fire, 120 children were saved by sheltering underneath water-soaked blankets while the firefighters played water over the roof to stop the building catching fire.

The firefighters worked all through the afternoon and the following night. Inevitably, many of them found themselves in extremely dangerous situations, surrounded by fire. Twelve of them died at Mount Gambier as they tried to quell a raging fire with too little water at their disposal.

Some small coastal settlements disappeared in the flames. People at Anglesea and Lorne abandoned their cliff-top homes and ran down to the beach. They had to stay there, stranded, while the fire enveloped their homes on the cliffs above.

The fire almost reached Melbourne. If it had reached the city, the fire would have been an even bigger human disaster than it was. From Melbourne it was possible to see the ominous pall of smoke, and the huge flames licking along the wooded ridges twenty miles away. There were emergency plans to send fleets of bulldozers in to create huge firebreaks to stop the fire from reaching the city, but given the ferocity of the fire it might easily have leap-frogged the firebreak.

The bush fire raged for two full days before it was finally under control. When it came, the 1983 fire was notable in several different ways. The sheer ferocity and heat of the fires was one. Another was the high level of loss. As well as killing seventy-one people, the fires killed 200,000 sheep and cattle, destroyed 150,000 acres of forest and farmland, and made 8,500 people homeless. It was far worse than anything Australia had experienced before.

THE LAKE MONOUN DISASTER

(1984)

IN 1984, A terrible disaster overtook the people living near a lake in Cameroon. They fell victim to one of the rarest and most insidious types of eruption of all. It is an event that is so rare that there is no everyday name for it; it is known to scientists as a 'limnic eruption' or a 'lake overturn'.

What happened in Cameroun in 1984 was that a huge quantity of carbon dioxide was suddenly released from the bottom of a lake, Lake Monoun, overwhelming and suffocating all the animal life in the area. Thirty-seven people who happened to be living close to the lake were killed. Carbon dioxide is denser and therefore heavier than air, so when released from the lake it settled on the ground, pushing the breathable air out of the way. So as the carbon dioxide cloud spread out across the landscape it choked all the animal it engulfed. The victims instinctively gasped for air, but this only made them ingest carbon dioxide all the faster.

A pre-condition for this type of disaster is that the water filling the lake needs to be saturated in carbon dioxide. The bed of the lake also needs to be cool, and the layers within the lake have to have different amounts of carbon dioxide. The lake also needs to be close to volcanic activity. The pre-conditions required are therefore quite special, and they are not going to occur very often or in very many locations. This is why lake overturn is such a rare type of disaster. It has in fact only been observed to happen twice. Lake overturns have almost certainly happened several times in the past, but it is in the nature of the event that we would know nothing about it.

The lethal carbon dioxide released in a limnic eruption comes from two sources. One is volcanic gas that has been given off from a magma chamber somewhere below the lake. The other is organic: the decay of dead material accumulating on the lake bed. The carbon dioxide is dissolved in the lake water and, as in a bottle or can of soft drink, more of it can be dissolved when the gas and liquid are under high pressure. The bottom layers of the lake are at a much higher pressure because of the water weighing down on them, so the bottom layers of a deep lake can contain much more carbon dioxide in solution. Low temperatures also aid solution, so if the bottom layers are cold they hold more carbon dioxide.

When the lake water is saturated with carbon dioxide, really any change in conditions may trigger an eruption. An increase in temperature in theory might do it. More likely is the sudden disturbace of the bottom layers so that they are no longer at the bottom. That disturbance might be in the form of a landslide, a volcanic eruption nearby, an earthquake, an explosion, possibly even a violent storm. The result, whatever the exact trigger, is that the pressure is released from the bottom water. The effect is like unscrewing the cap of a bottle of tonic water. The release of pressure causes a lot of the carbon dioxide to turn to gas, hence the formation of lots of bubbles, or 'fizz'. The bubbles give the bottom water buoyancy, so it rises higher in the lake body, where it is under even less pressure, so even more bubbles are formed, and so on. A column of gas is created and the bottom water is sucked up, losing its dissolved carbon dioxide in a feedback process. Carbon dioxide fountains up into the air, displacing the lake surface to form tsunamis.

THE MEXICO CITY EARTHQUAKE

(1985)

IN SEPTEMBER 1985, a massive earthquake measuring 8.1 on the Richter scale hit Mexico City, a city of eighteen million people, destroying about one-third of it. The historic city centre was badly damaged. Schools, cathedrals and hotels were levelled. An eight-storey apartment block folded up like a telescope. Some multi-storey buildings remained standing but leaning dangerously to one side.

Among many terrible scenes were the destruction of the central hospital. The building had partially collapsed in the earthquake, then various medical supplies such as cotton wool and surgical spirit caught fire. Over 1,000 people had been inside the hospital at the time of the earthquake, and hundreds of them were trapped between the floors as the building crumpled and burned. At least 150 mothers and babies died, along with the heads of obstetrics, surgery and intensive care, who stayed to help instead of saving themselves.

It was not just Mexico City that suffered: the towns of three provinces in Mexico were damaged. The shock was felt as far north as Houston in Texas, more than 700 miles away, and as far south as Guatemala City, over 600 miles away.

In the mountainous areas, there were landslides. At Atentique, part of a mountain side broke away and the resulting landslide killed many people preparing themselves for a day's work.

One problem was looters pretending to be rescue workers. Another was the stench of rotting bodies. A baseball pitch had to serve as a temporary morgue. There was a real fear that disease would spread through the ruined towns and raise the death toll even higher. Medical teams inoculated people against typhoid and tetanus in the streets. Meanwhile, efforts to rescue people from the rubble continued unremittingly. Teams of sniffer dogs were flown in from North America and Europe. The diggers worked for two days to rescue a medical student who had been looking after a patient at the time of the quake. A team of firemen from Miami worked with Mexican miners for seven days to dig three tunnels to reach a twenty-two year old woman who was buried. They eventually pulled her out to safety along the forty-foot passageway that they had dug.

The rescue workers were amazed to find fifty-eight new-born babies still alive in the ruins of Mexico City's central hospital. One premature baby was dug out, still alive though dehydrated, after being buried for seven days. It seems that babies survive being buried alive in earthquakes far better than adults because they have no idea what has happened to them. They are not psychologically traumatized; they are not terrified as we adults are.

THE LAKE NYOS
DISASTER

(1986)

THE FIRST RECORDED, the first known lake overturn eruption
happened in Cameroon in 1984. The second, and to date the only
other known lake overturn eruption, happened in Cameroon just
two years later. The statistical chances of an event, not known to
have happened anywhere else in the world at any other time,
happening twice in the same African country within two years are
almost zero. Yet that is what happened.

There was another lake overturn eruption, causing a very
similar disaster, at Lake Nyos, also in the 1980s and also in
Cameroon. Lake Nyos is a beautiful, tranquil lake nestling among
verdant hills, with picturesque cream-coloured cliffs in places
rising from the water's edge.

The eruption at Lake Nyos was far deadlier than the one at Lake
Monoun in 1984. This eruption is believed to have been caused by
a landslide on the lake shore. A huge volume of carbon dioxide,
estimated at more than 800 million cubic feet, was released without
warning from the lake. It descended from the lake into a village,
where it asphyxiated and killed 1,750 people. Some people living as
much as fifteen miles from the lake died. Thousands of cattle and
other livestock were killed. Many wild animals perished, too,
though nobody counted. The massive disturbance within the lake
churned up the lake-bed sediment, so that for a time after the
disaster the lake water was pale and cloudy with silt. The
vegetation of the area was unaffected, except immediately around

the lake, where it was damaged or destroyed by the fifteen-feet high tsunami which was generated by the lake overturn.

This type of disaster leaves few clues as to how it happened, or even what happened. The only evidence afterwards is the corpses lying about. But post mortem examination would only tell you that they died because they were deprived of oxygen, that they died of suffocation, even though they died out in the open air. After the disposal of the dead bodies, there is nothing in the landscape to show that a disaster has happened at all. But if the geological and environmental conditions have been right for a lake overturn eruption to happen in Cameroon in 1984, and then again in 1986, they must have been right on earlier occasions even if we have no direct evidence.

Perhaps the most important question to ask is, 'When and where is a lake overturn disaster likely to happen next?'

Scientists have identified another African lake, Lake Kivu on the precarious border between the Congo and Rwanda, as the likeliest location for the next lake overturn eruption. Professor Robert Hecky from the University of Michigan examined lake-bed sediments from Kivu. The sediments showed that something has happened to kill every living thing in the lake roughly every 1,000 years. When these massacres occurred, for some reason vegetation from the lake shore was swept back into the lake. Obviously the release of huge volumes of carbon dioxide from the lake bottom would result in huge bubbles disrupting the lake surface and produce tsunami waves. Big waves crashing over the lake shore could easily uproot vegetation and drag it back into the lake. So the evidence is very strong that lake overturn eruptions have happened at Lake Kivu in the past. And as we have seen over and over again in this book, disasters have a habit of repeating themselves, often cyclically.

Now that this type of natural disaster has been newly identified, we need to consider how we should respond to it. It seems, after the research on Lake Kivu, that scientists can identify the lakes that are likely to be dangerous. An early-warning or evacuation system would obviously be completely inappropriate, not least because the disaster is sudden, almost instantaneous, leaving no chance for escape. It may prove to be possible to remove the gas from the lakes artificially, and prevent the build-up of carbon dioxide to lethal levels.

In 1990, French scientists started experiments at Lake Monoun and Lake Nyos, They used siphons to degas the lake water in a controlled way. The experiments were successful but each pipe could only deal with a limited quantity of gas, and several pipes would be needed to degas each lake enough to make it safe. Another problem is that the carbon dioxide dissolved in the lake water makes the water acidic; this corrodes the pipes and electronics, adding considerably to maintenance costs. It could also be a problem if the carbon dioxide brought up through the pipes settled as a thin layer on the lake, where it would cause difficulties for wildlife. Possibly the degassing process needs to be undertaken only when there is a wind blowing, to disperse the extracted carbon dioxide. In 2001, a single pipe was installed on Lake Nyos. The following year Lake Monoun was given a second pipe. The hope is that this technology will be sufficient to stop the carbon-dioxide levels increasing any further. A proposal to degas Lake Monoun completely seems to have been shelved.

The prospect of a future disaster at Lake Kivu remains a great worry. The level of carbon-dioxide saturation is not yet dangerous, but as it increases obviously the danger of a major disaster will increase. In theory, the same degassing technology could be applied to Lake Kivu as is being used at the other two lakes, but Lake Kivu is a much bigger problem. It is 2,000 times larger than Lake Nyos, which will make it very difficult to degas. There are also more than two million people living along the lake shores, so the death toll would be utterly overwhelming. A further problem is that a natural degassing could happen earlier than the scientists are expecting, simply because there is an active volcano close by,

Mount Nyiragongo, which could erupt and trigger a lake overturn eruption in Lake Kivu. From what happened at the other two lakes, there is every probability that everyone living along the shores of Lake Kivu would be killed: no one would survive.

THE NEVADO DEL RUIZ ERUPTION

(1985)

NEVADO DEL RUIZ is the northernmost and highest volcano in the Colombian Andes, with a summit covered with about ten square miles of snow and ice. Every volcano has its own character, its own life cycle, its own style of erupting. Nevado del Ruiz has a history of small-scale eruptions, which nevertheless give off a lot of heat, melting the snowcap and releasing lethal volcanic mudflows, known as lahars. In 1595, one of these lahars poured down the valleys of the Rivers Guali and Lagunillas, killing 636 people. In 1845, a lahar inundated the Lagunillas Valley, killing 1,000 and flowing on for fifty miles down the valley before spreading out across a plain. It was on the surface of this 1845 mud deposit that the settlement of Armero was built. It was a disastrous choice of site, given the known history of the volcano: more lahars would be bound to follow.

Armero expanded and became a successful town with over 27,000 inhabitants. It was nevertheless doomed. On 13 November 1985, volcanic history repeated itself. There was another eruption and another deadly lahar came sweeping down the Lagunillas Valley. This time, because of the population of Armero, the death toll was very high indeed, 23,000 people were killed – most of the population of the town of Armero. It is very clear that this disaster need not have happened. Nothing could have stopped the lahar, but Armero need not have been built in its path.

The 1985 eruption started at 9 am on 13 November. There was

an explosion and an eruption column. Shortly afterwards, ash began to fall along with heavy rain; the two together produced the lahars. These began as many small rivers of mud, but after descending thousands of feet down the mountain at forty mph they converged into six major river valleys. By this time they were as much as 150 feet deep, having picked up soil and rocks along the way; they made a terrific rumbling noise. Houses and villages that were up on the valley sides were safe from the lahars. But Armero was down on the valley floor at the exit of the Lagunillas Canyon, and within four hours of the eruption, 23,000 people were dead.

Armero was hit by three main pulses of flowing water and debris. The first, arriving at 11.25 am, was a thin sheet of fairly clean water that had been displaced from a lake not far above the town when the lahars entered it. The second pulse arrived ten minutes later. This was the major mudflow, which destroyed most of the buildings and swept most of the people away. The third pulse arrived fifteen minutes later.

When Nevado del Ruiz began to reawaken in 1984, there was no team of troubleshooting volcanologists that could be mobilized to visit the scene of the impending emergency and give advice on evacuation. Within a year of the Armero disaster, and very much as a response to it, the US Geological Survey had set up a team that could set off to the scene of any imminent eruption anywhere in the world. Two important lessons were learned from the Nevado del Ruiz disaster. One was that on snow-capped volcanoes catastrophic lahars can be triggered by relatively minor eruptions. The other was that landscape studies can help us to make reasoned choices for settlement locations; clearly Armero should never have been built on an old lahar.

THE *HERALD OF FREE ENTERPRISE*

(1987)

On 6 March 1987, the roll-on-roll-off car ferry *Herald of Free Enterprise* started out on what should have been a routine English Channel crossing from the Belgian port of Zeebrugge. It was out of season, so the ship was sailing only half full. In an attempt to make the sailing more worthwhile, the ship's owners, P & O, had offered a cheap day excursion, so there were large numbers of British day trippers on board who had crossed the Channel for a day's shopping. There were also 100 British soldiers who had been serving a tour of duty in Germany but were going home on leave.

Many of the passengers, exhausted by their day's shopping, headed for the ship's cafeteria as the *Herald of Free Enterprise* left the quayside and crossed the harbour. She was a distinctive ship, with a green funnel, white superstructure and orange hull. The name of the shipping line, Townsend Thoresen, was painted proudly in huge white letters along her side.

The ship turned and was just leaving the harbour when she developed a sudden list to port. One minute later, she keeled right over on her side. The water was shallow, which prevented a complete capsize.

Inside the ship, chaos broke loose as decks instantly became walls and walls became floors. Everyone was disorientated and confused. In the cafeteria, people were thrown on top of one another in a heap, screaming and fighting for breath. Some people suffocated. Others were drowned as the water poured in. The ship had heeled over so fast that there had been no time to lower lifeboats. Some of the crew threw life jackets overboard to passengers and crew who had been on deck and thrown into the sea. But it was a cold day, and the water was very cold; many in the sea were too numbed by the cold to put the life jackets on.

The starboard side of the ship was now its upper deck. The crew tried hard to reach those who were on the port side of the ship and therefore in or under the water. There were scenes where people fought like animals for survival. There were also scenes of heroism. One of the passengers, Andrew Parker, allowed others to use his body as a human bridge so that they could climb over him to safety; his wife, twelve-year-old daughter and several other passengers owed their lives to him.

Helicopters appeared and a fleet of small boats. They worked to lift people out of the water or off the ship and took them to shore. Then there was confusion about who had survived and who had not. The survivors were landed at different places, and then dispersed to different hospitals. There was also no passenger list, so no one could even estimate how many had survived or how many had been lost.

Recovering the bodies from the overturned ship proved to take a long time. Divers were able to retrieve bodies from the upper decks fairly quickly, but those on the lower decks were much harder to get out. To their relatives' distress, they had to be left there until the ship had been taken back into harbour and all the accumulated layers of mud had been pumped out.

The *Herald of Free Enterprise* was a very ordinary roll-on-roll-off ferry, a ship of a very common design. It was a design that a number of experts had commented on as very unsafe. The problem was the huge open car decks low down in the ship's hull. Once water got onto those decks it would gravitate to one side or the other and give the ship an instant list, which is exactly what was observed. The water got onto the car decks by the simplest route possible, through the ferry's open bow doors. The ship had left her berth with her bow doors still wide open. The moment she left the shelter of the harbour for the rougher water outside, water started spilling onto the car decks. Once the ship started listing, water poured into the ship faster and faster, leading to the catastrophic capsize. It was a very obvious case of negligence on the part of the officers and crew. At an inquest on the 187 victims of the disaster, there was verdict of unlawful killing. In June 1989, the parent company, P & O European Ferries were charged with corporate manslaughter.

That really should have been the end of ferries leaving port with their bow doors open, but survivors were subsequently amazed – and horrified – when they watched other ships doing exactly the same thing. The lesson had not been learned.

DROUGHT IN THE UNITED STATES

(1987-89)

THE UNITED STATES was hit by a three-year drought in the 1980s. At its peak, it affected more than one-third of the country. This was very serious, though it is as well to remember that the Dust Bowl drought affected two-thirds of the United States at its peak.

The drought of 1987–89 was nevertheless the worst drought ever to hit the United States in terms of its financial cost. If the losses in water, energy, ecology and agriculture are all added together, the total cost of the three-year drought was thirty-nine billion dollars. That makes it the most expensive natural disaster ever to have affected the country. Western Canada was similarly affected.

The drought started on the west coast, extended into the north-west of the United States and had a devastating effect on the Great Plains. By 1988, the effects of the drought were being felt across much of the eastern half of the United States as well. Crops of wheat, maize and soybean were badly affected. Low river levels along the Mississippi made the river difficult for barges to navigate. The very dry conditions prepared the way for some serious forest fires too, including the catastrophic Yellowstone fire of 1988.

The drought of 1987–89 was the first persistent and widespread drought to hit the United States since the 1950s and it took people by surprise. A generation was affected that had not been affected before. It is a possibility that three-year droughts, or much longer droughts, are a regular and recurring part of the current climate regime. The Dust Bowl was such a drought; there was a persistent drought in the 1950s; here it was happening again in the 1980s. The clear implication is that it will happen again, perhaps three or more times in the twenty-first century. There is also the thought that, although a federal government might bail out 100,000 farmers in a particular drought year, it would be far less likely to do so if the drought went on for five or ten years.

The 1987–89 drought changed things, in that many people suddenly realized that part of the problem was that parts of the country were being farmed that were really marginal, and maybe should be abandoned. It was also becoming clear that pumping huge volumes of irrigation water onto farmland to make it productive was a poor solution. More and more evidence was coming forward that irrigating dry marginal lands was actually causing salinization. Not just in the United States, but in many parts of the world, soils were being sterilized and even poisoned by the use of irrigation. Fresh water always contains small amounts of minerals in solutions. When that water is continually spread onto fields where it evaporates, the mineral concentrations gradually increase, often to a point where they kill vegetation – and sometimes poison wildlife too. Archaeology too was beginning to show that ancient cultures that depended on irrigation systems had collapsed because of salinization, that there was, after all, a lesson to be learned from the past.

The three-year drought was a rite of passage for the United States, making land managers more aware that cultivating every possible parcel of land at any cost was no longer a sensible option. The full environmental costs of irrigation were just being realized. People became more respectful of drought. It was not, after all, just an inconvenient natural phenomenon to be overcome with modern technology.

THE ARMENIAN
EARTHQUAKE

(1988)

THE ARMENIAN EARTHQUAKE happened in the last days of the Soviet Union, and Soviet geologists were expecting it to happen because a major earthquake was long overdue in that region. It had been quiet for too long. The big earthquake struck on 7 December 1988, and it was much more powerful than expected, scoring 9.0 on the Richter scale.

The quake's focus was very near the surface, and consequently caused enormous damage to the towns in the area. Leninakan, the second largest city in Armenia, with a population of 300,000, stood just thirty miles from the epicentre and eighty per cent of its buildings were destroyed. Spitak, a town of 20,000 people, was completely destroyed. A survivor said, 'Spitak has perished. It is an ex-city. It is not possible to describe the dimensions of the catastrophe.' The high-rise buildings were inappropriately built of prefabricated panels, and under the force of the earthquake they were reduced to piles of rubble, entombing all of their occupants. Many of the specialist aid workers who arrived in the aftermath of the earthquake commented that the generally low standard of building design had a great deal to do with the high death toll. If the high-rise buildings had been fitted with steel reinforcement frames, they would have withstood the quake better. Many would have remained standing, giving those trapped inside, a better chance of surviving.

When rescuers arrived at Leninakan, they saw appalling scenes. Survivors sobbed as they clawed at the piles of rubble marking the places where they had live, and the pathetic sounds of relatives trapped underneath could be heard. When they realized that there was nothing they could do to free their families, the survivors ran about in a frenzy of frustration. The local rescue operation was inadequate. Everything needed was in short supply, from blankets to bulldozers. But the streets blocked with rubble from fallen buildings made rescue very slow in any case.

Once the world outside Armenia was involved, the scale of the rescue operation expanded and improved. President Gorbachev was on a visit to the United States at the time. Gorbachev recognized that the Soviet economy was in meltdown and the nuclear arms race with the West was something his country could no longer afford. The Cold War had to be ended. He extended a hand of friendship to the West. As if in part-payment for this major diplomatic gesture, the American government promised him lavish emergency aid. Gorbachev expressed his 'deep gratitude and profound appreciation' for the promised aid. The relief operation became the biggest ever mounted in the Soviet Union, as relief workers flew in from many countries. The sky over Leninakan was full of planes ferrying people and equipment in. A military transport plane collided with a helicopter, killing seventy-eight Russian servicemen who were arriving to swell the rescue teams. Shortly after that, a Yugoslav plane flying medical supplies in crashed, killing the seven crew. It was inevitable, given the number of flights in and out.

The official Soviet death toll for the earthquake was 55,000 people, though aid workers from outside estimated that the figure was more likely double that. So many bodies were being dug out from the rubble that stacks of coffins lined the streets. As the coffins were filled, they were taken off to the football pitch that served as a mortuary. Survivors trooped around, looking into the coffins and trying to identify their relatives.

THE *EXXON VALDEZ* DISASTER

(1989)

TWO MAJOR OIL spill disasters struck the English Channel during the twentieth century: the *Torrey Canyon* in March 1967 and the *Amoco Cadiz* eleven years later, in March 1978. Far and away the worst oil spill disaster to affect North America was the *Exxon Valdez*, which ran aground another eleven years later, in March 1989. This oil tanker ran aground about twenty-five miles from the port of Valdez in Alaska.

The officers on the bridge of the *Exxon Valdez* were worried about ice. They used their radio to ask the coastguards if they could leave the shipping channel they had been allocated. They were given clearance by the coastguards to leave their channel and use another route a mile away. For reasons that remain unclear, when the ship hit the rocks, it was in neither the first nor the second shipping channel. At 12.27 on Good Friday 1989, the captain of the *Exxon Valdez* sent the message, 'Evidently we're losing some oil and we're going to be here a while.'

It was an understatement. Oil poured out of the tanker – around eleven million tons of it – devastating the Alaskan coastline around the entrance to Prince William Sound. Within ten days, the oil slick had spread out to cover 500 square miles of sea and coat 800 miles of coastline. Wildlife of every kind perished along every foot of those 800 miles: birds, sea otters, limpets, deer, bears. It was and still is a remarkable wilderness area, with glaciers, fjords, forests and alpine tundras. It is also a highly vulnerable area that suffers continual threats not only from the endless procession of tankers passing along the coast but from increasingly intrusive tourism.

Within a matter of hours of the oil spill beginning, environmental workers were on the shoreline, collecting the bodies of hopelessly oiled seabirds. It is believed that as many as 40,000 of them may have died. The deer and bears that also died were poisoned by eating oiled food. Oil entered the food chain of Prince William Sound and remained there like a slow poison for ten years.

A particular problem with this oil spill was the low temperature. In the warmer air and warmer water of southern England and northern France, the spilt oil breaks down faster. Under the colder conditions of Alaska the processes of decomposition are much slower and the oil remains in the landscape for much longer, so the effects of an oil spill go on for much longer and are consequently far more damaging. One positive outcome of the *Exxon Valdez* disaster was that the US government was made more aware of the need to protect its national parks and other wildernesses from pollution and other damage.

THE ERUPTION OF MOUNT PINATUBO

(1991)

ON 15 JUNE 1991, Mount Pinatubo in the Philippines erupted. It was the second biggest volcanic eruption of the twentieth century, and the biggest by far to affect an inhabited area. The eruption triggered avalanches of ash, giant lahars and above all a gigantic billowing cloud of grey ash that spread for hundreds of miles. The eruption was big enough in scale to have major regional effects, and even to have effects on global climate.

On 16 July 1990, there was a violent (magnitude 7.8) earthquake about sixty miles north-east of Mount Pinatubo. The effect of this on Pinatubo was to trigger a major landslide, some local earth tremors and an increase in steam emissions, but the volcano otherwise remained dormant. But by March 1991, it was evident that lava was forcing its way to the surface from twenty miles beneath Pinatubo, causing many small earthquakes and generating steam explosions that made three craters on the volcano's northern flank. The activity continued into April, May and June with huge quantities of sulphur dioxide gas given off. By 12 June 1991, huge clouds of ash and steam rose over Mount Pinatubo. The pre-eruption sequence was monitored by geologists from the US Geological Survey's newly created trouble-shooting team and scientists from the Philippine Institute of Volcanology. Their warnings facilitated the safe evacuation of the people living close to the volcano, saving the lives of over 5,000 people and possibly 250 million dollars' worth of property.

Commercial aircraft were warned to stay away because of the ash cloud, but some jets flying far to the west of Pinatubo flew into ash and sustained 100 million dollars' worth of damage.

The catastrophic main eruption came on 15 June, Philippine Independence Day, 1991. Over one cubic mile of lava and rock was ejected. Huge volumes of ash were thrown up into a eruption column twenty-two miles high, and from there they rained down on the fields and villages around the volcano. The roofs of thousands of houses collapsed under the weight of the ash; others were completely buried. A lot of the fallen ash was then picked up by heavy rains and turned into lahars, causing even more destruction than the explosion of the volcano itself. In the lower atmosphere, a lot of ash was blown about by a typhoon, which coincidentally happened at the same time as the eruption. Fine ash fell far away in the Indian Ocean, and the ash was blown into a thin veil that circled the globe several times.

On the slopes of Pinatubo itself, pyroclastic flows caused massive destruction. These avalanches of scalding gas, ash and rock fragments raced down the mountain slopes filling valleys and ravines with up to 650 feet of debris. The eruption was so violent that the magma chamber completely emptied itself and the summit collapsed in on itself to form a caldera 1.6 miles across. After the main eruption sequence was over, in July–October 1992, a lava dome was built inside the caldera.

The effects of the eruption continued for a long time. Because the pyroclastic flow deposits were so thick, they kept their heat for several years afterwards. Five years after the eruption, they were still 500 degrees Celsius, and will remain hot for decades. There is so much loose ash lying around in the area that every rainstorm mobilizes it and produces fresh lahars; these too will continue to be a problem to the 200,000 people who returned to live near Pinatubo for a long time to come. Another 20,000 people have still not returned home; these were the Aeta highlanders who lived on the slopes of the volcano. Rice and sugar-cane fields buried under lahars will remain out of use for many years to come. The two biggest US military bases in the Philippines were severely damaged in the eruption by heavy falls of ash, and the Americans abandoned them that year.

The climate system of the world was affected. The huge volume of ash put into the stratosphere and spread around the world by high-altitude winds lowered temperature. The atmosphere was polluted by the emission of twenty million tons of sulphur dioxide and this too contributed to the global cooling, by half a degree Celsius for the next two years.

TYPHOON THELMA

(1991)

TYPHOON THELMA WAS one of the most destructive tropical storms to strike the Philippines in the twentieth century. The typhoon arrived in early November, causing landslides, dam failure and flash flooding affecting wide areas. The death toll of 6,000 people was greater than that caused by the eruption of Pinatubo, another major disaster that hit the Philippines in 1991. Thelma was by typhoon standards a weak storm, with winds of only fifty mph. Because it moved slowly across the central Philippines, it brought large quantities of rain to a large area. Thelma gradually moved westwards, reaching the mainland of Asia on 8 November, when it hit Vietnam.

Most of the fatalities occurred on Leyte Island. Intensive tree-felling for timber over the previous few years had left the hillsides denuded. Forests are good at retaining large volumes of water; once felled, the run-off into streams is greatly increased – and so is flooding. One result of Thelma was that a list of illegal loggers and their financial backers was compiled and passed to President Aquino. The people living in the hill country knew that illegal logging was responsible for the massive mudslides that devastated the hill sides. One of the local governors tried to press the government to put a total ban on logging, but he was unsuccessful.

The 1991 typhoon season in the Pacific was unusually active. Typhoons are commonest in the north-west Pacific from June to December. In 1991, twenty storms reached typhoon or hurricane intensity, and five were classified as super-typhoons. One was

478

called Typhoon Yunya. It was not an exceptional typhoon, except that it coincidentally hit Luzon at the moment when the colossal eruption of Pinatubo happened. Under normal conditions the ash from the eruption would have been dispersed over the oceans, but the spiral winds of the typhoon and the heavy rain helped to deliver large quantities of ash onto the island of Luzon, causing far more damage. In places it rained mud.

Another typhoon that season was Typhoon Amy, which skimmed the coast of Taiwan on 18 July, causing severe flooding. Ninety-nine people died, 5,000 people were injured and 15,000 were made homeless. Amy sank a merchant ship called *Blue River*, causing another thirty-one deaths. Only four days later Typhoon Brendan struck Luzon, bringing more flooding to the area already devastated by the Pinatubo eruption; it also reached China, where 100 people died. A month later, Typhoon Gladys hit southern Japan and South Korea, where it killed over 100 people and made 20,000 people homeless. A month after that, Super-typhoon Mireille moved in from the Pacific to strike southern Japan on 27 September. It was awarded super-typhoon status because at one point its wind speed reached 150 mph; it caused three million dollars' worth of crop damage in Japan. As is the custom with extremely severe typhoons and hurricanes, the name was 'retired' after this event; after this season the name Mireille was replaced by Melissa. In November, Thelma followed Mireille.

After Thelma came Super-typhoon Yuri, with winds of over 150 mph racing round a central eye with air pressure as low as 885 millibars. Yuri ranks as one of the twelve most powerful tropical storms ever recorded. In Guam, Yuri caused severe beach erosion, destroyed over 200 buildings and caused thirty-three million dollars' worth of damage.

HURRICANE ANDREW

(1992)

JUST THREE HIGHEST category, Category 5, hurricanes were to hit the United States in the course of the twentieth century. Hurricane Andrew in 1992 was one of them: the others were Camille in 1969 and the Labor Day Hurricane of 1935. Appearing in August 1992, Andrew was the first storm of the hurricane season and it left a trail of damage in the Bahamas, southern Florida and Louisiana. It killed sixty-five people and caused twenty-six billion dollars' worth of damage in 1992 dollars; the cost today would be twice as high. This enormous cost was only surpassed by Katrina in 2005.

The severity of the storm gave it historic status, and the name Andrew was accordingly retired; it was replaced by Alex in 1998.

Andrew had modest beginnings over the tropical Atlantic off the West African coast on 14 August, tracking westwards, then north-westwards. It strengthened to become Tropical Storm Andrew on 16 August. After that, it almost dispersed, then strengthened again to reach hurricane strength on 22 August. 'Hurricane strength' means sustained wind speeds above seventy-four mph. On 23 August it reached Category 5 status, when winds peaked at 175 mph. The actual peak wind speeds were not measured, as the measuring instruments themselves were destroyed, though one automated weather station was able to record gusts of 200 mph and the speed was probably above that when the instrument was destroyed. The air pressure at the centre of the hurricane was as low as 922 millibars. The Labor

480

Day Hurricane had the lowest pressure of all at 892 millibars. An unusual characteristic of Hurricane Andrew was its small size. It had a radius of only ninety miles.

This very violent storm touched land twice as it crossed the Bahamas, sweeping across Eleuthera and Great Harbour Cay with winds of 150–160 mph. After that the storm weakened slightly, then regained its strength as it smashed across southern Florida with 165 mph winds on 24 August. After crossing Florida south of Miami, Hurricane Andrew moved out into the Gulf of Mexico and swung gradually northwards to make landfall in Louisiana near Morgan City. By this stage it had weakened to a Category 3 hurricane. After that it swung north-eastwards and merged with a mid-latitude low-pressure system on the north-eastern seaboard.

There were plenty of severe weather warnings, and these probably explain the relatively low death toll. Residents in the Bahamas were warned that there could be a storm surge up to eighteen feet high and evacuations were ordered. A storm surge up to ten feet high was predicted for the east Florida coast, though it turned out to be seventeen feet high. In Florida, 1,500 troops were mobilized to stop looting. Flights in and out of New Orleans were cancelled.

The worst damage was not done by the straight-line winds, but by eddies within those winds. These whirlpools of wind were rather like tornadoes embedded within the hurricane, travelling for several miles and often flattening everything in their path.

The nuclear power station at Turkey Point suffered a direct hit by the hurricane. More than ninety million dollars' worth of damage was done to the power station, though this was mainly damage to a chimney on a fossil fuel unit and a water tank. The nuclear containment buildings were not affected; the plant had been designed to withstand winds up to 235 mph. In the light of the measured speed of the gusts, the winds may have closely approached 235 mph, which may mean that nuclear powers stations have not been designed to high enough specifications – in itself an alarming thought. A huge amount of damage was done at the Homestead Air Force Base, which is located close to the place where Andrew came ashore in southern Florida. The base had to be closed. Subsequently it was partly rebuilt as a US Air Reserve Base; the aircraft were moved to Aviano in Italy. Inevitably, power lines were brought down, leaving areas without electricity. Both the Florida Keys and Louisiana suffered in this way. The rural areas in Louisiana experience a great deal of crop damage, and it was estimated that 200 million dollars' worth of sugar cane was lost.

The natural environment suffered, too. The high energy waves generated by the hurricane cause moderate damage to coral reefs down to a depth of seventy-five feet off the Florida coast. The increased turbidity of the water lowered the oxygen level, which must have compromised marine life. In the Gulf of Mexico, over nine million fish died. On land, there was extensive damage to the Florida Everglades, where twenty-five per cent of the trees were knocked over. Interestingly, replacement tress were seen to be growing within twenty days of the passage of the hurricane. Evidently the Everglades have an inbuilt resilience to hurricanes. In the Atchafalaya River basin, the western part of the Mississippi Delta, Hurricane Andrew knocked over more than three-quarters of the trees; large areas of marshland were destroyed, too.

Great events generate their own legends. One that came out of Hurricane Andrew was the rural legend that thousands of migrant workers in Dade County (southern Florida) had died and their deaths were excluded from the official version of the disaster. A Miami newspaper looked into this story and found that it was completely untrue. Its origin lay in the Okeechobee Hurricane of 1928, when it was certainly true that the deaths of migrant workers at first were not counted; it was an historical issue that was being discussed at the time of Hurricane Andrew and for a few days past and present disasters became merged into a single mythic event.

Federal authorities were slow to provide aid in southern Florida and this led Kate Hale, the emergency management director for Dade County to protest, 'Where in hell is the cavalry on this one? They keep saying we're going to get supplies. For God's sake, where are they?' The president replied, 'Help is on the way,' and the supplies then started rolling in.

Hurricane Andrew was a disaster for insurance companies. The claims were enormous. Eleven insurance companies went bankrupt and had to close. Thirty more were put into serious financial difficulty. The Florida Legislature created new insurance agencies so that property owners could set up adequate cover for their properties. Both householders and authorities blamed poor building practices and poor building regulations for the scale of the damage. There was an inquiry, and the conclusion was that although stricter building codes had been in force since 1986, they had not been enforced. A side effect of the disaster was that many residents of southern Florida who lost their homes moved to undamaged areas further north and west, creating a sudden unanticipated housing boom in Broward County.

THE MISSISSIPPI RIVER FLOOD

(1993)

On 1 August 1993, the American Midwest experienced its worst flood in recorded history, worse even than the 1927 flood, with twenty million acres of farmland submerged and 48,000 homes seriously damaged or destroyed. The Mississippi is a long river with a long history of floods, yet the scale of this one took Americans by surprise. There was extensive flooding not only along the Mississippi itself but most of its tributaries, too.

It may be that the unusually heavy rainfall in the central part of the United States in the year-long run-up to the flooding was the result of the Pinatubo eruption. The particles of volcanic dust that were spread all around the world acted as condensation nuclei, helping to generate rain. For whatever reason, the autumn of 1992 was very rainy in the Mississippi catchment area, saturating the soil. In the winter that followed, there was heavy snowfall, and in the spring a sequence of heavy rainstorms. The 1993 flood is what is sometimes known as a 'slow-rise flood'. It had its origins in the previous autumn, when soils across the centre of the United States were already wet. Winter rain saturated them, so that the spring snowmelt and rainfall had nowhere to go except to run off into streams and rivers. By early June, river levels were very high. Then came a series of major summer thunderstorms bringing twice as much rain as normal in June, July and August.

At St Louis the river was flowing nineteen feet above its flood level, and over six feet higher than its previous record, set in 1973.

River water poured out of the Mississippi at St Louis for more than two months. Industry and the entire transport infrastructure were disrupted along the Mississippi for several months. The flood lasted from April until October.

Americans had understandably been proud of the Mississippi's flood defences, developed as they were over the course of many decades and at great expense, but now they saw seventy-five per cent of the levees fail. Flood water poured over, through and around the artificial earthen banks. The cities, such as St Louis, were protected by their massive flood walls.

The disruption caused by the 1993 flood was enormous. Some places along the Missouri, the Mississippi's largest headstream, were under water for 100 days; some places on the Mississippi, such as Grafton, Illinois, were under water for 200 days. More than 70,000 people had to move because of the flooding. One saving grace was that only fifty-two people lost their lives. One notable characteristic of natural disasters in more economically developed countries is the tendency for the death toll to drop and the cost of property damage to rise. The 1993 flood is estimated to have cost up to twenty billion dollars.

THE SINKING OF
THE *ESTONIA*

(1994)

THE HUGE, NEW, white German-built ferry was acquired for the
Estonian fleet at the beginning of 1993. At 15,000 tons, she was
the biggest ship in that fleet and for many she represented
Estonia's new-found self-confidence and independence. It was
fitting that, as a symbol of Estonia's nationhood, she should have
been named 'Estonia'. Her name was emblazoned in big letters
along her hull. Seeing her steaming by on the Baltic Sea seemed
to Estonians a way of flaunting their new sense of nationhood,
their independence of the old Soviet Union. For many Estonians
it was the *Estonia* that carried them on their first trip outside the
old USSR. Under Communist rule there was a folk tale that one
day a white ship would deliver the Estonians from tyranny; many
Estonians joked that this was the ship they had been waiting for.

The trauma experienced by Estonians, when they heard on the
morning of 28 September 1994 that the *Estonia* had sunk, can
only be imagined. At first, people could not believe it was true. As
more information came out, the more horrific the tragedy turned
out to be. The death toll itself was unbelievable; 852 people had
died when the ship sank. Almost everybody used the Tallinn-
Stockholm ferry, so it became less a question of whether people
knew any of the victims, more a question of how many.

Investigators came to the conclusion that it was a faulty bow
door that caused the ship to sink in very rough weather. Huge
waves smashed into the visor-shaped bow door, loosened it,

opened it. Water poured inside the ship. The entire sequence of events may never be fully known, partly because so many of the witnesses died, partly because all of the officers on the bridge died, partly because the ship capsized and sank so quickly.

Some bizarre versions of the disaster have been circulated, including one that has the ferry colliding with a Russian submarine. The sinking of the *Estonia* has gathered to itself its own stock of legends, some possible, some highly improbable, like those surrounding the Kennedy assassination or the death of Princess Diana. But it has also been the subject of a large-scale international investigation, which produced an 800-page report on the sinking and which seemed to answer most of the important questions.

The run-up to *Estonia*'s last voyage began at six-thirty pm on 27 September 1994, with passengers gathering at Terminal B at the port of Tallinn. They included fifty-six people who had recently retired, who were celebrating with an outing, and twenty-one teenagers from a school; there were also most of the town councillors from the Estonian town of Voru. In all, 989 passengers boarded the *Estonia*, mostly of Swedish or Estonian nationality, along with the 189 crew members.

The ship sailed out of Tallinn at seven-fifteen pm, into bad weather. The sky was overcast and there was a strong wind blowing. Most of the passengers had experienced rough conditions like this before and coped in their various ways, whether by retreating to their cabins with sea-sickness pills, walking round the ship, or heading for the duty-free shops for cheap drink. By eight pm, the ship was still close inshore. The sea was choppy but not so rough as to stop people drinking or dancing.

At nine pm, the *Estonia* sailed into a storm that generated waves twenty feet high. By this stage, most of the passengers were fairly subdued and many were suffering from nausea. During the next two hours the sea became even rougher, though the dance band somehow kept playing. By eleven pm, the *Estonia* was halfway to Stockholm. By twelve-thirty, the ship was pitching so violently that the band had to give up and very few of the passengers were able to sleep. A male dancer, Risto Ojassaar, went to an upper deck bar to relax after performing and looked out at the sea. Huge waves were approaching the ship, some reaching as high as Deck Eight. He enjoyed the savage spectacle of it.

It was at twelve fifty-five am that the *Estonia* began to get into serious difficulties. The visor-shaped bow door, which weighed fifty tons, was fixed to the hull by poorly designed and badly made attachments. When the visor was hammered repeatedly by powerful waves, they eventually snapped. Many of the passengers heard a metallic banging sound coming from the bow door, but apparently none of the ship's officers knew that something very serious had happened. A crew member on the car deck, inside the bow door, heard the clang, reported it to the bridge and inspected the inside of the bow door. He could see nothing unusual and assumed that all was well.

At this time the *Estonia* was still travelling at full speed, fourteen knots, which maximized the amount of energy that the now-vulnerable bow door had to absorb. On Deck Five, a member of the crew was leading a karaoke session. It was supposed to end at 1 am, but because everyone was having so much fun it was extended for another fifteen minutes.

At five past one in the morning, the visor's attachments failed completely and the visor hung loose, pushed and pulled by the waves, and banging against the inner door. It was now this inner door that critically separated the *Estonia*'s car deck from the Baltic Sea. If the inner door had remained intact, the ship could have made it safely to Stockholm; the problem was the renegade visor that was banging against it. The repeated banging broke the locks on the inner door, which then leaned slightly forward. Still no one realized that something was seriously wrong with the bow, though some passengers were woken up by the banging. A handful of passengers who had sailed on the *Estonia* before were aware that the noise was abnormal; they got up and anxiously left their cabins. The banging noises were reported to the bridge (once more) and the crew member who first reported them was sent down to examine the car deck. With hindsight, it is clear that the officers on the bridge should have slowed the ship's speed down as soon as they knew there was something amiss with the bow door. Slowing down at this moment might still have saved the ship.

At one-ten am, small quantities of water started to wash through the inner door, which was now slightly ajar. A crew member in the engine room saw water on a CCTV picture. Thinking it was just rainwater, he switched on the pumps to get rid of it. What he should have done was to report it to the bridge. It soon became apparent that the pumps were not able to cope with the amount of water, so the engineer went to the car deck, where he was horrified to find that he was up to his knees in seawater.

At one-fifteen am, the bow door ripped away completely from the ship, bouncing off the bulbous bow that stuck out in front of the ship below the waterline before continuing to the bottom of the Baltic Sea. A lot of the passengers heard the noise, a reverberant sound like a sledgehammer hitting the hull. One passenger joked nervously, 'We've hit an iceberg!' On its way, the bow door snagged the inner door and pulled it open. The *Estonia* was now doomed. The ship was powering into heavy seas at 14 knots with a gaping hole in her bows, as if trying to gulp down as much seawater as possible. Tons of water crashed into the car deck. Loose water on an open deck like this always gravitates almost immediately to one side or the other, and when it does it makes the ship heel over. Without warning, the *Estonia* developed an immediate list to starboard, initially by fifteen degrees.

In his cabin, Risto Ojassaar tried to persuade himself everything was all right. The ship had rocked one way, so in a moment it would rock the other. But it didn't.

The officers on the bridge at last realized that something serious was happening, but they did not know what it was. From the bridge, the bow door had never been visible, so naturally they could not see that it had gone. The indicator lights on the panel remained green, misleading the officers into thinking that both bow door and inner door were in place. Because they did not understand what was happening, the officers did not sound the alarm. If they had done so, more passengers might have been able to get out of the doomed ship. A crew member was detailed to find out what the metallic banging sounds were, but he found his way blocked by panicking passengers streaming up the stairs. They shouted that there was water on Deck One. The crew member fell down, and while lying on the floor sent a radio message to the bridge about the water.

Because the ship's officers did not know why the ship was listing, they then made a fatal mistake. They reduced the ship's speed, a sensible but overdue decision, but also turned the ship to port in the hope of counteracting the list; their idea was to make the wind and waves push the ship back onto an even keel. From this moment, water started pouring through the accommodation decks as well as through the open bow. The *Estonia* was taking on water at an even faster rate than before, at perhaps twenty tons a second. Turning the ship had not worked. The list to starboard increased and some members of the crew and many of the passengers understood that this meant that the ship was sinking. Some passengers shouted to others to head for the lifeboats.

Ojassaar went out into the hallway, towards the main stairwell, but the leader of his dance group grabbed him and pulled him towards the side stairs. She had worked out that because of the ship's severe list only the side stairs would get them out. As he said later, she saved his life. The severe list was causing some passengers to lose their footing and slide sideways into bulkheads.

At one-twenty am, the ship's engines stopped, leaving the *Estonia* totally at the mercy of the huge waves battering her as the storm roared on. Vehicles crashed against the walls of the car deck. The ship listed further to starboard as yet more water poured in. Passengers trapped on the lower deck had no chance of escape and by this point many of them were already dead. The tilted stairways became hard to negotiate. On the upper decks, some passengers formed a human chain to help one another reach the exit. It became increasingly obvious that the ship was going to capsize and it was imperative to get outside as quickly as possible. Not everyone tried to get out. Quite a lot of passengers, probably guessing that they would die in a life-raft in the Baltic, even if they managed to reach and board one, gave up hope and just stayed where they were.

Then the *Estonia* belatedly sent its first distress call, 'Mayday, *Estonia*', which was picked up by several ships in the Baltic. An alarm was also belatedly sounded. Only a few minutes later, one of the officers made an unsatisfactory final call to the other ships: 'Yes, we have a problem here now, a bad list to starboard. Really bad, it looks really bad here now.'

Ojassaar reached the top of a side staircase and looked back down to see water coming in fast at the bottom. There was no one behind him. As a dancer, he was naturally very fit and cut out for survival. Even so, he nearly did not manage to climb the tilting, lurching stairs and commented that most people on the ship were just not athletic or strong enough to get out of the ship under such conditions. Once outside, Ojassaar was swept straight off the ship by a giant wave before he could put on a life jacket. He was under water for what seemed a long time. Then, when he eventually surfaced in the icy sea, he found himself surrounded by empty life jackets and climbed into a raft. He had become separated from his director, who had not survived.

The ship tilted over further and further until it was on its side. Inside, it was complete chaos, floors had become walls, walls floors, and escape became almost impossible. Passengers on the wrong side of the broad foyer found themselves facing the prospect of scaling the floor, which had become a cliff, to get out of the hull. One young man successfully struggled up, only to turn around and see that his parents and girlfriend were still at the foot of the slope. They had given up, accepting that they were going to die there, trapped inside the ship, but urged him to go on and escape without them. By one-thirty, those still left inside the *Estonia* had absolutely no chance of getting out alive; they had in fact had only fifteen minutes to save themselves. Fewer than 300 people had managed to get out – 750 were left inside.

Getting the lifeboats and rafts free of the ships was very difficult. Some passengers were drunk; some were traumatized; some were understandably overwhelmed by a sense of futility. It was also very dark, though there was now some moonlight. The ship went on turning over and sinking at the same time and there was a mad scramble to get the boats and rafts into the sea, then to climb into them, passengers fighting other passengers off just to have a chance of surviving. At one-fifty the big white ship slipped under the Baltic like a sounding whale. She went down stern first and the survivors noticed – only then – that the bow door was missing. Some people were still instinctively hanging onto the ship, unable to let go as she sank. Sending up thousands of bubbles, the *Estonia* went down more than 200 feet to settle on floor of the Baltic.

During the next few hours, most of those struggling in the water died of hypothermia. Some of the survivors in the rafts also died of hypothermia. And still the storm continued, with winds of fifty or sixty mph tossing the rafts about. Ojassaar and two other people in a lifeboat decided to stand knee-deep in the water. They were afraid that if they sat down in the cold water they too would die of hypothermia.

It was just after two in the morning when the passenger ferry *Mariella* arrived at the scene of the disaster. The *Mariella* had great difficulty in pulling perhaps as few as a dozen people out of the water. All the other survivors were left to go on drifting, waiting to be spotted by the helicopters, which arrived an hour later. But the rescue operation was very messy. When the helicopters tried to lift the heavy water-filled rafts from the sea, some of the cables broke, sending the rafts plunging back down into the sea. By the time the helicopters had returned to the scene after flying home for fresh equipment, more of the passengers in the rafts had died. The scenes in the rafts were terrible. Some passengers held up the heads of injured friends to prevent them from drowning. One deranged man called hysterically on God for hours on end, while other passengers tried in vain to quieten him.

By this time, news of the loss of the *Estonia* had reached Tallinn and Stockholm. One woman rushed down to the docks in Tallinn clutching a teddy bear. She said, 'My husband and son were on their way to Sweden. My son has left his teddy bear behind.' At 9 am the last survivors were rescued, Ojassaar among them. The helicopter crews were frustrated and disappointed at how few people they had managed to rescue. They saw forty life rafts floating in the Baltic Sea, but most of them turned out to be empty. Only ninety-four bodies were found. Most of the 852 dead were trapped inside the ship when she went down and they remained there. Most of the people who survived were fit young adults; the elderly stood no chance of escaping from the ship; the eleven child passengers (ie those under the age of twelve) all died.

Three years later, the international team of investigators came to the conclusion that, apart from the appalling weather conditions and the powerful waves, there had been some terrible human errors. The investigators in particular blamed the German shipyard where the *Estonia* had been built. 'The visor attachments were not designed according to realistic design assumptions.' They did not go so far as blaming the officers and crew, which as we have seen they might well have done, but suggested that they were bad at exchanging information at a critical moment. There was a moment when saving the ship might still have been possible, but the crew had been too disorganized.

THE KOBE EARTHQUAKE

(1995)

PLATE MARGINS, THE joins between the various segments of Earth's crust, are dangerous places – places where volcanoes erupt and where earthquakes occur. Japan is a doubly dangerous place because it stands at the junction of three plates, the Pacific plate to the north-east, the Philippine Plate to the south-east and the Eurasian Plate to the west. The Philippine Plate is a relatively dense oceanic plate, and it is sliding underneath the Eurasian plate at a speed of four inches a year. The friction between the rock layers is such that this movement is not smooth; the pressure builds up for years or tens of years and then the plates jump a foot or two all at once, generating earthquakes. The Japanese have become used to earthquakes, some of them very violent. On 17 January 1995, a big earthquake struck Kobe at 5.46 in the morning. Kobe is the most industrialized and heavily populated region of Japan after Tokyo, with an overall population of around ten million.

The earthquake did not last long, perhaps twenty seconds, but in that short time it caused an enormous amount of damage. Five thousand people died, 300,000 people lost their homes, and property damage amounting to around one hundred million pounds was done. The huge amount of damage was due to the fact that the earthquake's focus was near the surface, in fact only ten miles down, and shallow earthquakes normally cause enormous structural damage. The situation was made worse by an accident of geology. The big shock waves from the earthquake

495

ran along a major crack in the rocks, the Nojima Fault, and this directed a great deal of the earthquake's energy from the epicentre on the island of Awaji into the cities of Kobe and Osaka.

The immediate impact of the earthquake was the destruction of buildings, bridges, flyovers and other structures. The ground moved as much as four feet up and down and two feet sideways, which was easily enough to bring large buildings down. Office buildings that had been built in the 1960s out of concrete and steel tended to collapse in the middle, so that one entire storey was crushed while the floors above and below remained intact. Later buildings, designed to be earthquake-proof, generally suffered little damage. Some of them remained intact but sank into the ground when it liquefied; this left them standing but partly buried and leaning. Wooden buildings of traditional design were completely destroyed. In Kobe, it was possible to see all three types of building side by side.

The earthquake also caused fires to break out all over the city as gas pipes were ripped open and electric cables sparked. Far more people were killed as a result of the fires than because of the collapse of buildings. Over 7,500 wooden homes were destroyed in fires. There was also major disruption of the road system, which was blocked in many places by the rubble from collapsed buildings.

Businesses had to close, people were homeless, and then there the aftershocks – more than 1,000 of them – which prevented any return to normality. Many people suffered major problems afterwards because they were uninsured; it is very difficult and very expensive to get insurance cover in such an earthquake-prone area. As many as 300,000 people were left homeless by the Kobe earthquake. Providing immediate emergency shelter was essential as it was winter and the temperatures were below freezing. The homeless people were given shelter in schools and town halls, but the conditions were seriously overcrowded, unsanitary. The housing shortage also meant that people had to endure these very unsatisfactory and unhealthy living conditions for a long time. Even food and blankets were in short supply for the first few days. The scale of the disaster had taken the authorities by surprise. The Japanese expect earthquakes and are, by comparison with most other people, well prepared for them, but the scale of the Kobe disaster caught even the Japanese out.

Kobe is a major route centre, with both railway lines and motorways passing through it. It has a large and busy modern port. The earthquake damaged, disrupted and disabled all of these important transport facilities. Several sections of motorway that were carried above ground on pillars collapsed vertically or toppled sideways. One result of this was the complete closure of the motorway. Railway tracks were buckled and stations were damaged. A 100-mile stretch of the bullet train network had to be shut down. At the port, cranes fell over and nearly all the quays were destroyed.

Kobe lay at the heart of a major industrial centre. Level land is in short supply in mountainous Japan, so Kobe's industrial complex had been extended out onto reclaimed land near the port. The vigorous shaking by the earthquake caused the made ground to settle and liquefy. The damage to factories and warehouses was very severe indeed. The destruction of the adjacent port and the land communications as well made continuing production extremely difficult in any case. Many well-known companies such as Panasonic and Mitsubishi were in serious difficulties.

The work on clearance and rebuilding began at once. Water, gas, electricity and phone services were fully reinstated within six months and the railways were back in service within seven. One year after the earthquake the port was working at eighty percent of its normal capacity, though the motorway was still closed. Within four years, the authorities had organized the building of only 134,000 new homes, and many people were still living in temporary accommodation. There was widespread criticism of the inadequate preparations for a disaster of this magnitude. Buildings had been built to what were supposed to be earthquake-proof designs; schools and factories regularly held earthquake drills. Yet still there had been a huge amount of damage and disruption. New legislation was introduced to make both buildings and motorways more resistant to earthquakes. The large number of old-style buildings in Kobe meant that many roads were blocked as they collapsed, holding up the relief effort. It turned out that although the city was partially prepared for earthquakes, it was not in a thoroughgoing and comprehensive state of preparedness. Both the Kobe city authorities and the Japanese government were criticized for their slowness in organizing the rescue of earthquake victims and organizing proper accommodation for the survivors. There was a lot of collateral and largely invisible damage from the Kobe earthquake. No statistics can tell us how much additional unemployment was caused, how many children's education was significantly impaired by disrupted schooling, how many elderly people had their deaths hastened by the hardship and distress, how many ordinary people's lives were irreparably damaged by the trauma.

THE VATNAJÖKULL
ICE-CAP ERUPTION

(1996)

THE ERUPTION IN Iceland in 1996 was spectacularly different from all the other volcanic disasters in this book – because it happened beneath an ice cap.

The eruption started on the evening of 30 September 1996 after a series of warning earthquakes, several of them of magnitude 3. Geologists suspected from the earthquake sequence that an eruption was about to take place, then the site of the eruption was spotted from an aircraft flying over the ice cap. The heat from the lava rising from a fissure three miles long had melted the 500-feet thick ice cap from below, and made it sag in two places. These huge areas of subsidence, each about a mile across and ringed by tensional crevasses, were clearly visible from the air. Observers watched as the surface of the ice sagged as much as 150 feet in four hours. The ice cap was on the flank of the Grímsvötn volcano and the meltwater drained into the Grímsvötn caldera.

On the third day of the eruption, the area of subsidence had grown to about six miles long and one mile wide. The melting of the ice cap continued, producing a huge volume of meltwater that remained trapped out of sight under the ice cap. On 1 October, the water level in this lake stood at about 4200 feet above sea level. Two weeks later it stood at 4500 feet. The lake level had risen 300 feet.

Meanwhile, lava erupting from the fissure was piling up on the ground surface beneath the ice cap, building a mountain ridge 600 feet high. On 2 October, the melting above one of the craters made a hole right through the ice and a huge column of steam rose up to a height of 30,000 feet.

On 16 October, geologists observing the eruption warned that the huge volume of water trapped underneath the ice cap in the Grímsvötn caldera lake could burst out at any moment in a catastrophic flood. The Icelanders have a special name for a spectacular glacial outburst flood like this – jökulhlaup. On 5 November, the Grímsvötn jökulhlaup began.

Enormous quantities of meltwater trapped beneath the ice were suddenly released as the ice barrier thawed. They poured towards the sea in a spectacular torrent, sweeping away a stretch of the vital coast road. The flood was so violent that it was able to bowl along huge blocks of ice and rock as big as houses. Fortunately there were no settlements in the area and no one was killed, but the sheer natural violence of the event took everyone by surprise.

TEN-YEAR DROUGHT
IN AUSTRALIA

(1996–)

MANY TROPICAL COUNTRIES, especially those with well-marked dry seasons, experience occasional droughts. They may cause crop failures, and create serious economic problems for many farmers. But the really serious droughts are those that continue for a second or even a third year. Australia is especially prone to drought. It lies across the southern subtropical high-pressure belt. This is a zone of subsiding air. Sinking air tends to warm up and increase its capacity to hold water vapour, so it produces a region of dry, cloudless conditions with very high temperatures. There are moist winds arriving from the south-east, but they have to cross the Great Dividing Range close to the east coast, and so shed their moisture as rain in the east: the rest of Australia is really a huge rain shadow.

The Murray-Darling Basin in south-eastern Australia is a huge region that is naturally covered by temperate grassland, but it has been converted on a grand scale to agriculture. It is a key region in the Australian economy. It is also a key region in terms of Australia's water supply. Although it normally receives only four per cent of Australia's rainfall, it supplies seventy-five per cent of the country's domestic and industrial water needs. Very serious problem arose when the rainfall across the region fell to only five per cent of its normal level. Supplies of drinking water are threatened, with reservoirs only half full.

The drought meant very poor crop yields. Wheat crops halved from one year to the next. The government's response was to allocate over 200 million Australian dollars (eighty million UK pounds) to businesses supporting drought-affected farmers – on top of the 910 million dollars paid directly to the 72,000 worst afflicted farmers.

The farmers were psychologically as well as financially affected by the drought. A mental health organization revealed that every four days an Australian farmer kills himself. The suicide rate among farmers, which was already twice the national average, rose alarmingly. Some of them sank into despair as the conditions worsened and they found themselves trying rear emaciated cattle in a dust bowl. The farmers are known for their toughness, and very few seek psychiatric help or counselling; their geographical isolation makes their predicament worse still. It was not surprising that they sank into depression, alcohol abuse and family breakdown. Many farmers were forced to sell up, in some cases moving from farms that had been in their families for several generations.

The Australian government has tended to be sceptical about climate change and especially about the environmental effects of global warming, refusing to sign the Kyoto agreement setting targets for greenhouse gas emissions. It is sensible to be sceptical about the causes of climate change (man-made carbon dioxide may well not be the cause), though not sensible to deny that warming has taken place. Unfortunately, the two issues are usually confused. The Australian prime minister has courageously and quite rightly insisted that there is no evidence to support the claims that the drought was the result of greenhouse gas emissions. Now that there is a major environmental change under way in Australia, the issue of greenhouse gas emissions is raised as 'the solution'. The drought has caused a significant shift in public opinion in Australia, a movement towards faith in the man-made greenhouse.

The Australian prime minister conceded that climate change was taking place, announced a number of green-energy projects, but argued that the Kyoto accord was a wrong turning because the world's biggest polluters, India, China and theUnited States, were not signatories. It was an embarrassment when figures subsequently issued by the United Nations showed that Australia was actually the second biggest polluter in the world (in greenhouse gas emissions per head of population), next to Luxembourg. Australia puts out as much greenhouse gas as France, which has three time the population.

Alarmingly, Australia's drought problem could get much worse if the trends in climatic change continue. The Commonwealth Scientific and Industrial Research Organization has predicted that parts of eastern Australia could experience a fall of forty per cent in rainfall totals by 2070. There is also predicted temperature rise of seven degrees Celsius, which would mean that much of the rain would be evaporated off. Streams and rivers are likely to dry up and the desert is likely to expand eastwards. In other words, the drought Australia was experiencing was only a taste of what was to come. One water management expert commented that Australia had been 'built on the assumption that it was going to be wetter, as we haven't been prepared to make the change back to a much drier regime.'

There had been droughts in Australia before – there was one in 1914 – but this was by far the worst in the 200 years of Australia's modern history and according to some statisticians may be a 'once-in-a-thousand-years' drought. But this Big Dry is a ten-year drought. And it may turn out not to be an anomaly, a blip in the old climate, but the beginning of a new climatic regime altogether. It has prompted questions about the future of the Murray-Darling basin. Should farmers in the worst-hit areas simply leave them for rainier areas?

EL NIÑO

(1997–98)

EL NIÑO IS A whole collection of environmental changes that occur every so often in the tropical Pacific. Normally, there is an anti-clockwise movement of water around the South Pacific, with cold Antarctic water flowing northwards along the west coast of South America, the Peru Current, then turning west to flow along the equator as a westward-flowing Equatorial Current. This 'cold tongue' of Antarctic water gradually warms up as it passes from the East Pacific to the West Pacific, and delivers warm water to the West Pacific, reinforcing the warmth and humidity of Indonesia. There is a tendency for the trade winds to reinforce this flow, pushing the surface water westwards and producing a slight piling-up of warm surface water in the West Pacific. The sea surface is about two feet higher in Indonesia than it is on the coast of Ecuador. Meanwhile, at the eastern end of the equator, the cold surface water of the Peru Current – about eight degrees colder than the sea in the West Pacific – is very rich in nutrients and brings a wealth of plankton to the coast of Peru, where it forms the basis of an important food chain. It is also the basis of a commercial fishing industry. It is the cold water that brings health and prosperity to the coast of Peru.

That is the normal state of affairs, in a non-El Niño year. In an El Niño year, such as 1997–98, the trade winds weaken, leaving the piled-up warm water at the western end of the equator unsupported. The warm water surges back along the equator towards the coast of Peru, 'bouncing' off the South American coast and rippling backwards and forwards along the equator before coming to rest against the coast of South America. One major effect of this reversal of equatorial water is that the cold water next to the Peruvian coast becomes buried under a thick layer of warm water, causing a collapse of the regional ecosystem. There is insufficient plankton to support the fish population; the seabird population suffers; so too does the human population. El Niño is a disaster.

The reversal of the Equatorial Current also means that there is less warm air, less water vapour and less rain in the West Pacific. This in turn has led to catastrophic bush fires in Australia. So El Niño is an environmental disaster for the whole tropical Pacific belt.

On the local scale, Peruvian villagers experienced weeks of unceasing rain and rising river levels, and this in a region that was normally bone-dry. By February, the rivers were overflowing their banks, sweeping away houses, livestock, wild animals, people. It was no surprise to the villagers, as this was a cyclical event. Every three to seven years for as long as anyone could remember this had happened, when a vast slick of warm seawater the size of Canada arrived on the Peruvian coast. El Niño had been recognized long before by the fishermen of the Pacific coast, when the unusually warm water arrived. El Niño means 'The Little Boy' or more specifically 'The Infant Christ', and the name was given because the phenomenon tended to begin at Christmas time. La Niña means 'The Little Girl'; other names for La Niña are El Viejo, anti-El Niño or non-El Niño.

The heavy rains in Peru poured into the Sechura Desert, turning arid scrubland into a huge lake ninety miles long and ten feet deep. Ponding of water elsewhere made temporary new habitats for mosquitoes, causing 20,000 additional cases of malaria.

Far away in Indonesia, there was the opposite problem – intense drought. Fires spread totally out of control in the dried-out forests that were being burned by loggers. The huge clouds of smoke from the forest fires covered Indonesia and Malaysia, to the extent that drivers in the cities had to switch their headlights on in the middle of the day. The smoke haze spread right across the Indian Ocean to the Maldive Islands, where visibility was at times reduced to half a mile. In Mongolia, the temperature soared to forty-two degrees Celsius in the summer of 1998.

The effect of El Niño was strongly felt even in Europe, where the chain reaction through the volatile and unstable climate system produced heavy rain and large-scale flooding. River floods killed fifty-five people in Poland and sixty in the Czech Republic. In North America, flash floods damaged townships from California across to Mississippi.

The El Niño phenomenon has become of great interest to climatologists in recent years, now that they have realized that it has knock-on effects well outside the Pacific basin, that it has global significance. During El Niño years, there is more rain in Peru and in the south of the United States as well. Increased awareness of the importance of El Niño has led to the setting up of a monitoring system in the Pacific to collect information about the changing conditions in the ocean. A network of buoys has been installed. Each buoy is a floating environmental station, taking continuous measurements of the winds and air temperature, but also more importantly of the direction and speed of ocean currents and the temperature of the sea surface. The buoys transmit data continuously to climatologists all around the world. The monitoring system enables researchers to forecast developments as an El Niño event is about to get under way and as it is about to terminate, as it did during 1998.

December 1997 was the peak of an unusually strong El Niño. Twelve months later came the peak of an unusually strong non-El Niño. During the December 1998 non-El Niño, the East Pacific cold tongue was three degrees Celsius colder than normal. In the nineteenth century, El Niño years were fairly well spaced. For some reason, they have become more frequent in the recent past: 1986–87, 1991–92, 1993, 1994, 1997 and 2002 were all El Niño years.

THE SARNO MUDSLIDE

(1998)

IN THE AFTERNOON of 5 May 1998, after two days of continuous rain, the southern slopes of Mount Sarno in the Campania region of southern Italy started to collapse. One of the problems of the area is that over the last 20,000 years nearby Vesuvius has dropped volcanic debris over the mountain sides. This coating of loose material becomes very unstable, especially on steep slopes, and especially after heavy rain.

By midnight, what had begun as rivulets of muddy water had turned into a wave of mud twenty feet deep, racing down the valleys at thirty mph and burying parts of five small towns.

Because it was dark, the inhabitants of the towns did not understand what was happening, and as a result hundreds of them were buried under the mud. Some who were sufficiently alert to what was happening managed to escape to the upper floors of their houses. Some of them were then buried inside their houses when the mudflow undermined them. The mud reached as high as the second floors of some buildings, though the levels of flooding and damage were very varied. In some areas, the houses were inundated with mud and knocked down or buried; in other areas, the houses were left unscathed. Hundreds of cars were swept away by the filthy flood. Trees forty feet high were knocked over and swept away by the mud. The extreme local variations seem to have been due to variations in the speed of the mudflow; wherever that peaked, there was total destruction.

The rain stopped for a while on 9–10 May, and a general evacuation was planned as more rain was expected in a few days' time. Observers in helicopters could see that there had been at least thirty major landslides on the slopes of Mount Sarno, and also that there were twenty-three further sites where it looked as if landslides might easily be triggered by further heavy rain. The rescue operation was difficult. The mud that had knocked over and buried houses, entombing their occupants, also filled the streets and made it very difficult to reach people who were trapped.

In the immediate aftermath, there was so much confusion that it was believed that 245 people had died, but three weeks later it emerged that 137 had died and eighteen were unaccounted for. The loss to property, by contrast, was initially underestimated and was eventually calculated at more than 500 million dollars. Enormous costs were involved in replacing damaged public buildings. Journalists and politicians competed with one another to apportion blame for the lack of preparation for the disaster and for the slowness of the rescue operation. It was American troops from a NATO base who expertly and efficiently cleared the towns of the clogging mud.

In fact, there was a strong human element in this natural disaster. The hill sides that were naturally clothed in forest had been deforested, partly by deliberate clearance, partly by accidental forest fires, partly by uncontrolled grazing. Down in the valleys there had been a lot of illegal building. Many local people had made unwise decisions about land utilization, but the authorities were also to blame for allowing those decisions.

Following the disaster, there have been repeated warnings that there could be a repeat of the 1998 mudflow, and the local population of 70,000 holds itself in readiness to evacuate the area as soon as the next emergency comes. Campania is clearly disaster-prone – there have been 631 landslides since 1954 – though only because it has specific natural characteristics that happen to have collided with specific human mismanagement. As with many 'natural' disasters, there is a strong sociocultural element. If, over the past century or so, different decisions had been made, more environmentally-sensitive decisions, the danger of landslides and mudflows would have been greatly reduced. In the mountain valleys of Campania, corrupt government and local government decision-making created not so much a disaster as a disaster-prone sociocultural system. This emerged from a detailed investigation of the Sarno disaster. On the day when the disaster happened, no preparation for the disaster was undertaken whatever. The mayor of Sarno, for reasons that are not clear, did not alert either the regional or national authorities until it was too late. Instead, he gave the inhabitants of Sarno and the authorities repeated assurances that everything was under control. The result was that the mudflows did maximum damage in the town of Sarno – 126 people were killed there.

HURRICANE MITCH

(1998)

HURRICANE MITCH WAS one of the most powerful and destructive tropical storms of modern times, a truly historic storm. There were sustained wind speeds, not gusts, of 180 mph. Strong those these winds were, they were exceeded in 2005 by Hurricane Wilma. Tropical storms are a regular feature of the global weather system, and Mitch was the thirteenth such storm of the 1998 hurricane season.

Mitch developed over the western Caribbean on 20 October, where it quickly gained in strength up to Category 5, the highest possible rating. Mitch reached hurricane intensity on 24 October, south of Jamaica. A peculiarity of Mitch was its wayward track. Perhaps the commonest track for a hurricane in that region is a long curve beginning out in the Atlantic, travelling south-westwards, then west, then north-westwards, then north. This common behaviour is a response to the rotation of Earth. But Mitch did not behave like this. It first travelled north, then north-west, west, north-west, west, south then west again. It was a route without pattern, a meandering that defied logic or prediction.

In a situation like this, it was difficult to give adequate weather warnings. Two days before Mitch made its first landfall, the meteorologists were very uncertain where that landfall would be. To be safe, government officials issued hurricane warnings along a very long coastline that included several states. The government of Honduras did everything possible to save lives, evacuating people from islands. The Belize government issued a red alert and advised people on offshore islands to come to the mainland for safety. It looked as if the hurricane could hit Belize City as a Category 4 hurricane, so a large area of the city was evacuated; the fear was that there might be a repeat of the carnage experienced in Hurricane Hattie thirty-seven years before. The government of Guatemala advised people not to embark on boats; there was also a warning about the danger of flooding from rivers. By the time Hurricane Mitch reached land, 100,000 people in Honduras had been evacuated, 20,000 in Mexico, 10,000 in Guatemala. This was an impressive state of preparedness.

The hurricane hit Honduras, then wandered through Central America. After its tour of Central America, Mitch started off on a new, almost dead straight, track towards the north-east, heading for Florida, which it hit as a strong tropical storm. Then it went on into the North Atlantic.

Between 29 October and 3 November, Mitch moved very slowly across Honduras and Nicaragua and deposited record quantities of rain on those countries. The rainfall total was seventy-five inches, which is as much as the hills of western Great Britain receive in an entire year. The historic rainfall raised rivers to unprecedented levels and produced disastrous river flooding. The flooding was responsible for enormous numbers of deaths. In spite of all the warnings and the preparation, more than 11,000 people are known to have been killed, and another 8,000 went missing. The breakdown of the known death toll is as follows: Honduras 7,000, Nicaragua 3,800, Guatemala 268, El Salvador 240, at sea 31, Belize 11, Mexico 9, Costa Rica 7, Jamaica and Panama 3 each, United States 2.

Huge numbers of people were swept away by rivers, drowned and their bodies swept far out to sea, where they would never be found. Enormous amounts of property damage were done too, more than five billion dollars' (1998 dollars). In the Choluteca district, the high intensity rainfall peaked at thirty-six inches of rain in all, with more than eighteen inches of rain falling in one day, the average rainfall for about eight months. The Choluteca River was overfilled by this excess rainfall, swelling up to six times its normal width. The flooding was made even worse, though, by the history of land use in the area. The once extensive forests had been cleared for slash-and-burn agriculture, so the land could no longer absorb moisture. There would have been flooding with rainfall of such high intensity, but the inappropriate land use made the flooding far worse. Even higher intensity rainfall in the mountain areas caused mudslides there.

Hurricane Mitch intensified abruptly during 24-25 October. During that time, the pressure in the centre fell more than fifty millibars. By the next day, 26 October, the peak intensity in terms of central low pressure had been reached. The pressure of 905 millibars was among the lowest pressures encountered in an Atlantic hurricane (compare the lowest, 882 millibars in Hurricane Wilma in 2005). At the same time the wind speeds reached their maximum, too – 180 mph. Just before reaching the Central American mainland, the hurricane piled up seawater into a storm surge, sending waves up to twenty-two feet high against the coastline.

When Mitch made landfall with Honduras, Mitch weakened slightly. This is because hurricanes are fundamentally sea creatures. They are fed by water vapour rising off the surface of a warm sea and as they pass over land they are cut off from their source of energy. Mitch made landfall eighty miles east of La Ceiba in Honduras on 29 October. Here it was only a Category 1 hurricane, and the wind speeds had dropped to eighty mph. As it wandered over Central America it continued to weaken.

Then Mitch reorganized over the Bay of Campeche on 3 November, travelled north-eastwards as it strengthened again, and hit the Yucatan peninsula on 4 November. Once again it weakened as the centre travelled over land, but regained strength as it passed out over the Gulf of Mexico. When it reached Florida on 5 November, its winds were a mere sixty-five mph. After that it gradually lost its identity as a tropical storm, eventually disappearing north of Great Britain on 9 November.

The impact of Hurricane Mitch on people was unparalleled in the last 200 years. Mitch was the deadliest hurricane since the Great Hurricane of 1780, and it shouldered the Galveston Hurricane of 1900 aside as the second-deadliest on record. Most people died as a result of river flooding and mudslides in Central America. Even though people were warned of rivers flooding, they could not have imagined the severity of the flooding that actually occurred. The worst flooding was on the Ulua River near Chinda, where the flood water was forty feet deep. The floods and mudslides destroyed tens of thousands of houses, too.

President Carlos Roberto Flores of Honduras commented that fifty years of progress in his country had been destroyed at a stroke by Hurricane Mitch. Seventy per cent of the country's crops were destroyed. Seventy per cent of the road system was destroyed, including nearly all the bridges. The damage to the communications system would cost 529 million dollars (1998 US dollars). The damage was so great that the maps were obsolete and useless. Twenty-five villages had been completely annihilated by mudslides and landslides triggered by the storm. About 33,000 houses had been completely destroyed; twice as many again had been damaged. And the danger was not yet over; the landscape was scarred, in many places denuded, bare, vulnerable to yet more mudslides. Thirty per cent of the food-producing arable land in Honduras had been damaged. There were severe shortages of food crops, such as maize, sorghum, rice and beans. There were also severe losses of commercial crops destined for export, such as bananas, sugar cane, melons, coffee. In addition, 50,000 cattle had been lost and sixty per cent of the country's chickens.

The losses were incalculable. Twenty per cent of the population of Honduras had been left homeless, and the disruption of the water supply and sanitation systems led to outbreaks of malaria, dengue fever, cholera.

Hurricane Mitch did not actually pass over Nicaragua, but its cloud systems delivered massive falls of rain. The crater lake in the Casita volcano overflowed, causing the crater walls to collapse, creating a huge mudslide that killed over 2,000 people – a major disaster in its own right. The heavy rain destroyed 24,000 house, damaged almost as many again. There was damage on a similar scale to schools, health centres, sewerage systems, roads and bridges. About 50,000 head of cattle died. Nicaragua was in almost as bad a state as Honduras. In some ways the problem was worse. 75,000 live land mines left behind from the insurgency of the 1980s were washed out by the flood water and relocated, no one knew where.

Out in the Caribbean there were losses, too. The windjammer sailing ship Fantome was sunk off the Honduran coast after experiencing waves fifty feet high. All thirty-one of her crew members were drowned.

In Costa Rica, Guatemala and El Salvador, the pattern of damage was similar again, with floods and mudslides causing widespread damage to arable land, livestock, houses, roads and bridges. Food crops were seriously damaged and cash crops lost. In Guatemala, a plane crashed in the storm, killing another eleven people. In Belize, the damage caused by Mitch was actually far less than initially predicted, though there was still heavy rainfall and many of the country's rivers overflowed their banks; but the death toll was startling low compared with the story in Honduras.

When the storm reached Florida, with winds gusting to fifty-five mph, the levels of damage were far lower than in Central America, though the property damage still amounted to forty million dollars (1998 dollars). One curious feature of the Florida episode was the way Mitch spawned five tornadoes across the state.

The aftermath was a deluge of international aid, in fact 6.3 billion dollars' worth of aid. Many of the people who lost their homes took the opportunity to rebuild to a higher standard, to make their houses more resistant to a future storm. But there were inevitable outbreaks of disease. Over 2,300 cases of cholera were reported, mostly in Guatemala, where people had eaten contaminated food. Overall, Honduras was worst affected by this multiple disaster, and it was the main recipient of the international aid. The Mexican government was quick to send aid in the form of rescue planes, search dogs, medicine and 700 tons of food. The main shock was the US government's offer of only two million dollars in aid. Neither the Hondurans generally nor their president could quite believe that so little was being offered by their rich neighbour. The US government later raised the sum to seventy million.

Hurricane Mitch was one of the largest scale disasters of recent years. Mitch was responsible for such an appalling amount of destruction that the World Meteorological Organization decided never to use the name again. When it might have been reused in 2004, it was replaced with the name Matthew.

THE IZMIT
EARTHQUAKE

(1999)

AT 3 AM ON 17 August 1999, one of the most powerful earthquakes to strike Turkey hit the industrial town of Izmit. Most of the residents were in bed at the time, and many were trapped as their homes collapsed around them. Few of the buildings were built to withstand earthquakes, and whole districts of the town were flattened by the quake, which measured 6.7 on the Richter scale.

The earthquake happened in the extreme north-west of Turkey, only fifty miles from Istanbul, and it was severe enough to destroy some buildings there, too. Sections of the motorway from Ankara, the capital, to Istanbul were buckled, causing a number of road traffic accidents.

As with all major earthquakes, there were powerful aftershocks, ten in the space of the next two hours. These also caused a great deal of damage and killed more people. Rescue teams worked hard to find people who might have survived under the rubble; frantic relatives scrabbled at the ruined buildings with their bare hands. The prime minister of Turkey, Bulent Ecevit, visited the disaster area and said it was the worst he had seen: 'The loss is huge. May God help our country and its people.'

The Izmit earthquake was a major disaster in itself. But it also had serious implications for the future. Geologists analyzing the earthquake realized that it was only a matter of time before a violent earthquake struck Istanbul itself. Pressure from the African Plate and the Arabian Plate, both moving northwards, is forcing

Turkey westwards, towards Greece, at an average rate of one inch a year. The friction between the rock layers prevents a smooth slide, and there is a sudden jump after years of inactivity. In the Izmit earthquake, Turkey jolted about three feet closer to Greece.

Before the Izmit earthquake, geologists did not really understand the dynamics of the region, but studying it has led to some frightening conclusions. Geologists had, before 1999, seen the Sea of Marmara area as criss-crossed by a series of small separate faults. One conclusion of their new research was that they were dynamically linked, making a single fault continuing for 1,000 miles. Each time there is a major quake in the area in the fault, it transfers stress further along the line of the fault.

It is known that Istanbul has experienced a sequence of earthquakes during its long history. In fact, since AD 400 the city has been damaged by major quakes no less than twelve times. The most recent was at the end of the nineteenth century. The Anatolian Fault, which runs from the interior of Turkey westwards towards Istanbul, has become more active in recent decades. There have been seven major earthquakes along it, and they form an ominous pattern, a sequence progressing from east to west – towards Istanbul.

The geologists estimate that Istanbul will be devastated by a major earthquake measuring at least 7.6 on the Richter scale before 2030. A 590-feet high tower block, the premises of a bank, carries the slogan, 'We are here for ever.' The building may be built to the most up-to-date specifications for earthquake-resistance, and it may be built on the solid rock of the business quarter, but it is still a rash boast given that the city stands very close to one of the most seismically active faults in the world. The North Anatolian Fault runs under the Sea of Marmara, just a few miles away from the city. The tower may survive the big earthquake when it comes, but the areas of poor housing built on sand and mud are very unlikely to remain standing.

The realization that Istanbul faces disaster has fuelled a boom in steel-reinforced houses and flats that are 'guaranteed' to withstand earthquakes. But not every building in Istanbul can be made earthquake-proof – there are 1.6 million of them. It is certain that many buildings will collapse and equally certain that many people will die. Istanbul is a city of fifteen million people, growing at a rate of an extra 400,000 every year. The people of Istanbul are responding to the prospect of the disaster in one of two different ways. Some are fatalistic, taking no action whatever and leaving everything to destiny. Others are busily organizing street committees to stop antisocial parking that obstructs the exits from buildings, and they are nailing their furniture to the walls and floors of their homes.

The World Bank is supplying huge amounts of money to enable the Turkish authorities to set up an appropriate earthquake response. There has been a tightening up of building regulations in Istanbul, but buildings are still going up that flout them. More than half of the buildings in Istanbul will fail under the impact of a major earthquake.

Nor would the earthquake be the only problem. The shock of a 7.6 quake on the bed of the Sea of Marmara could devastate half of the city on its own, but it is likely to generate a small tsunami twenty-two feet high as well, which would inflict further large-scale damage. Often we talk of so many people killed, or so many buildings destroyed, or so much financial cost inflicted; but the emotional and psychological costs are incalculable. A big earthquake striking Istanbul is likely to leave huge numbers of people in a very poor psychological state. It is estimated that perhaps ten per cent of the population of Istanbul – 1.5 million people – would be left gravely traumatized.

THE MOORE
TORNADO

(1999)

THE MOORE TORNADO of 1999 has a special place in tornado history, because somebody succeeded in measuring, not just estimating, its speed. For a very long time, before the arrival of home movies and Doppler radar, there was little to go on except estimates for the rotating speed of a tornado. It was fairly easy to arrive at the forward speed, by noting the clock time when the tornado reached each township along its path, but the speed of its rotation was more difficult. People were so impressed by the spectacle of the tornado, that they estimated speeds of 500 mph, or even supersonic speeds.

Just as the Richter scale was devised for earthquake magnitude and the Beaufort scale for ordinary wind speeds, in 1971 the Fujita scale was devised for tornadoes. It was the invention of Tetsuya Fujita, with the help of Allen Pearson. The Beaufort scale deals with everyday winds and the Fujita scale overlaps with its upper end. Force 11 on the Beaufort scale corresponds with F0 on the Fujita scale, Force 12 with F1. F12, the upper end of the Fujita scale, is the speed of sound, 738 mph. In practice, it is only the lower end of the scale that is in use, F0 to F5, simply because it is virtually impossible to measure winds above that level in reality.

An F0 tornado is not really strong enough to do direct structural damage to buildings. It can tear branches off trees, though, and the falling braches can do quite a lot of damage. If a falling branch causes a roof to cave in, it may injure or kill people, so even an F0 tornado can kill.

An F3 tornado causes serious structural damage. Typically, some of the walls of a brick-built building are knocked down, and the roof is demolished. Usually, people with experience of tornadoes take shelter in an enclosed space in the middle of their house, and this is usually sufficient protection against an F1, 2 or 3 tornado.

An F5 tornado cause incredible levels of destruction. It sweeps flat almost anything in its path, including timber-built houses, brick-built schools and factories. Virtually nothing is left standing. It ought not to be possible for people to survive an F5 tornado, but they do. People have survived direct hits by F5 tornadoes by, for instance taking shelter by lying down in a bathtub. The first actual measurement to prove that F5 tornadoes really exist was taken on 26 April 1991, in a tornado at Red Rock, Oklahoma. Climatologists used a portable Doppler radar device to measure the wind speed. As the tornado reached its peak intensity, a speed of 268 mph was registered. This confirmed that tornadoes do really reach F5, which is a force not reached in any other way in the lower atmosphere.

But the measurements with the Doppler radar also implied that tornado wind speeds had been seriously overestimated or exaggerated in the past – 268 mph was nowhere near the 500 mph that some had estimated for tornadoes, and far below the speed of sound. It looked as if tornadoes never achieve speeds in the upper parts of the Fujita scale. Probably F10, F11 and F12 never occur in tornadoes. The overestimation is quite a common phenomenon in human observations of extreme situations. Survivors of the Mount St Helens eruption overestimated the temperature of the hot blast from the volcano. We regularly overestimate the gradients of hills when we find ourselves struggling to walk up them; we think they must be sixty-degree slopes, when they are only thirty degrees. The exaggeration is probably a function of stress.

Once the upper half of the Fujita scale appear to be theoretical rather than real, the American Meteorological Society adapted it, renaming it the Enhanced Fujita Scale. This new 'EF' scale runs only up to 5, and comes into use at the beginning of 2007.

A team of observers monitored the outbreak of tornadoes in Oklahoma on 3 May 1999, and found that one of them was exceptionally violent. This was the Moore tornado. It eventually killed thirty-six people. At seven o'clock in the evening on 3 May, they measured a wind speed of 318 mph, which was fifty mph faster than anything previously recorded. Interestingly, this is only fractionally short of Fujita F6, so it may be that the American Meteorological Society was too hasty in capping the tornado intensity scale at EF5. I suspect that in time people will revert to the Fujita scale, simply because it makes such a natural bridge between the Beaufort scale and the Mach scale (Mach 1 being the speed of sound, F12). The higher numbers in the Fujita scale may be useful in the study and description of upper air winds, which reach higher speeds.

For a long time it has been seen that tornadoes function rather like miniature hurricanes. They both have high winds spiralling in towards the centre. It has been assumed that tornadoes have very low air pressure at the centre, to account for the wind spiralling inwards; there must be a steep pressure gradient. But it had not been demonstrated. Certainly hurricanes have very low pressure at the centre, but they are large enough and move at a stately enough speed for orderly measurements to be taken. Do tornadoes have low pressure at the centre? Some domestic barometers that somehow survived the passage of tornadoes showed measurements as low as 810 millibars, which proves that tornadoes do indeed have intense low pressure at their centre, but a broken barometer found in the wreckage of a house is scarcely the best evidence. In June 2003, some meteorologists successfully dropped devices called 'turtles' into a tornado with an intensity of F4, and what they found was that the atmospheric pressure fell more than 100 millibars as the tornado passed.

FOREST FIRE
IN ALASKA

(1999)

In 1999 THERE was a forest fire that was small in scale, but important in leading to a breakthrough in our understanding of the environment. The fire broke out in a forest in the Donnelly Flats in the centre of Alaska and destroyed the trees across an area of about seventeen acres.

A minor disaster, but one that recurs throughout the boreal or northern forests. In fact, unusually large-scale fires have broken out across Alaska, Canada, Norway, Sweden and the Russian Federation over the past ten years. One reason why these northern forest fires have become more frequent could be that the climate generally has been warmer, drier and the summers have been longer. As the forests have been dried out, they have become more prone to fires, and indeed fires that spread through large areas of forest.

There has been an understandable assumption among environmentalists that the burning must be enhancing the greenhouse effect by releasing more carbon dioxide into the atmosphere. In other words, global warming has produced more forest fires; more forest fires release more carbon dioxide; more carbon dioxide means more global warming. This, if a real effect, would be a feedback effect, or a loop. Such feedback effects are a major component of the current global warming scare, as they imply that once global warming is under way it becomes self-running, self-enhancing.

But a team of seventeen American and Australian researchers has found that this is not so. The team looked at the various effects of the Donnelly Flats fire and came to a surprising conclusion. Some scientists looked at the way the fire changed the colour, tone and texture of the landscape and therefore how it absorbed or reflected the Sun's radiation. Some scientists looked at the changes in greenhouse gas emissions from the area of the fire. Their results were fed into a computer model, so that a projection could be made up to eighty years into the future. The reason for choosing eighty years was that within that sort of time period it is likely that another forest fire would happen in the same area.

The computer model showed that the climate warms up for about twelve months following the forest fire, but then cooled down again within ten or fifteen years. Moving on eighty years into the future, there was a net cooling. The cooling is explained mainly by the change in the tone (darkness or lightness) of the area. The northern evergreen trees are dark, and therefore absorb the Sun's heat. When the trees are burned, the landscape is snow-covered, at least for many months of the year, and this very light surface reflects heat as well as light back into space. As a result the cleared area became cooler – regardless of the carbon dioxide emission during the burning. The black soot and charcoal coating the ground immediately after the fire, explains why there is an initial warming effect for the first year. The overall cooling effect cancels any impact of greenhouse gases.

This interesting result does not mean that it is a good thing to burn down forests. On the contrary, there may be all sorts of ecological reasons for wanting to conserve the forests. But the main implication of the new research must be that forest fires after all do not cause any warming of the global climate. They may alternatively cause regional cooling. On a global scale, forest fires do not make any difference to the climate at all.

THE CARACAS FLOOD

(1999)

ON 19 DECEMBER 1999, torrential rainfall in the mountains of Venezuela caused massive floods in Caracas and other towns. Water flooded down from the mountains towards the coast. Whole buildings and whole areas of towns were washed away by the flood along Venezuela's Caribbean coastline. So many people were displaced by the destruction of their homes – tens of thousands of them – that Caracas was overwhelmed by refugees. Three days after the worst of the rain ended, flood water was still draining down from the mountains and pouring through the towns, following routes where previously there had not even been rivers, tearing away houses and depositing huge volumes of mud. Many people were drowned and washed away by the water or buried irrecoverably under the mud. Lists of missing people were posted on the walls of municipal buildings, alarming lists with thousands of names.

As the flood subsided, digging out and reburying the dead became an urgent priority, as the risk of disease spreading among survivors was very high. At least 10,000 people died and more than 150,000 were made homeless. It is hard to be sure of even an approximate death toll, because many bodies were washed out to sea, or buried and never found. The outskirts of Caracas were also an area where transients lived, migrants who were not on anybody's list. Many people from the interior also travelled to the coast for recreation. How many of them died it would be impossible to know. For this reason, some Venezuelan officials were speculating that the actual number of deaths in the Caracas floods might have been twice as high as the official figure.

THE MOZAMBIQUE FLOOD

(2000)

IN FEBRUARY AND March 2000, heavy rain continuing for five weeks led to catastrophic flooding in Mozambique. Unprecedented falls of rain produced unprecedented flooding.

It was on 9 February that the river floods started. Although much of southern Africa was affected by the heavy rain, it was Mozambique that was most seriously affected. The capital, Maputo, was flooded, along with the road that connected it with Mozambique's second city of Beira. The continuing rain caused the River Limpopo to overflow its banks; this caused very serious damage. A bad situation was made worse when the region was hit by a tropical storm, Cyclone Eline, on 22 February. The cyclone struck the coast close to Beira, bringing yet more rain. On 27 February, there were flash floods that flooded low-lying agricultural land round the towns of Xai-Xai and Chokwe.

The flooding was on an epic scale and the effects spread out through entire populations. Two million people were affected in one way or another by the floods. Approximately 800 people and 20,000 cattle lost their lives, and 25,000 people were made homeless. It was the worst flood Mozambique had experienced in fifty years.

The rescue operation mounted was (eventually) on a similarly unprecedented scale. The rescue workers managed to save more than 45,000 people who had taken refuge on anything sticking out above the rising flood water: hills, trees, rooftops. Television news pictures of people perched helplessly in the branches of trees above a sea of silt-laden flood water. One of the most memorable images of the flood was a woman, Sofia Pedro, giving birth while she was stranded in a tree. She was then flown to safety with her new daughter by the South African Air Force.

Initially the people of Mozambique were left to organize their own rescue effort. The governments of neighbouring countries were slow to offer help. The response from international aid agencies was slow, too. Equipment arrived from Europe and North America three weeks after the flood began.

The after-effects of the flood were severe. Virtually all of the country's irrigation system was damaged, which affected agricultural production. Huge areas of arable and grazing land were destroyed, and 113,000 farmers and their families were left without a livelihood. Enormous numbers of livestock had been washed away into the Indian Ocean. Many schools and health centres, including Beira Central Hospital, were put out of action.

But something positive came even out of this disaster – Rositha Pedro.

THE PERU EARTHQUAKE AND TSUNAMI

(2001)

AT 3.33 PM ON 23 June 2001, a severe earthquake struck Peru. It measured 8.1 on the Richter scale and its epicentre was five miles below the seabed, off the coast at Ocona and 375 miles south-east of Lima. This is a seismically active zone. The west coast of South America marks a major plate boundary, where the Nazca Plate (forming the ocean floor under this part of the Pacific) dives beneath the South American Plate. The line is marked by the Peru-Chile Trench, the western edge of the continent of South America, and the Andes Mountains. The particular seismic zone where the 2001 earthquake originated is in the mantle, and forms a narrow belt about seventy miles wide on the continental shelf between the Andes and the Peru-Chile Trench. The earthquake foci are usually quite shallow here, less than 100 miles down, and they have the potential to generate dangerous tsunamis. Under the Andes, the earthquake foci may be 400 miles under the surface. These depth differences reflect the position of the flap of Pacific Ocean floor as it slides diagonally down into the earth beneath South America.

The ground moved vigorously for over a minute. The quake cause extensive damage throughout southern Peru, but especially in the provinces of Arequipa, Moquegua and Tacna, where eighty per cent of the houses were damaged. Roads were seriously damaged, and the Pan-American Highway was closed. The whole infrastructure of the agricultural economy was wrecked, with the destruction of reservoirs, bridges and irrigation canals. The quake was strongly felt throughout Peru and across its frontiers in northern Chile and Bolivia. The earth movements were so energetic that even in Lima, the capital of Peru, houses were shaken down and people were injured – and Lima was nearly 400 miles from the epicentre.

Arequipa was the worst damaged city. It is the second largest city in Peru with a population of over a million. At least seventy-three people died there. Many houses were destroyed, and many historic buildings including churches were destroyed, many of them after being rebuilt after the 1886 earthquake. In the southern city of Tacna, many adobe houses were shaken down.

The overall death toll of the Peru earthquake reached 118 and another fifty-three were unaccounted for. In addition, 1,578 people were injured and 47,700 people were left without homes.

The main quake was followed by dozens of aftershocks, some of them major earthquakes in their own right; they went on for several days.

Among the many effects of the earthquake, several landslides were caused in hill and mountain country. Some small tsunamis was observed, and they particularly affected the coast close to the epicentre. They hit the Peruvian coast twenty minutes after the main earthquake shock was felt. In some low-lying areas, the tsunamis swept up to two miles inland. These were far-travelling tsunamis, reaching Japan right across on the other side of the Pacific. A large area of farm land was flooded at Camana, a summer resort 560 miles south of Lima. Camana was particularly hard-hit by both the earthquake and the tsunamis, which swept half a mile inland across the town and the surrounding rice and sugar cane fields. Twenty people were drowned by the tsunamis and another sixty were reported missing.

THE EUROPEAN HEATWAVE

(2003)

A MAJOR HEALTH crisis unexpectedly struck central and western Europe in the summer of 2003 when temperatures soared to record levels. It was much hotter than usual, especially in southern England, France and Germany. The worst affected region was the centre and south of France. Curiously, Portugal, Spain, Italy, Scandinavia, Poland and northern England were rather cooler than average. The problem was by no means continent-wide.

In France, the death toll as a result of the heat was very high, and 14,802 people, most of them elderly, died from the heat. A specific problem was that people were not careful about re-hydration: they were not drinking enough. It was also a problem that most of the retirement homes did not have air conditioning. Many younger people were able to get some respite from the heat by visiting air-conditioned shops, malls and public buildings such as libraries. The elderly were trapped in their homes, unable to cool down. There were contingency plans in place, as in other rich countries, for many kinds of natural disaster, but extreme heat was a hazard that had simply not been planned for.

The heatwave happened in August, when many young and middle-aged people are away on holiday. As a result, many families did not know that their elderly relatives had died. Bodies had to be stored for several weeks until appropriate funeral arrangements could be made when the families returned. The mortuaries filled up and undertakers had to resort to using a refrigerated warehouse outside Paris. On 3 September, fifty-seven bodies had still not been claimed.

Then there was the question of blame. The French president, Jacques Chirac, and the Prime Minister, Jean-Pierre Raffarin, blamed family doctors taking their holidays in August, the uncaring families who left their old relatives behind. The opposition politicians and the press blamed the health minister for remaining on holiday when the heatwave became serious. They also blamed his civil servants for impeding emergency measures in hospital, which might have included the compulsory recall of doctors on vacation.

Although Italy as a whole did not experience above average temperatures, it did get very hot in the cities, where the temperatures hovered at forty degrees Celsius (104 degrees Fahrenheit) for weeks on end. In total, 20,000 people died of the heat in Italy.

In England, the highest temperature was 38 degrees Celsius (100 degrees Fahrenheit), in Kent. For a day or two, London was as hot as Cairo. People arriving at Heathrow in an airliner from Jamaica thought they had been taken to the wrong country. As in France, the main problem was that people were not accustomed to the heat and perhaps did not respond in the best way. As a result of the heat, 2,139 people died in England.

The heatwave in Portugal caused extensive forest fires. Ten per cent of Portugal's forests were destroyed. Eighteen people died as a result of the fires.

In Germany, the temperatures were high, but the death toll was much lower than might have been expected: only sixty died, mostly elderly people. It was very dry in Germany, with around half average rainfall, so rivers levels were at their lowest for 100 years. The water levels were so low in the Elbe and the Danube that they became unnavigable.

In Switzerland the main problem was the melting of glaciers and snow, and the resulting avalanches. It was the first time – ever – that temperatures above 40 degrees Celsius had been experience in Switzerland.

In Europe as a whole, at least 35,000 and possibly as many as 50,000 people died as a result of the exceptionally hot conditions.

The heatwave had a major impact on crop production. In southern Europe food production was adversely affected, but in northern Europe the hotter, sunnier conditions actually improved that year's harvests. Many countries had crop shortfalls, Moldova's wheat shortfall of eighty per cent was exceptional.

There was much discussion about the causes of the heatwave in Europe. It was noticeable that there were various kinds of extreme weather in other parts of the world at about the same time, such as the worst-ever drought in Australia, which struck the previous summer, and severe floods in North America. It was the fashion, not just among journalists but among academics, who should know better, to blame all extreme weather on global warming. Climatologists at the Hadley Centre for Climate Prediction boldly claimed that human activity had increased greenhouse gases in the atmosphere and [therefore] more than doubled the risk of record-breaking hot European summers such as that of 2003. Blaming people for the heatwave seems to me to be going too far. It is safer to regard extreme weather events such as the heatwave as random. Extreme events of one kind or another, as we have seen throughout this book, have happened in every period. 'Global warming' cannot be used as an abracadabra to explain (or explain away) all the events that are happening, any more than the Millennium could explain what was happening in the eleventh century.

THE DESTRUCTION OF MOUNT STROMLO OBSERVATORY

(2003)

BUSH FIRES AND forest fires are the greatest natural hazards in the south-east of Australia. In grasslands and woodlands, fires occur naturally from time to time. The dry season is the likeliest time for the fires to spread, when both the vegetation and the litter of leaves and twigs underneath it are dry and can easily catch fire. Lightning strikes during thunderstorms can then easily set light to the vegetation.

In Australia, there is also a human element in bush and forest fires. People naturally put fires out when they start, or at least try to put them out. This may mean that a 'well-managed' woodland area may be protected from burning for a long time. That will mean that fallen leaves, twigs, branches and other debris will accumulate on the woodland floor to a greater depth. That in turn may make the forest fire much worse when it eventually occurs. Instead of the fire passing quickly through the area, burning up the leaf litter as it goes, it stays for much longer in each place, not only burning for longer but burning to a higher temperature. This leads to the total destruction of the trees, instead of what might have been a light searing. The problem seems to be an insoluble one, as letting fires burn in a region where there are settlements is not really an option.

People are also involved directly in forest fires because they frequently start them. This may in some cases be a deliberate act of vandalism. In other cases, it is an accidental fire caused by a camp fire getting out of control, or simply a discarded cigarette.

One major forest fire raged round Australia's capital, Canberra, on 18 January 2003, devastating huge areas of beautiful woodland. The Mount Stromlo Observatory was first built in 1910 up on top of a ridge overlooking a tract of pine forest. It was home to the historic Great Melbourne telescope, which was built in 1868 and modernized in the 1990s. The observatory staff were given twenty minutes' notice to leave the observatory complex, and there was just one road out of the area. The fire swept through the pine forest, a wall of flames twenty miles long, surrounded the observatory and destroyed it. The observatory and all of its equipment were completely gutted. The Australian prime minister, John Howard, said, 'I have been to a lot of bush fire scenes in Australia, but this is by far the worst.'

At the observatory, five astronomical telescopes were completely burned out, along with the main dome, eight homes for staff and the observatory workshops. One of the astronomers who used the Mount Stromlo telescopes said, 'This is a tragedy. Although some of the buildings have survived, all the domes and telescopes have been gutted.' Professor John Norris, who is Associate Director of the Mount Stromlo Observatory, said the place had been obliterated.

In the recent past, the historic Great Melbourne telescope made pioneering observations of faint objects orbiting our galaxy close to its outer edge; it is thought by astronomers that these compact objects, which had not been seen before, might make up a great deal of the universe's unseen mass. Only a month before the disastrous fire, the observatory had made a start on a digital survey of the entire southern sky. One particularly distressing loss was the destruction of state-of-the-art detectors that were being assembled in the workshops for two of the biggest telescopes in the world, the large Gemini telescopes in Chile and Hawaii. The detector for Hawaii had just been completed and was ready for shipment; it had cost five million dollars to build.

The firefighters who tried to deal with the forest blaze described it as 'a once or twice a century event' and said that there was little that they could have done to stop it. Four people were killed and nearly 400 homes were also destroyed.

THE ELK CREEK
FLOOD

(2004)

IN MAY 2004 there were heavy rains in Iowa, USA, and the water raised Elk Creek to flood level. The river overflowed an embankment and overwhelmed the small village of Elkport, washing many of its buildings away. The flood water rose to a height of fifteen feet inside the buildings that were left standing. When the flood subsided it was clear that the surviving buildings were so filthy and so badly damaged that they were beyond economic repair.

That was not the first time Elkport had been under water. Only five years earlier, in 1999, the Turkey River and the Volga River overflowed their banks and flooded the township. The embankment raised in 1949 had been built to prevent this kind of flooding, but clearly it did not. The 1999 flood damage was not too severe. The buildings had been repaired and life continued as before. In 2004 the flood damage was far worse. This time there would no bouncing back.

Often the story told is of repeating disasters, of villages, towns and cities undergoing the same trauma again and again. Often the damaged settlements are rebuilt only to be damaged all over again. With Elkport it was different. With only eighty-six residents, it was a small enough settlement to close down completely.

The Federal Emergency Management Agency (FEMA) agreed to buy the damaged properties at Elkport and the neighbouring settlement of Garber, at a cost of 1.6 million dollars. The process took a long time. It was not until one year after the flood, June

2005, that the agency gave its final approval to the plan, and it took a further year for the money to reach the owners of the wrecked properties. The residents, or ex-residents, of Elkport became impatient with the slowness of the agency, and angry that meanwhile they were expected to continue to pay taxes on properties that were worthless.

The FEMA arrangement was an offer. Acceptance by the owners was entirely voluntary, but they felt that they really had no alternative but to accept it, not least because many had no property insurance.

In September 2006, bulldozers moved into Elkport and razed the settlement. The elementary school, the general store, businesses, twenty-seven houses – everything was destroyed except a few houses right on the edge that happened to be above the flood level. The small handful of residents who are left hope that Elkport can still survive as a community, but it seems very doubtful.

Was there any alternative? Could Elkport have been saved? The damaged buildings could only have been restored or rebuilt at high cost. They would then in any case have been vulnerable to a future flood disaster with a similar end result, so they would have needed some sort of flood protection to make the reconstruction worthwhile. One way of achieving that would have been to raise the height of the buildings, in effect raise them fifteen feet, and that would have been both prohibitively expensive and impractical. To make matters even worse, Elkport had been built in a particularly bad location. It stood on the floodplain of not just one but three streams, so there was a very high likelihood that the settlement would be flooded again at some time in the future.

Bulldozing Elkport was the only realistic solution. It was very hard for the residents to have to abandon not just their own properties but their entire township like this, and they felt that the entire history of their settlement had been thrown away. An orderly retreat from the floodplain was the sanest and in the long-term the happiest solution – and not just for Elkport, but for other settlements and sectors of settlements that have unwisely been built on the floodplains of rivers. Elkport was not the first settlement in Iowa to be completely erased. In a very similar situation in 1999, properties in Littleport were bought out after a flood on the Volga River – and demolished.

THE BOSCASTLE
FLOOD

(2004)

A FLASH FLOOD hit the Cornish village of Boscastle on 16 August 2004. Homes, shops, roads and bridges were destroyed or badly damaged and 115 cars were swept away. No one was killed, thanks in large part to a helicopter which lifted 130 people to safety. The flood was caused by heavy rain over the moorland above the town. The waters rushed down the steep valleys sides, raising the River Valency, which tore through the middle of Boscastle.

The villagers were taken completely by surprise. But should they have been? In 1952, a flash flood tore through the lower part of Lynmouth in a very similar way. There are inherent dangers in building a settlement in the floor of a steep-sided valley, especially near its outfall, where the discharge from a storm may be very large. Many houses in Boscastle are built higher up and they re-mained completely unaffected by the disaster. The relatively few buildings that were damaged were at the bottom of the village, the picturesque area next to the harbour. This is a tourist honeypot in summer, and there are compelling commercial reasons for having shops there - but the risk was always very great.

In fact, Boscastle had been hit by floods before, more than once. In 2004, the heaviest rain fell over a watershed that separated four rivers, of which the Valency was one. The four rivers therefore shared the run-off from this storm. If the high-intensity rain had fallen only a mile away, so that all the water had fallen into the Valency's catchment area, the Boscastle disaster could have been far worse. In the high summer of 1827 there was a very similar flood, which was described shortly afterwards:

> *The whole street was filled with a body of water rolling down and carrying all materials with it. At Bridge teams of Wagon Horses were saved with difficulty. Pigs also belonging to the Cottagers were taken out of ye Roofs of Houses.*

That was Boscastle in 1827. Other floods followed in August 1847, August 1950, June 1957, June 1958 and June 1963. Nature always follows patterns, and the pattern at Boscastle is a very clear one – and a very clearly documented one, too. The River Valency needs the bottom of its valley for high storm flows. An Elk Creek solution would be better, removing the buildings altogether from the bottom of the valley.

THE BOXING DAY
TSUNAMI

(2004)

CHRISTMAS DAY IN 2004 came to a peaceful end, but not long after midnight the worst natural disaster of modern times was under way.

At 12.59 am Greenwich Mean Time on Boxing Day 2004, on the seabed 100 miles west of Sumatra a colossal earthquake was unleashed as two of the earth's plates slipped past each other along a split half a mile long. The earthquake measured 9.1 on the Richter Scale, making it the biggest since the Anchorage earthquake of 1964 and the fourth biggest since recordings of earthquake magnitude began in 1899. The energy released in the Sumatra earthquake was the equivalent of detonating 190 million tons of TNT.

The two tectonic plates that slipped past each other were the Australian-Indian Plate and the Eurasian Plate. Generally the plates that make up the earth's crust are moving imperceptibly slowly, at speeds around two inches per year, the speed at which our fingernails grow. The Australian-Indian Plate moves northwards at about that speed in relation to the Eurasian Plate, and the line separating the two runs north-south just west of Sumatra. But the movement is not smooth. The great slabs of rock are jammed against one another by friction for decades at a time, the pressure building and building until at last they jump past one another. In the Boxing Day earthquake, the pressure had been building up over the past 100 years. The focus of the big earthquake was on the same plate boundary as the big Toba eruption of 75,000 years earlier, and within 100 miles of the huge forgotten crater left by that ancient eruption. Banda Aceh and the other coastal towns wrecked in the Boxing Day disaster were arranged in a ring round the edge of the Toba crater.

Slabs of rock over a mile long were shaken loose from ridges on the seabed and swept up to seven miles in a series of underwater landslides triggered by the earthquake. Underwater photographs taken by a British survey ship show what observers described as an 'alien landscape'. Some chunks of rock as big as St Mary's in the Scilly Isles were swept down ridges and across plains on the seabed at 70 mph.

After the earthquake, Sumatra itself was in a different place; it had moved 120 feet to the south-west, along with the chain of islands along its west coast. The plates on each side of the plate boundary had moved 200 feet vertically in relation to each other.

The earthquake was in itself a major event. It lasted ten minutes, when most earthquakes last only a few seconds. There were many aftershocks, with epicentres scattered along the plate boundary from Sumatra northwards, and some of the aftershocks were above magnitude 7 on the Richter Scale, big events in their own right. Perhaps surprisingly it was not this gigantic earthquake that caused death and destruction around the Indian Ocean basin on Boxing Day 2004 – it was the tsunami that it triggered. The submarine disaster created chaos on the ocean floor, and during the earthquake one of the plates was jerked up 200 feet under water in a few seconds, pushing a huge volume of water up and then outwards at the surface. This is what unleashed the tsunami.

The earthquake happened just before one in the morning, and just eight minutes later it was picked up by seismographic instruments in Australia. Australian seismologists immediately alerted the Pacific Tsunami Warning Centre in Hawaii about the earthquake, because of the possible danger of a tsunami crossing into the Pacific. Just seven minutes after that the Warning Centre in Hawaii sent a bulletin alerting all the member states participating in the Tsunami Warning System in the Pacific. Unfortunately the system did not extend to the Indian Ocean. India, Sri Lanka, Thailand and the Maldives were not member states, so they were not informed of the impending tsunami. At three-thirty am, the Warning Centre heard about the Indian Ocean tsunami, not from their scientific instruments, but through the Internet, where the first news of casualties from Sri Lanka was breaking. By then, tens of thousands of people had already been drowned – by the tsunami that the scientists had known would be generated by the seabed earthquake. The lack of a formal warning system has been offered as an explanation, but the lack of an informal warning has still not been satisfactorily explained.

The people on the island of Simeulue, which was very close to the epicentre, felt the force of the big earthquake and headed for the hills, expecting that a tsunami would follow. They were right, and they were safe. But no one else round the Indian Ocean basin had any warning or took any precautionary measures at all. The victims were all taken by surprise – except on one beach on Phuket. There a ten-year-old British girl, Tilly Smith, applied what she had learned in a Geography lesson at school. She had been taught that just before a tsunami the sea draws back a long way. Tilly saw the sea receding and knew what it meant. She and her family managed to persuade everyone on the beach to head for higher ground and they were all safely evacuated by the time the tsunami arrived. But on many other beaches, people were intrigued by the sea drawing back a mile or more, and went out onto the seabed to have a look and catch stranded fish; few of those who did so lived. If only more people lived their lives like Tilly Smith. She saw the knowledge she had acquired in school as connected to what she was seeing happening in front of her, understood and was ready to put it to immediate practical use.

The tsunami travelled outwards from the epicentre in a series of huge concentric oval ripples. They travelled at enormous speed

in open water, around 500 mph, but as very broad low waves –
too low to be noticeable. Satellites that happened to be passing
overhead measured them as being only two feet high. As the
waves approached the coasts, they slowed down and the water
piled up into towering 100-feet high waves, though still moving at
a dangerous forty mph. The waves that hit Aceh (pronounced
arch-ay), the province of northern Sumatra nearest to the
epicentre, smashed into coastal towns and villages with un-
imaginable force, huge volumes of water sweeping inland, pushing a maelstrom of debris along with them. People who were
caught by the tsunami were dashed against buildings and trees
and in many cases killed by the mass of floating debris hurtling
along in the water.

First Aceh in Sumatra, then Thailand and Myanmar (Burma),
then Sri Lanka and India were hit by the tsunami. The waves
spread ever-wider, eventually reaching the Maldives, Somalia,
Kenya and Tanzania. Even though the tsunami struck at different
times in different places, no one had any warning. Even in the
Maldives, beyond Sri Lanka and India, there was no warning.

The worst affected area was the province of Aceh in northern
Sumatra. The town of Banda Aceh at the northern tip of Sumatra
was flattened, and so were the towns of Meulaboh and Calaya on
the west coast. Inevitably, the greatest death toll was in the
country closest to the earthquake epicentre, the source of the
tsunami, and in Indonesia 126,000 people died; the next highest
was Sri Lanka, where 30,000 died. Along the African coast, where
the waves were much lower, the danger was much reduced; only
one person is thought to have died in Kenya. The most distant
death to be caused by the tsunami was at Port Elizabeth in South
Africa, 5,000 miles away from the epicentre and sixteen hours
after the earthquake – ample time, one would have thought, for
the warning to stay off the beaches to have reached everywhere
along the coastline of the Indian Ocean. The tsunami spread
across the Pacific Ocean, and was even detected in Chile and

Mexico, where there were waves six feet higher than normal.

Many bodies were buried under the debris swept along and deposited by the tsunamis. Bodies were still being dug out of the debris at a rate of 500 a day in February 2005. The task of finding and identifying the often mutilated and decomposed bodies was overwhelming. Many bodies were swept out to sea when the force of the great waves was spent and the huge volumes of water drained back into the sea; they will never be found. It will never be known for certain how many people died altogether, but it is thought to be in the region of 287,000. A quarter of a million people unexpectedly wiped out in one morning, on 26 December 2004. One-third of those who died were children. This is partly because many of the countries affected were poor countries where the birth rate is still high. Of the children who survived, many were in a traumatized state. The charity organisation, Oxfam, pointed out that four times as many women died in the disaster as men, probably because they were waiting on beaches for the fishermen to return from the open sea, or were in their coastal huts looking after their children; in other words, they were in the most vulnerable location.

Little that was positive came out of the Boxing Day tsunami disaster. At Mahabalipuram, just to the south of Madras, the tsunami scoured the sand off the seabed, exposing a long-forgotten city half a mile out from the shore. It was the lost City of the Seven Pagodas, dating from the Pallava dynasty of Hindu kings 1,500 years ago.

The response to this terrible disaster from the rest of the world was immediate and unstinting. Huge amounts of money were given in donations by private individuals, overshadowing the government aid that was offered. This response was partly prompted by the fact that the disaster was entirely natural, and partly by the fact that so many already poverty-stricken communities were affected. But 9,000 foreign tourists also died. The British film producer Lord Attenborough lost three members of his family. The hardest hit

European country was Sweden, but people from all over the world were swallowed up by the tsunami. The Boxing Day tsunami disaster was felt, perhaps uniquely in human history, as a global natural disaster, an event that brought the world together.

HURRICANE KATRINA

(2005)

WE HAVE SEEN repeatedly in this book how the seeds of tragedy were sown decades or centuries ahead of disaster, by people founding their villages, towns and cities in the wrong places: Tokyo, Boscastle, Sarno, San Francisco, Pompeii, Naples. New Orleans is another. The Mississippi Delta is at or fractionally above sea level. New Orleans was built on perilously low-lying land between the main channel of the Mississippi and Lake Ponchartrain, and that land is a bowl up to eight feet below sea level. It is a place that is bound to flood.

On 29 August 2005, Hurricane Katrina hit New Orleans with 125 mph winds. The strong winds piled up the sea into a storm surge that swept up the Mississippi. The water spilt into the bowl, flooding it very rapidly. The hurricane track had been followed by satellite and the city had fair warning. Mandatory evacuation was declared. Everyone had to leave. But of course some people stayed regardless. Half the city of New Orleans was flooded in twenty-four hours and normal city life – normal civilized life – fell apart immediately. In the immediate aftermath of the hurricane, there were fires, looting, rape, robbery, anarchy.

The emergency services were all preoccupied with the overwhelming need to find and rescue people from the rising water. The crime rate in New Orleans was normally high, but it soared as the normal levels of policing were relaxed. The diversion of police attention to rescue provided the ideal environment for crime of every kind. By 30 August, the day after the hurricane, there was already widespread looting, often in broad daylight, and often with police officers looking on, powerless to intervene. The frustration of the police was intensified by the extra difficulty involved in trying to rescue people in a city where the normal transport and communication systems had been brought to a halt. The looting could not be controlled. Shopkeepers were abandoned to defend their property as best they could without police support. Some of the looting was individual opportunism, simply deprived and desperate citizens trying to gather essential food, merely scavenging. Some of the looting was more alarming, and organized by armed gangs.

There were even incidents of snipers firing at rescue helicopters, police officers and relief workers. It is not clear what the snipers were doing, but perhaps they were just people who were frightened at the prospect of being forcibly evacuated. In spite of the rising water, many people did not want to leave. One incident involced a gang attacking contractors employed to repair a breached canal wall; the police intervened, shooting six of the gang.

Looters also hindered the evacuation of Tulane University's medical facility. While staff tried to organize the evacuation, armed looters in boats tried to break in, presumably in the expectation of finding drugs. The hospital staff were diverted into defending the facility from the marauders. Another problem was the insistence by the city's 750 nuns that they should stay. They took the view that the clergy should remain in the city at a time of suffering, even though the authorities wanted a general evacuation. The safety of the nuns became a preoccupation the authorities could have done without.

An attempt was made to pump the water out of the bowl, but the levees surrounding the bowl had been badly damaged, so it was now impossible to keep the water out. The flood water quickly turned toxic with sewage, chemical pollution and decomposing corpses.

Many of the refugees from the lowest-lying areas of the city were taken to the Superdome. This was one of the biggest roofed structures in the city and seemed like the ideal gathering-point pending evacuation from the city. Katrina had ripped two gaping holes in its roof, but its was still seen as an attractive refuge – at first. By the evening of 30 August there were between 15,000 and 20,0000 people sheltering inside it. As the water level rose, it became clear that it was not a safe place to be after all. The land around the Superdome was flooded to a depth of three feet and if the water level equalized with the water level of Lake Pontchartrain, as was likely eventually, that would increase to seven feet. But the number of people gathering in the Superdome continued to grow and conditions inside became squalid. The people became hysterical and started spreading exaggerated rumours that 100 people had died of heat stroke, that a man who had committed rape in the Superdome had been beaten to death by a crowd. None of this was true. Six people died in the Superdome, one of a drug overdose and one committed suicide. Fortunately, before mass hysteria set in, the Superdome was evacuated; by 4 September all of the people had been moved on, out of New Orleans altogether.

By 31 August, the 1,500-strong police force had to be diverted from the search and rescue operation towards restoring order in the city. The looting had reached such a scale that it became the priority. Mayor Nagin desperately called for greater federal assistance because the city's police force was unable to control the looting unaided.; it was 'a desperate SOS'. A state of emergency was declared. On the same day, Governor Kathleen Blanco made it known that the military had arrived; she said they knew how to shoot to kill and fully expected that they would. But in spite of this stepping up of law enforcement, criminal activity went on being a major problem. There were more attacks on helicopters, bus convoys and police officers. The soldiers, the Louisiana National Guard, were not in the strongest position to help as more than one-quarter of their number had been posted to Iraq.

Curiously, after this tsunami of crime was over, the crime rate in New Orleans subsided. Before Hurricane Katrina, the crime rate in New Orleans had been ten times higher than the US average; afterwards, it was lower. Nevertheless, one of the outstanding features of Katrina and its effect on New Orleans is the frightening speed at which an apparently civilized community can descend into barbarism. A natural disaster can bring out the best in a community, or it can bring out the worst.

Most of the normal services in the city ground to a halt, but it was still possible for people to send e-mails out.

One read, 'My neighbourhood is under water. There are corpses all over the city. The stores are being looted. All residents of New Orleans are now refugees. Now I have a taste of what people in war-ravaged countries go through. Please pray for us. My children cannot grasp the scope of this catastrophe. My friends are missing. Take me away from this madness.'

Another message ran, 'I stayed in New Orleans because I didn't have anywhere else to go. I was in a friend's house and a couple of windows were blown in, but in the Garden District uptown we escaped the worst of the winds. Most of the damage seemed to be confined to downed trees and power lines. The flooding only followed afterwards . . . There was an atmosphere of lawlessness. I was frightened, to be honest.'

Another survivor escaped to Baton Rouge, reflecting that he had probably lost everything. He remembered that his work place was in an area prone to flooding and was probably now under water.

On 2 September a makeshift emergency hospital was set up at New Orleans airport. It was fairly chaotic, but up to 5,000 people received treatment there.

Within the city, the awful task of searching for bodies in the polluted and increasingly foul water continued. For two weeks the authorities fought to dissuade people from returning; they desperately wanted people to stay away until the normal services had been restored. On 19 September, hundreds of people returned to New Orleans. Some areas were dry enough for that to be possible, but the return was still premature. Health care in the city was at a virtual standstill. Several of the hospitals had been severely damaged and polluted and would not be back in use for some time.

Even after several major floods through the twentieth century, American citizens and engineers alike have a naive faith in levees. These artificially raised river banks were designed many decades ago to contain storm flows within the Mississippi's channel. Time and again it has been shown that the levees do not work. Either they safely contain the storm flow and deliver the problem to points further downstream, where the flooding becomes even more destructive than it would naturally have been, or they fail as the river rises and release huge volumes of water onto the floodplain all at once. Once overtopped, the levees trap the excess water on the wrong side, prolonging the flooding. Levees are a poor solution, yet because so many millions of dollars have been invested in making and maintaining them it is hard for the authorities to admit that they are unsatisfactory.

The question is now being asked, as it has been asked many times before – why did the levees fail? The US Corps of Engineers analyze the situation and try to understand. The levees round the New Orleans bowl were revetted in concrete and therefore should have stood up to the force of the storm surge – but the energy involved was too great. The concrete flood walls collapsed and the water pouring into the bowl swept the disintegrated walls into the residential areas, smashing and annihilating all the houses for several hundred yards. The flood walls were not designed to deal with so much water pushed by such a strong wind. Katrina was a Category 5 hurricane, the most powerful so far experienced, and the flood defences of New Orleans were not even designed to withstand a Category 1 hurricane.

It is now clear that New Orleans was a doomed city, badly located and provided with totally inadequate defences. The flood walls were only designed to hold back rising flood water in the Mississippi travelling south after rain in the interior; they were not designed to deal with the hurricane threat and a storm surge coming upriver at all. Outside the city, fifteen square miles of wetlands in the delta were destroyed.

If the Mississippi floodplain and Delta were in a natural state, the river would have carried large volumes of silt down to the Delta and built it up. The various engineering works along the way, including revetting the channel to prevent it from migrating, have reduced the amount of silt arriving in the Delta. To keep the site of New Orleans dry, pumping goes on all the time; this in turn reduces the volume of the delta. The result is that the Delta is waning and subsiding at a rate of one inch per year.

The New Orleans flood is the worst ever natural disaster ever to strike the United States. It cased seventy-five billion dollars' worth of damage, killed 1,300 people, rendered 500,000 people homeless. Six months after the disaster, only twenty-five per cent of the population has returned. Many people whose homes were completely obliterated have decided that there is no point in returning, especially since the same thing could happen again. Often, when a great disaster strikes a city, people show a spirit of resilience, a determination to make good, and the city is rebuilt. This geographical inertia is, in an objective sense, undesirable. Places that are prone to severe disasters are very bad places to build cities, and the optimum response would be to give in to the forces of nature and move the city somewhere else. Unusually, in this case, many people are saying that New Orleans should not be rebuilt. Now is the time to close this city down.

New Orleans is not a city with a long history. It was founded as recently as 1718. It was struck by severe floods in 1735 and 1785, and these led to the construction of artificial levees, first three feet high, then six feet. By 1812, over 200 miles of levees had been built along the banks of the Mississippi. When the levees collapsed under the weight of flood waters, as they often did, the flooding was even more disastrous. In 1850, thirty-two levees were breached and hundreds of people were killed. In 1882, in the most destructive Mississippi flood of the nineteenth century, the flood waters breached 280 levees.

In spite of its appalling history, there are people who have gone on writing about the city in startlingly optimistic terms. One apparently well-informed writer commented, only shortly before the catastrophic 2005 flood, that 'New Orleans is safe from the flood that comes every 100 years.' This shows a common misunderstanding of the recurrence interval. Recurrence interval is a statistical term attached to floods of particular magnitudes. The 'once-in-a-hundred years' event gives the average reader, and the average resident, the reassuring feeling that once that event has happened New Orleans will be safe from it happening again for another 100 years (ie not in my lifetime). In reality, the event could recur again and again in consecutive years. Common sense should tell us that most types of disasters – except perhaps geyser eruptions – do not occur at regular time intervals.

EARTHQUAKE IN
KASHMIR

(2005)

THE KASHMIR EARTHQUAKE occurred at 8.52 am on 8 October 2005. It was a major earthquake scoring at least 7.6 on the Richter scale (the Japanese estimate slightly higher, at 7.8): in other words, as violent as the 1906 San Francisco quake. Although there have been larger earthquakes in purely geological terms, there have been few in recent years with such a high death toll. The official number of dead in Pakistan, as given by the Pakistan government, was 73,276, while another 1,400 people died just across the border in India. A few died in Afghanistan. That brings the total, government-originating death toll to about 75,000 people. Aid agencies working in the area believe this is an under-estimate and that as many as 86,000 may have died.

Kashmir is in the heart of the zone of collision between the Indian and Eurasian plates, the collision which was responsible for the formation of the Himalayas. The earthquake shows that the northward drive of the Indian Plate beneath the Eurasian is still continuing. The epicentre was 100 miles north-north-east of the capital of Pakistan, Islamabad, and the earthquake's focus was sixteen miles below the surface. Afterwards there were lesser earthquakes in the same region. The aftershocks were unnerving for the survivors, but also made the task of rescue work more difficult and dangerous as workers picked their way through ruined buildings, searching for more survivors. The city of Karachi had an aftershock that reached 4.6 on the Richter scale. In the first twenty-four hours following the main earthquake there were 147 aftershocks, one of them reaching 6.2. The aftershocks went on for months after the earthquake. A full year after the Kashmir earthquake, there have been at least 978 aftershocks.

Saturday is a normal school day in Kashmir, so most children were at school at the time the earthquake struck and consequently many of them were buried under collapsed school buildings. As it was Ramadan, most adults were resting indoors after their pre-daybreak meal and were therefore caught inside their collapsing homes. Entire towns and villages in northern Pakistan were completely destroyed with all their inhabitants. So the earthquake itself and the building collapses that it caused led directly to an enormous number of deaths.

Rescue workers dug into as many wrecked buildings as they could to bring out those who were buried but still alive. But after the first few hours there was little chance of finding any more people alive. Even so, on 10 October, two days after the earthquake, several people were still being found alive, including a little girl of two in Islamabad. On 12 October, another little girl, this time aged five, was dug out of wreckage in the town of Muzaffarabad.

The buildings throughout the region were themselves partly to blame for the high death toll. When engineers from Peshawar looked at the damaged buildings in Muzaffarabad, the town closest to the epicentre, they concluded that sixty per cent of the buildings in the town were made of unreinforced concrete blocks. It was the collapse of a great many of these block buildings that was responsible for most of the deaths and injuries.

Then the survivors were in danger. On 20 October, the Secretary-General of the United Nations, Kofi Annan, pointed out that there were people stranded in 1,000 remote mountain villages, desperately in need of shelter, food and clean water; 'a second, massive wave of death will happen if we do not step up our efforts now.'

A major factor in the high death toll from this earthquake was the isolation of victims in the aftermath. Most of the victims were living in high mountain areas, where roads were blocked by landslides triggered by the earthquake. Even the Karakoram highway was blocked in several places. Many people were left homeless: over three million in Pakistan and probably over four million people in the Himalayan region as a whole. Ongoing political tensions between Pakistan and India regarding territorial claims to Kashmir meant that the border was closed, but the exceptional circumstances and the desperate need to improve access to stricken communities led to the opening of five crossing points along the 'Line of Control' (border). This made it easier to get medical and other humanitarian aid to those who needed it.

On 26 October, the prime minister of Pakistan appealed to surviving villagers in the mountains to come down to the valleys and the towns for help, because the relief workers were having great difficulty in reaching every house. He also pointed out that winter was about to set in, snow would fall, and they would be even more cut off.

The damage was not restricted to Pakistan. India suffered, too. The Moti Mahal fort in Poonch district fell down, along with many houses. Buildings in Amritsar and Delhi were damaged. The earthquake caused widespread panic. Of the four who died in Afghanistan, one was a little girl who was killed in the town of Jalalabad when a wall fell on her. The earthquake was felt in the capital, Kabul, but there was no damage.

The onset of winter filled everyone with apprehension, and it began almost at once. Temperatures fell, and the first falls of snow came on 13 October, only five days after the earthquake. The disaster was about to be compounded as whole areas were in danger of being completely cut off from aid. By the beginning of January 2006, heavy snow in the mountain areas was having a serious impact on the relief work.

The international response to Kashmir's tragedy was quick,

generous and appropriate. Some of the aid was large-scale, and governmental in level; this was in the form of money, blankets, tents, food, medical supplies. Other aid was small-scale and personal, but no less useful. Three Harley Street doctors went to Pakistan for a week to help treat earthquake victims and set up a field hospital at Bagh. This external support enabled the Pakistani government to organize the movement of injured earthquake victims efficiently by helicopter to hospitals in Islamabad and Rawalpindi on a daily basis. But the aid task was made more difficult by distraught and disoriented relatives trekking from hospital to hospital in the hope of finding a lost member of their family.

The resilience of Pakistan in the face of this overwhelming disaster has been remarkable. One year afterwards, the Pakistan government proposed an optimistic and highly ambitious comprehensive development scheme for the earthquake-damaged region; it will cost twenty billion dollars. The president, Pervez Musharraf, promised that most of the reconstruction work would be finished in two years, though many commentators have said that they do not believe this is achievable. The government of Pakistan government won widespread praise for the way the initial aftermath of the disaster was handled, but subsequently there were long delays due to bureaucracy and allegations of corruption. There has even been disagreement about the best design for the earthquake-proof houses that are to be built throughout the quake zone.

Exactly one year after the earthquake struck, the anniversary was marked by special prayers and the placing of a wreath at a memorial by. He said, 'With the grace of God, things are heading towards much improvement.' People crowded into mosques, bent their heads in prayer, and many considered how slow the pace of reconstruction had been. There was a mixture of sadness, frustration and impatience. At the moment of the anniversary, a second harsh winter was just weeks away for the hundreds of thousands of poor people who were still living in tents or shacks.

TYPHOON BILIS IN NORTH KOREA

(2006)

IN JULY 2006, a typhoon struck North Korea in the region surrounding the town of Yangdok. The tropical storm was accompanied by torrential rain. It was reported that more than twelve inches of rain fell on Yangdok during this one storm. The rivers were quickly swollen by the excessive rain, overflowing their banks, and there were mudflows too. Large areas of agricultural land were ruined. Fields, roads and farm buildings all suffered severe damage. Supplies of food during the succeeding months would be endangered by such a high level of damage to a landscape of subsistence agriculture.

The North Korean government gave out an official death toll of 549, with a further 295 people unaccounted for. But observers in South Korea claimed that the situation was far worse, claiming that as many as 57,000 people had died.

As a result of these conflicting claims, European researchers commissioned a sample satellite image of the region, in particular the area round Yangdok. This showed that flooding and landslides had caused widespread devastation. Many apartment blocks were destroyed; roads and railways were wrecked; bridges were swept away by flood waters. It was difficult to establish from the photograph how much damage had been done to buildings that remained standing, because the image only showed roofs, but it was reasonable to infer that people were buried or drowned in the lower floors of buildings that remained standing. That was, after all, what had happened in the Sarno floods in Italy.

The analysis of the satellite image showed large-scale devastation on the ground, and this did not match the low official casualty figures. According to the image analysis, the typhoon disaster was on an epic scale. Given that the flood peak arrived in the middle of the night, when many people living in the residential blocks were asleep, a great many more people must have perished than 594. The South Koreans who had claimed the disaster was more serious than the North Korean government admitted seemed to be correct, and a death toll of 10,000 seemed more likely than 594.

Politics constantly surface in natural disasters. The implication here is that the North Korean deliberately underplayed the scale of the disaster for the outside world, much as the Chinese government hushed up the Tangshan earthquake many years earlier. The Typhoon Bilis disaster is a particular breakthrough in the application of satellite imagery to the analysis of disasters. In this case, it was a useful way of cutting across what seemed to be a propaganda version of what had happened. In the future, it may play a valuable role in planning relief operations when there are large-scale complex disasters in difficult terrain.

DROUGHT
IN CHINA

(2006)

SICHUAN PROVINCE IN China has a long history of severe droughts and spectacular famines. In August 2006, Sichuan province and the urban area of Chongqing were hit by the severest drought in modern times. Low rainfall was part of the problem, but the exceptionally high temperatures and high evaporation rates made the situation much worse. On 15 August, a temperature of 44.5 degrees Celsius was recorded, and this was the highest temperature known in China for over 100 years.

The city of Chongqing itself was very severely affected, with its population of around twenty million people. The rural area surrounding the city was also hit hard. Two-thirds of the streams and rivers in the region dried up. Nearly 300 reservoirs dried up. As a result eight million people and seven million cattle were short of water.

Those who had air conditioning naturally used it, and the massive increase in usage put a big strain on the electricity supply.

The very hot dry conditions led to the outbreak of forest fires. There were over ninety separate fires that August, and they destroyed thousands of square miles of forest.

TYPHOON
DURIAN

(2006)

AT THE BEGINNING of December 2006, Typhoon Durian swept across the centre of the Philippines, bringing high winds, heavy rain and flash floods to a wide area. There were also mudflows that surged down mountain sides, knocking down trees, ruining fields, destroying roads and burying villages. Albay province was particularly badly affected. Rescue workers struggled to pull as many living victims from the debris as they could. The president, Gloria Arroyo, ordered out the military in an attempt to rescue people in villages submerged by flood waters.

Over 100 people died when mudslides on the slopes of the Mayon volcano hit several villages. The mudflows were very violent. There were reports of the people in Padang village having their clothes torn off as they were swept away by the mudflows of volcanic ash. They had very little chance to save themselves; it all happened at such enormous speed.

Immediately after the typhoon, the Philippine civil defence office declared that 198 people had died and that another 260 people were missing. This low death toll was almost certain to rise, and the director of the local Red Cross said that it was likely the death toll would double within a few hours.

After crossing the central Philippines, Typhoon Durian went on to hit the southern coast of Vietnam on 6 December. The typhoon had been expected to weaken before reaching Vietnam, but it still inflicted terrible damage. Almost 100 people were killed there. The situation was serious enough for the prime minister of Vietnam, Nguyen Tan Dung, to postpone his planned visits to Singapore and Malaysia and instead tour the damaged areas. Over 212,000 homes were damaged or destroyed and 808 fishing vessels were lost.

Typhoon Durian was just one of the many environmental crises Vietnam had to endure in 2006; the typhoon was its ninth tropical storm of the year. In May, hundreds of fishermen died in Typhoon Chanchu. In October, hundreds of thousands of homes were flooded when Typhoon Xangsane hit the coastal city of Danang. Every year in Vietnam, hundreds or sometimes even thousands of people lose their lives as a result of the effects of these ferocious tropical storms.

GLOBAL WARMING

(2007–)

THE GRADUAL WARMING of Earth's atmosphere is a large-scale ongoing global disaster. It receives an enormous amount of attention every day from the media and politicians and yet global warming has never been fully explained in terms that ordinary people can understand. It frequently comes up in discussions as an aside, a presumption, often as the justification for some questionable political decision – yet the underlying complexities are never adequately explained, let alone questioned.

Global warming is the upward trend of temperatures in the lower atmosphere over the last hundred years, and graphs of temperature measurements show this warming as an overall increase of half a degree Celsius. The conventional explanation of global warming is, to put it at its simplest, man-made greenhouse effect. This is the trapping of ever-increasing amounts of solar radiation in the atmosphere by ever-increasing amounts of carbon dioxide released into the atmosphere by human activity. Man-made emissions of carbon dioxide started in a small way when people started making fires for cooking and heating. They started to accelerate with the start of the Industrial Revolution in about 1750 and have now reached a high level; seven gigatonnes of carbon from carbon dioxide are released into the atmosphere every year. The additional carbon dioxide going into the atmosphere comes from power stations burning coal, oil and gas, from factories burning fossil fuels and from vehicles powered by fossil fuel. It must therefore be economic development starting with the Industrial Revolution that is to blame.

This widely accepted conventional explanation carries with it an implicit prediction that more warming is to come, because carbon dioxide emissions continue to increase, though the predictions of increases of one-and-a-half or even five degrees over the next 100 years are conspicuously not simple projections into the future of what is happening now.

A lot of the predictions as well as the message that man-made carbon dioxide is causing the temperature increase have come from a single organization, the Inter-Governmental Panel for Climate Change, the IPCC.

Earth's climate has certainly warmed up measurably and noticeably, and the consequences will be serious if the warming continues. It has been predicted that eighty per cent of South Africa's unique collection of wild flowers will disappear, ninety per cent of coral reefs will be killed, and polar bears will be wiped out. It has also been predicted that the sea level will rise and low-lying areas will have to be evacuated. The sea level has risen by about six inches over the last 100 years and may rise by another one or two feet in the next 100 years. A sea level rise of one-and-a-half feet by 2080 will put another seventy-five million people living on low ground at risk from annual flooding.

The world's climatic regions will change, too. Noticeable seasonal changes that have happened already include the very mild British autumn of 2005, when temperatures were two-and-a-half degrees Celsius above the thirty-year average and sunshine was fifty per cent above the average; as a result it was an unusually green autumn and early winter. In England, oak leaves now regularly fall one week later than they did thirty years ago. South-east England will suffer permanent water shortages. Much more serious is the possible shutdown of the Atlantic Conveyor, the huge figure-of-eight circulation of water around the North and South Atlantic Oceans, and the diversion of Gulf Stream, which at the moment bathes the British Isles in warm tropical water and keeps British winters mild. The diversion of this warm water away from Great Britain, towards Portugal, could have catastrophic effects on the climate of Northern Europe, even plunging Great Britain into a new cold stage. Ironically, global warming could lead to a sudden regional cooling on a grand scale, with glaciers reappearing in the mountains of Scotland and Wales.

The changes that are under way in the climate certainly appear to be having disastrous consequences all around the world. But some of the predictions that are commonly published in the media are based on false assumptions. More extreme weather has often been predicted. It is often said that there are more storms these days and that global warming will bring even more. Yet even the IPCC confirmed in 1996 that there is no evidence of an increase in extreme weather events in the twentieth century. In 2001, the IPCC modified this slightly by saying that there has been an increase in precipitation and in high-intensity rainstorms. On the other hand, hurricanes and cyclones actually weakened slightly during the second half of the twentieth century; they show an overall decrease in wind speeds, from forty-one m/sec in 1945 to thirty-eight m/sec in 1995.

One way the case for severer weather conditions has been argued up has been to cite the growing cost of storm damage. Global damage related to weather increased from between two and five billion US dollars in the 1960s to between thirty and a hundred billion in the 1990s. On the face of it this could be interpreted as showing that the weather became twenty times worse during that period. But the increase can be explained in other ways: by population increase, the great increase in settlement on low ground, and inflation. Bigger financial losses could reflect greater wealth almost everywhere, but better warning systems are in place so that people are able to defend themselves better against disaster. Interestingly, when hurricane damage cost is adjusted for inflation, what emerges is an overall decrease during the period 1960–2000.

But does this mean that the case for global warming and its predicted intensification has been exaggerated? The statistics are powerfully influential. One newspaper reported in February 2006 that 'a top climatologist', Michael Coughlan of the Australian Bureau of Meteorology, commented on Nasa figures for 2005: 'the world is now hotter than at any stage since prehistoric times.' The problem with this type of comment is that, although there may be general indications of prevailing temperatures on a century or millennium scale in the prehistoric past, there are no temperature measurements as such – there is no fine detail in the archaeological record on the scale that we as people experience or measure. Further on in the same newspaper report, it emerged that this was based on CO_2 readings, which are twenty-seven per cent higher than the highest level recorded (in the rocks) for the last 650,000 years – but that presupposes that CO_2 controls temperature, so there is a catch in the reasoning. The case for CO_2 controlling temperature has not been proved, and therefore the argument that people (who are blamed for the current 'excessive' output of CO_2) are to blame for climate change has not been proved either. The reasoning is disastrously flawed.

Another part of the global warming story is the feedback effect. In other words, as it gets warmer, the world warms itself up. As it gets warmer, more water is evaporated into the atmosphere and water vapour is a greenhouse gas, a gas that traps heat. Another feedback effect is related to the area of the world under permanent snow and ice. Ice caps and glaciers reflect the Sun's heat back into space, helping to keep the Earth cool. The warmer the atmosphere gets, the smaller the area of snow and ice becomes, and less heat is reflected back into space, so the Earth gets warmer – and so on. It is thought that the opposite feedback effect explains why the onset of ice ages is quite sudden. It may also explain why the ending of the last cold stage 10,000 years ago, which we must remember was an entirely natural event, was very abrupt. These are natural components in the global warming process, even according to the conventional scenario.

The feedback effect is a very important part of the story, as it becomes, in itself, a warming factor, obscuring the effects of other factors. In February 2006, newspapers were running a major story that the planet had reached a point of no return, the 'tipping point'; climate change was unstoppable, irreversible. The British newspaper, *The Independent*, ran a front page declaring that a 'special investigation reveals that critical rise in world temperatures is now unavoidable.' This included some alarming statistics, including the idea that a two degree rise in global temperature (not above the present temperature but above the temperature in the pre-industrial era, before the Industrial Revolution of the eighteenth century) was unavoidable and that this would produce a wide range of serious environmental effects, including the extinction of polar bears, the loss of over half the Arctic tundra, and the killing of ninety-seven per cent of the coral reefs. The news story was fuelled in part by the publication of a new book by the environmentalist James Lovelock, in which he stated that it was too late to reverse global warming.

The Toronto Conference of 1980 led to the creation of the Intergovernmental Panel on Climate Change (IPCC), which was set up jointly by the World Meteorological Organization and the United Nations Environmental Programme. At the Rio Earth Summit in 1992 the IPCC made a devastating report to world's political leaders. Since then the IPCC has repeatedly developed the case for a man-made greenhouse effect underlying the increase in temperature during the twentieth century, each time with more frightening prognoses for the future. Other causes than greenhouse gas emissions have scarcely been mentioned in the press releases issued by this very single-minded and influential body.

Although represented in the press as a scientific think tank, the IPCC has a very particular remit that is often overlooked. Its role is specifically 'to assess the scientific basis of the risk of human-induced climate change.' That is in reality a fairly narrow remit. It is not interested in exploring or highlighting any natural changes in climate. The IPCC has in effect been commissioned to make the case for the prosecution, and like any good lawyer it has down-played any evidence that might benefit the defence. The result has been a stream of imposing-looking reports that mention what are called 'natural forcings' of the climate but give far more space to the dangers of man-made effects. The IPCC's major publication, Climate Change 2001, is representative in that it contains chapters on solar variations but gives huge emphasis to man-made greenhouse effect. It uses language that is dense with scientific terms and therefore makes unsuitable reading for journalists or the general public; what the journalists are given is a summary, which zooms straight in on man-made greenhouse effect.

The conventional IPCC explanation for global warming presents it as a man-made disaster. But there are good reasons for thinking that it is not, that natural processes are behind it. Temperature has increased during the twentieth century, but only overall, not consistently and not in every decade. In fact, some very significant things emerge when the temperature graph is extended back to around 1870. There were several temperature troughs, around 1885, 1905 and 1965, when it was significantly cooler while carbon dioxide levels were rising either slowly or rapidly. There is, in short, no connection between temperature and carbon dioxide.

There is, on the other hand, a very close connection between the Earth's temperature and solar activity. The heat received at ground level from the Sun is referred to as total solar irradiance (TSI) and it is controlled by two things: the amount of energy arriving at the edge of the atmosphere from the Sun and the amount of dust put into the atmosphere by volcanic eruptions. All the major temperature changes, on the decade scale, over the last 400 years are exactly paralleled by the TSI graph. This was discovered back in the 1970s, and more recent research has confirmed it. There are even graphs that show it in the IPCC report Climate Change 2001, but the text does not draw attention to them.

The long-term changes in temperature have been due to astronomical variations: the changing tilt of Earth's axis, the circular movement of Earth's poles of rotation, and changes in the shape of Earth's orbit. These cyclical changes explain the pattern of glaciations and warm stages of the Pleistocene Ice Age. It is the short-term changes within the last 500 years that are of more concern to us, and they must be caused by some other variable.

Volcanic activity is one important variable. The large-scale nineteenth-century eruptions of Tambora (1815) and Krakatoa (1883) produced huge amounts of ash and large-scale cooling. The Pinatubo eruption of 1991 was big by twentieth century standards, but not by long-term standards, and by no means as big as the Krakatoa eruption. The lack of big ash eruptions in the twentieth century allowed the atmosphere to warm up. More important still are the variations in the Sun, as we saw earlier. The Sun's radiation varies measurably. Records of sunspot numbers exist from the seventeenth century to the present day. The number of sunspots increases and decreases in an eleven-year cycle. There are also eighty-year and 180-year cycles. Each peak in the sunspot cycle is associated with warmer and wetter weather. In the twentieth century, the sunspot number peaks got gradually higher. In other words, the Sun has become more active, drenching Earth with more radiation, and could easily be the main cause of the warming.

The temperature trough lasting from 1885 into the 1890s was not due to any human effect – there was no de-industrialization. Instead it could have been caused by the ash veil from the Krakatoa eruption of 1883, or a shutdown of sunspot activity. Both happened and most likely Earth cooled as a result of these two factors acting together. A model of global temperatures from 1600 to 2000 can be constructed, 'predicting' temperature from a combination of sunspot numbers and dust veil index. Excitingly, and bewilderingly, it replicates the actual global temperatures remarkably closely – including the otherwise very hard to explain temperature troughs of 1815, 1885, 1905 and 1965.

The Sun itself seems to be the major factor; the dust veil index is a less important factor. Very big volcanic eruptions can produce enough dust to blot out the Sun and reduce temperature. A model of temperature change using a combination of sunspots and volcanic activity is all that is needed to 'predict' the climate changes of the last 400 years, including the cold phase of the seventeenth century and the global warming of the twentieth century. A number of scientists have explored this theory and been convinced by it, though their views do not see the light of day in the IPCC reports. In the IPCC's 1990 report, it was actually admitted that the views of a minority of its writers 'could not be accommodated'.

One reason why some climatologists refuse to accept that solar variations are responsible is that the amount of energy emitted by the Sun only varies by 0.1 per cent, which they think is too little to explain the lively response of Earth's atmosphere.

Maybe they are wrong; Earth's climate system does appear to be extremely sensitive and volatile, with a level of instability that could easily be tipped one way or the other by relatively small changes in input. But a new discovery gives us a mechanism. The link between variations in solar activity and terrestrial warming might be mainly indirect. When the Sun becomes more active, as measured by numbers of sunspots, its magnetic field swells right out to a distance of nine billion miles, way outside the orbits of the outermost planets. The magnetic field of the Sun acts as a gigantic protective cage, fending off the cosmic rays that are continuously flying towards us from interstellar space. When the Sun's magnetic field is distended like this, fewer cosmic rays reach Earth. Cosmic rays give an electrical charge to the dust particles in the lower atmosphere, making them more likely to produce clouds, so more cosmic rays mean more clouds and lower temperatures, fewer cosmic rays mean less clouds and higher temperatures.

When the cosmic rays reach the ground they leave traces of two isotopes, carbon-14 and beryllium-10. Carbon-14 is absorbed by trees, beryllium-10 is absorbed by ice sheets, so tree rings and ice ayers, which can both be dated, can tell us how many cosmic rays were reaching the Earth and therefore the level of solar activity at any time. A solar activity graph stretching back over the past 11,000 years shows a pattern. After maybe 100 years of high-level activity the Sun slumps and its magnetic field contracts to 7.5 billion miles, letting more cosmic rays into the solar system. This boom-and-bust cycle in the Sun's activity explains the global warming we are experiencing; we are simply living through a solar boom period. It will be followed shortly by a bust. The Little Ice Age was really two separate solar busts, the Spörer Minimum centred on 1520 and the Maunder Minimum centred on 1720.

What does the future – our future – hold?

Astronomers tells us that we can expect fewer sunspots over the next ten years, and fewer still over the ten years after that, and that decrease in sunspot activity will be enough to bring global warming to an end. The doom-mongers' dire predictions for the next 100 years will evaporate and vanish, just like the now forgotten predictions of the 1970s that the next ice age is about to start. If global warming is a disaster it is a natural disaster, with a natural ending in the not-too-distant future. Two important messages come out of all of this. One is that there is no need for the present climate of fear. Another is that it makes a huge difference to our human responses, to the way we live, and a huge difference to the outcome, whether we perceive a disaster as natural or man-made.

The forces of nature are, whatever we think, still in control, still shaping our destinies. Sometimes the forces of nature are destructive, sometimes they are creative, and often as we have seen they are both destructive and creative at the same time. So when we witness a natural disaster it is a major psychological event; we are being reminded that those forces are still present in our lives and still very potent.

APPENDIX:
THE SEVENTY WORST
NATURAL DISASTERS

THE SEVENTY WORST
NATURAL DISASTERS

Event	Date	Location	Death toll
Toba eruption	73,000 BC	Sumatra	90% of human race?
Black Death	AD 1333-	Eurasia	100,000,000
Spanish influenza	1918-19	Global	20-100,000,000
Three Difficult Years famine	1958-61	China	25,000,000
AIDS pandemic	1981-	Global	25,000,000
Famine	1907	China	20,000,000
Bubonic plague epidemic	1892-96	China	10,000,000
Yellow River flood	1931	China	1-4,000,000
Yellow River flood	1887	China	1-2,000,000
Antonine plague	165-180	Roman Empire	5,000,000
Famine	1936	China	5,000,000
Asian flu pandemic	1957	Global	4,000,000
Famine	1900	India	3,000,000
Famine	1928-30	China	3,000,000
Famine	1941	China	3,000,000
Bengal famine	1943	India	2,500,000
River flooding	1959	China	2,000,000
Irish potato famine	1846-49	Ireland	1,500,000
Famine	1965-57	India	1,500,000
Famine	1995-98	North Korea	1,200,000

Event	Date	Location	Death toll
East Mediterranean earthquake	1201	Levant	1,000,000
Hong Kong flu pandemic	1968	Global	1,000,000
Shensi earthquake	1556	China	830,000
Bhola cyclone	1970	Ganges Delta	500,000
Cyclone	1839	Indonesia	300,000
Haiphong cyclone	1881	Vietnam	300,000
Yangtse River flood	1642	China	300,000
Boxing Day tsunami	2004	Indian Ocean	287,000
Tangshan earthquake	1976	China	242,000
Aleppo earthquake	1138	Syria	230,000
Super-typhoon Nina	1975	China	229,000
Damghan earthquake	856	Iran	200,000
Gansu earthquake	1920	China	200,000
Xining earthquake	1927	China	200,000
Ardabil earthquake	893	Iran	150,000
Yangtze flood	1935	China	145,000
Great Kanto earthquake	1923	Japan	140,000
Cyclone	1991	Bangladesh	138,000
Smallpox epidemic	1775–82	North America	130,000
Ashgabat earthquake	1948	Turkmenistan	110,000
Lisbon earthquake	1755	Portugal	100,000
Chihli earthquake	1290	China	100,000
Yangtze flood	1911	China	100,000
River floods	1971	Vietnam	100,000
Tambora eruption	1815	Indonesia	92,000

EVENT	DATE	LOCATION	DEATH TOLL
Kashmir earthquake	2005	Pakistan	87,000+
Shemakha earthquake	1667	Caucasus	80,000
Tabriz earthquake	1727	Iran	77,000
Great Plague	1665	London	70,000
Ancash earthquake	1970	Peru	66,000
Calcutta cyclone	1864	Ganges Delta	60,000
Typhoon	1922	China	60,000
Quetta earthquake	1935	India	60,000
Calabria earthquake	1783	Italy	50,000
Typhoon	1912	China	50,000
Cyclone	1942	India	40,000
Bam earthquake	2003	Iran	40,000
Krakatoa eruption	1883	Indonesia	36,000
Heat wave	2003	Europe	35,000
Erzincan earthquake	1939	Turkey	32,700
Storm surge	1362	Netherlands	30,000
Tokaido tsunami	1707	Japan	30,000
Yangtze flood	1954	China	30,000
Mt Pelée eruption	1902	Martinique	29,000
Tsunami	1826	Japan	27,000
Tsunami	1896	Chile	22,070
Great Hurricane	1780	Caribbean	22,000
Cyclone	1963	Ganges Delta	22,000
Cyclone	1965	Ganges Delta	22,000